What Does It Mean
to Be White?

COUNTERPOINTS

Studies in the
Postmodern Theory of Education

Shirley R. Steinberg
General Editor

Vol. 497

The Counterpoints series is part of the Peter Lang Education list.
Every volume is peer reviewed and meets
the highest quality standards for content and production.

PETER LANG
New York • Bern • Frankfurt • Berlin
Brussels • Vienna • Oxford • Warsaw

Robin DiAngelo

What Does It Mean to Be White?

Developing White Racial Literacy

REVISED EDITION

PETER LANG
New York • Bern • Frankfurt • Berlin
Brussels • Vienna • Oxford • Warsaw

Library of Congress Cataloging-in-Publication Data

Names: DiAngelo, Robin J., author.
Title: What does it mean to be white?: developing white racial literacy /
Robin DiAngelo.
Description: Revised edition. | New York: Peter Lang, 2016.
Series: Counterpoints: studies in the postmodern theory
of education; vol. 497 | ISSN 1058-1634
Includes bibliographical references and index.
Identifiers: LCCN 2016005919 | ISBN 978-1-4331-3110-3 (paperback: alk. paper)
ISBN 978-1-4539-1848-7 (e-book)
Subjects: LCSH: Whites—Race identity. | Race relations. | Racism.
Classification: LCC HT1575.D53 2016 | DDC 305.809—dc23
LC record available at http://lccn.loc.gov/2016005919

Bibliographic information published by **Die Deutsche Nationalbibliothek**.
Die Deutsche Nationalbibliothek lists this publication in the "Deutsche
Nationalbibliografie"; detailed bibliographic data are available
on the Internet at http://dnb.d-nb.de/.

The paper in this book meets the guidelines for permanence and durability
of the Committee on Production Guidelines for Book Longevity
of the Council of Library Resources.

© 2016 Peter Lang Publishing, Inc., New York
29 Broadway, 18th floor, New York, NY 10006
www.peterlang.com

Printed in the United States of America

This book is dedicated to Deborah Terry-Hays and Darlene Flynn, two of the most brilliant and committed leaders in the cause for racial justice I have ever known. You have been my mentors and guides on the most profound intellectual, emotional, and political journey of my life. Thank you for never giving up on me and for your immeasurable trust, patience, love, and support. To stand by your sides as a white woman in the struggle is the greatest of honors.

CONTENTS

ACKNOWLEDGMENTS

I extend my most heartfelt thanks to the numerous friends and colleagues who supported me in this project. Jason Toews, for the *hours* of astute and vigilant editing you generously donated; my colleagues Anika Nailah, Özlem Sensoy, Holly Richardson, Carole Schroeder, Malena Pinkam, Lee Hatcher, William Borden, Kelli Miller, Ellany Kayce, Darlene Flynn, Deborah Terry, Jacque Larrainzar, Darlene Lee, Sameerah Ahmad, Nitza Hidalgo, and Kent Alexander for your support, insight, and invaluable feedback. Thank you Amie Thurber for your perceptive and detailed reading of the final draft and help with the discussion questions. Thank you Brandyn Gallagher for your insight and patience in working to raise my awareness of cis-supremacy. Thank you to Dana Michelle, Thalia Saplad, and Cheryl Harris for all I learned from you in the beginning of this journey.

Thank you to all of the scholars whose work has been foundational to my understanding of whiteness, particularly Peggy McIntosh, Richard Dyer, Charles Wright Mills and Ruth Frankenberg. Any errors or omissions in interpreting or crediting that work are my own.

A special thank you to Robin Boehler—a fellow white ally—for the countless hours we spent debriefing our training sessions and working to put the racial puzzle together. Your support and brilliance were invaluable.

Thank you Todd LeMieux for all of your design and graphic work, Andrea O'Brian for your Frames of Reference illustration, and Katherine Streeter for the beautiful cover art.

This text addresses whiteness within the context of what is now known as the United States, originally known as Turtle Island by some Indigenous peoples. The theft of Indigenous lands was the starting point of our current racial system. A key argument of this book is that we must know where we came from in order to understand where we are now. For a powerful overview of this history, see *Bury My Heart at Wounded Knee* and *A People's History of the United States*. In honor of the Indigenous peoples whose ancestral territories I stand on and write from, I offer my sincerest respect.

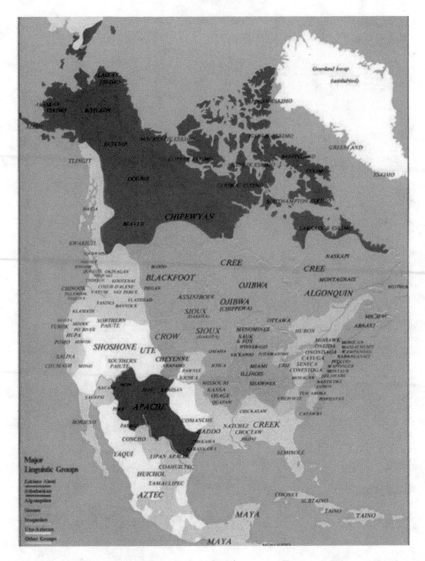

Figure 1. Map of Indigenous peoples at time of 15th-century European contact.

INTRODUCTION

I grew up in poverty, in a family in which no one was expected to go to college. Thus I came late to academia, graduating with a BA in Sociology at the age of 34. Unsure what I could do with my degree, I went to my college's career center for help. After working with the career counselors for several weeks, I received a call. The counselor told me that a job announcement had just arrived for a "Diversity Trainer," and she thought I would be a good fit. I didn't know what a Diversity Trainer was, but the job description sounded very exciting: co-leading workshops for employees on accepting racial difference. In terms of my qualifications, I have always considered myself open-minded and progressive—I come from the West Coast, drive a Prius, and shop at natural food markets such as Whole Foods and Trader Joe's (and always bring my own bags). I will admit that I have on occasion told an ethnic joke or two (but never in mixed company) and that I was often silent when others told similar jokes or made racist comments. But my silence was usually to protect the speaker from embarrassment or avoid arguments. Thus, confident that I was qualified for the diversity trainer position, I applied and received an interview.

The interview committee explained that the State's Department of Social and Health Services (DSHS—the "welfare" department) had been sued for racial discrimination and had lost the suit. The federal government had determined that the department was out of compliance regarding serving all clients equally across race and, as part of the settlement, had mandated that every employee in the state (over 5,000 people) receive 16 hours (2 full workdays) of diversity training. DSHS hired a training company to design and deliver the trainings, and this company wrote the curriculum. Part of the design was that inter-racial teams would deliver the trainings. They needed 40 trainers to be sent out in teams of two. The interview committee, composed primarily of other (open-minded) white people such as myself, agreed that I was qualified, and I got the job. Initially elated, I had no idea that I was in for the most profound learning curve of my entire life.

I showed up for the Train-the-Trainer session with 39 other new hires. We would be working together for 5 full days to learn the curriculum and get ready to fan out across the state and lead the workshops. The challenges began almost immediately. On the first day, as we sat in the opening discussion circle, one of the other white women called out, "All the white racists raise your hand!" I was stunned as virtually every white hand in the room shot up. I was smart enough to realize that for some unfathomable reason this was the "party line" and that I should raise my hand like everyone else, but I just couldn't. *I was not racist*, and there was no way I was going to identify myself as such. Over the next 5 days we spent many hours engaged in heated discussions about race.

This was the first time in my life that I had ever talked about race in such a direct and sustained way with anyone, and I had *never* discussed race before in a racially mixed group. My racial paradigm was shaken to the core as the people of color shared their experiences and challenged my limited racial perspective. Indeed, I had never before realized that I *had* a racial perspective. I felt like a fish being taken out of water. The contrast between the way my colleagues of color experienced the world and the way I did worked like a mirror, reflecting back to me not only the reality that I had a racial viewpoint, but that it was necessarily limited, due to my position in society. I did not see the world objectively as I had been raised to believe, nor did I share the same reality with everyone around me. I was not looking out through a pair of objective eyes, I was looking out through a pair of *white* eyes. By the end of the 5 days I realized that regardless of how I had always seen myself, I was deeply uninformed—even ignorant—when it came to the complexities of race. This ignorance was not benign or neutral; it had profound implications for my sense of identity and the way I related to people of color.

The next point on my learning curve began when my co-trainer (a black woman) and I began leading the workshops in DSHS offices across the state. I had been expecting these sessions to be enjoyable; after all, we would be exploring a fascinating and important social issue and learning how to bridge racial divides. I have always found self-reflection and the insights that come from it to be valuable, and I assumed that the participants in the workshops would feel the same way. I was completely unprepared for the depth of resistance we encountered in those sessions. Although there were a few exceptions, the vast majority of these employees—who were predominantly white—did not want to be in these workshops. They were openly hostile to us and to the content of the curriculum. Books slammed down on tables, crossed arms, refusal to speak, and insulting evaluations were the norm.

We would often lead workshops in offices that were 95–100% white, and yet the participants would bitterly complain about Affirmative Action." This would unnerve me as I looked around these rooms and saw only white people. Clearly these white people were employed—we were in their workplace, after all. There were no people of color here, yet white people were making enraged claims that people of color were taking their jobs. This outrage was not based in any racial reality, yet obviously the emotion was real. I began to wonder how we managed to maintain that reality—how could we not see how white the workplace and its leadership was, at the very moment that we were complaining about not being able to get jobs because people of color would be hired over "us"? How were we, as white people, able to enjoy so much racial privilege and dominance in the workplace, yet believe so deeply that racism had changed direction to now victimize us? Of course, I had my own socialization as a white person, so many of the sentiments expressed were familiar to me—on closer reflection I had to acknowledge that I had held some of the same feelings myself, if only to a lesser degree. But I was gaining a new perspective that allowed me to step back and begin to examine my racial perceptions in a way I had never before been compelled to do.

The freedom that these participants felt to express irrational hostility toward people of color when there was only one person of color in the room (my co-facilitator) was another aspect of how race works that I was trying to understand. As a woman I felt intimidated when a white man erupted in anger. But at least I wasn't the only woman in the room, and the target was ultimately not me, but people of color. The lack of white concern for the impact our anger might have on my co-facilitator, who often *was* the only person of color in the room, was confusing. Driving home, I saw the devastating effect of this hostility on my co-facilitator as she cried in hurt, anger, and frustration. How could these white participants not know or care about this impact? How could we forget the long history of angry white crowds venting racial rage on an isolated person of color? Where was our collective memory? And what about the other white people in the room, those not openly complaining but supporting the complainers nonetheless through their silence? How might the ability to act so insensitively across racial lines depend on the silence of other whites? If we as white people did not speak up to challenge this, who would? How much more emotionally, intellectually, and psychically draining was it for my co-facilitator to speak back to them, than for me? Yet it had always been socially taboo for me to talk directly about race, and in the early days of this work I was too intimidated and inarticulate to raise these questions.

We had 5,000 employees across the state to train, and the project took 5 years to complete. As the years went by and I was involved in hundreds of discussions on race, clear and consistent patterns emerged, illustrating the ways in which white people conceptualize race and thus enact racial "scripts." Once I became familiar with the patterns, it became easier for me to understand white racial consciousness and many of the ideas, assumptions, and beliefs that underpin our understanding of race. I also had the rare gift of hearing the perspectives of countless people of color, and—in time—I became more articulate about how race works and less intimidated in the face of my fellow whites' hostility—be it explicitly conveyed through angry outbursts or implicitly conveyed through silence, apathy, and superficiality.

Because I grew up poor and understood the pain of being seen as inferior, prior to this experience I had always thought of myself as an "outsider." But I was pushed to recognize the fact that, racially, I had always been an "insider"; the culture of whiteness was so normalized for me that it was barely visible. I had my experience of class marginalization to draw from, which helped tremendously as I struggled to understand racism, but as I became more conversant in the workings of racism, I came to understand that the oppression I experienced growing up poor didn't protect me from learning my place in the racial hierarchy. I now realize that poor and working-class white people don't necessarily have any "less" racism than middle- or upper-class white people. Our racism is just conveyed in different ways, and we enact it from a different social location than the middle or upper classes. (I will discuss this in more depth in Chapter 11.)

As the foundation of the white racial framework became clearer to me, I became quite skilled at speaking back in a way that helped open up and shift perspectives. Although I learned a tremendous amount from all of the trainers

I worked with over those years, by the end of that contract there were only two of us left: myself as a white trainer and my African American co-trainer Deborah Terry-Hays. I had been given an extraordinary gift in having the honor of working with Deborah, a brilliant, compassionate, and patient mentor. She and I went on to lead similar workshops with other groups, including teachers, municipal workers, and police officers. Over the years I realized that I had been given an opportunity that few white people ever had—to co-lead discussions on race on a daily basis. This work had provided me with the ability to understand race in a profoundly more complex and nuanced way than I had been taught by my family, in school, from the media, or by society at large. Nothing had previously prepared me in any way to think with complexity about race. In fact, the way I was taught to see race worked beautifully to hide its power as a social dynamic.

I wanted to apply my new knowledge beyond these workplace discussions in order to impact a wider audience. I decided to earn my doctorate in Multicultural Education and Whiteness Studies so that I could disseminate what I had learned through teaching and writing. I completed my doctorate in 2004. My graduate study added more layers to my knowledge—6 additional years of scholarship and study. I now had empirical research and theoretical frameworks to support all I had experienced in my years of practice. In graduate school I co-led courses that trained students to lead interracial dialogues. For my dissertation study, I gathered an interracial group of students together to engage in a series of discussions on race over a 4-week period. A trained interracial team of facilitators led the discussions. I sat quietly in the back, observing while the sessions were video-recorded. This observation was the first time I was not in the position to either lead or participate in the discussion, and the opportunity to simply observe provided yet more insight into how whites "do" race.

I now understand that race is a profoundly complex social system that has nothing to do with being progressive or "open-minded." In fact, we whites who see ourselves as open-minded can actually be the most challenging population of all to talk to about race, because when we believe we are "cool with race," we are not examining our racial filters. Further, because the concept of "open-mindedness" (or "colorblindness," or lack of prejudice) is so important to our identities, we actually *resist* any suggestion that there might be more going on below the surface, and our resistance functions to protect and maintain our racial blinders and positions.

Today I am a writer, speaker, consultant and former associate professor of teacher education. Whether I am leading classes or workshops for college students, university faculty, social workers, government workers, youth, or private sector employees, each population I work with considers itself somehow unique, and when I am brought in I am often told that I must know such and such in order to understand this specific group. Yet in my years of experience working with all of these populations, the racial patterns are remarkably consistent. The specific norms of the group may vary—some groups may be more outspoken than others, or the discussion may center on education versus business, or there may have been some past conflicts I should know about—but the larger society has collectively shaped us in very predictable ways regarding race. Thus, although this book begins with the example of the teaching force—because education is such a primary site of racial socialization and my field of study—the larger points apply across all disciplines. I ask readers to make the specific adjustments they think are necessary, rather than reject the evidence because it isn't specifically based in their context. *Please note: This book is grounded in the context of the United States and does not address nuances and variations within other socio-political contexts.*

The Dilemma of the Master's Tools

Audre Lorde (1983), a writer, poet and activist, wrote that "The master's tools will never dismantle the master's house" (p. 94). She was critiquing feminists of the time who claimed to represent all women but who focused their concerns on white, middle-class women. This focus rendered women of color invisible and reinforced the race and class privilege enjoyed by white, middle-class feminists. Lorde and other feminists of color argued that race, class, and gender were inseparable systems and must be addressed together. She argued that by not addressing race and class, these feminists were actually reinforcing the system of patriarchy and its divisions—re-inscribing racism and classism (among other forms of oppression) in the name of eliminating sexism.

Lorde's famous quote also speaks to the dilemma of challenging the system from within. For example, can one authentically critique academia while employed by it and thus invested in it? This is one of the major challenges I face as a white person writing about race. While my goal is to interrupt the invisibility and denial of white racism, I am simultaneously reinforcing it by centering my voice as a white person focusing on white people. Although some people of color appreciate this, others see it as self-promoting and narcissistic. This is a dilemma I have not yet resolved, but at this point in my journey toward greater racial awareness and antiracist action, I believe the need for whites to work toward raising their own and other whites' consciousness is a necessary first step. I also understand and acknowledge that this focus reinforces many problematic aspects of racism. This dilemma may not make sense to readers who are new to the exploration, but it may later on.

Another "master's tools" dilemma I face is that race is a deeply complex socio-political system whose boundaries shift and adapt over time. As such, I recognize that "white" and "people of color" are not discrete categories and that nested within these groupings are deeper levels of complexity and difference based on the various roles assigned by dominant society at various times (i.e., Asian vs. Black vs. Latino vs. Immigrant; Jewish vs. Gentile; Muslim vs. Christian). By speaking primarily in macro-level terms—white and people of color—I am reinforcing the racial binary and erasing all of the complexity within and between these categories. For example, what about bi- or multiracial people? What about a religion (e.g., Islam), which in the current post-9/11 era has been racialized? As will be discussed, race has no biological meaning; it is a *social idea*. Therefore, one's racial experience is in large part dictated by how one is *perceived* in society. Barack Obama is a clear example. Although he is equally white and black in current racial terms, he is defined as black because he looks black and therefore (at least externally) will have more of a "black experience"; society will respond to him as if he is black, not white.

Thus, for the purposes of this limited analysis, I use the terms *white* and *people of color* to indicate the two macro-level, socially recognized divisions of the racial hierarchy. I ask my readers who don't fall neatly into one or the other of these categories to apply the general framework I provide to their specific racial identity (I will explore specific racial groups in more depth in Chapter 17). Again, at the introductory level my goal is to provide basic racial *literacy* and, as such, understanding the relevancy of the racial binary overall is a first step, albeit at the cost of reinforcing it. To move beyond racial literacy to develop what might be thought of as racial *fluency*, readers will need to continue to study the complexities of the racial construct.

Chapter Summaries

Chapter 1: Race in Education

This chapter provides an overview of current demographic trends in teacher education. I explain why I believe that most white teacher education students (like most whites in general) are racially illiterate. I share some of my most common student essays on the question of racial socialization in order to illustrate white racial illiteracy. The challenges of a growing white teacher education population are discussed.

Chapter 2: Unique Challenges of Race Education

This chapter clarifies the differences between opinions on race and racism that all of us already hold, and informed knowledge on race and racism that only develops through ongoing study and practice. The common conception of racism as a good/bad and either/or proposition is challenged. An overview of race and whiteness as social constructs that have developed and changed over time is provided.

Chapter 3: Socialization

This chapter explains the power of socialization to shape our identities and perspectives. Using popular studies, I show the ways in which our cultural context functions as a framework through which we filter all of our experiences. This filter is so powerful it can shape what we see (or what we *believe* we see). This chapter will begin to challenge the concept of unique individuals outside of socialization and unaffected by the messages we receive from myriad sources.

Chapter 4: Defining Terms

This chapter provides a shared framework for defining key terms such as prejudice, discrimination, systematic oppression, and racism. Differentiation is made between dynamics that operate at the individual level (i.e., prejudice and discrimination) and systematic oppression, which is an embedded and institutionalized system with collective and far-reaching effects. This chapter provides the overall theoretical framework for understanding racism.

Chapters 2, 3, and 4 are adapted from *Is Everybody Really Equal? An Introduction to Key Concepts in Critical Social Justice Education* by Sensoy & DiAngelo (2012).

Chapter 5: The Cycle of Oppression

This chapter continues the discussion of oppression. The elements that constitute oppression are explained: the generation of misinformation; acceptance by society; internalized oppression; internalized dominance; and justification for further mistreatment. The treatment of children with learning disabilities (a form of ableism) is used to illustrate each point on the cycle.

Chapter 6: What Is Race?

A brief historical overview of the development of race as a social construct is provided. Dynamics of perception are discussed. The interaction between ethnic identity—e.g., Jewish or Portuguese—and race is explored. The development of white as a racial identity is traced over time. I introduce the idea of whiteness as a form of property with material benefits.

Chapter 7: What Is Racism?

Using the framework of oppression explained in Chapter 3, this chapter defines and describes racism. This chapter also distinguishes between the dominant conceptualization of racism as a binary (a person is either racist or not racist; if a person is racist, that person is bad; if a person is not racist, that person is good), and the antiracist conceptualization of racism as an embedded system of unequal power in which all are complicit—in varying ways and regardless of intentions. Examples are used to illustrate these key points. The concept of Whiteness is also introduced.

Chapter 8: "New" Racism

This chapter explains many of the ways that modern or "new" racism manifests. I address different forms of racism such as aversive and colorblind, and trace some of the ways that racism circulates today through media and social dynamics such as segregation.

Chapter 9: How Race Shapes the Lives of White People

Using the example of my own life, this chapter guides the reader through the daily processes, expectations, entitlements, privileges, messages, and norms that function to uphold Whiteness. By explicating dynamics that will be recognizable and indisputable for most readers, this chapter illuminates modern forms of racism.

Chapter 10: What Makes Racism So Hard for Whites to See?

This chapter explains common perspectives, conceptualizations, and ideologies that obscure racism for whites. These include: conceptualizing racism as a racist = bad/not racist = good binary; the ideologies of individualism and universalism; racial segregation; the tendency to focus on intent rather than impact; colorblindness; and lack of white racial humility.

Chapter 11: Intersecting Identities: The Example of Class

Using two of my own social group memberships—race and class—I explore the intersection of identities to argue that being oppressed in one axis of life does not mean that you cannot be privileged in another. These locations interact in complex ways that must be addressed together.

Chapter 12: Common Patterns of Well-Meaning White People

This chapter presents common patterns of well-intentioned white people. These patterns include: guilt, seeking absolution, objectifying, ignoring, minimizing, rushing to prove ourselves, and feeling unfairly "accused."

Chapter 13: White Fragility

Most white people in North America live in a social environment that protects and insulates them from race-based stress. This insulated environment of racial protection builds white expectations for racial comfort while at the same time lowering the ability to tolerate racial stress, leading to what I refer to as *white fragility*. This chapter overviews the dynamics of white fragility.

Chapter 14: Popular White Narratives That Deny Racism

This chapter explains several common misconceptions about racism, including the ideas that racism is in the past, that only bad people are racist, that I haven't been involved in racism if I didn't personally own slaves, and that people of color can be just as racist as whites.

Chapter 15: Stop Telling That Story! Danger Discourse and the White Racial Frame

This chapter illuminates *danger discourse*: narratives that reinforce the association of people of color—and blacks in particular—as inherently dangerous, while simultaneously reinforcing whites and the spaces associated with whites as the embodiment of safety and innocence. I examine the effects of these narratives and the racial capital they accrue. I conclude by asking white people to stop telling stories that reproduce racism and white supremacy.

Chapter 16: A Note on White Silence

This chapter analyzes a common dynamic in inter-racial discussions on race: white silence. I explicate common white rationales for this silence and challenge each from an antiracist framework. These rationales include: "It's just my personality—I rarely talk in groups"; "Everyone has already said what I was thinking"; "I don't feel safe"; and "I already know all this."

Chapter 17: Racism and Specific Racial Groups

This chapter provides a more specific overview of six major racial groups: Asian heritage, Latino/a heritage, African heritage, Native heritage, Arab or Muslim heritage, and multiracial heritage. A brief overview of some of the specific ways that racism manifests for each group is provided, along with a list of specific ways an ally can work to interrupt them.

Chapter 18: Antiracist Education and the Road Ahead

This chapter provides an overview of the basic tenets of antiracist education and addresses the question of where to go from here. Characteristics of allies and the skills whites need to develop in order to build cross-racial relationships are identified. Strategies for the lifelong continuing education necessary for interrupting racism are reiterated and summarized.

· 1 ·

RACE IN EDUCATION

The most recent data about U.S. teachers show that despite the fact that the public school population is becoming increasingly racially diverse, more than 80% of elementary and secondary school teachers are white (U.S. Department of Education, 2012). Almost half of the schools in the United States do not have a single teacher of color on staff and therefore many students, regardless of their own race, will graduate from high school having been taught only by whites (Picower, 2009). These racial demographics are not shifting; 80% to 93% of all current teacher education students are white, and they are being instructed by a teacher education profession that is 88% white (Picower, 2009). This racial homogeneity is compounded by unabated racial segregation in schools and housing, and it may be assumed from these statistics that the majority of whites have not lived near or attended school with people of color, have had few if any teachers, friends, family members, or authority figures of color, and do not interact with people of color in any direct or equal way in their lives or in their teacher preparation programs. Yet as evidenced in many studies, while most teacher education students live their lives in racial segregation, they believe that racism is in the past, that segregation "just happens," that they were taught to see everyone the same and therefore they don't see color, and that being white has no particular meaning.

The overwhelming majority of whites in the teaching field, particularly as classrooms are increasingly filled with children of color and immigrants in a country marked by racial inequality, has profound implications for the role white teachers play in reproducing racial inequality. These implications are intensified by the fact that few—if any—white teacher education students can answer the question, "What does it mean to be white?" Yet it is critical that future teachers understand racism's modern manifestations if they are to interrupt it—rather than reproduce it—in schools. This book will provide the conceptual framework necessary for the majority of readers to think critically about race and answer the essential question: *What does it mean to be white in a society that proclaims race meaningless, yet is deeply divided by race?*

Consider an exercise I use in my teacher education classes (adapted from Nitza Hidalgo). On the first day of the semester, before I go over the syllabus or talk to my new students beyond introducing myself, I pass out a sheet of paper with the following questions and ask them to write their anonymous reflection:

> Discuss what it means to be part of your particular racial group(s). How racially diverse was your neighborhood(s) growing up? What messages have you received about race from your family, friends, schools, and neighborhoods about race? In other words, how has your race(s) shaped your life?

I tell the students that we will return to these at the end of the semester, pass them around (with no names), and read them out loud. But to add another layer of anonymity, theirs will be read in one of my other course sections, and we will be reading another section's reflections in our class, so nothing they write will be read in their own class.

After about 10 minutes I collect the reflections in an envelope and set them aside. I then tell my class that I am going to make some predictions about what their reflections say. These are my predictions: "You grew up in mostly white neighborhoods and went to mostly white schools. Your teachers were mostly white. Race hasn't shaped your life because race is not important. You believe that people should be judged by their actions, not the color of their skin. The messages you have received about race have come primarily from your family; if your family was not prejudiced, then they taught you not to be prejudiced. If your family *was* prejudiced, then you rejected their teaching and are not prejudiced. Perhaps you had a friend or two growing up or a family member who is not white, or you traveled outside of the United States, and that is why you are not prejudiced. If there were a few students of color in your school, they were your friends, or at least no one had any issue with them. Some of you felt that no one should get *special* treatment because of race, and had programs such as Affirmative Action in mind. Perhaps you know some people other than yourself who are racist, but you don't approve of that. Further demonstrating how unimportant race has been to your life, many of you found it difficult to come up with enough ideas or interest to write more than just a few sentences. The majority of the reflections will add up to the same conclusion: race is not and should not be important." (My students tell me later that my predictions irritated them because they were correct, suggesting that I can know something about them based solely on the fact that they are white, and thereby poking not only at their racial narratives but also at their sense of themselves as individuals.)

The following anonymous student responses (ASR) are representative of most I receive, both in content and length. Students are answering the following three questions: (1) How racially diverse was your neighborhood(s) growing up? (2) What messages have you received about race from your family, friends, schools, and neighborhoods about race? (3) How has your race(s) shaped your life? As you read, keep in mind that these students are in their junior and senior years of college and will be going on to be our nation's teachers:

> I don't believe that my particular race has had much impact on my life. I don't feel that I strongly identify with it. There was only one black family in my neighborhood of 30+ houses. The message I received about race in high school was very limited. I personally do not think that my race is a factor in the way I live my life. Race is not something that I often acknowledge. (ASR)

> My first neighborhood, racially, was pretty (not meaning nice) diverse. These being apartments, you could find different races. My second neighborhood, where I live now, is not very racially diverse. Messages? Not really any. Impact? I don't know. (ASR)

> My neighborhood in itself was not that diverse, however, much of my hometown is. I have always been taught to treat everyone no matter what their race is equally. My grandparents have a much different thought than my own parents do and they made sure to bring us up treating everyone with respect. Overall, I do not think race has shaped me much at all because it really doesn't matter to me. When I look at someone, I do not look at the color of their skin but rather the person that they are. (ASR)

> My neighborhood was not racially diverse at all growing up. Maybe freshman year of college was when diversity appeared, yet still very small. I am not sure [how race

shapes my life], it seems similar because I am white and I feel like I am constantly hearing racial slurs or people using the race card, that it just makes me thankful for who I am, and don't have to deal with that. (ASR)

Growing up my neighborhood was not that diverse at all, basically almost everyone was white with no other backgrounds. I honestly don't think about my racial group too much, I try not to discriminate against people of another race. Where I work, however, we have a lot of diversity. People speak more than one language, come from different countries. I found it very interesting and since I've been there for so long I am used to it. Even when I first started I never felt weird or anything. In school we were taught to never discriminate, and learned about different cultures. (ASR)

I taught in an education program that is 97% white, and it was rare for me to have any students of color in my classes. Thus, this typical insistence that race doesn't matter comes from white students sitting in an all-white classroom, who grew up in primarily white neighborhoods and attended primarily white schools, and are currently being taught by a virtually all-white faculty (including me). These racial realities testify to a society separated by race. Yet how do so many white people manage to position race as meaningless even as we live, work, study, love, and play in racial separation? Further, this separation is not benign; racial disparity between whites and people of color is measurable in every area of social life—health, income, net worth, educational outcomes, criminal justice, infant mortality, and life expectancy. If race is meaningless, how do we explain that separation and disparity?

My students' answers, which are the same answers I get regardless of where I ask the question—schools, workplaces, social gatherings—or the age of the participants, indicate that the vast majority of whites are racially *illiterate*. Of course we don't realize that we are illiterate because we have been taught that these are the correct answers to questions of race in public (what we say about race in private will be discussed later in this book). But I use the term illiterate because we are only able to articulate the most predictable, superficial, and distorted understandings of race. Most white people have never been given direct or complex information about racism before, and often cannot consciously recognize, understand, or articulate much about it. I open each chapter of this book with excerpts from my students' responses in order to illustrate this point.

People of color are generally much more aware of racism on a personal level, but due to the wider society's silence and denial of it, often do not have a macro-level framework from which to analyze their experiences. Further, dominant society "assigns" different roles to different groups of color, and a critical consciousness about racism varies not only among people of color within groups, but also across groups. For example, many African Americans relate having been prepared by parents to live in a racist society, while many Asian heritage people say that racism was never directly discussed in their homes (hooks, 1989; Lee, 1996). While this book focuses on white racial socialization, it may be helpful to people of color because so much of the experience of a person of color in this society is predicated on adapting to the ways in which whites understand and perform race.

Returning to the exercise, at the end of the semester we gathered in a circle and I passed around another section's reflections. We each read one aloud. My predictions all came to pass, with a few variations (occasionally a white person will acknowledge that whites have benefited from a system that privileges them or admit to holding some racial stereotypes) and depending on whether there were any students of color in the group (students of color rarely say that race has no meaning in their lives). But now my students could see that the way that white people conceptualize race plays a key role in how racism flourishes. At this point in the course, many students were better equipped to critically analyze the fundamental question addressed by this book—how the vast majority of whites can live in racial segregation even as we insist that race has no meaning in our lives. They had also begun to see what is required of them if they want to change these dynamics. In short, they have gained some degree of racial literacy. My goal for this book is to take my readers on that same journey.

Speaking as a white person to other white people, *and within the context of the United States*, I will explicate how we are able to position racism as something that happened in the past at the same time that so many of us live racially segregated lives today. I will also address why it is urgent that we understand and can identify current manifestations of racism. Starting with a framework for understanding racism as a system of unequal social, cultural, and institutional power, rather than as individual acts of prejudice, I will take my readers through an analysis of white socialization. I will provide a conceptual framework for understanding the power of race in our lives, and information on the skills and perspectives needed to build cross-racial awareness in a society that is deeply segregated at the same time that it is positioned as "post-racial."

Some may ask why white people need to develop racial literacy when these simplistic answers clearly work for us and allow us to be comfortable in the face of so much racial inequality. One important reason is that our illiteracy limits our intellectual, psychic, and emotional growth. Bonilla-Silva (2009) documents a manifestation of white racial illiteracy in his study of color-blind white racism. He states, "Because the new racial climate in America forbids the open expression of racially based feelings, views, and positions, when whites discuss issues that make them uncomfortable, they become almost incomprehensible: 'I, I, I, I don't mean, you know, but …'" (p. 68). Probing forbidden racial issues results in verbal incoherence—digressions, long pauses, repetition, and self-corrections. Bonilla-Silva suggests that this incoherent talk is a function of talking about race in a world that insists that race does not matter. This incoherence is one demonstration that many white people are unprepared to engage—even on a preliminary level—in an exploration of their racial perspectives that could lead to a shift in their understanding.

However, an assertion that whites do not engage with dynamics of racial discourse is somewhat misleading. White people do, of course, notice the race of others and invariably mark it ("the Asian teacher …"). We also discuss race somewhat freely among ourselves, albeit often in coded ways. But our refusal to directly acknowledge this race talk results in a kind of split consciousness that leads to the incoherence Bonilla-Silva documents above. This denial also guarantees that the racial misinformation that circulates in the culture and informs our perspectives will be left unexamined. But most importantly, this lack of preparedness results in the maintenance of racial inequality, for if whites cannot engage in an exploration of both their own and people of color's racial perspectives, we hold the racial order in place and continue to impose our racial perspectives and experiences as universal. This imposition works to obscure the workings of race in our lives, leaving us to explain racial segregation and inequality in ways that blame and punish people of color. The continual retreat from the discomfort of authentic racial engagement in a culture infused with racial disparity limits our ability to challenge racial inequality and results in a perpetual cycle that works to hold racism in place. Perhaps most profoundly, racial illiteracy prevents us from building and sustaining authentic relationships across racial lines.

· 2 ·

UNIQUE CHALLENGES
OF RACE EDUCATION

I just see us all as part of the human race, not necessarily different groups of people. Whether people see it or not we are all the same with one objective, to survive. My neighborhood is mostly white. My family doesn't talk about race because we have a lot more important things to do than worry about the color of people's skin because I like all people. (ASR)

My neighborhood growing up was not racially diverse at all. Every family in my neighborhood was also Caucasian. Throughout my time in school I have continually been taught that skin does not matter. (ASR)

My neighborhood wasn't very diverse at all, mostly white middle class. From my parents and schools I have been taught to be tolerant of other races and to accept others for their differences. (ASR)

Racism is among the most emotionally and politically charged issues in society. This makes it challenging to discuss for many reasons: widespread miseducation about what racism is and how it works; a lack of shared language and frameworks for discussing racism; deep institutional and economic investments in the maintenance of racism; ideologies such as individualism, meritocracy, and colorblindness; fear of losing face or self-concepts; and an emotional attachment to protecting (rather than expanding) our worldviews.

At the same time that most whites have a very limited understanding of race and racism, I have never met a white person who does not have an *opinion* on race and racism. In fact, I have seldom met a white person who didn't have a strong, *emotional* opinion on race and racism. If you are white and are unsure that white people have strong opinions about race, at your next family dinner or social gathering ask a direct question about race, for example, "I am reading a book on what it means to be white. What do you think it means to be white?" Or perhaps, "How do you think race shapes white people's lives?" or even simply "What are your thoughts on race?" Try to move people past superficial and trite answers ("I don't think it means anything to be white—I see people as humans") by continually asking them to "say more about that ..." and see what happens. The direct question itself will make many white people uncomfortable, and most will start out with the usual declarations that it doesn't or shouldn't mean anything. As you continue to probe however, you will likely begin to see the emotions concealed just beneath the surface—discomfort or anxiety or anger or resentment. These emotions are an indicator that there is more going on than our initial responses would imply, and much of this book will address this below-the-surface level. But for now consider the surface level of race dynamics for whites—our *opinions*.

Any white person living in the United States will develop opinions about race simply by "swimming in the water" of our culture. But these opinions will necessarily be superficial because mainstream society—schools, media, films, family discussions—addresses race in very superficial ways (at least when addressing race directly; we address race indirectly in much more complex ways). Unfortunately, we confuse these opinions with informed knowledge and lose sight of the fact that this is a social-scientific field of research and scholarship that is ongoing, ever deepening and expanding. Many people feel that taking a class, reading a book, attending a workshop, having a friend, or just being a generally nice person are sufficient to "cover it" and thus lack the humility that is afforded other disciplines. But informed knowledge and opinions are not the same. Informed knowledge on racism for whites only comes from intentional long-term study and practice.

Consider, for example, other fields of social science such as anthropology, archaeology, economics, geography, history, linguistics, and political science. Although I have opinions (thoughts, ideas, assumptions) about each of these fields, I also understand that my opinions are based in the most elementary understanding. I would not presume to offer these opinions to scholars in these fields, knowing that I would embarrass myself in my ignorance. Instead, I would acknowledge their expertise and seek to learn from them by asking questions. If I had specific ideas or had heard something interesting about their field of study, I might share my ideas, but with humility, possibly prefaced with, "I was taught ... or I heard that ..." and closely followed by "What are your thoughts on that?"

Try this thought experiment: You are in a course that fulfills a university science requirement. The professor holds a PhD in Astronomy. He has written several books and is widely published in peer-reviewed journals, and has a national reputation in his field. The course objectives include defining physical concepts and terms used in modern astronomy; gaining an understanding of the physical nature of various astronomical bodies and phenomena; and exposure to the practices, methodology, and conceptual basis of the modern physical science of astronomy. The professor is presenting the established theory in the field. He raises the issues of the number of planets and states that, based on currently accepted criteria for constituting a planet, there are officially 8 planets.

One of the students raises his hand and insists that there are 9 planets, because that is what he learned in school, and he has seen many books with pictures of the planets, and there are always 9. He had a map of the sky in his bedroom as a child and it showed 9 planets. Further, he says, his parents taught him that there were 9 planets, and many of his friends also agree that there are 9. When the professor tries to explain to the student that to engage with the planet controversy one must first demonstrate understanding of the criteria for what constitutes a planet, he is cut off by the student, who declares, "Well, that's your opinion. My opinion is that there are 9."

The professor tries once more to explain that there are scientific criteria for classifying celestial bodies as planets, and although at one time the scientific community believed that Pluto qualified, with further study they now understand that it doesn't, in large part based on its shape. To which the student replies, "I don't care what Pluto is shaped like, it's a planet, and there are 9 planets."

Do you imagine that this student would be seen as credible by the rest of the class? Would the class admire him for standing up to the professor and expressing the same opinions they held? Even if his peers did share his opinion, would that make his argument credible? Or is it more likely that he would be seen (at the minimum) as immature, not particularly bright, and even somewhat disrespectful? Would it be assumed that he might have trouble passing the class? Most people would not see this student as credible or seek to align themselves with him.

But something interesting happens to our humility when the topic is race. Like this student, many of us feel completely confident—indeed, even a bit righteous—about sharing our opinions. And like the student above, we cite anecdotal evidence and family teachings to support it. But when we understand how complex race relations are, we may realize that our opinions on race and racism, unless supported by ongoing cross-racial relationships, study, continuing education, and self-knowledge and reflection, are as naïve and ignorant as those of this hypothetical astronomy student.

For example, I have had some version of the following interaction many times: I am in the grocery store and run into another white person whom I haven't seen in many years. As we catch up I mention that I have earned my doctorate in Whiteness Studies and that I now research, write, and teach on the topic of racism and race relations. Invariably, they will reply with some form of this platitude: "Oh, people just need to ... get along, get over it, take responsibility, see each other as individuals," and so on. Rarely does anyone ask me my thoughts on the topic, or what I have learned, or what the latest research or theory is. I can't help but notice that we are usually surrounded by white people, in a grocery store that is in a primarily white neighborhood, and that the person who just gave me the "answer" leads a primarily white life.

Critical thinking in the study of race includes the ability to recognize and analyze the ways in which meaning (knowledge) is historically, politically, and socially constructed and infused with political investments. These investments have concrete outcomes for people's life opportunities. Whether you agree with the ideas expressed here or not, other scholars who are experts in the topic have found the arguments to be credible and relevant, and you must be prepared to engage critically and constructively with those arguments. Your "common-sense" opinions alone will not enable you to do that.

Thus, to make the time spent reading this book as constructive as possible, I only ask that readers be willing to grapple with difficult and challenging ideas. Grappling means to receive, reflect upon, practice articulating, and seek deeper clarity and understanding. Grappling is *not* rejecting out of hand, refusing to engage, debating, or playing "devil's advocate." The goal is to move us beyond the mere sharing of the uninformed opinions we already hold and toward more informed engagement. I urge my readers to remember the distinction between opinions and informed knowledge as I proceed to raise some challenging and politically charged issues. As the book unfolds, I will work to show you why whites lose their humility as well as their curiosity when it comes to race. For now, I ask you to hold your opinions lightly and to be willing to look beneath the surface of your racial beliefs.

In order to meet the challenges of race education, I offer the following reminders, adapted from Sensoy & DiAngelo (2012):

- A strong opinion is not the same as informed knowledge.
- There is a difference between agreement and understanding: When discussing complex social and institutional dynamics such as racism, consider whether "I don't agree" may actually mean "I don't understand."
- We have a deep interest in denying the forms of oppression which benefit us.
- We may also have an interest in denying forms of oppression that harm us. For example, people of color can deny the existence of racism and even support its structures. This denial may keep them from feeling overwhelmed by the daily slights or protect them from the penalties of confronting white people on racism. However, regardless of the reason, this denial still benefits whites at the group level, not people of color.
- Racism goes beyond individual intentions to collective group patterns.
- We don't have to be aware of racism in order for it to exist.
- Our racial position (whether we are white, a person of color, or multiracial) will greatly affect our ability to see racism. For example, if we swim against the "current" of racial privilege, it's often easier to recognize, while harder to recognize if we swim with the current.
- Putting our effort into protecting rather than expanding our current worldview prevents our intellectual and emotional growth.

Unfortunately, dominant society teaches us that racism consists of individual acts of meanness committed by a few bad people (McIntosh, 2012). The people who commit these acts are considered racists; the rest of us are not racist. These ideas construct racism as an individual binary: Racist/Not Racist (Trepagnier, 2010). A binary is an either/or construct that positions a social dynamic into two distinct and mutually exclusive categories. Virtually all people know how to fill in the two sides of the racism binary: if you *are* a racist, you are ignorant, bigoted, prejudiced, mean-spirited, and most likely old, Southern, and drive a pick-up truck (working-class). If you are *not* a racist, you are nice, well-intentioned, open-minded, progressive, and "don't have a prejudiced bone in your body." Most of us understand, at this moment in our cultural history, which is the "right" side of this binary to be on. But these categories are false, for all people hold prejudices, especially across racial lines in a society deeply divided by race.

Racist = Bad	Not Racist = Good
Ignorant	Progressive
Bigoted	Educated
Prejudiced	Well-intentioned
Mean-spirited	Open-minded
Old	Young
Southern	Northern

Figure 2. The racist/not racist binary.

I may be told that everyone is equal by my parents; I may have friends of color; and I may never tell a racist joke. Yet I am still impacted by the forces of racism as a member of the society; I will still be seen as white, treated as white, and experience life as a white person. My identity, personality, interests, and investments will develop from a white perspective. In a society in which race clearly matters, our race profoundly shapes us and if we want to challenge it, we have to make an honest accounting of how it manifests in our own lives and in the society around us. Although racism does of course occur in individual acts, *these acts are part of a larger system of interacting and interlocking dynamics*. The focus on individual incidences prevents the personal, interpersonal, cultural, historical, and structural analysis that is necessary in order to challenge this larger system. In the chapters that follow, I will explain this system. For now, strive to consider a different way of thinking about racism, rather than strive to maintain the concepts you already hold. Set aside the common beliefs that racism only occurs in specific and intentional incidents and that only bad people participate in racism. In order to understand how racism works as a system, we must start with an understanding of socialization.

Discussion Questions

1. What does Audre Lorde mean when she says "The Master's tools will never dismantle the Master's house," as discussed in the Introduction? What are some of the ways in which the Master's Tools Dilemma is operating when white people attempt to challenge their own racism? When we use terms such as *white people* and *people of color*?

2. Why do so many white people lose their humility when the topic is race and racism?

3. Discuss the "Good/Bad Binary." What are some examples of how you have seen the "Good/Bad Binary" at play in your own life? In the larger society?

4. What parallels do you see between the analogy of the Astronomy student and how white people often engage with education on race and racism?

5. Discuss the list of reminders the author offers in order to meet the challenges of race education. Which are the most difficult for you? Why? How will you work to address that difficulty?

6. If you are working through these questions as part of a white discussion group, how will you keep the discussion on track (focused on *ourselves* and our *own* participation)? How will you ensure that when common white patterns surface (distancing, intellectualizing, rationalizing), you will work to identify and challenge them rather than ignore or avoid them?

· 3 ·

SOCIALIZATION

The messages I've received have all been from home, school, or working and are all the same, which is that race doesn't matter. There is no way to choose or control what race you are so everyone is the same in that way, which means everyone should be treated the same. I don't know how my race has shaped my life at all. (ASR)

My neighborhood wasn't diverse at all. In my school of 500-plus students there was only a handful of non-white students. My family hasn't sent me messages on race. I guess my schools have sent the message that the non-white students have behavioral problems. Overall, race doesn't mean that much to me or my life. (ASR)

What Is Socialization?

We are born into a particular time, place, and society—into a particular *culture*. Culture refers to the characteristics of everyday life of a group of people who are bound together in time and place, and through shared systems of meaning. Some of these characteristics are visible and easily identified by the members of the culture (dress, food, customs, language), but the vast majority of meaning is below the surface of everyday awareness. Many educators use the metaphor of an iceberg to capture the concept of culture. The iceberg's tip, which shows above the water line, can be thought of as the superficial and easily identified characteristics of culture.

But below the surface of the water, hidden from our sight, is the majority of the iceberg's massive bulk (see Figure 3). This represents the aspects of culture that are so deeply internalized that they are taken for granted. These aspects include: notions of modesty; patterns of non-verbal communication; meanings attributed to emotions and rules governing their public expression; approaches to problem-solving; beliefs about pain tolerance; medical frameworks; definitions of obscenity; relationship to animals; gender roles; norms of sexuality; concepts of the individual versus the collective; what constitutes ownership; beliefs about aging; and concepts of childhood, time, normalcy, deviancy, beauty, family, race, the body, and death. We rarely consciously reflect on these aspects of culture, yet we just *know* when someone is crying too loud, acting strange, or not fitting in.

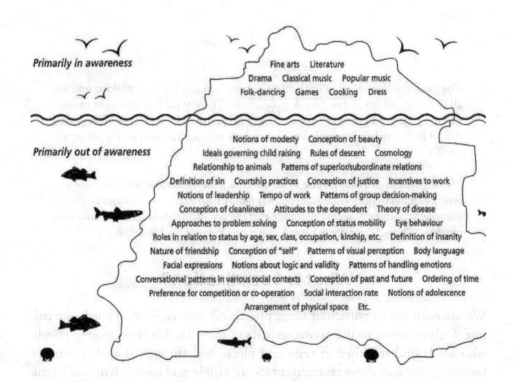

Figure 3. The iceberg of culture.
Reprinted with Permission: p. 14, *AFS Orientation Handbook* Vol. 4, New York: AFS Intercultural Programs Inc, 1984.

Although the cultural norms governing our interactions and behaviors come to feel natural, we aren't born knowing them. We are *socialized* into them. Socialization is the process of being trained into our culture; learning the norms, meanings and practices that enable us to make sense of the world and behave appropriately in a given culture. We are taught these norms in myriad ways, by a range of people, and through a variety of mediums. Further, this training is not complete after childhood; it continues throughout our lives. Much of this training is non-verbal and is achieved through watching and comparing. This will be important to remember when we begin to consider our racial socialization, because there is a vast difference between what we verbally teach our children and all of the other ways we train them into the norms of their culture.

Let's take gender roles as an example of socialization's ongoing nature across the lifespan. *Sex* refers to physical aspects of the human body. *Gender* is a social role defined by the *meaning* that a given culture assigns to those physical aspects. In other words, penises and vaginas are body parts used as an indicator of your sex. But gender is the *meaning* society enforces on those body parts: the roles and behaviors expected of you based on the sex you are assigned at birth. The term for people whose sex assignment at birth is aligned with their current gender identity in accordance with their socialization into dominant norms—e.g., they were assigned "male" at birth and grow to identify as a man, or assigned "female" at birth and grow to identify as a woman— is "cisgender." Cis is Latin for *same* and indicates that one's gender assignment and identity are the same or in agreement. Another way to think about this is that a person who is cisgender is *not* transgender.

People who are transgender have a gender identity that is different from their assigned sex at birth. A transgender woman is someone who was identified as male at birth but whose gender identity is female and lives, or desires to live, her life as a woman. A transgender man is someone who was identified as female at birth but whose gender identity is male and lives, or desires to live, his life as a man. (And there are some people who don't identify with either of the gender categories; they are *non-binary*.)

One thing we all have in common, regardless of our gender identity, is that we live in a society that is set up to enforce the gender roles imposed on us from birth. In several chapters I make parallels between sexism and racism in order to make points that most readers will be able to recognize and understand. In doing so, I acknowledge that the terms I use—"man," "woman," "male," "female"—are neither natural nor unchanging. What I seek to accomplish by using these terms, limited and inadequate as they may be, is to reveal the process of *socialization*: what society tells us it means to be a man or a woman/ male or female, and *how* it tells us. In so doing, my intent is not to invalidate or dispute the validity of anyone's gender identity. Rather, I intend to illustrate the process of socialization within a cisnormative gender binary, the lasting effects it has on us as individuals, and how seeing this system of compulsory gender socialization can help us see the process of our racial socialization.

> **Cisgender:** The term for people whose sex assignment at birth and subsequent socialization are the same as their gender identity. The majority of people are cisgender.
>
> **Transgender:** The term for people whose sex assignment at birth is different from their gender identity.

As an example of gender socialization, I might tell my daughter that her intellect and character are much more important than her physical appearance. Yet as she watches me get ready for work, observes my grooming habits, watches me shop, sees what magazines I read, picks up differences in tone and content between the way I talk with men versus women, sees me worry about my weight and constantly check myself in the mirror, hears the comments I make about other women, and senses my anxiety about what to eat or not eat, she is receiving powerful implicit messages that are counter to those I give her explicitly. Through my behavior, I am effectively training my daughter in her gender role. The very fact that I feel the need to tell her that her looks don't matter, but don't feel the need to tell this to her brother, is also communicating something powerful.

Indeed, I can't actually raise my daughter entirely free from my culture's gender socialization because I am not free of it. I can work hard to challenge this socialization in myself and to raise her in a way that counters these gender scripts, but I can't inoculate her from it. These messages about our roles as females are too deeply entrenched in all aspects of culture. Of course my implicit messages that indeed her looks do matter are reinforced (and often much more explicitly) throughout the rest of society; when her relatives buy her "pretty clothes" and praise her appearance, when she watches television and movies, passes by the magazine rack in the grocery store, walks down the toy aisle at the local department store, and plays with Barbie & Bratz dolls with her friends. All of these activities will reinforce the message that in this culture, a girl's looks *do* matter, and these messages can easily overpower the few that counter them.

Socialization begins at birth, but the forces of socialization are gearing up even before birth when our families begin to project their dreams and expectations onto us. For example, in an earlier career I was a childbirth educator, and this career afforded me great insight into the socialization process and how all-encompassing it was. I worked at a hospital and taught the classes that prepared expectant mothers and their partners for childbirth. Participants would often come to class and tell me that they had an ultrasound that week (an ultrasound uses sound waves to create a picture of the baby inside the womb). I would ask these couples if they had the ultrasound because there had been an indication of a problem with the baby. Invariably, they would answer, "No. We wanted to know the sex of the baby so we could prepare the room."

I ask my readers to imagine what this preparation might look like if the baby was going to be a girl. What if it was going to be a boy? We all know the answers to these questions. The sex of the baby would determine the colors the room would be painted, the clothes that would be purchased, and the toys that would be waiting. Babies are born into an environment already infused with cultural meanings. Later, physical rituals that altered the baby's body based on gender roles may also take place, for example circumcision for the boy, perhaps pierced ears for the girl. Even if the parents wanted to try a more "gender-neutral" approach, it would be very difficult to control the friends and relatives around them and the pressure they would exert to let them reinforce gender roles through clothes, toys, and other gifts.

Research has shown that even the way that mothers hold babies in their arms is influenced by the gender roles of their culture (Martin, 1998). For example, one important study (Bernstein, 1983) gave new mothers a baby wrapped in a blanket. The mother could not see the actual sex of the baby, but she interacted differently with the baby based on what she was *told* the sex was. If she thought she was holding a girl, she handled the baby gently, held it more closely to her body, and made cooing sounds. If she thought she was holding a boy, she held the baby less gently and further away from her body, for example, holding the baby out toward a football and moving his body side to side to simulate walking toward it. Although babies can't walk, if the mother thought she was holding a boy, she would interpret the baby's movements through the lens of gender, for example, "Look! He wants to play with the football!" Overall, mothers encouraged babies to interact with the world based on what we believe about gender—boys to be more active and girls to be more passive. This encouragement is further reinforced through, for example, restrictive clothing for girls such as tights, dresses, shoes with heels, hair ribbons, and jewelry. In these ways, gender gets coded into our very bodies and how we gesture, sit, stand, run and throw (Martin, 1998; Messner, 1995).

If, from the time my mother first held me in her arms, I was being socialized to hold my body in gender-specific ways, these ways would come to feel natural to me. If almost everyone else of my sex also used their bodies in similar ways, and the society around me told me that was natural or biological, my belief would be reinforced. But consider, for example, what happens to a boy who doesn't use his body in socially prescribed ways—a boy who crosses his legs while sitting, gestures with his wrists, and throws "like a girl." He gets teased and corrected.

Although all babies cry regardless of their sex, parents respond to their crying differently (Condry, Condry, & Pogatshnik, 1983; Malatesta & Haviland, 1982), as does the society around them. Boys learn very early that they shouldn't cry. Over time, not feeling like or not being able to cry becomes so ingrained that it seems *natural*. But it isn't. We are trained or socialized into gender-appropriate emotional expressions from the day of our birth. This is what it means to say that gender is *socially constructed*. Socially constructed refers to social meaning that is not inherently *true*, but believed by a society and thus *real* in its consequences for our lives. Gender conditioning begins so early that it becomes very difficult to say what is natural and what is socially constructed. It is naïve to say that one is free of this socialization just because one wishes to be.

> **Socially Constructed**: Meaning that is not inherently true, but agreed upon by society. Once society agrees to this meaning, it becomes real in its consequences for people's lives.

Many educators use the metaphor of a fish in water to capture the all-encompassing dimensions of socialization. A fish is born into water and so simply experiences the water as one with itself; a fish has no way of knowing that it is actually separate from the water. And although the fish *is* separate, it still can't survive without water. In the same way that a fish cannot live without water, we cannot make sense of the world without the meaning-making system that our culture provides. Yet this system is hard to see, because we have always been swimming within it; we just take for granted that what we see is real, rather than a particular *perception* of reality.

As we are socialized into our culture's gender roles, we are similarly socialized into our culture's racial roles. Our parents might tell us that race doesn't matter and that we shouldn't see color, but as with gender socialization, this explicit teaching is not enough to inoculate us against all of the other messages circulating in the culture. For example, if race doesn't matter, why do we live so racially separate? We do so because in our culture race *does* matter, regardless of what we say to our children. The hypothetical mother who doesn't need to teach her son that his intellect and character are the most important things about him is most likely white. The mother of a black son may indeed need to give her son the same message a white mother needs to give her daughter. This is because unlike the white son, his character and intellect will not often be affirmed throughout the culture. Race and gender won't *appear* to matter for those whose race and gender are not devalued in the society.

Frames of Reference

The concept of a frame of reference is another useful way to think about the forces of socialization. Although we live in a culture that emphasizes science and objectivity, human objectivity is not actually possible; humans are social, cultural creatures. We can only make meaning of the world through the cultural frameworks we've been given. Our frame of reference is our meaning-making system, the cultural glasses put over our eyes starting at birth through which we view and make sense of the world. These glasses allow us to see some things while blocking out others. For example, if we are born into one culture and then move into another, we will likely see more than someone who is mono-cultural. Our glasses are not fixed; over our lifetime we may adjust our prescription or even switch between multiple lenses depending on our environment.

The power of our frames of reference to shape meaning and experience was also brought home to me during my years as a childbirth educator. Prior to becoming involved in the field of childbirth, I assumed that some aspects of life were universal—that all people regardless of their culture experienced them similarly. The ultimate example of a universal human experience, it seemed to me, was childbirth. This was not merely a cultural custom; this was a biological process necessary to human survival. How could race or class or language interfere here? If we brought 5 pregnant women together from around the world, what would it matter what their customs were or what color their skin was? They all had a uterus with a baby inside, and that baby had to come out. With minor variations, if a baby is being born vaginally, then it has to move down the birth canal in a certain way, the mother's body has to stretch in a certain way, and so on. Wouldn't all women experience this physical process similarly? Wouldn't they describe it similarly (long, hard, and very painful)? But when I began to witness women giving birth in different cultures, I was astounded by just how profound the differences in their experiences were. I soon realized that the experience of something as physical as childbirth was fundamentally shaped by what we *believed* about it; how we made meaning of that physical process through our cultural glasses or frames of reference.

During my training, I watched a film of women giving birth in Brazil. These women were laboring at home without medical intervention. They were calm during labor. When it came time for birth, they squatted down and pushed their babies out on their own, and then picked them up and held them to their chests. Although they often seemed tired afterwards, they didn't cry, scream or otherwise indicate that they felt extreme pain. Women in the United States, however, generally labored in hospitals, with various machines attached to them, given I.V. drips of drugs to speed their labors up, and with limited sensation from the waist down due to pain medications. If they weren't using medication or their medication had worn off, they were usually expressing a great deal of pain. Taken aback by these differences, I began to explore the relationship between socialization and the experience of childbirth. In my classes, I would ask the couples, "How many of you have some anxiety about the upcoming labor?" Consistently, every hand in the room shot up. I would then ask them to free-associate with me their first thoughts when I said "birth." Invariably, the first or second word would be "pain."

When we began to unpack this association, we saw that throughout their lives virtually every story they heard or media depiction they saw portrayed birth as "the most painful thing they would ever experience." Thus, they were socialized to view birth through the cultural lens of pain. This does not mean that the women in Brazil did not experience pain in childbirth, but "pain" was not the primary lens through which they had been socialized to view birth. For them, pain was only one part of a larger whole. In the United States, however, we do reduce childbirth in large part to pain. Needing to manage this pain contributes to the movement of birth into hospitals, where it is defined as a medical event that must be controlled by experts. The vast majority of childbirths in the United States occur in hospitals, and the cesarean section rate in 2014 was 32%, with more than 1 in 3 mothers giving birth surgically. (It is also important to note that infant mortality rates have not decreased in relation to the rise in c-sections.)

Having the opportunity to witness the rituals of birth in two different cultures, I was able to adjust my prescription. This adjustment allowed me to see birth differently. It also allowed me to reflect on the cultural lens I had *previously* viewed birth through. Without the contrast that came from being exposed to a different cultural lens, I wasn't aware I had a cultural view of birth at all; I just assumed the way we did it was normal, natural, and universal. Notice if you had a reaction to my description of birthing women in Brazil squatting down, pushing their babies out by themselves, and picking them up on their own (yes, still covered in the mother's body fluids), with no doctor's hands in the scene. Did the image of the women squatting bother you a little? What about the thought that a medical expert was not orchestrating the process? Many people in the United States do have these reactions, and that helps illustrate the power of our cultural lenses. We may actually feel physically and emotionally upset when our norms are violated.

Another example of how our cultural lenses shape our actual physical perceptions has been demonstrated in studies of orchestra auditions (Klein, 2007). For many years it was believed that women musicians just didn't have the hand strength to play certain instruments as well as men. This wasn't seen as any kind of gender bias, but just a physical fact; women were naturally smaller and weaker, and this was evident in their playing. But then orchestra auditions began to occur behind screens, preventing the judges from knowing the gender of the musician they were listening to, and an astonishing thing happened. Suddenly, many more women were hired in orchestras. Before the screens, when the judges knew the musician was a woman, they actually *heard* her differently based on their cultural *beliefs* that women were not as skilled as men. Again, cultural beliefs are so powerful that they shape physical perceptions. These studies have shown that women are more likely to be chosen if the judges don't know they are women. Based on this research, many auditions now take place behind screens, which has been attributed to a 25% increase in women orchestra musicians (Klein, 2007).

In each of the examples above, people are viewing an experience or event through their cultural glasses. These glasses have two significant parts: the *frames* and the *lenses*.

Our Frames

The *frames* of our glasses are the big picture (macro) ideas about group identities, as identified in the chart below (adapted from Sensoy & DiAngelo, 2012).

Examples of Group "Frames"	Examples of Identities within Group Frames
Race	White, Black, Indigenous, Asian, Latino, Filipino, South Asian, Multiracial, People of Color
Class	Poor, Working Class, Middle Class, Upper Class, Owning Class
Gender	Cis-Men, Cis-Women, Transgender
Sexuality	Lesbian, Gay, Bisexual, Two-Spirited, Heterosexual
Ethnicity	Irish, Italian, Métis, Greek, Taiwanese
Religion	Hindu, Buddhist, Jew, Christian, Muslim, Atheist
Ability	Able-bodied, People with physical disabilities, People with developmental disabilities
Nationality	Immigrants, Indigenous people, Citizens

Figure 4. Group identities.

This chart illustrates some of the significant social groups in our society. Regardless of our protestations that these groups don't matter and we see everyone the same, we know that to be a man as defined by dominant culture is a different experience than to be a woman, to be old is different than to be young, to be rich is different than to be poor, to be able-bodied is different than to have a disability, to be gay is different than to be heterosexual, and so on. These groups matter, but not *naturally* as we are often taught to believe. They matter because the socially constructed *meaning* ascribed to these groups creates a difference in lived experience (e.g., the belief that women musicians are not as skilled as men results in different kinds of encouragement and opportunities for men than women).

We are socialized into these groups *collectively*. This means that in mainstream culture, we all receive the same messages about what these groups mean; *why* to be one is a different experience than to be another. And we also know that it is *easier* to be in one rather than the other. Further, if we asked 100 people in the United States to brainstorm common characteristics for each group, the lists would be very similar. We gain our understandings of group meaning collectively through aspects of the society around us that are shared and unavoidable: television, movies, news stories, song lyrics, magazines, textbooks, schools, religion, literature, stories, jokes, traditions and practices, history, and so on. These dimensions of our culture shape the *frames* of our glasses—our *group* identities.

Our Lenses

Within our frames are our *lenses*. Our lenses are aspects of identity that are more unique to us—what we think of as our personality, our family influences, our birth order, and our unique experiences. For example, my sister and I are only 1 year apart, both white, U.S. citizens, English-only speaking, middle-aged, able-bodied, raised poor but currently middle-class females who lost our mother when we were children. We have a great deal in common and share the same cultural references. At the same time, we are considered different from one another. She is more extroverted, artistic, and organized, and I am more introspective, intellectual, and unorganized. In addition to the socialization we share (our frames), we each have unique character traits and have had experiences that the other has not (our lenses), which accounts in part for our differences.

Putting Our Frames and Lenses Together

Figure 5 may be a useful way to conceptualize our cultural glasses; the social group filters through which we view the world. In order to begin the process of identifying and articulating your frames and lenses and *how they interact*, reflect on the following overarching questions: (a) How have my cultural glasses shaped how I view myself and others? (b) What might my glasses make it easy for me to see? What might my glasses prevent me from seeing? (c) How might my glasses shape my expectations in life and what I do or do not take for granted?

The following are more detailed questions to explore regarding our social identities. Notice that these questions combine individual experiences (our lenses) with larger social patterns (our frames), because our frames and our lenses are inseparable.

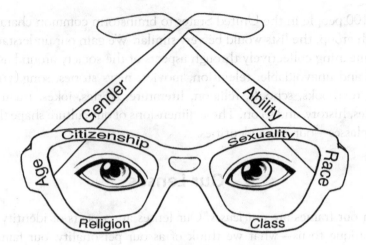

Figure 5. Frames of reference (illustration by Andrea O'Brian).

Family: How did your family shape you? Consider birth order, size of family, specific family members, whether your family was biological, and changes in the composition of your family over time.

Place: How did the neighborhood/region/country(s) in which you grew up influence how you see the world? Was it urban, suburban, or rural? Did you move a lot or seldom? Was your neighborhood racially integrated or racially segregated? Was it considered a "good" neighborhood or a "bad" neighborhood, and why?

Class: How did your class background (i.e., poor, working-class, middle-class, upper-class) shape your expectations about your future? Where you believe you can go? What resources you have access to? What kind of employment you have or assume you will have? How you view those in different class groups?

Religion: Were you raised within a certain religious tradition? How did it shape your worldview? What kind of framework did (does) it provide for you? Did your religion give you a sense of yourself as an "insider" or an "outsider"? What were you taught about people outside of your religion?

Race: Did you grow up with a sense of yourself as a member of a racial group(s)? Did other people respond to you that way? How did your race(s) shape your sense of place in the world? If you did not have a sense of yourself as a member of a racial group, how did that shape your identity? Who did you learn had race, if you didn't? How did you learn this?

Body: How do aspects of your body influence your orientation to the world? Athletic ability? What about your skin color? Ability? Age? Health?

Height and weight? Are you considered physically "normal" or abnormal? What can you or can't you take for granted based on your body and how it functions in relation to other bodies?

Gender: What messages did you get about your assigned gender? What roles and expectations did others have for you based on your gender (one way to surface gender socialization is to consider the consequences of being perceived as acting "too much" like the other gender)? What appears to be open to you based on your gender and how others perceive it? How does your own gender identity shape your daily experience and routine?

Sexuality: How does your sexuality shape how you define yourself? How does it shape your expectations for your life, your partners, your family? How others see you? What privileges do or don't you have access to? For example, can you openly discuss your relationship status, in virtually any situation, without risk of social penalty? What assumptions do people make about you based on what they perceive to be your sexuality?

Experiences: Are there key experiences you have had that shape how you see the world?

As you can see, these questions are not simple, and it can take a lifetime to uncover the answers. Further, as we have new experiences, our perspectives change; our glasses are not fixed. Often in multicultural education endeavors, we learn about the experiences of people who are in marginalized groups, but seldom are we asked to consider what it means to be in a dominant group. For example, if I am learning about the experiences of people who grew up in poverty and I was raised middle-class, I can use this contrast in our experiences to gain more insight into the experience of poverty. But I can also use it to gain more insight into what it means to have been raised as middle-class. The contrast in our experiences can help me see my own frames. Without that contrast I can't fully understand differences between social classes. This is one of the great challenges of social segregation. Because our society separates us based on key differences such as age, race, and class, we have limited opportunities to contrast our experiences with others, and thus, limited opportunities to understand how our frames shape our perspectives.

Many of us are taught that we have to "walk a mile in someone else's shoes" in order to understand their perspective. But walking in someone else's shoes is not truly possible. Many of us who wear glasses have had the experience of someone taking our glasses and trying them on, then exclaiming, "You can't see at all!" By this they mean that our glasses make their vision very blurry. This is because we have a different "prescription" than they have. We may share the frames—the socialization or "big messages" we all collectively receive from the wider society through schools, media, movies, literature, and so forth—but we don't share the lenses. Although we can't fully walk in others' shoes, we can learn to draw connections, contrasts, and parallels between their experiences and our own. But in order to do this, we must first begin with an understanding of our *own* glasses; considering those of others requires that we are able to consider our own.

Social Groups Are Given Different Value

Our lenses and the frames that hold them are *inseparable*. They interact in important and dynamic ways. Yet in U.S. society, it is the lens that is emphasized—our so-called uniqueness or individuality. Indeed, advertisers, who depend on as many people as possible buying the same products, consistently appeal to our individuality to get us to buy their products: "Show how unique you are by wearing this designer's name on your jeans." These advertising techniques work precisely because they appeal to a *culturally shared* value—to be seen as an individual who is different from everybody else. Because our society emphasizes our lenses over our frames, many of us are not skilled in reflecting on our group memberships. As race is one of these groups, developing racial literacy requires that we push against our socialization and temporarily suspend our focus on our lenses and focus on our frames. This will go against our conditioning because we have been taught that only the lenses matter, not the frames.

If we reflect on this frame/lens dilemma for a moment, we might begin to see why so many aspects of social life are confusing. On the one hand, we know that our group memberships (the frames) profoundly matter, but on the other hand, we are told that the lenses are the most important part of ourselves and we should deny the significance of the frames. This is because each group membership has an opposite group, and one is *valued* more highly than the other. Further complicating identity, we only need to deny the significance of our frames if we are in the more socially valued group. For example, if I am a white middle-class male, I am more likely to deny that race, class, or gender matters than if I am poor, Asian, or female. On the other hand, some social groups are more acceptable to denigrate than others, based on the specific historical moment. For example, many of us who are younger and thus in the more socially valued group, openly make fun of the elderly, and getting old is represented in our culture as a terrible thing (if you doubt this, go to the humor section of the birthday card display in any store or read a women's magazine). We know these differences matter, but *acknowledging* that they matter is a nuanced social dance, based on what is socially acceptable in a particular context. These contradictions, which often require us to deny something that we know is true, create internal conflict. Thus, we need practice in openly and honestly examining aspects of our frames we have been taught to deny.

Our identities (or glasses) are a complex intersection of the personal, historical, and cultural; they are formed within a social context. An identity depends upon others; we know who we *are* by knowing who we *are not*. The sociologist Charles Cooley (1922) termed this dynamic *the looking glass self*. By this he meant that our identities develop based on what others reflect back to us. These others include our parents, care-givers, teachers, peers, images in the media, authority figures, role-models, and more. Understanding of ourselves is necessarily based upon our own comparisons to others. The concept of *pretty* has no meaning without the concept of *ugly*; the concept of *smart* has no meaning without the concept of *not-smart* or "stupid"; the concept of *deserving* has no meaning without the concept of *undeserving*; the looking glass self is a continual process of comparing ourselves to others in order to understand who we are. Thus a student who tells me, with some pride, that he doesn't care what others think about him and that he is not influenced by others is still dependent on others to know who he is. This statement only has meaning because it is in contrast to (and implies judgment of) those who *do* care about what others think. Ironically, that he has pride about his presumed independent thought is precisely because in our culture, we teach that being an individual is important. This same statement would not be made with pride in a collectivist culture, in which seeing oneself as a member of a group (rather than as an independent individual) is most highly valued.

We learn very early in life which parts of our frames are valued and which are not. Recall the earlier example of the white mother who doesn't need to tell her son that he can be anything he wants. "Anything he wants" refers to the careers deemed *valuable* in society. She doesn't need to tell him he can be a doctor because the assumption that this career is within his reach will be embedded in all aspects of society. For example, the habit of assuming doctors are male that causes us to use "he" when talking about doctors in general; the gender tracking in school that will provide the educational background he needs in the sciences; and the abundance of role-models he will see in the medical profession, all enable him to take for granted that this career is open to him. (This assumes, of course, that he has the economic means to go to medical school, which adds another layer: class.) Now notice that the mother *does* need to tell him that other careers are open to him, such as nursing, early childhood education, elementary school teaching, secretarial work, and so forth, as he won't see many male role models in these careers. But it is highly likely that the mother (and certainly the father) will *not* encourage him to pursue these careers, as worthy and fulfilling as they are. This is because they are associated with women and thus are of *less value* in our society. They pay less and have less status because they are seen as "women's work." Men who do go into these fields are often assumed to be gay, another group membership that is not valued in our society.

However, if the son does go into a female-dominated career, research shows that he will most likely quickly rise to the top and eventually take leadership over the women (Williams, 1992, 1995; Muench et al., 2015). These patterns will occur regardless of whether any one individual agrees that they should, because these patterns occur at the collective level—they are outside the control of any one individual person. Further, while I may not consciously believe that men are superior to women, I could not have avoided that message because it's embedded in all aspects of the cultural water in which I swim. In fact, on a subconscious level, I am very likely contributing to a male's rise over me in an organization.

> **Remember:** Our parents might tell us that aspects of identity such as race and gender don't matter, but this is not enough to inoculate us against all of the other messages circulating in the culture.

Our socialization takes place through both our daily personal interactions with those around us and our exposure to the larger society as we watch television, movies, music videos, advertisements, and news programs, read school textbooks, celebrate national holidays, and follow rules made by courts and politicians said to represent us. Socialization is ongoing throughout our lives; it is not complete after childhood. As we are exposed to new information and as social forces around us shift and change, we shift and change with them. For example, when I was growing up, the technology we take for granted today did not exist. Telephones were stationary and communication was done primarily through hand-written letters. But changes in technology have changed the way we communicate, how we hold our bodies, how we define and conduct relationships, and how we see and present ourselves to others (among many other changes). Technology has socialized us into new norms and practices that are not the same as those we were taught in childhood.

Because our frames are composed of the large social groups into which we are born (i.e., race, class, gender), they remain fairly stable over our lives and continually impact our adaptation to social changes. For example, if we are of a lower social class, we might not have the same access to new technology that those of the middle and upper classes take for granted, and thus we may not develop the same skill set. If we are female, subtle bias in schools may track us away from courses in advanced technology, or we may have less confidence or interest. Our frames are always impacting our lenses.

Most importantly for the purposes of understanding racism, while we remain in the racial group into which we were born, our *lenses can shift* (expand and deepen) as we reflect on our racial frames; gain new experiences, information, and self-knowledge; and practice new patterns of behavior. The goals of this book are rooted in this understanding; as we gain deeper insight into what it means to have the racial frames that we have, our perspective on race deepens, we gain a more nuanced and complex understanding, and we can begin to act in new and more equitable ways. In order to increase our racial literacy we must be able to reflect upon the whole of our cultural glasses—the lenses *and* the frames.

Discussion Questions

1. What does it mean to say that race and gender are socially constructed?
2. Why can't human beings be objective?
3. Why can't we simply decide to override the aspects of our socialization that we don't like?
4. How can we make generalizations about the messages we have received when we don't know each person's individual story?
5. How would you respond to someone who said, "Doesn't it all come down to what your parents taught you?"
6. In your reading group, take a few minutes to share some of your answers from the Frame of Reference reflection questions. What patterns do you notice? What surprised you? (These questions can be downloaded as a handout from www.robindiangelo.com.)

· 4 ·

DEFINING TERMS

My neighborhood is pretty much dominantly white. There are some parts of my town however, that are dominantly Spanish and/or African American. Lately, my town has become much more diverse than when I was younger. The media, history, word of mouth has shown me that there is a certain sense of racism in everyone, even if it's unintentional. Although segregation is in the past, I feel as if racism will always stick. I feel like my life is not affected by race. I grew up in an accepting household and was taught to love everyone. (ASR)

Once we understand the power and ongoing nature of socialization in our lives, we are ready to move on to the next fundamental building block of racial literacy: understanding the terms *prejudice*, *discrimination*, and *racism* and the key differences between them. These terms provide the overall theoretical framework for understanding what it means to be white.

In the following discussion, I am referring to social dynamics based on group memberships. In other words, we are social beings who learn to understand each other by the groups we belong to: old/young, male/female, heterosexual/gay, able bodied/person with a disability. In large part, we know what it means to be part of our own group by understanding that we are *not* a part of its opposite group. Thus when I discuss prejudice and discrimination, I am referring to social dynamics between *groups* of people. These dynamics are a function of socialization and based on a person's social group memberships in a given society. (While these terms are also used to indicate preferences such as those for food, and concepts such as "discriminating taste," this is not the context in which I use them.)

It is critical that readers understand that in speaking about patterns, I will necessarily be generalizing. There are of course exceptions to patterns, and not everyone will fit every pattern. But patterns are recognized as patterns precisely because they are recurring and predictable. One cannot understand modern forms of racism if one cannot or will not explore patterns of group behavior.

Prejudice

Prejudice is pre-judgment about another person based on the social groups to which that person belongs. Prejudice is based upon characteristics we *assume* others have due to their group memberships. We can sometimes pre-judge a person based on their resemblance to another individual (my neighbor is unfriendly; you remind me of my neighbor; I have an immediate dislike of you). But for the purposes of understanding racism, I will focus on prejudice that is based on the *group* to which someone belongs or is *perceived* to belong (you drive an old pick-up truck—I assume you are of a lower social class and therefore will be crude and uneducated). Prejudice is made up in large part by stereotypes that create bias or value judgments. This bias can be *toward* a group as well as against it; whether you view someone as better or as less than someone else based on a group to which they belongs, you are still attributing relative value based on the group.

> **Prejudice:** Learned prejudgment based on stereotypes about a social group that someone belongs to. Prejudice occurs at the individual level; all humans have learned prejudices.

Prejudice consists of thoughts, feelings, assumptions, beliefs, stereotypes, attitudes, and generalizations. The nature of prejudice is that it is based on little or no experience and then projected onto everyone from that group. For example, I have rarely interacted with people from Afghanistan, but my head is nonetheless filled with stereotypes about them, and those stereotypes will

be consistent with those held by most others in my society. If I asked a group
of people who also did not know any Afghani people to share the ideas they
had about Afghanis, our ideas would be similar because we swim in the same
cultural water and absorb the same messages.

So if we don't actually have to have any experience with a group of people
in order to hold prejudices about them, where do we get our prejudice? We
learn prejudice from the society around us. Anyone who grew up watching
Disney movies, for example, has absorbed ideas about ethnic "others": Arabs,
Native Americans, Mexicans, Asians, and so on. We learn prejudice from comments made by family members, from media, advertisements, magazines, song
lyrics, television, novels, textbooks, from teachers and classmates in school.
We also learn prejudice just as powerfully from the *absence* of information, for
example history lessons and textbooks that leave out groups such as women,
people of color, and the poor and working classes. The absence of information
conveys the implicit message that this group of people is not important. Figure
6 illustrates some of the sources of prejudicial messages we receive and absorb.

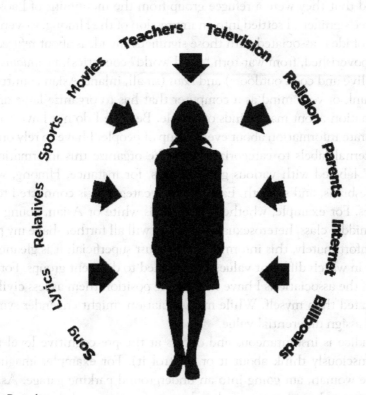

Figure 6. Prejudice.

Further, we tend to focus on information that reinforces our prejudice and to disregard information that counters it. For example, if I hold a stereotype that elderly people are bad drivers, I can be cut off in traffic all day long by a wide range of different kinds of drivers, but when I am cut off by an elderly driver, I will say, "A-ha! See, elderly people are bad drivers!" The 20 bad drivers I encountered previously do not cancel out my stereotype. I view them simply as individual bad drivers; they don't represent their group to me because I don't hold a stereotype about their group's driving ability. For example, I don't have a pre-conceived judgment that white people are bad drivers, or Latino/a people, or working-class people. But I do have a pre-conceived notion about elderly drivers.

All humans have prejudice; it is not possible to avoid. If I am aware that a social group exists, I have to have information about that group that I have gained from the society around me. This information helps me make sense of the group from my cultural framework. For example, when I first heard reference to Hmong people, I had no idea who they were or where they were from. I was told that they were a refugee group from the mountains of Laos. With these three signifiers, I settled into an impression of the Hmong, woven from a network of ideas associated with those signifiers: my ideas about *refugees* (victims, impoverished, from war-torn "third world" countries), *mountains* (rural, peasant, live and cook outdoors) and *Laos* (small, inland Asian country). You might think of your mind as a computer that has to organize large amounts of information about many kinds of people. Because I do not have complete and accurate information about every group of people, I have to rely on superficial external labels to categorize them. We organize this information into "folders," labeled with various group names, for instance, Hmong, women, elderly, lesbians, and so forth. Each of these categories is connected to other categories. For example, whether a woman is white or Asian, young or old, poor or middle class, heterosexual or lesbian, will all further shape my perceptions. Unfortunately, this information isn't just superficial; it is gleaned from a society in which different values are assigned to different groups. For example, all of the associations I have for Hmong position them as less civilized or sophisticated than myself. While my associations might engender sympathy, they still assign differential value.

Prejudice is instantaneous and occurs at the pre-cognitive level (before I can consciously think about it or control it). For example, imagine that I, a white woman, am going into an underground parking garage. As I walk toward my car, I see a man standing between my car and the car next to it, on my passenger side. If it's during the day and the man is white, I usually do not feel fear. I might, however, feel fear in this situation at night. If the man standing by my car is black, I will likely feel some level of fear whether it is day *or* night. If the man standing by my car is Asian, I will *not* feel fear whether it is day or night. I have these reactions instantly, before I can even think about them. This is because I have received relentless messages throughout my life about each of these kinds of men; for example, that black men are dangerous and highly sexual, and that Asian men are passive and nonsexual. As a white woman, I have had less experience with black men and Asian men, so I am more likely to rely on these messages; living in racial segregation, there has been very little in my life to counter them. However, I have a great deal of experience with white men, which is why I am less likely to feel afraid during the day but will have some fear at night—I have a more contextualized response.

But, you might say, as a woman alone you need to feel some fear—that is a healthy way to protect yourself. Yes, that is true. But the problem is that my assessments of safety in that situation are based on misinformation. Most personal crime occurs between people of the same race, so I am statistically at most risk from the white man. Thus, my misinformation is causing me to be off-guard when I shouldn't be and thus not actually keeping me safe (the infamous serial killer Ted Bundy, who was white, understood this well. He lured women into his car by pretending to have a broken arm. Seeing a well-dressed white man in need of assistance, the women were fooled.)

People who say, "I don't have a prejudiced bone in my body," are demonstrating a profound lack of self-awareness. Ironically, they are also demonstrating the power of socialization—we have all been taught in schools, through movies, from family members, teachers, and clergy that it is important not to be prejudiced. Prejudice, we are told, is bad. We wouldn't boast about our lack of prejudice if it weren't socially popular to insist we don't have it; if we hadn't been socialized into thinking we could and should avoid it. Unfortunately, this causes us to deny the unavoidable reality of prejudice. This teaching also works to guarantee our prejudices will be held in place, because we will put our energy into denying rather than examining and challenging them.

At the same time that we are taught to deny our prejudice overall, we are not taught to deny *all* of our prejudices. This is because at different historical and political moments in a given culture, some group prejudices are more acceptable than others. Two examples may illustrate this social dynamic. When I was growing up, it was perfectly acceptable in mainstream society to make fun of people with disabilities. One of my sisters, who has what we now understand to be a learning disability, was simply seen as stupid during our childhood. While it pains me to write that today, it was what everyone around me called her—other children, my parents, relatives, and teachers—and so did I. She was relentlessly teased, called a "retard," and even beaten up after school for being "dumb." I don't recall ever receiving feedback that this wasn't appropriate or that she didn't somehow deserve this treatment. Yet today this treatment would be seen as terrible (and I feel terrible about participating in it). As our knowledge of the learning process changed, we came to understand that people learn differently and we need to modify our teaching. This does not mean that we no longer look down on people with learning disabilities or that they don't grow up with a sense of shame, but there have been improvements, and most adults or teachers wouldn't as openly call someone stupid or punish them as they did in the past.

On the other hand, prejudice toward gay, lesbian, and gender non-conforming people is currently still socially acceptable. While today most people agree that shunning or denying basic rights to a person with a learning disability is unacceptable, I could easily get into a debate about the acceptability of shunning or denying gay people certain basic rights (such as marriage). Gay rights are debated all the time in social and political arenas. Context also plays a part—if I am liberal it is less acceptable for me to express my prejudice on this issue, but if I am conservative it is more acceptable. The fact that I could easily rouse people to debate the issue indicates that progress has been made; just 40 years ago there wouldn't have been a debate—homosexuality was unquestionably seen as wrong in mainstream society. Yet although progress has been made, those who consciously hold prejudice toward gay people generally have no compunction about admitting it. (We all *unconsciously* hold some prejudice toward gay people—even if we are gay ourselves—because like racism, it is embedded in the culture at large. These dynamics are termed *internalized dominance* and *internalized oppression* and will be discussed in the next section.)

There are also emotional dimensions to prejudice. As we are learning our prejudices throughout our lives, emotions are often involved in the process. For example, if I am a child watching a Disney movie such as *Mulan*, in which the scary bad guy is a large Arab man with a beard, turban, and a machete, I am learning the classic stereotypes associated with Arabs, as well as learning to associate the *fear that I'm feeling* with Arabs. These stereotypes and fears will be reinforced in other aspects of my life, such as when I am watching the news and hear about a suspected suicide bomber, or when I hear my parents angrily discussing the 9/11 attacks, or my school is debating whether to allow Muslim girls to wear head-coverings to class, or when the news is repeatedly showing images of strife in Muslim countries. None of my stereotypes have to be factual in reality in order to be "factual" in my mind. For example, I see Arabs and Muslims as interchangeable because they are presented as inter-changeable through the misinformation that circulates in the culture at large.

The negative emotions associated with prejudice range from hatred, fear, mistrust, and disgust, to discomfort and lack of interest. However, most of us are taught to think of prejudice as simply hatred, and because most of us don't consciously hate someone just because of their social group, we seldom relate to or see ourselves as prejudiced. But if we think of the emotions associated with prejudice as a continuum with hatred as the extreme at one end and discomfort at the other end, we may be more likely to admit that we do have prejudice (see Figure 7). For example, throughout all my years of education I have been separated from people with visible disabilities. I did not go to school with them because in U.S. society, people with disabilities usually go to separate schools and are hidden away. This in itself is a powerful message about their value, but it was reinforced by many other messages and indicators that they held less status and were less valuable than I was.

BLATANT					SUBTLE
Hatred	Fear	Disgust	Resentment	Discomfort	Lack of Interest

Figure 7: Emotions of prejudic.

Messages about children with disabilities included the ridicule about riding "the short bus," the teasing that they endured when they were encountered, jokes and slurs about "retards," the frustration and even anger my teachers showed with students who learned more slowly, and discussions in the news about parents getting amniocentesis to determine if their children had Down Syndrome so they could decide whether or not to abort. I grew up watching countless telethons about children with disabilities that portrayed them as tragic victims who would never lead meaningful lives without help. I was receiving the message that people with disabilities were less valuable, and I was also receiving the message that their lives were defined by suffering and limitation. These messages also came to me through stories about their amaz-ing courage to carry on in hopes of society finding a "cure" for their condition.

Understandably, I now feel awkward around people with visible disabilities because I am not sure how to act. If I'm walking down the hall in my building and a man is coming toward me using a wheelchair and we are reaching the door at the same time, I am often unsure about whether or not I should offer to hold the door open for them. What if I offend them by assuming that they needs help? On the other hand, to not offer them help may be insensitive. These conflicting feelings cause me discomfort, and I may simply opt to avoid the situation altogether and keep walking toward another exit.

Because I have so little authentic understanding of people with disabilities I have to rely on my stereotypes. These stereotypes may cause me to avoid the group altogether *without being aware that I'm doing so*; I simply won't be interested in getting to know people with disabilities. Certainly if someone comes into my life with a disability I will try to be open and accepting (in itself revealing my condescending attitude toward them). But I certainly won't seek them out or gravitate toward them in a social gathering.

Thinking back to Chapter 3, we know that we absorb information throughout our lives about social others. All humans have prejudice (in the above example, the person using the wheelchair is just as likely to have prejudice toward me, perhaps assuming that because I am able-bodied I will be ignorant and insensitive toward people with disabilities). Thus the goal to never pre-judge or to wipe out all of our prejudice is not humanly possible. The goal that *is* possible, however, is to become *aware* of our prejudice and the *misinformation* on which it is based and to do our best to correct this information. But if we refuse to acknowledge that we have prejudice because we have been taught that prejudice is bad, we only end up protecting our misinformation and holding it in place.

Discrimination

Discrimination is *action* based upon prejudice. All of the messages we have absorbed in the society at large "leak out" and manifest in our actions. If we think of prejudice as the internal filters through which we view social others— how we perceive them and the values attached to those perceptions—then discrimination is the *action* that results from those filters.

> **Discrimination:** Unfair action toward a social group and its members that is based upon prejudice about that group. Discrimination occurs at the individual level; all humans discriminate.

Figure 8. Discrimination.

These actions include ignoring, excluding, threatening, ridiculing, slandering, and violence. For example, if hatred is the emotion we feel based on our prejudice, extreme acts of discrimination may follow. These forms of discrimination are usually clear and recognizable. But if *discomfort* is the feeling, the discrimination is likely to be much more subtle, even hard to detect (see Figure 9). For example, most of us can acknowledge that we do feel some discomfort around certain groups of people, if only a heightened sense of self-consciousness, as with the person with the disability I avoid in the hallway. But this discomfort doesn't come naturally; it comes from our prejudices, which are learned. This is the result of living separate from a group of people while simultaneously absorbing incomplete or erroneous information about them. When the prejudice causes me to *act* differently—I avoid the person in the hallway—I am now discriminating.

PREJUDICE:	Hatred	Fear	Disgust	Resentment	Discomfort
					Lack of Interest
DISCRIMINATION:	Violence	Exclusion	Ridicule/	Avoidance	Segregation
			Blame		

Figure 9. Negative emotions and actions.

Putting prejudice together with discrimination, imagine that I am a store-owner who is worried about shoplifting. I may automatically give the benefit of the doubt to middle-aged, white, female customers who appear to be middle class. I don't worry about these customers or keep an eye on them as they shop.

> **Remember:** Prejudice and discrimination are always at play in human interaction. They are also operating for those people we see as *normal*, and thus *don't* mistrust or treat as less than.

However, if one of the variables here is changed—for example, if they are white, middle-aged women but appear to be homeless or dressed in a way that indicates a lower class status—my suspicion may be aroused. On the other hand, when young black female customers enter my store, regardless of what their class status appears to be, I am likely to feel suspicious and watch them more closely. I might not even be aware that I am doing this, but because the media and popular discourse constantly associate young blacks with crime, I will see these customers through this filter, and act accordingly.

This difference in my assumptions is not benign—it has an impact on both shoppers. Although my prejudice is *positive* for the white, middle-aged, middle-class shopper, it is still *unfair* in that this customer was automatically granted it based on assumptions about her age, race, and class. This allows her to have an enjoyable shopping experience wherein she feels respected and unself-conscious about her race or other aspects of identity. She is not likely to be aware that she is being viewed more favorably than other shoppers; she can take this privilege for granted. While I should treat all of my customers equally, the fact that I don't turns my positive treatment of this customer into a *privilege* that she can take for granted and enjoy, but others cannot.

PREJUDICE:	See as Superior	Prefer	Benefit of the Doubt		See as Normal/ Benign
DISCRIMINATION:	Defer to	Include	Gravitate toward	Trust	Treat as an individual

Figure 10. Positive emotions and actions.

The shopper that I do watch because I assume she has bad intentions will certainly not see my prejudice as fair. The social cues of mistrust that I convey, although they may seem subtle to me (if I am aware of them at all), will be easily read by this shopper because she has likely had this experience many times before. This raises another aspect of being on the receiving end of prejudice—while the shopkeeper likely sees herself as an individual and if confronted on her suspicion might insist that it only happened this once (if she can admit to it at all), for the suspected shopper this is *not* an isolated experience. Both shopper and storeowner, while individuals, are also swimming in their cultural water and represent their larger social groups and their collective experiences.

> **Remember:** The nature of an assumption is that I don't know I am making it. One need not be aware of their assumptions in order to hold them and act on them.

As another example of the more subtle aspects of discrimination, I may find myself in the rare work situation of standing in a group of African American colleagues and use a term that I often use (perhaps a term with the word "black" in it), but now I am suddenly very self-conscious that I have used that term in front of my black colleagues and begin to question whether or not it's appropriate or if I offended anyone. This causes me to feel awkward and ultimately to behave differently than I would around a group of white colleagues. It might even cause me to avoid being in that situation again.

Prejudice also manifests as discrimination in an even more subtle way—for example, simply being uninterested in a group of people. This lack of interest is not natural, or a fluke, or "just me." Because I rarely ever see or hear about this group in any consistent or positive way, I learn that they are not socially valuable, and therefore I do not value them. This allows me to feel comfortable living in segregation and not having any relationships with them. For example: if you are under 30 years old, consider how many relationships you have with elderly people (say, people over 60 or 70) who are not family members or friends of family members. Very few of us have cross-generational friendships. This is the result of a society that separates us by age, presents the elderly in very limited ways (if at all) in the media, and teaches us to feel contempt for aging and impatient with and dismissive of the elderly.

If we think about how we rationalize this lack of interest in the elderly, we will surface many of the prejudicial stereotypes, attitudes, and beliefs we hold. For example, I might rationalize the fact that I have no elderly friends by claiming that they aren't interested in what I am interested in; they are too slow; they are too conservative; it takes so long to do anything or go anywhere; they are boring; they are physically unpleasant; I don't know any elderly people; and so on. All of these beliefs translate into a basic lack of value of the elderly and I feel no loss in not having them in my life. These attitudes have been created and supported in large part by two key social dynamics: *segregation* and *limited representation* in society.

Who Discriminates?

Pause for a moment to reflect on this question: Can we have our social prejudices and *not* discriminate? Many people believe that we can, but the research shows differently (Dovidio, Glick, & Rudman, 2005). Just as all people have prejudices learned through socialization, all people discriminate. Because prejudice informs how we *view* others, it necessarily informs how we *act* toward others. This action may be subtle—as subtle as awkwardness, reserve, avoidance, and disinterest. But again, this disinterest is not natural, neutral, or benign; it is *learned*, and it results in (among other things) not developing relationships with people from particular groups.

To understand the power of our socialization and the unconscious prejudice and discrimination that results from it, consider an important study on racial discrimination in hiring (Bertrand & Mullainathan, 2004). Despite common claims that racism is in the past and that the playing field is now level, patterns of inequality between whites and blacks in the U.S. job market, in terms of both rate of employment and pay, are well documented. Seeking to understand these patterns, researchers at the University of Chicago conducted a large study in which they responded to over 1,300 help-wanted ads in Boston and Chicago newspapers. They sent out close to 5,000 resumes to a range of employers in both the public and private sectors. The qualifications on the resumes were consistent, but the researchers randomly assigned stereotypically white-sounding names, such as Emily Walsh or Greg Baker, to half of the resumes, and stereotypically African American–sounding names, such as Lakisha Washington or Jamal Jones, to the other half. They found that regardless of the employer, occupation, industry, or size of the company, the call-back rate for the resumes with white-sounding names was *50 percent higher* than for the resumes with black-sounding names.

Because mainstream culture often insists that if someone is having trouble finding a job the issue is just a matter of qualifications, the researchers also investigated how improvements in credentials affected the call-back rate. The resumes with white-sounding names received 30 percent *more* call-backs when the credentials improved. But there was *no* significant improvement in call-back rates for applicants perceived as black when their qualifications improved. In other words, even when the applicants perceived as black were *more* qualified, they were still discriminated against; there were no benefits to black applicants for improving their credentials. Discrimination against more qualified applicants but with black-sounding names remained consistent and did not vary based on occupation, region, or industry.

This study, among many others that were conducted following it, provides empirical evidence that—contrary to the beliefs of many whites—racial discrimination against blacks is real, pervasive, and ongoing. It also raises an important question: What happened when the human resource workers screened those resumes? It is highly likely that they were unaware that they were discriminating and would have vigorously (and sincerely) denied any suggestion that they were. They would not be intentionally lying when they denied that they were engaged in racial discrimination, and herein lies the power of socialization: we often have no idea that we are discriminating based on prejudice. Like the orchestra judges who simply believed women were less qualified musicians and thus heard their playing through that filter, what the screeners saw just appeared to be the *truth*: this candidate is less qualified than that one. But the screeners necessarily read the resumes through their cultural *lenses*, which were racially biased.

When the screeners opened the resumes and saw, for example, the name Lakisha Washington, a name traditionally associated in our culture with blacks, their racial filter for "blacks" was activated. From that moment on, they were reading her resume through these filters, which are filled with the

assumptions and expectations that circulate in the culture at large: her qualifications will be inferior because society tells us that blacks are inherently
less qualified than whites. This is a function of the unavoidable power of
socialization; it happens instantaneously and is almost always unconscious.
We will simply interpret Lakisha's resume in a way that fulfills our expectations that she is less qualified; the facts do not get in the way of our unconscious beliefs. Names such as Jennifer Nelson or Daniel Miller don't trigger
the same set of racial filters because they are associated with dominant
culture, and thus we will perceive them as neutral or *normal* names. (How
we have been socialized to associate white and normal will be discussed in
Chapters 6–9.)

    While the resume readers necessarily also read the resumes of applicants
with white-sounding names through a racial filter, these filters did not penalize the applicants; white applicants are the norm against which black applicants are measured. The racial filter for whites does not assume the person is
unqualified *based on race* the way that the filter for black applicants does. This
comparison is not dependent on our awareness of it.

    Regardless of the race of the human resource employees screening
these resumes, names convey ideas about race, class, gender, and ethnicity
to everyone, as we are all affected by the messages in mainstream culture.
Names are connected to group categories, and these categories are assigned
different values by society. This illustrates the power of our filters and the
dilemma of our denial of them; if we can't or won't admit that we have
them, we can't challenge them or put protections in place to help minimize
their impact. For example, because this study provided powerful proof of
racial discrimination, many companies now block out the names on resumes
before sending them to hiring committees, just as screens are now more
often used in orchestra auditions. Intentions alone are not strong enough to
overcome socialization; this takes study and practice. In the meantime, we
need to be willing to concede that they exist and put protections in place
against them.

    Most people assume that we are "in charge of" and able to control our
own behavior. This assumption, however, is wrong. Scientists estimate that
we have conscious access to only 2% of our brains' emotional and cognitive
process. Neuroscientists have also determined that we process 11 million bits
of information at a time but only have the capacity to be aware at best of
40 bits (Powell & Godsil, 2012). When reflecting on the racial messages
embedded in those 11 million bits of information circulating around us at

all times, consider how many implicitly reinforce whiteness as superior. For example, a news reporter's expression of surprise that a violent crime occurred in a white middle-class neighborhood. Or the ways in which only the white experience is celebrated nationally as we commemorate July 4th, 1776 as the day of American "freedom," even though it was the era of legal black enslavement. These narratives and omissions send powerful messages of white superiority and centrality. Further, these messages don't stand alone; they are reinforced through relentless depictions of ideal beauty and behavior as white. When we understand that the vast majority of our behavior is dictated by the 98% of our brain that works without our conscious awareness, we begin to understand the contradictions between what we profess and how we actually behave. Consider the resume readers who would likely insist that race had nothing to do with their assessments but were still clearly guided by their unconscious negative bias towards African Americans; we don't have to be aware of our bias in order to have it and we don't have to be aware that we are discriminating in order to discriminate.

> **Implicit Bias:** The largely unconscious and automatic prejudice that operates below conscious awareness and without intentional control. Implicit bias is absorbed from the messages surrounding us and results in acts of discrimination. Because implicit bias is below conscious awareness and often in conflict with what a person consciously believes, the person is unaware of the discrimination that results from it.

The Harvard Implicit Association Test (IAT) (Greenwald & Banaji, 1995) was developed in order to access aspects of bias that a person is either unaware of or cannot admit to. (Whereas the researchers use the term bias, I tend to use the term prejudice; thus they are used interchangeably here.) The test measures implicit bias toward a wide range of social groups. It is accessible to anyone online and guides the viewer through a series of rapid associations (implicit.harvard.edu). For example, test-takers are asked which of the two terms "Male" and "Female" is more strongly associated with the term "Logical." The more rapid your response, the more closely the terms are associated in your memory. The test has been highly researched and has consistently demonstrated validity (Greenwald, Poehlman, Uhlmann, & Banaji, 2009). After 7 years of administering the test, the following conclusions have been drawn (adapted from the Project Implicit website):

Implicit Biases Are Pervasive

Bias appears as statistically large effects that are often shown by majorities of samples of Americans. For example, over 80% of web respondents show implicit negativity toward the elderly compared to the young; 75–80% of self-identified whites and Asians show an implicit preference for whites compared to blacks.

Most People Are Unaware of Their Implicit Biases

People have been found to hold negative biases in relation to various social groups even while sincerely reporting that they regard themselves as not holding these biases. Implicit bias is found equally across all groups. No one group of people is any more or less biased than another.

Implicit Biases Predict Behavior

From simple acts such as friendliness and inclusion to more consequential acts such as the evaluation of work quality, those who display greater implicit bias have been shown to display greater discrimination. The published scientific evidence is rapidly accumulating. Over 200 published scientific investigations have made use of one or another version of the IAT.

People Differ in Their Levels of Implicit Bias

Although implicit bias is universal, levels vary from person to person. Certain experiences may make a person more aware of bias and thus able to challenge it in themselves—for instance, being from a minoritized group. In addition, consciously held attitudes interact with implicit bias and can help to mediate it. The level of bias existing in the immediate environment can also impact individual levels. This is why media literacy and other manifestations of critical thinking are so crucial.

All human beings have prejudice and all human beings discriminate toward other human beings based on that prejudice. Concepts such as "reverse discrimination" and statements such as "They are just as prejudiced as we are" don't really make any sense if you understand that prejudice and discrimination are universal. If you have this understanding, why point out that prejudice goes both ways or that "they" are also prejudiced? Pointing this out is often done as a way to justify one's own prejudice. Prejudice doesn't need justifying in the sense that one can't help but have absorbed it from the cultural water that surrounds us. However, acceptance of one's prejudices as they stand cannot in good conscience be justified; prejudice is hurtful and causes serious suffering to others. Prejudice can and should be addressed by taking steps to challenge the misinformation on which prejudice is based and the segregation that keeps that misinformation alive.

Understanding that prejudice and discrimination occur at the individual level and that all individuals have prejudices and act upon them is critical to understanding racism. But prejudice and discrimination are not the same as racism, and these terms should not be used interchangeably (the connections and differences between prejudice, discrimination, and *racism* will be discussed in Chapter 7).

Oppression

To oppress is to hold down—to press—and deny a social group full access to resources in a given society. Oppression describes a set of policies, practices, traditions, norms, definitions, cultural stories, and explanations that function to systematically hold down one social group to the benefit of another social group. The group that benefits from oppression is called the *dominant* (or agent) group, and the group that is oppressed is called the *minoritized* (or target) group. Scholars use the term *minoritized* (rather than minority) to indicate that the group's lower position is a function of socially constructed dynamics, rather than its numbers in society. In order to oppress, a group must hold institutional power in society. Holding institutional power enables a group to control resources and to impose its worldview throughout the society in ways that are difficult to avoid. Oppression is historical (long-term and ongoing) and thus becomes automatic and normalized. Thus, we are all socialized to see this group's position as normal, natural, and even necessary for the good of society.

> **Minoritized**: A social group that is devalued in society. This devaluing encompasses how the group is represented, what degree of access to resources it is granted, and how the unequal access is rationalized. The term *minoritized* (rather than minority) is used to indicate that the group's lower position is a function of active socially constructed dynamics, rather than its numbers in society.

Oppression is different from prejudice and discrimination in that prejudice and discrimination describe dynamics that occur on the individual level and in which anyone can (and does) participate. For example, people with disabilities can be prejudiced against the able-bodied, and the elderly can be prejudiced against the young. But oppression occurs when one group's *collective* prejudice is backed by social, political, economic, and institutional *power*. The elderly and people with disabilities are not in the position to impose their prejudices on the rest of society. Oppression is the result of prejudice *plus* the power to enforce that prejudice throughout the culture. The prejudice becomes embedded in the very fabric of society, in institutions such as media, family, religion, education, language, economics, and criminal justice, *and in cultural definitions of what is normal, real, correct, beautiful, and valuable*. This results in the *systematic* mistreatment of a targeted group.

Oppression: Group prejudice and discrimination backed by institutional power. The term "oppression" indicates that one group is in the *position to enforce* their prejudice and discrimination against another group *throughout the society*; the prejudice and discrimination have moved from the individual to the societal level and have long-term and far-reaching impacts. *Prejudice + Discrimination + Power = Oppression*.

Understanding the difference between discrimination and oppression will build a foundation for understanding racism. The history of women's suffrage (gaining the right to vote) in the United States illustrates several distinguishing features of oppression. Consider how women received the right to vote in the United States. Women played a primary role—they had to organize and fight for many years to gain the vote. Yet ultimately the ability to grant women the vote rested in the hands of men. Only men could actually grant the right to vote to women because only men occupied the institutional positions of power necessary to do so; women could not grant themselves the right to vote because they did not hold institutional power. Hence, while both groups could be prejudiced against the other, only men were in the position to oppress women throughout the whole of society. Women could discriminate against men in temporary and individual situations, but could not pass far-reaching legislation that limited *all* men's lives.

The question of suffrage was not isolated to the realm of politics; many other institutions—also controlled by men—worked together in interlocking ways to ensure that women were viewed as incapable of handling the responsibility of voting. Because men control all of the major institutions of society—government, media, economics, religion, medicine, education, police, and military—men as a group, from the founding of the United States, have been in the position to weave their prejudice into the very fabric of society. A society in which men are seen as having the inherent right to rule over women is termed a *patriarchy*. The United States was founded as a patriarchal system. Patriarchy and *androcentrism* are closely linked. Androcentrism is the belief that men are inherently superior to women, and it is based on the underlying idea that males represent the human norm, and females are a deviation from that norm. Patriarchy and androcentrism worked together to make it difficult for women to gain suffrage.

For example, because scientists began with the androcentric premise of female inferiority, their research questions and the interpretation of their findings were informed by that premise. Because they were in the institutional positions to disseminate their findings through journals, textbooks, and universities (patriarchy), they were able to reinforce and rationalize their positions. Other institutions worked to normalize male dominance: the clergy preached male superiority from the pulpit and rationalized it through the Bible; doctors used the male body as their reference point; psychiatrists based definitions of mental health on male norms for emotions and definitions of rationality; and male professors taught men's history, thoughts, and interests. Women's lack of voting rights was not an isolated issue: all of the institutions of society, which were built on patriarchy and androcentrism, worked together to enforce the idea that women were inferior and thus should not have the same rights as men.

Social Binaries

All major social groups are organized into binary (either/or) identities (i.e., male/female, black/white, straight/gay, rich/poor). Returning to Cooley's concept of the *looking glass self*, these identities depend upon one another because each identity is defined by its opposite (or *other*). The category "masculine" can have no meaning without an understanding of a category called "feminine," "rich" can have no meaning without "poor, "young" can have no meaning without "old," and so on. Not only are these identities constructed as opposites, but they are also ranked into a hierarchy of *value*.

Figure 11 illustrates the historical and current relationships of inequality between some of these key social groups in the United States and the term for that specific form of oppression.

Minoritized/Target Group	Oppression	Dominant/Agent Group
People of Color	Racism	White
Poor, Working-Class	Classism	Middle-Class, Wealthy
Women	Sexism	Men
Gays, Lesbians, Bisexuals, +	Heterosexism	Heterosexuals
Transgender, Gender Queer, Gender Non-Conforming, Intersexed	Transgender Oppression	Gender-Conforming; Cisgender
Muslims, Buddhists, Jews, Hindus, etc.	Religious Oppression	Christians
People with Disabilities	Ableism	Able-bodied
Jews	Anti-Semitism	Non-Jews (gentiles)
Immigrants (perceived), Indigenous peoples	Nationalism	Citizens (perceived)
Elderly	Ageism	Young Middle-aged
Children	Adultism	Adults

Figure 11: Oppression chart.

This hierarchical social arrangement is termed *social stratification*, a system in which one social group is positioned in society as more valuable than its opposite: men are more valuable than women; the rich are more valuable than the poor; the young are more valuable than the old. The identity group that is positioned as more valuable—the dominant group—will have more access to the resources of society. The group positioned as less valuable—the minoritized group—will receive less access to the resources of the society. People in the society will be taught to see the difference in access to resources as fair and legitimate (for example in the case of women's suffrage, men's greater access to resources was seen as legitimate based on rationalizations that men were able to disseminate throughout society). The terms used to describe these relationships of inequality between dominant and minoritized groups usually end in "ism," for example sexism and racism.

Most people find themselves in both dominant and minoritized group positions (i.e., in some categories on the left side and in other categories on the right side of the chart). One is not simply a woman, but a white woman, or a heterosexual, white, middle-class, able-bodied Jewish woman—and each of these group positions intersect in important ways that I will discuss in more depth in Chapter 11.

Returning to the struggle for women's suffrage, the concept of intersecting identities adds more layers of binary relationships. When we consider the dimensions of class and race, we see that white upper-class women were recognized as the legitimate leaders of the movement, and these women resisted the inclusion of black women. So while the "women" we commonly refer to as suffragists were oppressed as women, they were privileged as *white* women. This is a cogent illustration of how oppression works; because they were racially privileged as *white* women, their experience stands in as representing *all* women. Yet in practice they only represented white women's interests (and middle-/upper-class white women in particular). In fact, many leading suffragists, such as Elizabeth Cady Stanton, stated openly that white women were more worthy of the vote than blacks (Ginzburg, 2009).

Understanding Oppression

Understanding how oppression works and why it is different from prejudice and discrimination requires us to understand that oppression involves pervasive, historical, political relationships between social *groups*. Oppression goes well beyond individual or situational interactions. When scholars use the term oppression (or use the terms that refer to the forms oppression takes such as racism, ableism, heterosexism, and sexism), we refer to these large-scale, historical, political, and pervasive relationships. We are not referring only to individual acts of prejudice or discrimination, which all people can commit. Rather, we are referring to the dynamics of a group's *collective power over* the group that is seen as its less-valuable opposite: (men/women; heterosexual/gay). All people have prejudice, but only the dominant group is in the position of social, historical, and institutional power to back its prejudice with policies and procedures that infuse it throughout the entire society.

> **Remember:** Prejudice and oppression are not the same and these terms should not be used interchangeably. Oppression includes the dynamics of social and institutional power, while prejudice does not.

The ism words allow us to discuss these specific forms of oppression and to include the dynamics of unequal social and institutional power between dominant and minoritized groups. In this way, we avoid reducing oppression to individual acts of prejudice and claiming that these acts are comparable, regardless of who commits them. From this understanding, so-called "reverse racism" or "reverse sexism" do not exist, because racism and sexism refer to power relations that are historic, embedded, and pervasive—the same groups who have historically held systemic power in the United States continue to do so. For example, despite suffrage and women's numerical majority, in 2015 women were still less than 20% of the House and Senate, 33% of the Supreme Court, and have never held the highest office, the presidency.

The United Nations has concluded that a critical mass of at least 30% of women is needed before government policies begin to reflect women's priorities and before there is a shift in the governmental management style and organizational culture. Yet in the entire history of the United States, only 2.1% of members of Congress have been women. In 2012, the United States was 80th in an international ranking of women's representation in federal government Inter-parliamentary Union, 2011. At the current rate of progress, it will take *nearly 500 years* for women to reach fair representation in government. While numbers do matter, oppression isn't simply the result of a numerical majority (for example, women are the majority of the world yet do not hold institutional power, and blacks were the majority under South Africa's apartheid rule). Oppression is a multidimensional imbalance of social, political, and institutional power that is taken for granted and thus accepted by most people in the society.

Further, because inequality between groups is rationalized and justified by all of the institutions of society, oppression cannot be ended through legislation alone. Oppression is also embedded within individual and collective consciousness through socialization. Both dominant and minoritized groups are socialized into their roles, and these roles come to be seen as natural. When we believe the social hierarchy is natural, it is difficult to see our positions within it as unequal or problematic. For example, not all women were interested in gaining suffrage. Many women were taught to believe that voting was a man's domain and inappropriate for women. Thus the suffrage movement had to convince other *women*, as well as men, that it was in women's best interests to have a role in the political system that controlled their lives. This process of re-socializing the minoritized group is termed *consciousness-raising* and it was a fundamental piece in the struggle for women's suffrage. However, ultimately only men had the institutional power to actually grant women suffrage.

Oppression Is Historical

The underrepresentation of women in government is not simply the result of any single election and cannot be remedied by isolated changes in the law. Women received the right to vote in 1920 in the United States, but the oppression of women by men did not end the day suffrage was granted. Oppression has deep historical roots and does not change overnight based on a single victory. In fact, isolated victories, while important, often work to fool people into believing that the relationship of inequality has ended and thus no further effort is required. But even if the critical mass of at least 30% of women in government proposed by the United Nations was achieved overnight, the androcentric norms, traditions and beliefs embedded in our institutions would continue (indeed, in order for women to be elected, they have to play by the rules of men). Androcentrism is so taken for granted that most people can't see it even as they uphold it; this includes women. Change is slow and efforts must continue over time and throughout the whole of society. Understanding the historical dimensions of oppression may also help us to see why temporary and limited policies such as Affirmative Action (which continues to be deeply resented by many whites and has been systematically challenged and undermined since its passage) can't in and of themselves reverse the forces of oppression.

Oppression Is Institutional

Government is only one institution dominated by men. Men also dominate all other major institutions (military, medicine, media, criminal justice, policing, finance, industry, higher education, and science). These institutions are interconnected and function together to uphold male dominance across all dimensions of society. In the case of suffrage, women were not in a position to use any of the institutions in their fight and could only rely on a few sympathetic men to present their case for them or allow them limited opportunities to present it for themselves. This is another reason why victories in a single domain don't end oppression. Even when male government officials finally granted women the right to vote, women were not immediately accepted into the halls of power. The government remained male dominated, as did all of the other institutions.

While institutions are created and maintained by people, they have a life and a power well beyond those of individual members. Due to the institutional dimensions of oppression, no individual from the dominant group has to actively do anything unfair in order for the *system* to be unfair. Thus while individual members of a dominant group may support the rights of a given minoritized group, institutions still grant them privileges not made available to the minoritized group. This is another reason why oppression can be difficult to see; we are taught to focus on individual acts of cruelty rather than look at systems as a whole.

Oppression Is Ideological

Ideology refers to the big ideas that are reinforced throughout society. Ideologies provide the frameworks through which we represent, interpret, understand, and make sense of social existence (Hall, 1997). As such, they play a foundational role in the maintenance and reproduction of oppression. Because these ideas are constantly reinforced, they are very hard to avoid believing. Examples of ideology in the United Sates include: individualism; the superiority of capitalism as an economic system and democracy as a political system; consumerism as a valuable lifestyle; and meritocracy (anyone can succeed if they works hard). From the time we are born we are conditioned into accepting and not questioning these ideas. Ideology is reinforced in multiple ways, for example through schools and textbooks, in political speeches, through movies and advertising, in holiday celebrations such as Columbus Day and Independence Day, through words and phrases, and through the limited availability of alternative ideas.

> **Ideology:** The dominant ideas that are circulated and reinforced throughout society, making it very difficult to avoid believing them or questioning them.

Much of the ideology that circulates in the United States works to obscure and deny oppression. This ideology rationalizes social hierarchies as the outcome of a natural order resulting from individual effort or talent. Those that don't succeed are just not as capable, deserving, or hard-working. Ideologies that work to obscure inequality are perhaps the most powerful forces of oppression because once we accept our positions within social hierarchies, they seem natural and difficult to question, even when we are disadvantaged by them. In this way, very little external pressure needs to be applied; once the rationalizations for inequality are internalized, both sides of an oppressive relationship will work to uphold the social order. This may help us understand why gaining suffrage alone did not end oppression against women. The ideologies of patriarchy and androcentrism remained deeply embedded in our culture, in the foundations of our institutions, and in the consciousness of both men *and* women.

Oppression Results in Systematic Dominant Group Privilege

The term *privilege* refers to rights, benefits, and resources that are purported to be shared by all but are only consistently available to the dominant group. The fact that an assumed right is not granted to everyone turns it into a privilege—an unearned advantage. For example, prior to suffrage, even if individual men believed women should have the right to vote, as men they still benefited from women's exclusion. In this way, oppression is not personal and intentions are irrelevant.

If we are in a dominant group, we can think of privilege as the current in the water that is going in our direction; the society is set up to affirm, accommodate, and reward the norms of our group. Anyone who has ever swum with a current knows that the current makes swimming so much easier. You may still exert yourself, but your efforts take you twice as far as they would without the current. In fact, you could stop exerting yourself and you would still be moved along in the direction that you want to go. Conversely, when you swim *against* the current, you have to work twice as hard to get half as far. One of the distinguishing features of privilege is that it is usually not recognized as such by the dominant group. The dominant group either assumes the privilege is available to everyone, or that they personally earned it, or that it is simply good luck. Because the currents of privilege—pushing the dominant group forward while pushing against the minoritized group—are invisible to the dominant group, they can say, "I worked hard for what I have, why can't they?"

Oppression Does Not Go Both Ways

Members of a dominant group may be a numerical minority in a given context and experience short-term and contextual discrimination. For example, men in female dominated fields may experience feelings of isolation and disconnection from cultural norms in that context, and they may experience discrimination and exclusion from the women with whom they work. They may also be discriminated against based on stereotypes, such as the belief that they may be more likely to abuse vulnerable populations. However, while these are forms of discrimination and may be painful, they are not oppression because they are temporary and context-specific. The historical, ideological, institutional, and cultural dimensions of society are still patriarchal and androcentric and reward and advance men over women. In fact, in fields in which women constitute a majority (teaching, nursing, social work), men are most likely to rise to positions of leadership over women (principals, administrators, department heads, professors) (Williams, 1992, 1995; Muench et al, 2015).

The Forces of Oppression Are Interlocking

Scholar Marilyn Frye uses the metaphor of a birdcage to describe the interlocking forces of oppression (1983). If you stand close to a birdcage to press your face against the wires, your perception of the bars will disappear and you will have an almost unobstructed view of the bird. If you turn your head to examine one wire of the cage closely, you will not be able to see the other wires. If your understanding of the cage is based upon this myopic view, you may not understand why the bird doesn't just go around the single wire and fly away. You might even assume that the bird liked or chose its place in the cage (which, from this distance, wouldn't appear as a cage at all). But if instead of taking a close-up view, you stepped back and took a wider view, you would begin to see that the wires come together in an interlocking pattern—a pattern that works to hold the bird firmly in place. It now becomes clear that a network of systematically related barriers surrounds the bird. Taken individually, none of these barriers would be that difficult for the bird to get around, but because they interlock with each other, they thoroughly restrict the bird.

Figure 12. The birdcage.

The birdcage metaphor helps us to understand why oppression can be so hard to see and recognize: we have a limited view. Without recognizing how our *position* in relation to the bird defines how much of the cage we can see, we rely on single situations, exceptions, and anecdotal evidence for our understanding, rather than on broader, interlocking patterns. Although there are always exceptions, the patterns are consistent and well documented: oppressed groups are confined and shaped by forces and barriers that are not accidental, occasional, or avoidable. These forces are systematically related to each other in ways that restrict their movement overall.

Dominant groups, because of their social and institutional positions, necessarily have the most limited or myopic view of society. But because they control the institutions, they have the means to legitimize their view and impose it on others. Minoritized groups often have the widest view of society, in that they must understand both their own and the dominant group's perspective. In order to succeed in dominant culture they must develop what race scholar W. E. B. Du Bois, writing in 1903, termed *double-consciousness*. Du Bois was writing about race, but the term has relevance for other minoritized groups: in spite of their wider view or expanded consciousness, minoritized groups are at the bottom of the social hierarchy, and thus their view is seen as the least legitimate in society. Another challenge in seeing oppression is that both dominant and minoritized groups are socialized into seeing their positions in the hierarchy as natural. Scholars use the terms "internalized dominance" and "internalized oppression" to refer to this acceptance of our socialization into unequal groupings. Although this socialization can be resisted (and I have written this book to aid whites in resisting internalized racial dominance), resistance takes intentional effort and is not without personal and social costs.

Oppression Is Deeply Woven into the Fabric of Society

When I use the example of women's suffrage during a class or workshop, I end by asking this question: Today, if men—*as a group*—wanted to take away women's right to vote, could they? The vast majority of people answer no, that men could not take away women's right to vote today. I then show them the statistics discussed earlier. After hearing these statistics, most people quickly realize that indeed men could take away women's right to vote if they wanted to. This powerfully illustrates some of the key dimensions of oppression: it is historical and deeply embedded in all institutions and in the social fabric of society. Thus, it does not move back and forth, changing directions between groups. All of the groups who have been historically oppressed since the founding of the United States continue to be. Oppression adapts overtime so that it looks more acceptable to the culture at a given historical moment, but it does not end easily. Patriarchy and androcentrism did not end the day that women were granted the right to vote. Although I do not believe that men will take women's right to vote away, the point is that they remain in the institutional positions of power, so they could if they chose to. For example, the Equal Rights Amendment, which was proposed in 1923, has 3 simple sections:

- Section 1. Equality of rights under the law shall not be denied or abridged by the United States or by any state on account of sex.
- Section 2. The Congress shall have the power to enforce, by appropriate legislation, the provisions of this article.
- Section 3. This amendment shall take effect two years after the date of ratification.

Yet the Equal Rights Amendment did not receive the necessary number of endorsements by the final date of 1982 and although efforts continue, it has not been ratified and is not part of the United States Constitution. Indeed, in 2011, Supreme Court Justice Antonin Scalia stated that the Constitution—and the Fourteenth Amendment—does not protect women against discrimination, and was never intended to do so. In 2014 women make 77% of what a man in similar work earns, yet in 2014 Republicans *unanimously* voted against the Equal Pay Bill.

Remember: Oppression is a multidimensional imbalance of social, political, and institutional power that spans history and is taken for granted by most people in the society, particularly by those whom the oppression benefits.

Oppression Results in Internalized Dominance for the Dominant Group

Men and women are born into a society in which males are collectively privileged over females: men are the dominant group. The "ism" term for this form of oppression is *sexism*. For males, this means that from the time they are born, they are conditioned to see their positions as natural and earned, and most come to accept their place in the hierarchy. This process is termed *internalized dominance* (or internalized superiority). We don't need to consciously think of ourselves as superior to someone else based on their group membership, but because this superiority is embedded in the very framework from which we operate, it underlies and informs our daily thoughts and actions.

Internalized Dominance: The result of socialization in which members of the dominant group are conditioned into their roles. This socialization causes them to see themselves as naturally superior to the relationally minoritized group and more deserving of their superior positions and the resources of society.

For example, if I ask one of my heterosexual male students if he would be willing to put on a dress, drink a "fruity drink" at a football party, paint his fingernails, or otherwise enact norms associated with females, he would most likely (and quite emphatically) say, "No!" I can safely predict that the rest of the class would erupt in laughter, especially the other males. These males might even tease this student for the rest of the semester, simply because my suggestion *associated* him with female norms. This is because a heterosexual, cisgender male who associates himself with cultural norms assigned to females loses status in two social groups in which he has dominance: gender and sexuality. Yet if I asked him to explain why he has such a strong negative reaction—how he came to see these requests as beneath him—he would most likely not be able to answer. His position is so deeply internalized for him that he hasn't had to think about it. (My female, gay, and transgender students however, might have less trouble.) His reaction to my request and his difficulty in articulating the socialization that led to that reaction is the result of internalized dominance.

The specific ways in which racial superiority is internalized for whites will be discussed in Chapter 9. But to use a non-racial example to further illustrate the depth and acceptance of internalized dominance, consider society's relationship to animals as a food source. Other than vegetarians, most people eat animals every day without a second thought. At the same time, we know that animals suffer and feel pain, form attachments, bond with their offspring, and have a survival instinct similar to our own (in other words, they want to live). Yet in our culture, it is taken for granted that we are entitled to kill and eat animals. When asked how they could allow animals to be killed and eaten, most people would have no trouble answering (they may even scoff at the absurdity of the question). Their answers would likely include: they were put on the earth for us to eat; it's natural to eat them; survival of the fittest; nature is filled with predators; meat is delicious; meat is a necessary food source; hunting is an enjoyable sport, and so on. Notice the deeply held belief underlying these reasons: human needs and interests are elevated above those of animals, giving humans the right to kill and eat them.

Sometimes this right is rationalized through religion (God put them here for us; it's man's place to rule the earth), and sometimes as a function of nature (we have to eat animals for protein in order to survive; humans have always hunted). For the purposes of illustrating internalized dominance, I am less interested in whether these rationalizations are valid and more interested in the fact that we completely take for granted our right to kill and eat animals. This right, because it's deeply embedded in our collective unconscious, infuses all aspects of our relationship to animals, including the ease with which we can dismiss their potential suffering. For example, many advertisements for hamburgers and other meat products use the animals in their ads. Ads for hamburgers often feature a cow, and the cow may even have been anthropomorphized (infused with human characteristics) and is perhaps wearing clothes and speaking to us. Sometimes these ads even poke fun at the fact that the animal is going to end up in the frying pan. That these ads actually work to make the meat product *more* appealing to us—rather than turn us off when we think about eating animals with human characteristics—illustrates the depth and power of our fundamental cultural paradigm that we have dominion over animals.

If we were socialized from birth to see an animal's right to life as equal to our own, the belief that we should not kill and eat it would seem just as natural. For example, we don't see *all* animals as food sources that we have a right to kill and eat: cows but not dogs, tuna but not dolphins. A common reaction in the United States to the concept of eating dogs illustrates the *socialized* nature of our relationship to animals as a food source. We see cultures that eat dogs as uncivilized. An ad for a burger made of dog meat, in which the dog is wearing clothes and talking to us next to an image of himself made into a burger, would be unthinkable. Yet there are cultures that see us as barbaric for eating cows and pigs.

Consider our rationales for which animals we comfortably eat and which animals we don't. Do we not eat dogs because they are smart? Pigs are actually smarter. Do we not eat dogs because they are cute? Lambs are cute, too. Do we not eat dogs because they are our companions? They are not naturally human companions—we chose them and domesticated them as such, and many animals we eat in the West have been shown to be capable of being companions to humans—people have made pets of animals including goats, rabbits, and pigs.

My point here is two-fold. First, that our sense of ourselves as having dominion over others (be those "others" human or animal) is *socialized*, and thus arbitrary; this means we can challenge and change it. While it may feel natural to eat meat or dominate others, we are also able to live quite well (even healthier) without eating meat. It is also possible to live without dominating others. Second, this assumption of dominion is so deeply *internalized* and taken for granted that it isn't questioned; we just feel that we have the right to this position. Questioning or challenging this right often causes anger, resentment, dismissal, and ridicule.

For example, I asked several colleagues to read this section using the right to kill animals as an example of internalized dominance. All of them said that they completely understood my point and could find no loopholes in my argument, but that they feared it would make readers too defensive and it would, therefore, be dismissed. In other words, readers would get caught up in defending the right to eat meat and miss the larger point: once we are socialized into our position, it is so deeply internalized as to be outside the realm of *question*. Suggesting that dominant groups have not earned their positions or do not automatically have the right to them ("this is MY job or MY slot in college") challenges internalized dominance and raises similar defenses and dismissals. I ask my readers to use their reactions to the example of our relationship to animals as a window onto understanding the power of internalized entitlement to one's position in the social hierarchy.

Oppression Results in Internalized Oppression for the Minoritized Group

Minoritized group members are also born into a society that socializes them to accept their place in the hierarchy. While they may resist this socialization, they cannot fully avoid it and must constantly navigate it. *Internalized oppression* is the term for accepting and acting out (often unintentionally) the constant messages that you and your group are inferior to the dominant group and thus deserving of your lower position. Like internalized dominance, internalized oppression is deeply held. Once we accept our lower position in the social hierarchy, it doesn't seem like inequality at all but normal, natural, perhaps even preferred.

Internalized Oppression: The result of socialization in which members of a minoritized group are conditioned into their roles. This socialization causes them to see themselves as naturally inferior to the relationally dominant group and less deserving of the resources of society.

Claude Steele's work in *stereotype threat* (1997) demonstrates internalized oppression in action. Steele's basic premise is that a person's social identity as defined by group membership—age, gender, religion, and race—has significance in situations in which attention is drawn to that identity. Steele found that when a person's social identity is attached to a negative stereotype, that person will tend to underperform in a manner consistent with the stereotype. He attributes the underperformance to a person's anxiety that they will confirm the stereotype. For example, in a study in which black students were asked to identify their race before taking a standardized test, they consistently scored lower than black students who were not asked to identify their race before the test. Their lower scores did not correspond with their previously identified abilities. In another study, women taking a math test were randomly divided into three groups. One group was asked to answer a list of questions that clearly identified them as women; one was given a list that identified them as residents of the northeastern United States; and the third answered questions that identified them as students at an elite private college. The women who identified themselves as elite students consistently performed better on the test than the others—often even better than male students who have almost invariably scored higher than women (Steele, Spencer, & Aronson, 2002).

These results have been consistent in many other studies Steele and his colleagues have conducted. While Steele refers to this dynamic as stereotype threat, social justice educators term it *internalized oppression*—in which a person believes the negative information about their group and acts on it, fulfilling society's expectations. In light of this, consider the beliefs many teachers hold about children of color and the role these beliefs play in children's school performances. Constant focus on what is termed *the achievement gap* and pressure to perform on high-stakes standardized tests—*or else!*—surround these students and create a vicious cycle.

The high suicide rate for lesbian, gay, bisexual, transgender, queer/questioning, intersex, asexual, and others (LGBTQIA+) youth is another example of internalized oppression in action. Stereotypes about LGBTQIA+ people abound in the culture at large. These youth are most often portrayed in limited and negative ways in the media, expelled from families, subjected to psychiatric treatments and medications, bullied in schools, coerced into programs to "cure" them, beaten, and killed. Many of these practices are seen as legitimate by much of dominant culture. The Suicide Prevention Resource Center has estimated that 30–40% of LGBTQIA+ youth have attempted suicide (2011). They have internalized the message that they are abnormal and immoral and, believing society's messages that they are unworthy—that there is something deeply wrong with *them* rather than with *society*—seek to end their lives. While not all LGBTQIA+ youth feel this way, and progress such as federally recognized legal gay marriage has been made, the negative messages are still unavoidable, and these youth must expend a great amount of effort— effort that heterosexual youth don't need to expend—in order to navigate this treatment and maintain self-worth.

But we cannot discuss the internalization of homophobia, transphobia, and heterosexism without acknowledging how they intersect with racism. Trans women of color are the most targeted victims of violence among LGBTQIA+ people. In 2014, trans women made up 72% of hate and homicide victims, and 89% of these victims were people of color (Cox, 2014). LGBTQIA+ people of color must also deal with racism in the predominantly white-led and represented movement. Having to deal with racism from both the dominant culture and in one's own subculture intensifies the impact of internalized oppression on LGBTQIA+ people of color. This is not to diminish the impact of homophobia, transphobia and heterosexism on white LGBTQIA+ people, but to acknowledge that white and LGBTQIA+ people are not *also* dealing with racism, and that as white people, they will necessarily perpetuate racism in their communities if they don't intentionally seek to redress it.

Internalized oppression also causes members of a targeted group to devalue and more harshly criticize other members of their own group. Take, for example, the ways in which society blames women for their victimization when sexually assaulted. Some of the first questions both men and women ask a woman who was raped (assuming that we believe her) are where she was, what she was doing, and/or what she was wearing. We ask these questions in order to ascertain whether the assault was her fault, and we can assume that she will be asking the same questions of herself. Many rape victims feel a deep sense of shame and responsibility. This is reinforced by the way in which society focuses on the culpability of the rape victim but not on the rapist. It is estimated that 68% of sexual assault crimes go unreported (Rape Abuse & Incest National Network [RAINN], 2012) due to the social shame that rape victims feel, which is exacerbated by the treatment victims often receive in the male-dominated criminal justice system. The shame that male victims feel may be even greater, due to sexism and homophobia.

How many of us have seen warnings and safety tips for avoiding sexual assault? These warnings (even though they may be necessary) reinforce the idea that assault is preventable if women behave in specific ways.

These warnings also illustrate two other aspects of oppression. One, the dominant group (in this case, men) are *invisible*, and the focus is on the behavior of the *victims*—women—who must change their behavior to avoid assault, not men. Two, the dominant group enjoys privileges that the minoritized group cannot—in this case, freedom of movement and freedom of blame. It is estimated that 98% of rapists never spend a day in jail (RAINN, 2012).

Consider the following from http://feminally.tumblr.com/:

Sexual Assault Prevention Tips Guaranteed to Work!

- Don't put drugs in people's drinks in order to control their behavior.
- When you see someone walking by themselves, leave them alone!
- If you pull over to help someone with car problems, remember not to assault them!
- NEVER open an unlocked door or window uninvited.
- If you are in an elevator and someone else gets in, DON'T ASSAULT THEM!
- Remember, people go to laundry to do their laundry, do not attempt to molest someone who is alone in a laundry room.
- USE THE BUDDY SYSTEM! If you are not able to stop yourself from assaulting people, ask a friend to stay with you while you are in public.
- Always be honest with people! Don't pretend to be a caring friend in order to gain the trust of someone you want to assault. Consider telling them you plan to assault them. If you don't communicate your intentions, the other person may take that as a sign that you do not plan to rape them.
- Don't forget: you can't have sex with someone unless they are awake!
- Carry a whistle! If you are worried you might assault someone "on accident" you can hand it to the person you are with, so they can blow it if you do.

- And, ALWAYS REMEMBER: if you didn't ask permission and then respect the answer the first time, you are committing a crime—no matter how "into it" others appear to be.

These tips are so provocative because they make the *perpetrators* of sexual assault *visible* by turning the usual focus on its head and, in so doing, challenge the taken-for-granted *privileges*—such as freedom of movement—that men enjoy at the expense of women.

Internalized dominance and oppression create observable social group patterns in members of dominant and minoritized groups. While there are always exceptions and acts of resistance, *overall* these patterns are well documented, recognizable, and predictable.

Positionality

> Someone who does not see a pane of glass does not know that he does not see it. Someone who, being placed differently, does see it, does not know the other does not see it.
>
> —Simone Weil (1987)

Positionality is the concept that our perspectives (what we see or don't see; what we know or don't know) are based on our *positions* within the social hierarchy. Positionality recognizes that where you stand in relation to others in society shapes what you can see and understand. For example, my position as an able-bodied person, in a society that devalues people with disabilities, limits my understanding of the barriers people with disabilities face. I simply don't "see" these barriers, in large part because I don't have to. If I want to move through a building, I simply walk, take the stairs, or ride the elevator. If any of these means are unavailable to me due to a malfunction or repair work, I may actually feel irritated. This irritation is an indicator of my internalized dominance regarding my able-bodied status. I am so used to all of the privileges of access afforded by my status (including the privilege of being perceived and perceiving myself as normal)—that I have come to feel *entitled* to these privileges. My irritation indicates that I am not used to being "inconvenienced"; I take this privilege of access for granted. Because society devalues people with disabilities, I live segregated from them, so unless I know someone with a disability, I am unlikely to be aware of the barriers they face.

> **Positionality**: The concept that our perceptions are shaped by our positions within society. These positions allow us to see and understand some social dynamics while obscuring others.

Conversely, people with disabilities are much more likely to be acutely aware of, and informed about, the barriers, issues, norms, policies, and practices in dominant society that limit their lives. They are also much more likely to be aware of my assumptions and the privileges that I take for granted. This is due to our different social *positionality*. However, due to the differential of power between our groups, my perspective (although it is the more limited one) will be the perspective that is validated. My group, from its position of privilege and limited awareness, is the group in the position to make policy and set norms that profoundly impact the lives of people with disabilities. Due to the devaluing of people with disabilities and the resultant social segregation and lack of physical access, people with disabilities are not generally sitting at the tables of power in society and therefore have little, if any, say in issues that affect their lives.

> **Remember**: All individuals have prejudice and all individuals discriminate based on this prejudice. However, this is not the same as oppression. Only the dominant group is in the position to oppress the minoritized group.

Another familiar illustration of positionality and the power dynamics that inform our perspectives is the story of Columbus's discovery of America. The ad in Figure 13 uses the Columbus story as the backdrop to sell Costa Rican vacations. We can assume that the intended audience is white (as is the family featured in the ad). The copy says, "Costa Rica: Constantly Being Discovered Since 1502." Whose racial perspective is reflected in the idea that the continent was "discovered" when Europeans arrived? Whose perspective is rendered invisible? Which racial group may be invested in this story? Which racial group may be invested in challenging it? Asking questions such as these develops a clearer picture of how *what you know* is connected to *who you are* in the society at large and *where you stand* within that society; your *positionality*.

Figure 13. Costa Rica ad.

Discussion Questions

1. What is the difference between prejudice, discrimination, and systematic oppression?
2. Why can't we avoid discriminating against people based on the groups to which they belong?
3. What does it mean to say that dominant group members are granted privilege?
4. How can a group be oppressed if it is the majority in numbers?
5. What is positionality? Give an example of how you have seen positionality limit or expand someone's understanding of an aspect of oppression. How might your own positionality limit or expand your understanding of oppression?
6. How does Frye use the birdcage metaphor to illustrate oppression?

· 5 ·

THE CYCLE OF OPPRESSION

My neighborhood growing up was not diverse at all. Everyone is equal. There is no race that is better than another. I've never felt like my race was important in shaping my life. It's never been in my mind. It was never a limitation or an advantage or anything. (ASR)

One way to conceptualize oppression is through the image of a cycle, as illustrated in Figure 14. The result of this cycle is the systematic mistreatment of a minoritized group.

The Generation of Misinformation

The first dynamic that sets the cycle in motion is *misinformation* about and *misrepresentation* of a minoritized group. The group is presented in limited, superficial, and negative ways. Take, for example, the representation of black men on television. When we see black men, it is most often either in sports (and concentrated in specific sports such as basketball and football), or associated with the criminal justice system, be it in the role of criminal or cop. "Reality" shows about the daily life of police officers or prisoners in lockdown deeply reinforce these associations, as over and over we see the bodies of black

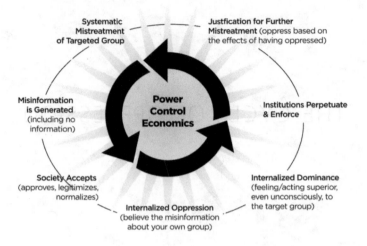

Figure 14. Cycle of oppression.

men (often shirtless) being forcibly contained. These constant negative representations reinforce prejudice toward black men and cause us to have skewed understandings about their lives.

It is also important to note that *invisibility* is a form of misinformation, because invisibility denies the minoritized groups' experience. To see virtually nothing testifying to an alternate experience from that of the dominant group is a form of misinformation. In other words, the group's history, interests, needs, perspectives—their voices—are minimized or absent from the history books, medical journals, media, movies—virtually nothing in dominant culture attests to the (positive) existence or value of the group.

Social Acceptance of the Mistreatment of the Minoritized Group

Once we have misinformation circulating in the culture at large, we have the next point in the cycle: social acceptance of mistreating the group. Society accepts the misinformation and mistreatment of the minoritized group because the dominant group has been socialized to see them as less valuable, if the minoritized group is considered at all. This misinformation is used to rationalize the lesser position (e.g., "They just don't value education" or "They are naturally prone to violence"). The misinformation becomes normalized and taken for granted, enabling it to continue to circulate and be reproduced through the society and, in turn, serve to justify the mistreatment of the minoritized group.

Ward Churchill, an American Indian activist, in his challenge to the ongoing use of Indian mascots in sports, uses an example from World War II to illustrate the power of representation and the social acceptance that results from it (2001). On October 16, 1946, Julius Streicher was sentenced to death at Nuremberg, Germany, for "crimes against humanity." He had not killed anyone or directly participated in Nazi genocide. But he had served as publisher and editor of the newspaper *Der Sturmer* during the early to mid-1930s, years before the Nazi genocide began, and had written a long series of extremely anti-Semitic editorials and "news" stories. These stories were often illustrated with cartoons and other images depicting Jews in profoundly degrading ways. The prosecution asserted that these stories and images played a powerful role in the dehumanization of Jews in the German consciousness, and this dehumanization played a part in enabling the average German to later participate in the genocide of Jewish "vermin." Thus, they argued, he was *just as guilty* as those who carried out the actual genocide. The tribunal agreed, holding Streicher complicit in genocide and deserving of death by hanging. While we might find the death penalty extreme, what is important in this example is the recognition that there is a powerful relationship between how we *perceive* people and how we then *treat* those people.

Internalized Oppression

As discussed in Chapters 3 and 4, the misinformation about the minoritized group is circulating throughout the cultural "water," and all members of the society absorb it to various degrees. At the same time that the dominant group is receiving the message that there is something *wrong with* the minoritized group—that they are *not* normal, valuable, or worthy of consideration—the minoritized group is also receiving this message about themselves. This results in *internalized oppression*, wherein the minoritized group comes to believe the misinformation and to feel that there is something wrong with them. This sense of inferiority is often not explicit (clear in the conscious mind) but internalized deep beneath the surface. Those from their group who "make it" are seen as exceptional. This internalization affects their expectations for themselves and weakens their sense of confidence, which in turn helps reinforce the dominant group's beliefs about them.

Internalized Dominance

We know that we learn who we *are* as social beings largely by learning who we are *not*. For the dominant group, being socialized to see the minoritized group as inferior *necessarily conveys* that the dominant group is *superior*. This sense of superiority is often not explicit but internalized deep beneath the surface. Across their life span and in every aspect of life, dominant group members are affirmed, made visible, and represented in diverse and positive ways. This process causes members of the dominant group to see themselves as normal, real, correct, and more valuable than the minoritized group, and thus more entitled to the resources of society.

Enforcement by Institutions

This step in the cycle concerns the role of institutions. Because oppression involves the prejudice of the dominant group plus the institutional power to maintain and enforce that prejudice, it necessarily becomes embedded within institutions. Continuing with the example of World War II and the German genocide of the Jews, we can see how institutions connect to and reinforce one another. Because German gentile scientists began with the premise of Jewish inferiority, their research questions and the interpretation of their findings were informed by that assumption. Because they were in the position to disseminate their findings through media (films, journals, speeches, editorials) they further reinforced and rationalized their superior positions. Other institutions were also constructed in ways that normalized German gentile superiority: the clergy preached Christian superiority from the pulpit and rationalized it from the Christian Bible; doctors used biased research to position the German gentile body as the reference point for good physical health; and German gentile professors taught from an anti-Semitic perspective. They were in positions that enabled them to deny Jews housing and employment, and to enact laws to restrict their movements. Anyone in any of these institutions who did not go along with German gentile superiority was penalized, in increasingly severe ways as the war progressed. Because German gentiles controlled the military, they could ultimately impose their beliefs through sheer force.

Justification for Further Mistreatment

Finally, oppression becomes justified in large part based upon the impact that generations of oppression has had on the minoritized group. Long-term systematic oppression in access to resources, social acceptance, housing, education, employment, health care, and economic development has devastating effects. Due to generations of being denied full access to the resources of society, the minoritized group occupies a much lower overall position. The minoritized group must develop survival strategies in order to cope with long-term oppression. Many of these patterns will be empowering to the minoritized group, but some of these patterns will not be healthy and will not support their survival. For example, there may be increased drug and alcohol use, or increased rates of suicide. The dominant group uses the position and patterns of the minoritized group to rationalize the oppression and blame the minoritized group for its condition, attributing the effects of historical oppression to the lack of a work ethic, personal, cultural or family values, biology, or an element in their genetic makeup. Thus, the dominant group justifies the oppression of the minoritized group *based on the effects of having oppressed them.*

One of the ways in which justification for further mistreatment manifests for many minoritized racial groups is through what is termed *cultural deficit theory*. This refers to the belief that the minoritized group's oppression is the result of cultural characteristics specific to them, rather than as the result of structural barriers. While in the past dominant culture was more likely to argue that the minoritized group was in a lower position because they were *biologically* inferior, today we are more likely to argue that their position is due to something problematic in the minoritized group's *culture*. But both of these explanations locate the problem within the minoritized group and not within the structures of society. For example, in a December 2011 GOP debate, presidential candidate and former Speaker of the House Newt Gingrich made this statement:

> Really poor children in really poor neighborhoods have no habits of working and have nobody around them who works. So they literally have no habit of showing up on Monday. They have no habit of staying all day. They have no habit of "I do this and you give me cash," unless it's illegal.

Although Gingrich didn't explicitly say poor *black* children, the association in the public mind between really poor neighborhoods and black neighborhoods is very strong. I am confident that most people immediately made the racial association and had a corresponding racial image. Indeed, as Gingrich's

comments were challenged, he made reference to the high black unemploy-
ment rate, making it clear he wasn't talking about poor communities in general but *poor black communities*. That a candidate for president of the United
States made this statement testifies to the perceived legitimacy of cultural
deficit theory. The belief is not unique to Gingrich—perhaps the only thing
atypical about the comment is that it was made in a highly public forum.

Cultural deficit theory is common with many of the teachers I have worked
with in schools, who often explain that the challenges faced by children of
color—and black and Latino/a children in particular—are due to their lack
of cultural values. The ways that schools are structured or the bias of teachers
and other school personnel are left unexamined. "They just don't value education," "There is nothing you can do when their parents don't care," "They
probably have drugs and guns at home which stresses them out and makes
concentrating in school too difficult" are common white teacher narratives."
Racial disproportionality in special education referrals, punishments, and
access to quality public school resources are ignored, and unequal outcomes
are attributed to the children and their families, in spite of the National Col-
laborative on Diversity in the Teaching Force's (2004) conclusion that:

> The evidence ... proves beyond any shadow of a doubt that children ... who come
> from families with poorer economic backgrounds ... are not being given an opportu-
> nity to learn that is equal to that offered children from the most privileged families.
> The obvious cause of this inequality lies in the finding that the most disadvantaged
> children attend schools that do not have basic facilities and conditions conducive to
> providing them with a quality education. (p. 7)

An example of cultural deficit theory circulating in education can be seen in
the work of Ruby Payne. Payne is a white, middle-class author who is very
popular with white, middle-class teachers (Gorski, 2008). She conducts trainings in which she argues that there is a "culture of poverty" with hidden rules
that teachers—who are primarily white and middle class—need to understand
in order to teach children of a lower economic status. For example, according
to Payne (2001) (adapted from Gorski, 2008):

> The typical pattern in poverty for discipline is to verbally chastise the child, or phys-
> ically beat the child, then forgive and feed him/her. (p. 37)

> Also, individuals in poverty are seldom going to call the police, for two reasons: First
> the police may be looking for them. ... (pp. 37–38)

> Allegiances may change overnight; favoritism is a way of life. (p. 74)

If students in poverty don't know how to fight physically, they are going to be in danger on the streets. (p. 100)

And for some, alcoholism, laziness, lack of motivation, drug addition, etc., in effect make the choices for the individual. (p. 148)

The poor simply see jail as a part of life and not necessarily always bad. Local jails provide food and shelter and, as a general rule, are not as violent or dangerous as state incarceration. (pp. 22–23)

And one of the rules of generational poverty is this: [women] may need to use [their bodies] for survival. After all, that is all that is truly yours. Sex will bring in money and favors. Values are important, but they don't put food on the table—or bring relief from intense pressure. (pp. 24–25)

The scenarios Payne uses to illustrate these so-called cultural traits are filled with African American and Latino/a characters and stereotypes, illustrating and reinforcing the association between race and class. Payne's work embodies the cultural deficit framework—or victim blaming—that is used to justify institutional oppression (Kunjufu, 2007). Yet we do not fund schools equally. The charts in Figures 15 & 16 are from Jonathan Kozol's book (2005), *The Shame of the Nation: The Restoration of Apartheid Schooling in America.*

School Funding in New York City Area 2002–2003

District	Spending per pupil	% Student Population by Race: B = Black; H = Hispanic W = White; O = Other		% Low Income
Manhasset	22,311	B + H	9	5
		W + O	91	
Jericho	19,113	B + H	3	1
		W + O	97	
Great Neck	19,705	B + H	11	11
		W + O	89	
Bronxville	18,788	B + H	1	0
		W + O	99	
Rye	16,132	B + H	5	1
		W + O	95	
Roosevelt	12,834	B + H	100	92
		W + O	0	
New York City	11,627	B + H	72	83
		W + O	28	

Figure 15. School funding New York.

Changes over 10 Years

District	1986–1987	2002–2003
Manhasset	11,372	22,311
Jericho	11,325	19,113
Great Neck	11,265	19,705
Bronxville	10,113	18,788
Rye	9,092	16,132
Roosevelt	6,339	12,834
New York City	5,585	11,627

Figure 16. Funding changes.

These charts are based on school funding for the New York City area, but the patterns are similar for all major school districts. Kozol published these charts in 2005, but based on changes in the economy in the last decade, these patterns have only gotten worse, not better. For example, schools in poorer New York districts overall spent $8,733 per pupil less in 2012 than those in wealthier ones, an inequity that grew by nearly 9% (while the 100 wealthiest districts spent on average more than $28,000 in state and local funding per student in 2012, the 100 poorest districts in the state spent closer to $20,000 per student (Alliance for Quality Education).

Yet when income and wealth levels across race are the same, rates of college graduation are the same, rates of employment and work hours are the same, and rates of welfare usage are the same (Conley, 2009). Patterns of inequitable outcomes are not the result of personal shortcomings or cultural deficiencies; they are the result of institutionalized inequality.

Following a Minoritized Group through the Cycle

Although the points on the cycle of oppression are presented as if they occur in order, there is no first, second, and third step. Once set in motion (and all current systems of oppression were set in motion long before we were born), they play out simultaneously and continually reinforce each other. Further, what differentiates oppression from acts of discrimination is that oppression is large-scale discrimination backed by institutional power. This results in the inequitable distribution of power, control, and resources. While anyone can discriminate, oppression is a one-way dynamic and only benefits the dominant group at the macro level. Again, members of a minoritized group can be prejudiced and discriminate against members of the dominant group in limited and contextual situations, but are not in the position to oppress the dominant group across the society because they don't control the institutions necessary to do so.

Let's follow a minoritized group through the cycle to illustrate how it works in our own lives in ways that should be recognizable to most readers. Using children with learning disabilities as the minoritized group (*ableism* is the name of this oppression), try the following experiment.

Reflect back to the years you spent in elementary school. Think of the kids whom today, with our adult perspectives, we might understand as having mild learning disabilities. But when we were children ourselves, many of us didn't have an understanding of learning disabilities and simply understood these children as not good at school. These were/are the children who did not get their work posted on the wall, who failed tests or assignments, whom everyone had to wait for, who were rarely if ever the first to raise their hands or have the right answer, and who were in the lowest-level reading groups. Perhaps they spent part of the day in a "special" class or with a tutor, or rode a different bus ("short," "special") to school. We ourselves may have been one of these children, or perhaps had a sibling that had this experience in school. Once you get an image of these children, reflect on the following questions:

- How were children with learning disabilities viewed, by other students and by the teachers?
- How were they treated?
- How was this treatment possible (what made it acceptable)?
- How did the children with learning disabilities often respond to all of the above?

Although there are some variations, and there are likely positive attitudes and experiences for children with learning disabilities that we can recall, the answers to these questions are overwhelmingly negative. I have led this exercise with thousands of people over the years, and regardless of the time period in which someone attended elementary school, the following are the most consistent answers I hear:

How were children with learning disabilities *viewed*?

They were seen as: stupid, dumb, retarded, lazy, stubborn, dirty, poor, a waste, a drain on resources, bullies, different, weird, ugly, victims, trouble-makers, from bad families, pitiable, unable to learn, unwilling to learn, and unfeeling.

How were children with learning disabilities *treated*?

They were: ridiculed, tricked, blamed, punished, ignored, excluded, teased, avoided, segregated, picked on, beaten, used as an example, medicated, and not given the benefit of the doubt.

How was this treatment possible (what made it *acceptable*)?

This treatment was made possible through: peer pressure, ignoring, silence, role models such as teachers who participated in it or did not stop it, the belief that it did not hurt the children (because their humanity was diminished) or that if it did, they brought it upon themselves. It was also made possible institutionally through the organization of schooling itself: standardized testing, tracking, labeling, misdiagnosis, definitions of intelligence, norms, expectations, rules, insufficient funding, and the priorities of a society that does not provide the resources to meet these children's needs.

How did these children often *respond* to this treatment (what was the effect on them)?

They: withdrew; gave up trying; became angry, depressed, and shameful; believed they were stupid, bad, and undeserving; acted out; fulfilled other's expectations; blamed themselves; were either drawn to others like them or avoided others like them; participated in mistreating others like themselves; developed low self-esteem. As they progressed through the grades they became at higher risk to drop out and sometimes developed unhealthy coping strategies such as self-medicating.

Once the cycle is in motion, it is difficult to say where it begins—each point reinforces all of the others. It is important to note that a given child might not have a learning disability at all; the child may be assumed to have learning challenges simply because their first language is not English, or based upon assumptions about the child's race and class (it is noteworthy that "poor" and "dirty" often come up when asked how these children were viewed).

The cycle of oppression illustrated in Figure 14 is a useful tool for identifying the specific ways that oppression manifests for specific groups. Each point on the cycle is a general dynamic of oppression experienced by all minoritized groups, but the brainstormed lists under each section will vary depending on the group. For example, if we follow another minoritized group through the cycle, such as gay and lesbian people, we would need to address each of the same points on the cycle, but we would get somewhat different answers at each point. We can also use the cycle to identify variations between groups within a category. For example, while we could follow "people of color" through the cycle and identify commonly shared dynamics of racism experienced by all groups of color, we could also follow each specific group through within the broad category of "people of color" in order to identify the specific way oppression plays out for that group (e.g., Asian heritage, African heritage, Latino/a, Indigenous). This is important to do because each group has different histories and struggles.

For example, the history of African heritage people in the United States is different from the history of Asian heritage people in the United States. Dominant beliefs and representations of each group are also different. Further, within categories such as "Asian" are myriad groups who also have different histories. Again, while it is important to understand the racial dynamics that all Asian heritage people must navigate within dominant white culture, a more advanced analysis would also consider the variations within this category. This is also a place to consider the intersections of class and how it impacts the history and current experience of a group within the United States. For example, coming to the United States as an international student from China, or as a Japanese business person, or as a refugee from Cambodia or Viet Nam due to conditions of war (and in the case of the Vietnamese, a war with the United States), or to be third-generation Japanese American with grandparents who were interned during World War II, are all very different experiences. These experiences create different degrees of access to resources. Yet all of this complexity is ignored under the broad category of "Asian."

Both Dominant and Minoritized Groups Have a Role in Challenging Oppression

Returning to the example of women's suffrage to illustrate the differences among prejudice, discrimination, and institutional oppression, I want to be clear that I do not believe that men *will* take away women's right to vote in the United States. My point in raising this question is to illustrate that oppression does not change direction overnight. Further, this example illustrates several other important dynamics of oppression. The first is how confused most of us are about power. The gender makeup of the power-holders in society is clearly visible, and the actual statistics are just a Google search away. Yet most people cannot answer the question: *Today*, if men as a group wanted to take away women's right to vote, could they? Oppression in large part depends on this lack of clarity about the reality of power. When I ask a group this question and the majority of them look at me with confusion or shake their heads, "no," many of them are women. It seems to me that this is a question that women might be invested in and should be able to answer. This confusion and lack of attention illustrates how both dominant and minoritized groups are co-conditioned to either not see, or not question, their positions.

Further, simply stating a demographic fact and its implications—that is, men are the vast majority of the holders of institutional power and decision-making in society and thus *can* make decisions that are contrary to the interests of women—often causes defensiveness in both men and women. This defensiveness further illustrates the dynamics of oppression. Many people hear this statement of fact as a statement that men are bad. But this good/bad binary conception of relations of power is not constructive. It is important to identify where one stands in dynamics of unequal power—to identify one's *positionality*—because it enables us to identify how we can challenge inequality from that position. In the example of suffrage, although all men benefited from women's lack of suffrage, certainly there were men who wanted to change that condition. Indeed, women could only have been granted suffrage by men; they couldn't grant it to themselves.

Women had to have their consciousness raised and come to believe that they should have the right to vote; that they *deserved* suffrage. Although this may sound obvious to us today, women were not raised to believe that they deserved suffrage. They had a great deal of socialization to overcome. They also had to organize themselves and find men who would be allies. Men also had a task. They had to talk to other men and convince them to align with pro-suffrage forces. They had to advocate and speak out on behalf of women. They had to build a critical mass of men to tip the vote. Ultimately, men had to grant women suffrage. This is why, although both groups had a task—women to challenge their internalized oppression and men to challenge their internalized dominance—the weight of the responsibility for change fell to men. The dominant group always bears the greatest responsibility to change the inequitable relationships.

In Conclusion

Lynn Weber (2010), a sociologist who studies social inequality, offers the following helpful criteria for differentiating systems of oppression from individual acts of discrimination:

Oppression is:	
Complex	Intricate and interconnected
Pervasive	Widespread throughout all societal domains—e.g., families, communities, religion, education, the economy, government, criminal justice, the media
Variable	Changing and transforming to adapt to cultural shifts
Persistent	Prevailing over time and across places
Severe	Serious consequences for social life
Power Based	Hierarchical, stratified, power based, benefiting and providing options for some by harming and restricting options and resources for others

Figure 17. Oppression criteria (Weber, 2010).

Weber reminds us that oppression can adapt to cultural changes and still maintain inequitable outcomes. These adaptations are accomplished in large part through ideology. Ideology is an important concept to remember as we grapple with problematic concepts such as colorblindness and reverse racism.

Discussion Questions

1. In your own words, explain each point on the cycle of oppression.
2. While everyone has prejudice and discriminates, only the dominant group can oppress. Why is this? What does it mean to say that, for example, only men can be sexist or only white people in the U.S. can be racist?
2. Provide some examples of how oppression is institutionalized.
3. What is ideology and what role does it play in maintaining oppression? Share some examples of ideologies that maintain oppression.
4. Think about a group you belong to that is a dominant group. What are some examples of your internalized dominance? How did you learn this?

· 6 ·

WHAT IS RACE?

Race means about as much as what I had for lunch today. Sure I noticed it, and sometimes people had a different lunch. I don't really care; it all goes the same way. Also, I am one of those people who don't hate anyone's lunch. Eat what you please I always say. I grew up in a three-house neighborhood in the woods. So, not much diversity. Messages I've received are that race doesn't matter. Be colorblind and all that good stuff. Race means very little to me. (ASR)

I come from a small town. It's not diverse in the slightest. Growing up the main messages I received were along the lines of: "Respect people of diverse backgrounds, meaning religion, race, etc." All the messages were positive ones. I'm not really sure what being white has meant to my life except that I am pasty and I burn under the sun. I'm a common white guy from the hills. (ASR)

Growing up my neighborhood was not that diverse at all, basically almost everyone was white with no other backgrounds. I honestly don't think about my racial group too much. I try not to discriminate against people of another race. (ASR)

Now that we have a framework for understanding how oppression works, we can focus on the form of oppression that is the topic of this book: racism. We begin with the very idea of race.

Many of us have been taught to believe that there are distinct biological and genetic differences between races. This biology accounts for differences we *can see* with our eyes such as skin color, hair texture, and eye shape, and traits that we *believe we see* such as sexuality, athleticism, or mathematical ability. The idea of race as biological makes it easy to believe that many of the divisions we see in society are natural. But race, like gender, is socially constructed. The differences we *do see* with our eyes, such as hair texture and eye color, are superficial and emerged as adaptations to geography (Cavalli-Sforza, Menozzi, & Piazza, 1994); there really is no race under the skin. The differences we *believe* we see (Lakisha is less qualified than Emily, or Jamal is more prone to violence) are a result of our socialization; our racial lenses. While there is no biological race as we understand it, race as a *social construction* has profound significance and impacts every aspect of our lives (Onwuachi-Willig, 2013). The impact of race as a social idea includes: where we are most likely to live, which schools we will attend, who our friends and partners will be, what careers we will have, how much money we will earn, how much education we will have, how healthy we will be, and even how long we can expect to live (Adelman, 2003; Johnson & Shapiro, 2003). In order to unpack the dynamics of racism, we first need to address our ideas about race itself.

Race as we understand it today is a relatively recent idea (Gossett, 1997). Humans have not been on the earth long enough to evolve into separate species. In fact, we are among the most genetically similar of species on earth. The external characteristics such as skin color that we use to define race are not reliable indicators of internal variation between any two people (Cooper, Kaufman, & Ward, 2003). However, the belief that race and the differences associated with it are biological is deep-seated. In order to challenge the belief in race as biology, we need to understand the social and economic investments that drove science to organize society and its resources along racial lines.

A Very Brief History of the Social Construction of Race in the United States

In the past, societies did not divide people into racial categories, although other categories of organization such as religious affiliation or class status were common. When the United States was formed, freedom and equality—regardless of religion or class status—were radical new ideas. At the same time, the U.S. economy was based on the enslavement of African peoples, the displacement and genocide of Indigenous North American peoples, and the colonization of Mexican lands. In order to reconcile the tension between the noble ideology of equality and the cruel reality of genocide, enslavement, and colonization, Thomas Jefferson (who owned hundreds of slaves himself) and others turned to science. Jefferson "suggested" that there were natural differences between the races and set science on the path to find them (Jefferson, 2002). If science could "prove" people of color were inferior, there would be no contradiction between our professed ideals and our actual practices. Drawing on the work of Europeans before them, American scientists began searching for the answer to the perceived inferiority of non-Anglo groups. Illustrating the power of our questions to shape the knowledge we validate, these scientists didn't ask, "*Are* blacks (and others) inferior?" They asked, "*Why* are blacks (and others) inferior?"

In addition to the moral contradiction between our ideals and our practices, there were enormous economic interests in justifying slavery and colonization. These social, political, and economic interests shaped race science and helped establish cultural norms and legal rulings that legitimized racism and the privileged status of those defined as white. For example, in the early to mid-1800s, skulls were measured in an attempt to prove the existence of a natural racial hierarchy. Samuel Morton, the first famous American scientist, claimed that brain capacity could be measured through skull size. However, his results reflected his biases as he concluded that Caucasians had larger skulls and thus had unquestioned superiority over all the nations of the earth (Gould, 1996). Because science claimed that blacks were naturally suited to slavery, the physician Samuel A. Cartwright (1793–1863) defined the attempts of slaves to escape as a form of mental illness which he termed "drapetomania." He wrote: "With proper medical advice, strictly followed, this troublesome practice that many Negroes have of running away can be almost entirely prevented" (1851). Anthropologists claimed that blacks were an inferior species and that miscegenation (inter-marriage) would produce weak offspring. (Early beliefs in the weakness of blacks compared with modern beliefs that blacks are stronger and more athletic show the socially constructed dimensions of our racial ideas; we see in others what we already believe about them in a specific cultural moment.)

Research such as this is termed *scientific racism*, which is the use of scientific means to "prove" the racial superiority of one race over another. In less than a century, Jefferson's suggestion of racial difference became commonly accepted scientific "fact" (Stepan & Gilman, 1993). But while race has no biological foundation, as a *social* idea it is very real and has profound consequences.

Scientific racism: The use of pseudo-scientific techniques to support the classification of individuals of different phenotypes into discrete races and to justify belief in the natural inferiority or superiority between these races.

As an illustration of race as an evolving social idea, in the late 1600s the term "White" first appeared in colonial law. By 1790, people were asked to claim their race on the census, and by 1825, the degree of blood determined who would be classified as Indian. From the late 1800s through the early 20th century, as waves of immigrants entered the United States, the idea of whiteness became more and more concrete (Gossett, 1997; Ignatiev, 1995; Jacobson, 1999).

While slavery in the United States was abolished in 1865, whiteness remained profoundly important as legal racist exclusion and violence continued. To gain citizenship and other rights, one had to be legally classified as white. Individuals from a range of non-white racial classifications began to challenge their classifications and petitioned the courts to be re-classified as white. These legal challenges put the courts in the position to decide who was white and who was not. Armenians, for example, won their case to be re-classified as white with the help of a scientific witness who claimed they were scientifically "Caucasian." In 1922 the Supreme Court ruled that the Japanese could not be legally white because they were scientifically classified as "Mongoloid." But a year later, the court stated that Asian Indians were not legally white, even though they were scientifically classified as Caucasian. In justification of this contradictory ruling, the court stated that whiteness was based on the common understanding of the white man. In other words, people already seen as white get to decide who is white (Tehranian, 2000).

Ta-Nehisi Coates (2015), in his powerful book *Between the World and Me*, eloquently explains:

> But race is the child of racism, not the father. And the process of naming "the people" has never been a matter of genealogy and physiognomy so much as one of hierarchy. Difference in hue and hair is old. But the belief in the preeminence of hue and hair, the notion that these factors can correctly organize a society and that they signify deeper attributes, which are indelible—this is the new idea at the heart of these new people who have been brought up hopelessly, tragically, deceitfully, to believe that they are white.

Many of us are familiar with the metaphor of the United States as "the great melting pot," in which immigrants from around the world come together and melt into one unified society through the process of assimilation; once we learn English and adapt to American culture and customs, we all become Americans. While the idea of the melting pot is a cherished one, in reality only European immigrants were allowed to "melt" or assimilate into dominant culture through the perception of whiteness; those who are seen as white are seen as belonging.

> **Race:** The false concept that superficial adaptations to geography (skin tone, eye shape) are genetic and biological determinants that result in significant differences among groups of human beings.

The Perception of Race

Because whiteness is a social construct, who is included in the category changes over time. European ethnic groups who today we see as white were not always included in the past. But where they may have been originally divided in terms of ethnic or class status, European immigrants became united in whiteness through the process of assimilation. For example, early Irish, Italian, and Polish immigrants were not initially considered white in the United States, but they "became" white as they assimilated into the dominant culture (Ignatiev, 1995; Jacobson, 1999; Roediger, 2007). This process of assimilation reinforced the concept of *American* as *white*. Racial identification in the larger society plays a fundamental role in identity development.

> **White:** The "top" classification of the socially constructed and hierarchically arranged racial categories. Those perceived and categorized as white are granted social, cultural, institutional, psychological and material advantages.
>
> **White identity:** To be socialized as a white person, enact whiteness by implicitly and explicitly upholding racism and white supremacy, and participate in the rewards of being perceived as white.
>
> **People of color:** Refers collectively to all of the socially constructed racial groups who are not perceived and categorized as white and do not have access to the social, cultural, institutional, psychological and material advantages of whiteness.

Today, if someone "looks white," they are *treated* as white in society. For example, people of southern European heritage, such as Spanish or Portuguese, especially if they are new immigrants or were raised by immigrants, will likely have a stronger sense of ethnic identity than someone of the same ethnicity whose ancestors have been here for generations. Yet while they may have a different sense of identity *internally*, if they look white, they will still have a white experience *externally*. In other words, if someone didn't tell me that they weren't white, would I know? If they *look* white the default assumption will be that they *are* white and thus they will be treated as white. Due to the incongruity between their internal ethnic identity (i.e., Portuguese, Spanish) and external racial experience (white), they may have a more complex or nuanced sense of identity than someone who doesn't question their whiteness. However, they will still be granted white privilege in dominant culture, and if they are committed to anti-racist practice, they will need to explore how that white privilege shapes them.

> **Remember:** While race has no biological meaning beyond very superficial differences in appearance, these differences have been given profound *social* meaning. To say that race is socially constructed is to acknowledge that the meaning assigned to these superficial differences is real in its consequences.

Race as a social construction has also manifested along class lines; poor and working-class people were not always perceived as fully white (Roediger, 2007). But because economic and racial forces are inseparable, poor and working-class whites were granted full entry into whiteness as a way to exploit labor; if they were focused on feeling superior to those below them in status, they were less focused on those above. In reality, the poor and working classes, across race, have a great deal in common. But racial divisions have served to keep them from organizing against the owning class who exploit their labor (for an astute analysis of this "bargain" between working-class whites and owning-class whites to unite across class lines, see Lillian Smith, *Killers of the Dream*, 1949). However, while working-class whites experience classism, they aren't *also* experiencing racism. The complexity of multiple identities is termed *Intersectionality* and will be explored in greater depth in Chapter 11.

> **Whiteness:** A term to capture all of the dynamics that go into being defined and/or perceived as white and that create and reinforce white people as inherently superior through society's norms, traditions, and institutions. Whiteness grants material and psychological advantages (white privilege) that are often invisible and taken for granted by whites.

The Unique Dynamics of White Identity and Anti-Semitism

Anti-Semitism is the term used for the specific form of oppression faced by Jewish people. Anti-Semitism is based on both religion and ethnicity, in other words on prejudice toward the religion and prejudice toward specific physical and cultural characteristics attributed to ethnicity. Unlike racism, which is a relatively new form of oppression, anti-Semitism has been around as long as Jews have. Anti-Semitism became more widespread with the rise and dissemination of the Christian Bible, in which Jews were blamed for the death of Christ. Because Christianity has been exported worldwide, so has anti-Semitism. Jews have faced persecution and extreme violence in virtually every nation on earth, and at one time or another nearly every one of the world's greatest powers with a Jewish population (the Roman Empire in the first century, the Christian world for over 15 centuries, the Nazi Reich, and the Soviet Union) has regarded Jews as an enemy despite the fact that they have never constituted more than a small percentage of the population. This speaks to the permanence of anti-Semitism, which culminated in attempted genocide during the Holocaust in Nazi Germany.

It is important to note that there is a great deal of geographic and ethnic diversity among the world's Jewish populations. In fact, the vast majority of Jews worldwide are people of color. Jews of Central European heritage—and thus white in racial terms—are referred to as Ashkenazic (this is differentiated from Sephardic Jews of Spanish and Portuguese ancestry, among others). While Ashkenazic Jews constitute approximately 20% of the world's Jewish population (Tobin, Tobin & Rubin, 2005), more than 90% of U.S. Jews are Ashkenazic. When I am addressing the relationship between whiteness and Jewishness, I am speaking about Ashkenazic Jews.

In the United States, covenants that were active through the 1960s excluded Jews from neighborhoods and other organizations. While explicit discrimination against Jews is illegal in the United States today, many stereotypes about Jews continue to circulate, including that they own the banking industry and Hollywood, have large or "hook" noses, and are loud, pushy, and greedy. Current examples of these stereotypes circulating in the culture at large are the expression, "He jewed me down on the price," jokes about "JAPS" (Jewish American Princesses), and negative literary descriptions in works considered classics such as *The Merchant of Venice* and *Oliver Twist*. Sporadic violence is still perpetrated against Jews in the United States. For example, in 2006 a man walked into the Jewish Federation of Seattle and shot six people—killing one—while stating that he was "angry at Israel." Due to the long history of anti-Semitism and recent incidents such as this, many Jews feel that they are in a constant state of threat. Thus, many Ashkenazic Jewish people don't identify as fully white because there are aspects of whiteness—for example, psychological freedom and freedom of movement—that they don't completely enjoy.

The unique aspects of Jewish identity illustrate the complex interaction between internal identity and external perceptions. For example, although the Jews of Europe are considered white by current racial classifications, Hitler focused "the Jewish problem" on the belief that Jews were a separate and inferior race from "Aryans." Because of this and the Holocaust that resulted, as well as the historic and current continuation of anti-Semitism, how Jews look at themselves racially is complicated. Yet while many Ashkenazic Jewish people may not feel fully white, if they are of European heritage they are *perceived* as white by the culture at large, and thus granted white privilege. In many ways the process of assimilation into whiteness for European Jewish immigrants was the same as that of other European immigrants (Brodkin, 1998). Under the current racial construction, while Ashkenazic Jews experience anti-Semitism, and anti-Semitism is in part based on perceptions of ethnicity, their *race* is white. In other words, Ashkenazic Jews can experience anti-Semitism and *also* benefit from white privilege. As for other groups of European heritage, the intersections for Ashkenazic Jews between ethnic identity and racial identity must be addressed in order to move forward in challenging racism.

White as a Position of Status

Reflecting on the social and economic advantages of being classified as white, critical race scholar Cheryl Harris (1993) coined the phrase "Whiteness as property." This phrase captures the reality that being perceived as white carries more than a mere racial classification. It is a social and institutional status and identity imbued with legal, political, economic, and social rights and privileges that are denied to others. Harris, tracing the evolving concept of whiteness across legal history, explains:

> According whiteness actual legal status converted an aspect of identity into an external object of property, moving whiteness from privileged identity to a vested interest. The law's construction of whiteness defined and affirmed critical aspects of identity (who is white); of privilege (what benefits accrue to that status); and, of property (what legal entitlements arise from that status). Whiteness at various times signifies and is deployed as identity, status, and property, sometimes singularly, sometimes in tandem. (p. 104)

Harris's analysis is useful because it moves beyond notions of property as merely material and shows how identity and *perceptions* of identity can grant or deny resources. Thus, identity is also a form of property if it grants resources. These resources include self-worth, positive expectations, psychological freedom from the "tether" of race, freedom of movement, the sense of belonging, and a sense of entitlement to resources. I will discuss these aspects of "property" in Chapter 9.

Whiteness as Property: The concept that being perceived as white is more than a racial classification; it is a social and institutional status and identity imbued with legal, political, economic, and social rights and privileges that are denied to others. These translate into *material* gains.

Given that race is socially constructed, the boundaries between groups are both rigid (in terms of their consequences for our lives) and fluid (because they are shaped by perceptions, politics, and other changing dynamics). For example, while racial categories are not "real" in the sense that there are no true biological racial groups among humans, racial categories play a profound role in social dynamics such as segregation and quality of life. Yet at what point does someone become "Black" or "Brown" or "White"? Why is U.S. President Barack Obama generally considered black but not white, when he has one parent from each racial group? His case illustrates how perceptions of race can be as powerful as a person's actual heritage. This is why scholars have developed concepts such as "racialization" and "minoritized." When we say that someone is from a *minoritized* group or is *racialized*, we are seeking to capture the active dynamics of race as a *social process*, rather than as a fixed condition. However, this should not be used to deny that race has real consequences for our lives.

Discussion Questions

1. What is scientific racism? Give some examples of how scientific racism is conveyed today.
2. How can someone experience both oppression and privilege?
3. What does it mean to say that whiteness is a form of "property"?
4. What is problematic about the idea of the U.S. as a great "melting pot"? How did the "melting pot" actually work?
5. Discuss Coates's statement that *race is the child of racism, not the father.*
6. *White identity* is defined as being socialized as a white person, enacting whiteness by implicitly and explicitly upholding racism and white supremacy, and participating in the rewards of being perceived as white. Can you explain these points in your own words?

WHAT IS RACISM?

Until about 4 years ago, literally everybody in my neighborhood was white. I've read and learned that most people are subconsciously at least mildly racist, they just don't outwardly express it. But there was basically no diversity in my life until college so I've never really had it affect my life. (ASR)

When I was growing up and still to this day, my neighborhood was not very diverse. Race was not really talked about in school, but through friends and family I was always taught that certain races can be very stereotypical. Race does not really mean much to me. I treat everyone equally. (ASR)

What it means to me to be white. To me it means that (at least where I live) I'll never be subjected to any negative racial stereotyping or foul words/racism. I'll also never benefit from any affirmative action grants/school acceptance etc. … I grew up in a school system where you could count the kids who were not white Americans on your fingers. Growing up in a small town like I did also means that I do have some of the "good old boy" mentality though I do not consider myself "racist" per se. (ASR)

Racism is a form of oppression in which one racial group dominates others. In the United States, whites are the dominant group and people of color are the minoritized group. Thus in this context, racism is white racial and cultural prejudice and discrimination, supported intentionally or unintentionally by institutional power and authority, used to the advantage of whites and the disadvantage of people of color (Hilliard, 1992). Racism encompasses economic, political, social, and institutional actions and beliefs, which systematize and perpetuate an unequal distribution of privileges, resources, and power between whites and people of color.

> **Racism:** A form of oppression in which one racial group dominates others. In the United States the dominant group is white, therefore racism is white racial and cultural prejudice and discrimination, supported intentionally or unintentionally by institutional power and authority, and used to the advantage of whites and the disadvantage of people of color.

As with all forms of oppression, racism operates on more than just an individual or personal level. Thus, while individual whites may be "against" racism, they still benefit from a system that privileges whites as a group. David Wellman (1977) succinctly summarizes racism as *a system of advantage based on race*. These advantages are referred to as *white privilege* (McIntosh, 2012). White privilege is a sociological concept referring to advantages enjoyed and taken for granted by whites that cannot be enjoyed and taken for granted by people of color in the same context (government, community, workplace, schools, etc.).

> **Remember:** A strong opinion is not the same as informed knowledge; We have a deep interest in denying those forms of oppression which benefit us; We don't have to be aware of racism in order for it to exist; Our racial positionality will greatly affect our ability to see racism; Putting our effort into protecting rather than expanding our current worldview prevents our intellectual and emotional growth.

Racism is deeply embedded into the fabric of our society. It is not limited to a single act or a single person. Racism does not move back and forth, one day benefiting whites and another day (or even era) benefiting people of color. The direction of power between whites and people of color is historic, traditional, and normalized in ideology. The critical element that differentiates *racism* from individual racial prejudice and racial discrimination is the historical accumulation and ongoing use of institutional power and authority to support the prejudice and to enforce discriminatory behaviors in systemic ways with far-reaching effects. People of color may hold prejudices and discriminate against whites, but do not have the social and institutional power backing their prejudice and discrimination that transforms it into racism; the impact of their prejudice on whites is temporary and contextual. Whites hold the social and institutional positions in society to infuse their racial prejudice into the laws, policies, practices, and norms of society in a way that people of color do not. A person of color may be able to refuse to wait on me if I enter her shop, but people of color cannot pass legislation that prohibits me from buying a home in a certain neighborhood.

People of color may also hold prejudices and discriminate against their own and other groups of color, but this prejudice and discrimination ultimately serves to hold them down and, in this way, reinforce the system of racism that benefits whites. Oppression is a society-wide dynamic that occurs at the group level. From an antiracist perspective, when I say that *only whites can be racist*, I mean that in the United States only whites have *collective social and institutional power and privilege* over people of color. People of color do not have *collective* social and institutional power and privilege over whites.

> **Remember**: Racism is more than race prejudice. Anyone across any race can have race prejudice. But *racism* is a macro-level social system that whites control and use to the advantage of whites as a group. Thus all whites are collectively implicated in this system.

Racism Today

Many whites see racism as a thing of the past. Yet racial disparity between whites and people of color continues to exist in every institution across society, and in many cases is *increasing* rather than decreasing. While segregation may make these disparities difficult for whites to see and thus they are often denied, racial disparities and their effects on overall quality of life have been extensively documented by a wide range of agencies, including federal (such as the U.S. Census Bureau, the United Nations), academic (such as the UCLA Civil Rights Project, the Metropolis Project), and nonprofit (such as the NAACP, the Anti-Defamation League).

White families, on average, have always been wealthier than black or Latino families. But the magnitude of the disparity is overwhelming: the median wealth of white households is now 20 times that of black households and 18 times that of Hispanic households (Pew Research Center, 2014). These wealth gaps are the widest in 25 years. The racial wealth gap is due to a combination of factors that vary somewhat for specific groups. For example, the century of legal discrimination following slavery essentially kept most blacks impoverished and unable to pass assets down to their children. Since the civil rights legislation of the 1960s, continuing and well-documented racial discrimination in employment, housing, education, and mortgage lending has systematically denied people of color the opportunity to build equity and other forms of wealth. While all families have been impacted by the current recession, people of color (and blacks and Latinos in particular) do not have the kind of economic safety nets that could tide them over in difficult economic times. Further, blacks and Latinos were specifically targeted for the subprime loans at the center of the market crash (Faber, 2013).

Over the past few decades, wealth has been concentrated into fewer and fewer hands. For example, in 1980 the chief executive officers (CEOs) of Standard and Poor's top 500 companies averaged 35 times the average American worker's annual salary. In 2014, CEOs of Standard and Poor's top 500 averaged *over* 300 times the average worker's salary. The top hedge fund and private equity fund managers averaged *19,000* times the annual salary (*Forbes*, 2015).

Contrary to popular ideology, these gaps in wealth and access to resources are not the result of some people working harder than others. They are the result of some people being in the institutional positions to exploit others. And while the majority of us are impacted by the inequitable distribution of resources, people of color are hit hardest because they have been systematically denied the opportunity to build economic safety nets. For example, consider the following range of statistics documenting current conditions of racial inequality:

Health Care

At birth, the life expectancy in the United States is as follows:

White males 75	Black males 69
White females 80	Black females 76

- Racism in health care has been well-documented. For example, black patients are taken less seriously and receive fewer recommendations for treatment than white patients with the same symptoms (Ansell & McDonald, 2015).
- Cooper et al. (2012) found that two-thirds of primary care doctors harbor biases toward their African American patients, leading those doctors to spend less time with their black patients and involve them less in medical decisions.
- Despite persistent racial disparities in health care, people of color continue to be left out of clinical trials. Most physicians and scientists are informed by research extrapolated from a largely homogenous population, usually white and male (Oh et al., 2015).

Wealth

- The gap between median household income for whites (about $91,000) compared to blacks (about $7,000) is staggering, and that gap has tripled in just the past 25 years. The median net worth of white families is about $265,000, while it was just $28,500 for blacks (*Nesbit* 2015).
- As they have been across history, blacks were discriminated against during the sub-prime loan rush that precipitated the housing crisis (Burd-Sharps & Rasch, 2015). The resulting economic downturn has adversely affected blacks to a much greater degree than white homeowners for two key reasons: blacks have historically been denied access to wealth-building programs; and, blacks were unfairly targeted for subprime loans. Faber (2013) found that banks knowingly preyed on black mortgage-seekers when it came to issuing subprime mortgages. Even when a black middle-class family could afford a prime loan, subprime loans were pushed on them. Faber states:

Relative to comparable white applicants, and controlling for geographic factors, blacks were 2.8 times more likely to be denied for a loan, and Latinos were two times more likely. When they were approved, blacks and Latinos were 2.4 times more likely to receive a subprime loan than white applicants. The higher up the income ladder you compare white applicants and minorities, the wider this subprime disparity grows. (p. 328)

United for a Fair Economy (2010) reports that:

- The average net worth of white families is more than six times higher than the average net worth of black families, and 5.7 times greater than the average net worth of Latino families.
- Between 2007 and 2010, the average net wealth of white families decreased by 6.7%. By comparison, black families lost 27.1% of their average net wealth and Latino families lost 41.3%.
- Black and Latino families came out of the Great Recession much more highly leveraged (holding more debt relative to their net assets) than white families. White families on average have a debt burden equal to just 17% of their net worth, while black and Latino families owe 53% and 58%, respectively.
- 53.6% of black households and 46.4% of Latino households are unbanked or underbanked (no one in their household has a checking account, or they have a checking account but also rely on a fringe banking sector to meet their financial needs).

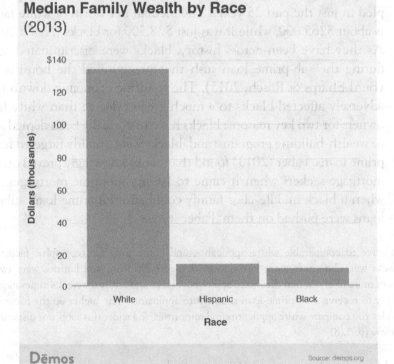

Figure 18. Racial wealth gap 2013.

- Both the unbanked and underbanked rely on a variety of "Alternative Financial Service Providers" (AFSPs) to provide some portion of their banking services via check cashers, payday lenders, auto title lenders, pawn shops, etc. For the underserved, there is little opportunity to create a credit history, have access to affordable, safe and sustainable financial services, or build assets over time.
- In the workplace, black college graduates are twice as likely as whites to struggle to find jobs—the jobless rate for blacks has been double that of whites for decades. As the resume study showed, people with "black-sounding names" had to send out 50% more job applications than people with "white-sounding names" just to get a call back.

Criminal Justice

From *U.S. News & World Report*, 2015:

- Black preschoolers are far more likely to be suspended than white children. Black children make up 18% of the preschool population, but represent almost half of all out-of-school suspensions.
- Once in K–12, black children are three times more likely to be suspended than white children. Black students make up almost 40% of all school expulsions, and more than two-thirds of students referred to police from schools are either black or Hispanic.
- About a fifth of children with disabilities are black—yet they account for 44% of students put in mechanical restraints and 42% placed in seclusion.
- Black children are 18 times more likely to be sentenced as adults than white children, and make up nearly 60% of children in prisons. Black juvenile offenders are much more likely to be viewed as adults in juvenile detention proceedings than their white counterparts.
- A black man is three times more likely to be searched at a traffic stop, and six times more likely to go jail than a white person. Blacks make up nearly 40% of arrests for violent crimes.
- Blacks aren't pulled over (and subsequently jailed) more frequently because they're more prone to criminal behavior. They're pulled over much more frequently because there is an "implicit racial association of black Americans with dangerous or aggressive behavior," the Sentencing Project found (U.S. Bureau of Justice Statistics, 2012).

- On the New Jersey Turnpike, for instance, blacks make up 15% of drivers, more than 40% of stops and 73% of arrests—even though they break traffic laws at the same rate as whites. In New York City, blacks and Hispanics were three and four times as likely to be stopped and frisked as whites.

- If a black person kills a white person, they are twice as likely to receive the death sentence as a white person who kills a black person. Local prosecutors are much more likely to upgrade a case to felony murder if you're black than if you're white.

- Qualified black jurors are illegally turned away as much as 80% of the time in the jury selection process.

- About a quarter of juries in death penalty cases have no black jurors, and more than two-thirds have two or less. When a black person is accused of killing a white person—and the jury consists of five or more white males—the odds rise substantially for a death penalty verdict. Defense lawyers and prosecutors know that having just a single black man on the jury considerably changes the odds.

- Black people stay in prison longer than white people—up to 20% longer than white people serving time for essentially similar crimes. They get much harsher sentences: black people are 38% more likely to be sentenced to death than white people for the same crimes.

- Whites and blacks represent about half of murder victims from year to year, but 77% of people who are executed killed a white person, while only 13% of death row executions represent those who killed a black person.

The Criminal Justice System

Let's look more closely at a specific institution in society with a devastating impact on people of color—the criminal justice system. The United States has the *highest* prison population in the world. Whereas there are on average 145 per 100,000 people in prison worldwide, the United States has 716 per 100,000, and those 716 are disproportionately people of color. The U.S. is 5% of the world population and has 25% of world prisoners. Consider that as the wealth gap grows and disproportionately impacts people of color, the prison population grows accordingly. Yet the reasons for this are not as simple as the belief that people of color commit more crimes.

Consider the following statistics, adapted from the NAACP Criminal Justice Factsheet 2009–2015 (retrieved from http://www.naacp.org/pages/criminal-justice-fact-sheet/ unless otherwise indicated):

People of color are overrepresented in the criminal justice system

- African Americans now constitute nearly 1 million of the total 2.3 million incarcerated population.
- African Americans are incarcerated at nearly six times the rate of whites.
- Together, African American and Hispanics comprised 58% of all prisoners in 2008, even though African Americans and Hispanics make up approximately one-quarter of the U.S. population.
- If African American and Hispanics were incarcerated at the same rates of whites, today's prison and jail populations would decline by approximately 50%.
- One in six black men had been incarcerated as of 2001. If current trends continue, one in three black males born today can expect to spend time in prison during his lifetime.
- Nationwide, African Americans represent 26% of juvenile arrests, 44% of youth who are detained, 46% of the youth who are judicially waived to criminal court, and 58% of the youth admitted to state prisons.
- About 14 million whites and 2.6 million African Americans report using an illicit drug.
- 5 times as many Whites are using drugs as African Americans, yet African Americans are sent to prison for drug offenses at 10 times the rate of whites.
- African Americans represent 12% of the total population of drug users, but 38% of those arrested for drug offenses, and 59% of those in state prison for a drug offense.
- African Americans serve virtually as much time in prison for a drug offense (58.7 months) as whites do for a violent offense (61.7 months) (Sentencing Project).
- Crime/drug arrest rates: African Americans represent 12% of monthly drug users, but comprise 32% of persons arrested for drug possession.
- In 2002, blacks constituted more than 80% of the people sentenced under the federal crack cocaine laws and served substantially more time in prison for drug offenses than did whites, despite that fact that

more than two-thirds of crack cocaine users in the U.S. are white or Hispanic.

- Of the nearly 2.1 million adult men and women imprisoned in the United States, roughly 70% are persons of color. Within the criminal justice system, people of color are imprisoned disproportionately and denied access to the rehabilitative options given to whites. Although people of color commit most crimes at the same rate as whites, the unequal targeting and treatment of people of color throughout the criminal justice system—from arrest to sentencing—results in disproportionate imprisonment of people of color.
- Latinos represent just 11.1% of the U.S. population and only 10% of U.S. drug users, yet make up 18.6% of the U.S. prison population and 22.5% of those convicted for drug offenses.
- On average, 1 in 25 adult American Indians is under the jurisdiction of the nation's criminal justice system—more than twice the number of white adults in the system.
- Women of color sentenced for drug crimes continue to be the highest-growing segment of the U.S. prison population.

People of color face harsher treatment in court

- Native people are disproportionately imprisoned compared to their population size. For example, in Montana 16% of prisoners are American Indians, even though they constitute just 6% of the state's population. In North Dakota, American Indians are 5% of the state's total population, but are 19% of the prison population.
- Blacks are more likely to be sentenced to prison for the same crime than whites. One-third of people of color sentenced to prison would have received a shorter or non-incarcerative sentence if they had been treated in court the same way as white defendants facing similar charges.
- Latinos and blacks who have no prior criminal record are far more likely to be incarcerated than white defendants with no criminal record. Latinos are twice as likely as whites to face prison time instead of probation, a fine, or time in a county jail.
- Black youth are more likely to be detained than white youth. Moreover, black youth with no prior admissions were six times more likely to be incarcerated in a juvenile facility than a white youth with a similar history. Latino youth were three times more likely to be imprisoned.

- Blacks are disproportionately placed on death row. While blacks constitute 12% of the total U.S. population, approximately 43% of the death row population is black.

Crack is the only drug with a mandatory prison sentence for a first offense of simple possession

- At the same time that crack has a mandatory prison sentence, the maximum sentence someone can receive for simple possession of powder cocaine is one year.

Stereotypes regarding who uses crack cocaine and who uses powder cocaine make mandatory minimums racist

- Not only are crack and powder cocaine simply different forms of the same drug, but crack is primarily thought of as a drug used in black, urban areas. Powder cocaine, on the other hand, is far more expensive than crack and is associated with wealthy white users.

Even though the majority of crack users are white, most people imprisoned because of crack offenses are black

- Roughly two-thirds of crack cocaine users are white or Latino, but 84.5% of defendants convicted of crack possession in 1994 were black, while 10.3% were white and 5.2% were Latino. The majority of persons charged with crack trafficking offenses in the federal system have also been black American (88.3%).

The School-to-Prison Pipeline

Although the previous statistics are from the criminal justice system, they illustrate the interlocking institutional forces that constitute oppression. Let's take what is termed *The School-to-Prison Pipeline* (STPP) as an example of these forces working in tandem. The STPP refers to the pattern of criminalizing rather than educating children, and poor children of color in particular. This pattern works as a kind of "pipeline" that channels these children into the prison system. Up until relatively recently, society drew a distinction between childhood and adulthood and made allowances for youth whose development was still in process. In recent years, this line has become blurred as children are treated and punished as adults in the system. Zero-tolerance policies in schools are a prime example of this increasingly inflexible and punitive rather than restorative response. These policies, which began in the 1990s, resulted in almost doubling the number of students suspended annually. In 2010, more than 3 million students were suspended from school. Meanwhile, more than a quarter-million were "referred" to police officers for misdemeanor tickets, very often for offenses that once would have elicited a stern lecture.

Black students are *three and a half times* more likely to be suspended as white students for the same infractions. Over 70% of students arrested in school or handed over to law enforcement are black or Latino. While there is no evidence that black students are more prone to violence, there is much evidence that the overrepresentation of black students is related to bias in referral on the part of school officials (C. Smith, 2009; Fenning & Rose, 2007; Nicholson-Crotty, Birchmeier, & Valentine, 2009; Solomon & Palmer, 2006).

Three major institutions are directly involved in creating the STPP: Criminal Justice, Education, and Social Services. School administrators rely on law enforcement to "police" schools with higher populations of students of color. The curriculum in these schools focuses on obedience and conformity rather than critical thinking and creativity. Social service agencies take a punitive rather than healing approach. Working together, these institutions force youth of color to face ever more layers of structural disadvantage.

Specifically, the criminal justice system contributes to the STPP through criminalization of truancy and zero-tolerance policies; public misperceptions based on racial stereotypes that cause the demand for ever harsher penalties at ever younger ages; the racial biases of police officers and judges; historical poverty, which makes it more likely that people of color will need to depend on public defenders; and district attorneys and public defenders who work together to encourage youth to take plea bargains that ensure they will have CORIs (Criminal Offender Records Information).

A report released by the Rennie Center for Education Research & Policy (2011) found that excessive disciplinary action for nonviolent offenses, such as tardiness and truancy, exacerbates the dropout rate. Testimony indicated that students already behind in school are often forced to miss additional days through suspension, which leads to a loss of credits and an inability to catch up. Out-of-school suspension is the most frequently used form of disciplinary removal. Particular segments of the student population (low-income,

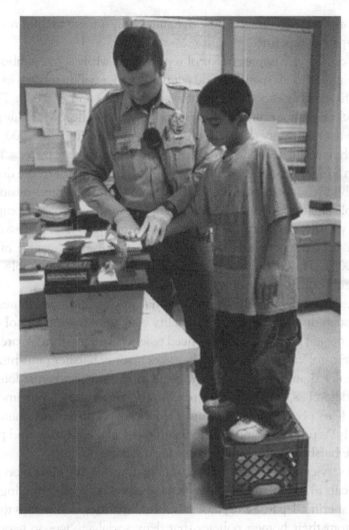

Figure 19. School-to-Prison Pipeline.

special education, male, black, Hispanic) are removed at disproportionately high rates.

In his powerful book, *The Shame of the Nation: The Return of Apartheid Schooling in America* (2005), Jonathan Kozol challenges the return to a deeply segregated and unequal school system. Rather than attribute unequal educational outcomes to families and communities who don't care about education, Kozol attributes unequal outcomes to a *society that doesn't care about poor children of color.* He identifies the institutional dynamics that account for these outcomes. These dynamics play a fundamental role in the school-to-prison pipeline.

As discussed in Chapter 5, Kozol reports that while some public schools in poor neighborhoods spend $8,000 per pupil, other public schools in suburbs and wealthy neighborhoods spend between $12,000 and $18,000. The salaries of teachers in poor and wealthy school districts follow a similar pattern. While the average salary of teachers in poor communities is $43,000, the salary of teachers in suburbs like Rye, Manhasset, and Scarsdale in New York can range from $74,000 to $81,000. Another contributing factor to the disparities among public schools in poor and wealthy communities is fund-raising activities schools organize to purchase school supplies and materials. Compared to schools in wealthy neighborhoods that have been able to raise up to $200,000, schools in poor districts have only been able to raise an average of $4,000 (Kozol, 2005). The amount of funding available to schools notably impacts the type and quality of schooling available to students.

Education works together with criminal justice and contributes to the STPP through disparity in access to quality education among school districts based on unequal funding; inexperienced teachers being sent to poorer school districts; zero-tolerance policies; high-stakes testing; harsher punishments for youth of color than for whites for the same infractions; and a predominantly white, middle-class, and suburban teaching force that does not understand and often fears people of color (Kunjufu, 2005) and disproportionately (and subjectively) sends black and Latino youth to special education and punishes them more harshly than white students for the same offenses.

Social services work together with criminal justice and education through continual cuts in federal funding that create the need to rely on funding streams from local sheriff's departments; race and class disparities in decisions to remove children from their homes; policies that deny social services to people once they have entered the system; and a predominantly white, middle- and upper-class social work population (Dominelli, 1989; Miller & Garran, 2007). These three institutions work together to create the School-to-Prison Pipeline. Of course corporations also play a role because they profit from prisons and thus work against efforts to minimize mass incarceration (Herival & Wright, 2008).

The following overview is adapted from the Anti-Defamation League's *School to Prison Pipeline: Talking Points* (2015):

- Children are far more likely to be arrested at school than they were a generation ago. The vast majority of these arrests are for nonviolent offenses such as "disruptive conduct" or "disturbance of the peace." For example, children as young as five years old have been led out of class-rooms in handcuffs for acting out or throwing temper tantrums. But the increase in school-based arrests cannot be attributed to an increase in youth violence. Between 1992 and 2002, school violence actually dropped by approximately half. Despite the fear generated by a hand-ful of highly publicized school shootings (mostly perpetrated by white males), schools remain the safest places for young people.

- Resources that could be invested in needed improvements for under-resourced schools are instead used for security. School districts spend millions of dollars for police officers and security personnel, despite the fact that some of these same schools are lacking basic educational resources like textbooks and libraries.

- Students who enter the juvenile justice system face many barriers blocking their re-entry into traditional schools, with life-long reper-cussions. The vast majority of juvenile justice–involved students never graduate from high school, and may be denied student loans, pub-lic housing, or occupational licenses because of their prior criminal records, virtually guaranteeing that they will end up back in the crim-inal justice system.

- According to the ADL (http://www.aclu.org/racial-justice/school-pris-on-pipeline-talking-points), students of color are disproportionately represented at every stage of the school-to-prison pipeline.

- African American students are far more likely than their white peers to be suspended, expelled, or arrested for the same kind of conduct at school.

- There is no evidence that students of color misbehave to a greater degree than white students. They are, however, punished more severely, often for behaviors that are less serious.

- Students with special needs are disproportionately represented in the school-to-prison pipeline, despite the heightened protections afforded to them under law.

- Children who have unmet special learning or emotional needs are par-ticularly likely to be pushed out of mainstream schools and into the juvenile justice system.

- African American students with disabilities are three times more likely to receive short-term suspensions than their white counterparts, and are more than four times as likely to end up in correctional facilities.

Remember: Institutions work together to produce predictable social outcomes. For example, the policies and practices of three major institutions—Education, Criminal Justice, and Social Services—together result in what is known as The School-to-Prison Pipeline. The STPP is an example of institutional oppression; it works systemically and cannot be isolated to a single person or act. The STPP is also an example of "new racism" in that it achieves the outcomes of prior incarnations of racism without overtly appearing to be racist.

Many people do not realize that once someone has a felony charge they can no longer vote in some states; can legally be discriminated against in housing and employment; can be denied educational loans; and can no longer receive food stamps or other public benefits, *even after having served the time*. These are permanent, life-long penalties that make it extremely difficult to survive, much less succeed, in society. Michelle Alexander (2010), a law professor and former director of the Racial Justice Project and former law clerk for Supreme Court Justice Harry Blackmun, refers to this as a "caste" system. The term caste means the position one is born into is permanent and cannot be changed. In her extraordinary book *The New Jim Crow: Mass Incarceration in the Age of Colorblindness* she argues that the criminal justice system is the "new Jim Crow" because it functions in the same way as Jim Crow policies did in the pre–civil rights era. (Jim Crow refers to the state and local laws that mandated racial segregation and discrimination.) Alexander illustrates that Jim Crow has not ended; it has simply been *redesigned* so that it accomplishes the same outcomes of social control and racial stratification. This legal discrimination is accomplished through institutions and the decision makers who comprise them in ways that cannot be isolated and appear to be colorblind. These are classic hallmarks of what has been termed "new racism" (Bonilla-Silva, 2009). In other words, racism has adapted to changes in society so that the same outcomes are produced but within the context of so-called colorblindness.

It is important to note that all of the institutions and decision makers within them that create the STPP are predominantly white. This means that we may assume that the majority of these decision makers have grown up in racial segregation and have not developed authentic cross-racial relationships or received quality information about people of color. Further, they have not been taught to value or to seek out these relationships or this information. Most of them have rarely (if ever) had a teacher of color or other role models of color. Thus, they rely upon very limited and problematic images and representations received in mainstream culture at large (recall the resume study). In other words, they have been taught in myriad and often very subtle ways that people of color either don't exist, are not valuable, or are dangerous and should be avoided. At the same time—and in large part through colorblind ideology—they have been taught to deny that they see and feel this way, making it very difficult to challenge their misinformation. Yet these are the people who have the institutional power to make lasting decisions about the lives of children of color. This limited and homogenous population will determine who is smart and who is intellectually limited, who is well-behaved and who is misbehaved, who has a correct attitude and who has a bad attitude, who is deserving and who is undeserving, who is capable of rehabilitation and who is incorrigible.

As our education system fails youth of color, we have put our resources into building more prisons rather than improving education. This results in profits for many corporations who are now invested in prisons and who in turn use their power to resist efforts for reform (Herival & Wright, 2008). All of these dynamics are examples of the ways in which racism works as an interrelated *system* to ensure racial disparity between whites and people of color.

As Coates (2015) so powerfully expresses:

> I, like every kid I knew, loved The Dukes of Hazzard. But I would have done well to think more about why two outlaws, driving a car named the General Lee, must necessarily be portrayed as "just some good ole boys, never meanin' no harm"—a mantra for the Dreamers if there ever was one. But what one "means" is neither important nor relevant. It is not necessary that you believe that the officer who choked Eric Garner set out that day to destroy a body. All you need to understand is that the officer carries with him the power of the American state and the weight of an American legacy, and they necessitate that of the bodies destroyed every year, some wild and disproportionate number of them will be black.

Coates refers to white people as "Dreamers" in "the Dream," falsely believing that they are actually white. I believe that by this he means that whites can only be white if someone is *not white*, or is its opposite: *black*. White is an identity of false superiority. In that sense, it isn't real. The Dream is the "perfect world," unpolluted by blacks; white identity and the Dream of whiteness is contingent on the absence of blacks. In order to construct this world, blacks must be *separated* and held away through State violence, but still *must exist*, for the existence of blacks provides the needed Other against which whites rise. Thus white identity depends on the oppression of blacks.

Discussion Questions

1. What is the difference between racial prejudice and racism?
2. Why does the author say that there is no such thing as reverse racism?
3. What is the *School-to-Prison Pipeline*?
4. What are some ways in which racism is "deeply embedded in the fabric" of society?
5. What does Coates mean when he says, "All you need to understand is that the officer carries with him the power of the American state and the weight of an American legacy, and they necessitate that of the bodies destroyed every year, some wild and disproportionate number of them will be black."

· 8 ·

"NEW" RACISM

I grew up in pretty much an all-white neighborhood. Every part of my life growing up told me that race is obsolete; it does not matter. Therefore, by being told this many times, I have taken away that everyone is equal and the way you look or the color of your skin does not matter. (ASR)

The town and neighborhood that I grew up in had basically no diversity. I would say 95% of the population in my town is Caucasian. However, my school and family have taught me never to look at someone differently just because of their race. I've believed in this all my life, so to me there is no difference how I am towards people based on their race. I try hard every day to live in a nice respectful manner to give my race a good name. (ASR)

Upon the election of the first biracial president of the United States, pundits declared that society was now "post-racial." This meant, presumably, that racism is in the past and race no longer has significance in our lives. This is a common dominant group narrative when there is a milestone in inter-group dynamics. I imagine that when women were granted the right to vote, sexism was declared dead; when civil rights legislation was passed, racism was declared dead (again); when the Americans with Disabilities Act was passed, ableism was pronounced dead, and so on. These milestones are of course very significant and worthy of celebration. But oppression is deeply rooted and it can and does adapt to challenges. In many ways these mile-stones enable society to obscure and deny oppression, as individuals from minoritized groups who publically succeed are held up as testimony that the system is open. But those of us who study inequality are not saying that the system is completely inflexible. What we *are* saying is that it is *far less flexible* than popular ideology would acknowledge, and that the *collective impact* of oppression—the inequitable distribution of resources between dominant and minoritized groups—continues, albeit in new forms. Upon reflection, it is highly superficial to claim that one minoritized group member's success proves there are no longer any barriers for any member of that group. In the case of Barack Obama, the entire social system didn't transform on the day of his election. For example, we (whites) might ask ourselves how his election impacted our actual lived experiences and relationships with peo-ple of color. On the ground, segregation and the inequitable distribution of resources persist, unabated. In this chapter, I discuss some of the ways that racism has adapted to social changes over time while still producing similar outcomes today as it did in the past.

Figure 20. The pier.

New Racism: The ways in which racism has adapted over time so that modern norms, policies, and practices result in similar racial outcomes as those in the past, while not appearing to be explicitly racist.

When I talk to white people about racism I hear the claims of new racism made again and again. As I listen, an image forms in my mind. I see a pier stretching out over water. The pier appears to simply float there. This image signifies for me the superficial or "surface" claims I consistently hear.

These claims include:

- I was taught to treat eveyone the same.
- I don't see color.
- I don't care if you are pink, purple, or polka-dotted.
- Race doesn't have any meaning to me.
- My parents were/weren't racist, so that is why I am not racist.
- Everyone struggles but if you work hard …
- … just happened to be black
- I work in a very diverse environment.
- I have people of color in my family.
- I was in the military.
- I used to live in New York.
- We don't like how white our neighborhood is but we had to move here, for the schools.
- I was in the Peace Corps.
- I marched in the '60s.
- Children today are so much more open.

Yet while the pier seems to float effortlessly, if we go under the surface of the water we can see the pillars that prop it up. The pier does not float at all; it is supported by a foundation of pillars (Figure 21).

In the same way as a pier is dependent on underlying pillars, typical white racial claims are dependent upon a framework of underlying meaning. The pillars in Figure 21 represent the framework that these claims are drawn from. Identifying these frameworks has been very useful to me in my understanding of how we manage to make such "surface" claims in the context of extreme segregation and racial inequity. For example, in a conversation of racism, when white people say that they work in a diverse environment or that they

Figure 21. The pillars.

have people of color in their family, they are giving me their evidence that they are not racist. If this is their evidence, how are they defining racism? In other words, what is underneath that claim? Clearly, they define racism as *conscious dislike*; racists is someone who does not like people of color and knows it. Further, a racist presumably cannot tolerate the sight of a person of color. But because they know or work with people of color, or lived in New York where they saw people of color all around them, they cannot participate in racism. When we go beneath the surface of these claims we can see their absurdity.

Someone who tells me that they were taught to treat everyone the same is simply telling me that they doesn't understand socialization. It is not actually possible to teach someone to treat everyone the same. We can be and often are *told* to treat everyone the same, but we cannot be *taught* to do so because human beings are not objective. Further, we wouldn't want to treat everyone the same because people have different needs and different relationships to us. Differential treatment in itself is not the problem (I wouldn't want to give a document with 12 point font to a sight-impaired person, even though someone else wouldn't have any trouble reading it). The problem is the *misinformation* that circulates around us and causes our differential treatment to be *inequitable* (recall the resume readers).

People who tell me that they marched in the 1960s—like those who tell me they know people of color—are telling me that they see racism as a simple matter of personal prejudice (which clearly they don't have or they would not have marched alongside black people during the Civil Rights movement). They are also telling me that they believe that racism is uncomplicated and unchanging. Therefore, based on an action they took over 50 years ago, their learning is finished for life; this action certifies them as outside of racism and there is no more discussion or reflection required.

As we explore the dynamics of new racism keep the image of the pillars in mind. The more we can see the meaning (beliefs, ideology) under the surface that support current racial narratives, the more effectively we can formulate strategies for deepening that meaning.

Colorblind Racism

What is termed "colorblind racism" is an example of racism's ability to adapt to cultural changes (Bonilla-Silva, 2009). This is the ideology that pretending that we don't notice race will end racism. This ideology comes out of the Civil Rights Movement of the 1960s and the parts of Martin Luther King's "I Have a Dream" speech focused on by dominant society. In many ways, King's speech symbolized a turning point in the adaptation of racism. Before the period leading up to his speech, many white people felt quite comfortable, even proud, to admit to their racial prejudices and internalized racial superiority. But one aspect of King's speech—that one day he might be judged by the content of his character and not the color of his skin—hit a moral chord with the public. Seizing on this part of King's speech, dominant culture began promoting the idea of "colorblindness" as a remedy for racism. But this was not the primary message of King's speech. King's speech was given at a march for economic justice, the "March on Washington for Jobs and Freedom," and he was there to advocate for the elimination of poverty, but few people today know the breadth and complexity of King's activism. Further, King did not mean that whites should *deny* that race mattered, but that they should actively work toward creating a society in which it *actually* didn't matter. But once the Civil

Rights Movement became more mainstream and civil rights legislation was passed, there was a significant change in dominant culture; it was no longer as acceptable for white people to admit to racial prejudice.

> **Colorblind Racism**: Pretending that we don't notice race or that race has no meaning. This pretense denies racism and thus holds it in place.

Of course the Civil Rights Movement didn't end racism; whites just became somewhat more careful in public spaces. But reducing King's work to the simplistic idea of "colorblindness" is a hallmark of the ways in which dominant culture resists movements for social change; they are co-opted, stripped of their initial challenge, and used against the very cause from which they originated. For example, today, in the name of colorblindness, to say that race is meaningful often results in the accusation that it is *you* who are racist for suggesting that race matters.

I was once co-leading a workshop with an African American man. A white participant said to him, "I don't see race; I don't see you as black." My co-trainer's response was, "Then how will you see racism?" He then explained to her that he *was* black, he was confident that she *could* see this, and that this meant that he had a very different experience in life than she did. If she were ever going to be able to understand or challenge racism, she would need to acknowledge this. Pretending that she did not notice that he was black was not helpful to him in any way as it denied his reality—indeed it *refused* his reality—and kept hers insular and protected. Further, this pretense assumed that he was "just like her," and in so doing, projected her reality onto him—for example, I feel welcome at work so you must too; I have never felt that my race mattered so you must not feel that yours does, either. Of course this denial that race matters rests on a foundation of deeply internalized messages about race; at the same time we deny that race matters we know that it does, especially if that race is not white.

A common statement from those who profess colorblindness and who are opposed to programs to support minoritized candidates is that they would hire the best person for the job regardless of their color. We may believe we are not seeing (or at least, ignoring) a candidate's race, but as the resume study demonstrated, this is not true in practice. Anyone who has had a conversation about race or hiring in the workplace has likely heard the common assumption that all people of color got their jobs (unfairly) via affirmative action programs. In my years as a workplace diversity trainer, I have rarely heard a white person assume that the person of color really was the most qualified. What I have heard is a deep-seated resentment that the person got the job that rightfully belonged to the white person doing the complaining. The assumption is that people of color are *inherently* unqualified for jobs that are of interest to whites (Bonilla-Silva, 2009). Further, I rarely hear white people express outrage about the myriad studies that show *empirically* that it is *people of color* who are discriminated against in the workplace, not whites (but they are discriminated against of course, *by* whites). This reveals the core contradiction between our desire to see ourselves as people who *would* hire the most qualified person regardless of race and the deeply internalized belief that the only qualified people are white.

We *do* see the race of other people, and that race has deep social meaning for us. Everyone receives value-laden racial messages *daily* that circulate in society; they are all around us. These messages did not end the day civil rights legislation was signed. While some of these messages are blatant (racist jokes, for example), we must understand that most of the racial messages we receive (and broadcast ourselves) are subtle and are often invisible, especially to whites. While we learn very early about race, much of what we learn is below the level of our conscious awareness.

Research over the past two decades indicates that children are vastly more sophisticated in their awareness of racial hierarchies than most people believe (Derman-Sparks & Ramsey, 2006; Quintana & McKown, 2008; Van Ausdale & Feagin, 2001). Even when race is not explicitly discussed, children internalize both implicit and explicit messages about it from their environment. For example, Monteiro, de Franca & Rodrigues (2009) tested 283 white children aged 6 to 7 and 9 to 10 years old. The children were asked to allocate money to white and black children, sometimes with a white adult in the room and sometimes without an adult in the room, to see if having an adult present impacted their behavior. They found that the 6- to 7-year-old children discriminated against Black children in both conditions, and the 9- to 10-year-old children discriminated against the Black children only when the white adult was not present. This is significant because it shows the older children clearly had racial prejudice and acted on it, but hid it when a white adult was present. Thus, the children showed that they did not become less racially biased with age, but that they had learned to hide their racism in front of adults. Van Ausdale & Feagin (2001) found racial hostility in white children as young as 3 years old. However, most white parents and teachers believe that children are colorblind. This false belief keeps us from honestly addressing racism with children.

Drawing on the iceberg metaphor from Chapter 3, we might think of the tip of the iceberg as the superficial aspects of our racial socialization: our intentions (always good!) and what we are supposed to acknowledge seeing (nothing!), while under the surface is the massive depth of racist socialization: messages, beliefs, images, associations, internalized superiority and entitlement, perceptions, and emotions. Colorblind ideology makes it difficult for us to address these unconscious beliefs. While the idea of colorblindness may have started out as a well-intentioned strategy for interrupting racism, in practice it has served to deny the reality of racism and thus hold it in place.

Aversive Racism

Colorblind racism may be seen as a form of aversive racism. Aversive racism is a term that describes the type of racism well-intentioned, educated, progressive people are more likely to enact (Hodson, Dovidio, & Gaertner, 2004). It exists under the surface of consciousness because it conflicts with consciously held beliefs of equality and justice among racial groups. Aversive racism is a subtle but insidious form, as the aversive racist enacts racism in ways that allow him/her to maintain a positive self-image ("I am not prejudiced/I am colorblind"). Some of the ways in which whites are able to enact racism while maintaining a positive self-image include: rationalizing racial segregation as necessary in order to access "good schools"; rationalizing a lack of cross-racial friendships as a result of few people of color living in the area; avoiding direct racial language and using racially coded terms such as "urban," "underprivileged," "diverse," "sketchy," and "good neighborhoods"; denying that one has few cross-racial relationships by proclaiming how diverse one's community or workplace is; and attributing inequality between whites and people of color to causes other than racism.

> **Aversive Racism:** Forms of racism which allow well-meaning white people to maintain a positive ("not racist") self-image while still perpetuating racism.

When you lay the racist = bad/not racist = good binary over this frame (racists are bad people; everyone else is good), our irrational reactions when confronted with the suggestion that we are complicit in racism begin to make sense. We believe we are superior at a deeply internalized level and act on this belief in the practice of our lives, but must deny this belief (even to ourselves) in order to fit in to society and maintain our self-identity.

A 2008 episode of the television show *20/20*, "What Would You Do: Racism," illustrates many aspects of aversive racism. While this was not an academic study, it did highlight many familiar dynamics of racism that have also been demonstrated in more rigorous studies. The show featured two sets of actors portraying vandals from different races: one set consisted of three young white men and the other of three young black men. The first set of white actors openly tries to break into a car that is parked in a suburban parking lot. While a hidden camera records the scene, they pry open the door with a crowbar, jump up and down on the hood, and spray-paint it with graffiti. Over the course of 3 hours, many people just walk by, ignoring the vandals and their actions. One woman says, "I hope that's your car" but doesn't stop and inquire further. One man questions the boys, and when they disrespect him, he becomes angry, but he doesn't call or threaten to call the police; his anger seems to be more about being disrespected. In the course of 3 hours, only *one* person calls the police.

However, during the time in which the white men are engaging in *open vandalism*, friends and relatives of the other set of actors, all of whom are black, are *sleeping* in a nearby car waiting for their friends/relatives to be filmed. The police are called *three* times to report the sleeping black men as suspicious. One caller states that the sleeping men look like they are "getting ready to rob somebody" (this caller was so concerned that he called twice). Once their scene starts and the black actors begin to vandalize the car, people immediately begin to call the police. A total of 10 calls are made, compared with 1 for the white vandals. One woman also wonders if the men have a gun, while this worry was never raised with the white men. This difference in reaction to the vandals should not be surprising to people. There is a deep association in people's minds between blacks and crime, and a corresponding feeling of resentment—those who report the black men exhibit outrage that the boys are in "their" neighborhood doing such things. And yet, all of the passers-by, when later questioned by the show's host, insisted that race had nothing to do with their response. Although there are countless studies with similar results, how can we "prove" that race informed a response if the person refuses to consider it? We can't challenge our racial filters if we can't consider the possibility that we have them.

> **Remember:** Racism is a complex, multifaceted system in which we are all involved, and which goes well beyond personal intentions.

Cultural Racism

The body of research about children and race demonstrates that children start to construct their ideas about race very early; a sense of white superiority appears to develop as early as pre-school (Clark & Clark, 1950; Derman-Sparks, Ramsey, & Olsen, 2011). This shouldn't be surprising, as society sends constant messages that to be white is better than to be a person of color. These messages operate on multiple levels and are conveyed in a range of ways. For example:

- Our centrality in textbooks and other curricular materials;
- Our centrality in media and advertising;
- Our teachers, role models, heroes, and heroines who all reflect us;
- The reduction of three centuries of slavery and genocide toward Indigenous people to sidebars in history textbooks;
- The hypocrisy of our pride in the 4th of July wherein we celebrate our independence and Thomas Jefferson, who held over 600 slaves;
- Our celebration of Columbus Day wherein we honor a man responsible for bringing slavery and genocide to the Americas;
- Everyday discussions about "good" neighborhoods and schools and the racial makeup of these quality locations;
- The return to pre-integration levels of racial segregation in schools and neighborhoods;
- Norms and standards of beauty that emphasize blonde (or at least straight) hair, blue eyes, slim hips, narrow noses, and almond-shaped eyes;
- Popular TV shows centered around friendship circles that are all white, even when they take place in racially diverse cities such as New York;
- Religious iconography that depicts Adam and Eve, other key Christian figures, and even God as white;
- Newscasters referring to any crime that occurs in a white neighborhood as "shocking";
- The lack of a sense of loss about the absence of people of color in most white people's lives.

Figure 22. Religious iconography.

These are examples of implicit (indirect) rather than explicit (direct) messages, all telling us that it's better to be white. While we may consciously reject the notion that we are inherently better than people of color, we cannot avoid internalizing the message of white superiority below the surface of our consciousness, *because it is ubiquitous in mainstream culture.*

Cultural Racism: The racism deeply embedded in the culture and thus always in circulation. Cultural racism keeps our racist socialization alive and continually reinforced.

Racism in Media

Media representations compound the impact of racial segregation on most whites' limited understanding of people of color. Movies, for example, have a profound effect on our ideas about the world. Key social concepts such as masculinity and femininity, sexuality, desire, adventure, romance, family, love, deviancy and normalcy, violence and conflict are all conveyed to us through the stories told in films. We can see the power of movies to shape children's desires, fantasies, identities, and play, as early as age two. In many ways it has become impossible to think and imagine outside the influence of movies. Now consider that the *vast* majority of all mainstream films are written and directed by white males. In fact, the 20 highest-grossing films of all time worldwide were all directed by white men (*Frozen* was co-directed by a white man and a white woman) (Box Office Mojo, 2010): *Avatar; Titanic; Jurassic World; The Avengers; Furious 7; Age of Ultron; Harry Potter & The Deathly Hollows: Part 2; Frozen; Iron Man 3; Minions; The Lord of the Rings: Return of the King; Transformers: Dark of the Moon; Skyfall; Transformers: Age of Distinction; The Dark Knight Rises; Toy Story 3; Pirates of the Caribbean: Dead Man's Chest; Pirates of the Caribbean: On Stranger Tides; Jurassic Park; Star Wars 1: The Phantom Menace.* Also consider race and gender in the story-lines and main actors of these films. Of the top 50 films, all were directed by men, 46 of whom were white (the exception is *Frozen*, which still had one white male director).

Because of the racial segregation that is ubiquitous throughout all levels of society, it follows that these men are very unlikely to have gone to school with, lived near, been taught by, or been employed by or with people of color. Therefore, like many of us, they are unlikely to have meaningful cross-racial relationships. Yet these men are society's cultural authors or storytellers; their imaginations, their desires, their worldviews, and their conceptions of people of color become ours. Consider the implications of this very privileged, homogenous, and racially isolated group essentially telling our culture's stories. These implications aren't problematic because privileged white men are bad people; they are problematic because their worldview is necessarily very *limited*, especially regarding race. Yet it is virtually the *only* worldview many of us see, and it unavoidably (and quite powerfully) shapes *our* worldview.

> **Remember:** A fundamental element of oppression is the ability to disseminate your group's worldview throughout the society.

Those who decide which films to promote and award are also primarily white. In fact, they are an extremely homogenous group in several interconnected dimensions. Of the 5,765 voting members of the Academy of Motion Picture Arts and Sciences, *nearly 94% are white* and *77% are male*. Blacks represent about 2% of the academy, and Latinos are less than 2%. Oscar voters have a median age of 62. People younger than 50 constitute just 14% of the membership (Horn, Sperling & Smith, 2012). Figure 23 shows the Academy Board of Governors, 2015–2016. Two out of 51 (3%) are persons of color.

Figure 23. Academy Board of Governors.

Over and over, white male directors depict people of color and their environments in narrow and stereotypical ways (*if* they depict them at all). This repetition creates familiar tropes (clichés) that directors rely on to quickly set up or convey racial meaning. Not having many—if any—cross-racial friendships, most whites come to rely on these images for their understanding of people of color, reinforcing the idea of a positive "us" versus a negative "them." I very often hear white people refer to neighborhoods as "sketchy." Yet what makes a neighborhood sketchy? It appears to be the presence of people of color and apartments or modest houses. In other words, low income and people of color automatically equal sketchy in white people's minds. And sketchy, of course, also means "dangerous."

Pornography is another rich site for racial analysis because the narratives that circulate within it are so uncensored. While it may be uncomfortable, we need to take porn seriously, especially if we care about challenging racism, because porn has become ubiquitous in popular culture and racism is ubiquitous in porn. In 2006 the worldwide porn industry was worth $96 billion (Dines, 2010). Each year over 13,000 porn films are released (compare to the approximately 600 Hollywood film releases in a given year, according to the Motion Picture Association of America's website). There are 420 million Internet porn pages, 4.2 million porn websites, and 68 million search engine requests for porn *daily* (Dines, 2010). The porn site LiveJasmin has more visitors worldwide than BBC Online, CNN, and *The New York Times* combined, and it ranks just after the most-visited sites such as Google, Facebook, and Craigslist (Alexa, 2010). Many porn directors and actresses are crossing over to direct and act in mainstream videos and movies.

Mainstream heterosexual gonzo porn (reality-based porn that places the viewer directly in the scene), also primarily directed by white men, regularly reproduces blatant and explicit racist discourses and images. While the majority of men in the United States are estimated to view pornography (Dines, 2010), many men don't openly talk about their viewing habits. Their silence enables the most base of racist stereotypes to circulate unchallenged. Mainstream porn is virtually all-white, and women of color are usually found in specialty porn. However, in all porn, only the race of people of color is typically named. I warn my readers that the text that follows is sexually graphic and explicitly racist.

When Asian heritage women appear in mainstream porn, they are often referred to as *Oriental*—an outdated racist term—or Lotus Blossom, China Doll, and Geisha. These women are described as submissive, passive, tiny (and thus ideal), and they are more likely to be depicted in bondage. The introductory text on *Hustler*'s website "Asian Fever" reads: "Asian Fever features scorching scenes of sexual excesses these submissive Far East nymphos are famous for. No one knows how to please a man like an Asian slut can, and these exotic beauties prove it" (Dines, 2010). The font on this site is formed from chopsticks, with stereotypical music in the background and the women speaking in broken English. "Asian sluts" are described as [receiving] "American" phalluses (American is a classic stand-in for white). At the same time, Asian men are virtually non-existent in mainstream hetero porn. Latina women are "Muchas Latinas," "exotic," "hot," "spicy," and "light skinned" with "dirty Spanish words spilling out of" their mouths, and often depicted on the beach or by the pool. Like Asian men, Indigenous women are virtually non-existent in porn.

But black men and women get the worst of porn's racism. Of all of the women depicted, black women are the least visible and shown as the least desirable. For example, if a club scene is being filmed, the camera will avoid focusing on the one or two black women present. Black women are paid less than white women for the same scenes (Ross, 2007) and rarely become stars. Inter-racial scenes are the one space in which the race of white women is highlighted, in order to emphasize their transgression with and violation by black men. White women with black men will be either labeled white outright, or be labeled as blonde to convey whiteness, for example: "Black on Blondes"; "White Pussy-Black Cocks"; and "White Sluts Black Snakes" (Dines, 2010). White women are sometimes described as "going black."

The racist narratives that accompany this type of porn are jaw dropping. While doing research for this book, I encountered one website that depicted black men in loincloths running with spears and chasing white blonde women through the jungle. The text explained that these natives were angry with the white man for slavery and thus were going to "destroy" the anuses of the white man's women, using their "huge" phalluses. Black men's phalluses are always described as "enormous" or "monster" with the ability to "tear up" white women, for whom they have an insatiable appetite. One interracial porn website is titled *Blackzilla*, and a film released in 2007 was titled *Long Dong Black Kong*, a frequent association of black men to gorillas that is continually repeated in mainstream films such as *King Kong* and dolls such as "Lil Monkey" (see Figures 32 and 33).

While white women are described as whores, black women are marked as *ghetto hos*. The racist stereotypes are rampant on sites that feature blacks, and in the names of the films themselves (e.g., *Ghetto Gaggers*; *Pimp My Black Teen*; and *Oh No! There's a Negro in My Mom*). Landscapes in porn that feature blacks are peopled with criminals, hos, pimps and gang-bangers [sic], and the copy that accompanies the films is degrading and unapologetically racist.

For example, *Ghetto Gaggers* explains that Vixen has "more attitude than Harlem has crack." She needs "a learnin' …" to "remove the sass from her chicken bobbin' back and forth ghetto ass … we destroy ghetto hos …" (Dines, 2010). The text on a site for interracial sex (white men/black women) invokes a long string of stereotypes: an angry black woman who hates white men, is poor, slovenly, and has kids she can't feed, has gang members as friends, and will engage in prostitution if offered money. It reads:

> What a … hot day it was when we found Carmen. She was walking out of the grocery store with her shirt up and her big fat tits hanging out. We had to say something to her, a fine black woman like this. But when we tried to approach her, she wasn't having it. This woman may be the most racist black woman we've ever met. She couldn't stand the white man. Calling them perverts, ingrates, honkeys, even threatening to get her gang members to kick the … out of them. But we had an angle. See Carmen has two kids and they need milk and Carmen is a little low on cash right now so we made her a proposition. One thousand bucks to … a white man. … She accepted alright and when we got back to the house she also got a mouthful … to wash down with that milk." (Dines, 2010, p. 129)

The degradation of people of color in pornography is widespread and extreme. There is no pretense of colorblindness in pornography. These are only a few examples (for a fuller analysis of racism and sexism in pornography see Dines, 2010, and Jensen, 2007).

The explicit racism in porn circulates unchallenged by the industry or consumers, illustrating one way that racism manifests in a purportedly colorblind and post-racial society: silence and denial in the face of explicit and repetitive racism. Because porn is an increasing presence in our lives, it is essential that we set aside whatever discomfort about or attachment to it we may have, and reflect deeply upon what porn tells us about the current realities of racism (in addition to misogyny and other forms of oppression), and the ways in which racism is maintained, disseminated, accepted, and internalized.

Front- and Backstage Racism

Even if we don't engage with illicit porn sites, we are still surrounded by friends and family who often make direct comments and jokes about people of color. For example, despite the claims of many white young adults that racism is in the past and that they were taught to see everyone as equal, research shows otherwise. Picca and Feagin conducted an important study published in 2007. They asked 626 white college students at 28 different colleges across the United States to keep journals recording every instance regarding racial issues, images, and understandings that they observed or were part of over the course of 6–8 weeks. They received over 7,500 accounts of blatantly racist comments and actions by the white people in their lives (friends, families, acquaintances, strangers). These accounts come from the generation most likely to claim they were taught to see everyone as equal. This study provided empirical evidence that racism continues to be explicitly expressed by whites, even those who are young and profess to be progressive.

But Picca and Feagin's study revealed something else—a pattern in the way that these comments and actions were expressed. The majority of incidences occurred in what the researchers describe as the "backstage"—in all-white company. Further, they found that whites involved in these incidences most often played predictable roles. Typically, there was a protagonist, who initiated the racist act, a cheerleader who encouraged it through laughter or agreement, the spectators who stood in silence, and (only very rarely) a dissenter who objected. Virtually all objectors were subject to a form of peer pressure in which they were told that it was "only a joke" and that they should "lighten up."

The journals documented that in "front-stage" settings (those in which people of color were present), the white students displayed a range of racially conscious behaviors including:

- Acting overly nice
- Avoiding contact (e.g., crossing a street or not going to a particular bar or club)
- Mimicking "black mannerisms and speech"
- Being careful not to use racial terms or labels
- Using code words to talk negatively about people of color
- Occasional violence

In "backstage" settings, in which people of color were not present, white students often used humor to reinforce racial stereotypes about people of color, particularly blacks, and occasionally made blatantly racist comments. Picca and Feagin argue that that the purpose of these backstage performances is to create white group solidarity and to reinforce the ideology of white and male supremacy. This behavior keeps racism circulating, albeit in less formal but perhaps more powerful ways than in the past. Today we have a cultural norm

that insists we hide our racism from people of color and deny it among ourselves, but not that we actually challenge it. In fact, we are socially penalized
for challenging it.

> **Remember:** Racism is a complex and interconnected system that adapts to
> challenges over time. Colorblind ideology was a very effective adaptation
> to the challenges of the Civil Rights Era. Colorblind ideology allows soci-
> ety to deny the reality of racism in the face of its persistence, while making
> it more difficult to challenge than when it was openly espoused.

In some ways, the ideology of racism and its adaptation over time is more
sinister than concrete rules such as Jim Crow, because it produces the same
outcome (people of color are blocked from moving forward), but by a dominant white society that won't or can't admit to its beliefs. This makes it very
difficult to address and stop racist practices. Based on my work with white
college students and other white people, I am confident that most of my readers would recognize all of the incidences documented in Picca and Feagin's
study. Indeed, although in the beginning of each semester my virtually all-
white students insist that they were taught that everyone is equal and nothing
else, later many will admit that all of the racist comments and interactions
recorded in the study are familiar to them and have also occurred throughout
their own lives. This makes for a very challenging dynamic in which whites
are both *unaware* of many aspects of their racism and *dishonest* about those
aspects of which they are aware: what we really think and do regarding people
of color.

Internalized Racial Superiority and the White Racial Frame

Sociologist Joe Feagin, after conducting extensive research on racism, coined
the term *white racial frame* to describe the way that whites make meaning of
race and racial difference. The concept of the white racial frame may be useful for explaining several white racial patterns, including the preference for
racial segregation, unconscious racial discrimination, the lack of interest in
challenging racism, feeling entitled to our position of dominance in society,
and defensiveness when white privilege is questioned. The white racial frame

includes racial images, interpretations, emotions, and actions, and has several levels. At the most general level, the racial frame views whites as superior in culture and achievement and views people of color as generally of less social, economic, and political consequence. People of color are seen as inferior to whites in the making and keeping of the nation.

At the next level of framing, because social institutions (education, medicine, law, government, finance, and military) are controlled by whites, white dominance is unremarkable and taken for granted. That whites are disproportionately enriched and privileged via these institutions is also taken for granted; we are entitled to more privileges and resources because we are "better" people. At the deepest level of the white frame, negative stereotypes and images of racial others as inferior are reinforced and accepted. At this level corresponding emotions such as fear, contempt, and resentment are also stored. This framing is so internalized (below the surface of the "iceberg") that it is never consciously considered or challenged by most whites. Further, taboos against talking openly about race protect this frame as whites collude in a tacit agreement not to question it. The frame includes both negative understandings of people of color and positive understandings of whites and white institutions; the justification of inequality involves two complementary strategies: the positive representation of the dominant group, and the negative representation of the marginalized group (Feagin, 2006).

The white racial frame is deep and extensive, with thousands of stored "bits." These bits are pieces of cultural information that are collected and passed along from one person and group to the next, and from one generation to the next. These bits circulate both explicitly and implicitly, through movies, television, news, and other media, and stories told to us by family and friends. By constantly using the white racial frame to interpret society, events, and relations, by integrating new bits into it, and by applying learned stereotypes, images, and interpretations in discriminatory actions, whites reinscribe the frame ever deeper into their minds.

White Racial Frame: The deeply internalized racist framework through which whites make racial meaning. This framework includes images, interpretations, perceptions, evaluations, emotions, and actions that position whites as superior and that are passed down and reinforced throughout society.

Whites typically combine racial stereotypes (the cognitive aspect), metaphors and concepts (the deeper cognitive aspect), images (the visual aspect), and emotions (feelings like fear, contempt, or curiosity), to assess and respond to people of color. It's important to note that the absence of people of color in one's environment (workplace, school, neighborhood) also fortifies the white racial frame, as other whites reinforce the concept that these spaces are of a higher quality precisely because people of color are absent.

To get a sense of what might be below the surface of your conscious racial awareness, try this thought experiment. At what point in your life were you aware that people from racial groups other than your own existed? Most people of color recall a sense of "always having been" aware, while most white people recall being aware by at least age 5. If you lived in a primarily white environment and are having trouble remembering, think about Disney movies, music videos, sports heroes, Chinese food, the Taco Bell Chihuahua's accent, and Apu Nahasapeemapetilon the South Asian Kwiki Mart proprietor from The Simpsons.

Once you identify the earliest age at which you were aware of the existence of people from racial groups other than your own, reflect on the following. Did your parents tell you race didn't matter and everyone was equal? Why did they need to tell you this? Where did people of color live? If they did not live in your neighborhood, why didn't they? What kind of neighborhood did they live in? Were their neighborhoods considered "good" or "bad"? What made a neighborhood good or bad? What images did you associate with these other neighborhoods? What about sounds? What kind of activities did you think went on there? Where did your ideas come from? Were you encouraged to visit these neighborhoods, or were you discouraged from visiting these neighborhoods?

What about schools? What made a school good? Who went to good schools? Who went to bad schools? If the schools in your area were racially segregated (as most schools in the United States are), why didn't you attend school together? If this is because you lived in different neighborhoods, why did you live in different neighborhoods? Were "their" schools considered equal to, better, or worse, than yours? If you went to school together, did you all sit together in the cafeteria? If not, why not? Were the honors or advanced placement classes and the lower-track classes equally racially integrated? If not, why not?

What about your teachers? When was the first time you had a teacher of the same race(s) as you? How often did this occur? When was the first time you had a teacher of a different race(s) than you? How often did this occur?

Most whites, in reflecting on these questions, realize that they almost *always* have had white teachers; they rarely if ever have had a teacher of color, and typically not until college. Conversely, most people of color have rarely *if ever* had a teacher who reflected their own race(s). Why is this important to reflect on in order to uncover our racial socialization and the messages we receive from schools?

As you answer these questions, also consider *which* races were closer in proximity to you than others. If your school was perceived as racially diverse, which races were more represented, and how did that impact the sense of value associated with the school? For example, if white and Asian heritage students were the primary racial groups in your school, your school was likely to be seen as better than a school with more representation from black and Latino/a students. What were you learning about race from all of these dynamics?

If you lived and went to school in racial segregation (as most people in the United States do), you had to make sense of this incongruity. If you lived and went to school in integration, you had to make sense of the segregation in the vast majority of society outside the school, especially those segments of society seen as being of higher value or quality. It is also highly likely that there was still racial separation within the school (e.g., the classic white question, "Why do all the black kids always sit together?").

In conclusion, what does it mean to say that all people are equal but live separately from them? Our *lived* separation is a more powerful message because the separation is manifested in action, while inclusion is not.

> **Remember**: Grappling with challenging concepts does not require agreement; you don't have to agree first before you can consider an alternate framework. I simply ask my readers to be willing to look below the surface to see what becomes visible that was not previously.

White Supremacy and Whiteness

When race scholars use the term white supremacy, we do not use it as popular culture does to refer to extreme hate groups such as the Ku Klux Klan or Aryan Brotherhood. Nor do we use it to indicate majority-versus-minority relations, for power is not dependent on numbers but on *position*. We use the term to refer to *a political-economic social system of domination. This system is based on the historical and current accumulation of structural power that privileges, centralizes, and elevates white people as a group.* The term allows us to capture the all-encompassing nature of white dominance, centrality, and assumed superiority. While the dominant racial/ethnic group in other cultures may not be white (for example, the Chinese rule Tibetans, and the Tibetans may experience racism from the Chinese), there is nonetheless also a global dimension of white supremacy.

> **White Supremacy:** The term used to capture the all-encompassing centrality and assumed superiority of people defined and perceived as white, and the practices based on this assumption.

The United States is a global power, and through movies and mass media, corporate culture, advertising, United States-owned manufacturing, military presence, historical colonialist relations, missionary work, and other means, white supremacy is circulated globally. White supremacy is also a powerful ideology that promotes the idea of whiteness as the ideal for humanity well beyond the West. This is especially relevant in countries that have a history of colonialism by Western nations.

In Charles W. Mills's brilliant, award-winning book *The Racial Contract* (1997), he describes white supremacy as "the unnamed political system that has made the modern world what it is today" (p. 1). He notes that while white supremacy has shaped Western political thought for hundreds of years, it is never named. Mills argues that while this political system is the most important in recent history, it is not identified as a system at all. In this way, white supremacy is rendered invisible while other political systems—socialism, capitalism, fascism—are identified and studied. In fact, much of its power is drawn from its invisibility—the unnamed and taken-for-granted aspects of white superiority that underwrite all other political and social contracts.

> **Remember:** White supremacy does not refer to individual white people per se and their individual intentions, but to a political-economic social system of domination. This system is based on the historical and current accumulation of structural power that privileges, centralizes, and elevates white people as a group.

A collection of papers from panels convened in the 1980s by the National Economic Association calculates some of the cumulative benefits to whites from white supremacy (not accounting for pain and suffering and the adjustment of these figures for inflation over the years since they were estimated) (Mills, 1997, p. 39):

- Labor market discrimination 1929–1969: $1.6 trillion;
- Diverted income from slave labor 1790–1860: $2.1–4.7 trillion;
- Unpaid slave labor prior to 1863, underpayment since 1863, and denial of the opportunity to buy the land and natural resources available to white settlers: possibly "more than the entire worth of the United States."

I would be remiss if I did not acknowledge the Indigenous peoples from whom the land and resources were originally taken, and Chinese laborers who in large part built the railroads that generated untold wealth for white owners. In light of these figures and the statistical reality of historical and continual white supremacy, white complaints about Affirmative Action and other programs intended to ameliorate the most basic levels of discrimination in hiring appear profoundly petty and illusionary. As Mills summarizes:

> Both globally and within particular nation states, then, white people, Europeans and their descendants, continue to benefit from the Racial Contract, which creates a world in their cultural image, political states differentially favoring their interests, an economy structured around the racial exploitation of others, and a moral psychology ... skewed consciously or unconsciously toward privileging them, taking the status quo of differing racial entitlement as normatively legitimate, and not to be investigated further. (p. 40)

White supremacy refers to the overarching and all-encompassing system of white domination and the assumed superiority that legitimizes it. Whiteness refers to the specific dimensions of racism that elevate white people over people of color. While these terms are used somewhat interchangeably, we might think of whiteness as all of the aspects of being white that go beyond mere skin color and which are related to the meaning and resultant material advantage of being white in society: what is granted and how it is granted based on that meaning. Instead of focusing on how racism hurts people of color, whiteness focuses on how it elevates whites. Whiteness refers to the basic rights, resources, privileges, and experiences that are assumed to be shared by all, but in practice are actually only available to white people.

Whiteness is similar to the previously discussed concept of androcentrism, applied to race. Whiteness is not simply the idea that whites are superior to people of color, but a deeper premise that supports this idea—the definition of whites as the norm or *standard* for human, and people of color as a *deviation* from that norm. Whiteness remains invisible in all contexts except when we are specifically referring to people of color, at which point an actress becomes a *black* actress, and so on. Dyer (1997) states that "There is a specificity to White representations, but it does not reside in a set of stereotypes so much as in narrative structural positions, rhetorical tropes and habits of perception" (p. 12). We might think of these structural positions, narratives, and tropes as rooted in what Feagin calls the white racial frame. The white position is represented in society as unracialized. This contributes to a kind of blindness, an inability to think about whiteness as a state of being that could have an impact on one's life and perceptions, and thus be a source of meaning. Whiteness is not recognized or named by white people, and a universal reference point is assumed.

People of color, including W. E. B. Du Bois and James Baldwin, wrote about whiteness as early as 1900. These writers urged white people to stop studying "the *Other*" and turn their attention onto themselves to explore what it means to be white in a society that is so divided by race. For example, in 1946, a French reporter asked expatriate writer Richard Wright his thoughts on the "Negro Problem" in the United States, to which Wright replied, "There isn't any Negro problem, there is only a white problem" (Lipsitz, 1995). Finally, by the 1990s, white scholars began to rise to the challenge. These scholars (as well as scholars of color) examine the cultural, historical, and sociological aspects of being white and how they are tied to white supremacy.

> **Remember:** When I use the term "white supremacy", I do not use it to refer to extreme hate groups. I use the term to capture the pervasiveness, magnitude, and normalcy of white dominance and assumed superiority.

Racism against people of color doesn't occur in a vacuum, yet ironically, this idea that racism in the United States can operate outside of white people is reinforced through celebrations such as "Black History Month" in which we study *their* history as if it occurred outside of our own. In addition to the general way this takes whites out of the equation, there are specific ways this idea is reinforced, such as the stories we tell about black cultural heroes. Take, for example, Jackie Robinson. Robinson is often celebrated as "the first African American to break the color line and play in major-league baseball." While Robinson was certainly an amazing ball player, this story line depicts Robinson as *racially* special; a black man who finally had what it took to play with whites, as if no black athlete before him was qualified enough to compete with whites. Imagine if instead, the story went something like this: "Jackie Robinson, the first black man whites allowed to play major-league baseball."

This is a critical distinction because no matter how fantastic a player Robinson was, *he simply could not play in the major leagues if whites—who control all of the institutions—did not allow it.* Were he to walk onto the field prior to being granted permission by white owners and policy makers, the police would have removed him. Narratives of racial exceptionality obscure the reality of ongoing institutional white control while reinforcing the ideologies of individualism and meritocracy. They also do whites a disservice by obscuring the white allies behind the scenes who worked hard and long to open the field. These allies could serve as much-needed role models for other whites.

The Jackie Robinson story is a classic example of how whiteness renders racism invisible by rendering whites, white privilege, and racist institutions invisible. This does not mean that I am against Black History Month. But it does mean that it should be celebrated in a way that doesn't reinforce whiteness. For those who ask why there is no White History Month, the answer illustrates how whiteness works. White history is implied in the absence of its acknowledgment; white history is the norm for "history." This is why we need to qualify that we are speaking about black history or women's history whenever we go outside this norm. In March 2003 the satirical newspaper *The Onion* ran a headline that humorously captured this dynamic: "*White History Year Resumes.*" The article opened with the tongue-in-cheek statement, "With Black History Month over, U.S. citizens are putting aside thoughts of Harriet Tubman and George Washington Carver to resume the traditional observation of White History Year."

The image in Figure 24 illustrates the white disconnect from our shared history. This image was taken from the 2015 College Jeopardy Champion Playoffs. As college champions, these 3 players—who appear to be all white—are our best and our brightest, certified as educated by our highest institutions of learning. The image shows the board at the end of their round. One category is left untouched, presumably because it was the hardest and no player wanted to risk a question from it. I would assume that category was something akin to astrophysics. But no, the category is *African American History*. This image powerfully and succinctly captures whiteness.

Figure 24. Jeopardy.

Ruth Frankenberg, one of the premier white scholars in the field of whiteness studies, describes whiteness as multidimensional. She states (1997), "Whiteness is a location of structural advantage, of race privilege. Second, it is a 'standpoint,' a place from which white people look at ourselves, at others, and at society. Third, 'whiteness' refers to a set of cultural practices that are usually unmarked and unnamed" (p. 1). Let's break this description down and clarify each of its three claims.

First, Frankenberg describes whiteness as a "location of structural advantage, of race privilege." By this she means that to be white is to be in a privileged position within society and its institutions—to be seen as an insider and to be granted the benefits of membership. This position automatically bestows unearned advantages. Whites control all major institutions of society and set the policies and practices that others must live by, while not allowing their voices or interests to be "at the table." While rare *individual* people of color may be inside the circles of power—Condoleezza Rice, Colin Powell, Clarence Thomas, Barack Obama—this is usually because they support the status quo and do not challenge racism in any way significant enough to be threatening, and certainly not in enough numbers to be threatening. While this does not mean these public figures don't experience racism—indeed, Obama has endured insults and degrees of resistance previously unheard of—overall the status quo remains intact. Thus, whites collectively control the resources and are in the position to decide how to allocate them. The American Express ad in Figure 25 succinctly captures the dynamics of structural advantage and racial inclusion.

Figure 25. American Express ad.

Second, Frankenberg describes whiteness as a "stand-point, a place from which whites look at ourselves, at others, and at society." By this she means that a significant aspect of white identity is to see oneself as an individual, outside or innocent of race—"just human." To be white means seeing white people and their interests as central to and representative of all of humanity. Whites also produce and reinforce the dominant narratives of society—opportunity is equal, anyone can make it if they just tries hard enough, and there are no structural barriers. Therefore we view society and the positions of the various racial groups within it through the lenses of individualism and meritocracy. Using these ideologies, we can congratulate ourselves on our success within the institutions of society and blame others for their lack of success.

Third, Frankenberg says that whiteness refers to a set of cultural practices that are unmarked and unnamed. By this she means that rather than isolated acts of individual race prejudice that only bad people engage in, racism is a network of norms and practices that consistently result in advantage for whites and disadvantage for people of color. These norms and practices include basic rights, values, beliefs, perspectives, and experiences purported to be commonly shared by all but which are actually only afforded in any consistent way to white people; they result in *white privilege*. When she says that these cultural practices are unmarked and unnamed, she means that the dimensions of racism that serve to advantage white people are usually invisible to whites. We are unaware of, or do not acknowledge, the meaning of race and its impact on our own lives. Thus we do not recognize or admit to white privilege and the norms that produce and maintain it.

Ta-Nehisi Coates (2015) expresses whiteness this way:

> The forgetting is habit, is yet another necessary component of the Dream. They have forgotten the scale of theft that enriched them in slavery; the terror that allowed them, for a century, to pilfer the vote; the segregationist policy that gave them their suburbs. They have forgotten, because to remember would tumble them out of the beautiful Dream and force them to live down here with us, down here in the world. I am convinced that the Dreamers, at least the Dreamers of today, would rather live white than live free.

As discussed in Chapters 3 and 4, major social groups are organized into binary (either/or) identities. These identities depend upon one another because each identity is defined by its opposite (or *other*). Not only are these identities constructed as opposites, but they are also ranked into a hierarchy of value. This means that one social group (or social identity) is positioned in society as more valuable than its opposite: men/women; rich/poor; young/old. In sum, racism is a system of *relations* between white people and people of color that are based in white supremacy. These relations are historically, socially, politically, and culturally generated, and produce an ongoing, dynamic, and adaptive condition of white racial domination. Understanding that racism is a *relationship* between white people and people of color is essential to understanding how racism works.

Internalized Racial Oppression

People of color absorb all of the same messages circulating in the culture at large about the meaning of racial difference. But these messages have a very different impact on them than on whites; they result in what is termed *internalized racial oppression*. Internalized racial oppression refers to the largely unconscious beliefs and related behaviors that are accepted by people of color raised in a white supremacist society. People of color come to believe, act on, or enforce the dominant system of beliefs about themselves and members of other non-white racial groups. While the term "people of color" merges groups that have different histories and different relationships to white supremacy, it also acknowledges that there are connections in terms of economic status, relationship to the institutions, lack of access to resources, experiences with institutional and internalized racial oppression and/or minoritized status. The following list of dynamics leading to internalized racial oppression is adapted from the Western States Center's *Dismantling Racism: A Resource Book for Social Change Groups* (2003):

- Historical violence and the ongoing threat of violence
- Destruction, colonization, dilution, and exoticization of their cultures
- Division, separation, and isolation from one another and from dominant culture
- Forced changes in behaviors to ensure psychological and physical safety and to gain access to resources
- Having individual behaviors redefined as "group" norms
- Denied individuality and held up as representative of (or occasionally as exceptions to) their group
- Being blamed for the effects of long-term oppression by the dominant group, and having the effects of that oppression used to rationalize further oppression

Internalized racial oppression includes feelings of:

- Self-Doubt
- Inferiority
- Self-Hate
- Powerlessness
- Hopelessness

- Apathy
- Generalized Fear/Anxiety

Studies conducted by Kenneth and Mamie Clark powerfully illustrate internalized racial oppression (Clark & Clark, 1939; 1950). The Clarks were interested in the self-esteem of black children. They found that by age 3, black
children had begun to internalize a sense that they were inferior to whites. By
age 7, this sense was firmly in place. They conducted their studies by asking
the children to choose which doll they preferred, a white doll or a black doll.
Their questions included, "Give me the doll that you like to play with," "Give
me the doll that is a nice doll," "Give me the doll that looks bad," and "Give
me the doll that is a nice color." The majority of the children preferred the
white doll to the black, and this preference was stable regardless of whether
they lived in the North or South United States, although Northern children
had a more definite preference for white skin. Similar studies have been informally conducted on both black and white children in recent years with the
same results. When asked why the black doll looks bad, both white and black
children consistently attributed it to the doll's blackness. As The Harvard
Implicit Association Test demonstrates, *everyone* is impacted by the racial
messages that circulate in the culture at large, albeit with different outcomes
based on their racial position.

In Conclusion

Antiracist educator Darlene Flynn uses the metaphor of a dance to capture
the collective *relationship* between whites and people of color. Using this metaphor, we might think of whites as the "lead" and people of color as the "follow." Internalized dominance and internalized oppression are the dance parts
that whites and people of color are given to play in society. The steps in the
dance are a kind of social default. Internalized racial oppression and internalized racial dominance work in tandem, reinforcing one another and creating
smoothness in the dance. For example, because I have been taught to see
myself *racially* as smart, deserving, and capable, I can effortlessly take over
when I am in a cross-racial setting; I don't even realize I am doing it. At the
same time, since people of color (and black people in particular) have been
given the message throughout society that *racially* they are not smart, capable,
or deserving, they can effortlessly step back and let me take over, also seeing

me as more capable. They, too, will likely not know they are doing this and may even prefer it. In these ways, both groups are having their social positions reinforced.

> **Remember:** While not all whites will take over and not all people of color will fall back, I am speaking about the collective patterns of social groups at the macro level. While there are always exceptions, these collective patterns are consistent, measurable, and predictable.

While whites are the dominant group, the smoothness of the dance depends on both parties playing their parts. This is important because either party can interrupt the dance—they do not have to depend on each other to do so. But interrupting the dance can only come from the development and implementation of new steps, and not from mere good intentions or a positive self-image.

Discussion Questions

1. How is the author using the term *white supremacy*?
2. Explain the concept of the *white racial frame*. What are some examples?
3. What does Coates mean when he says, "I am convinced that the Dreamers, at least the Dreamers of today, would rather live white than live free"?
4. What is the significance of white people not knowing our racial history? How is the disconnect from history necessary to maintaining white supremacy?
5. Frankenberg states, "Whiteness is a location of structural advantage, of race privilege. Second, it is a 'standpoint,' a place from which white people look at ourselves, at others, and at society. Third, 'whiteness' refers to a set of cultural practices that are usually unmarked and unnamed" Explain the 3 parts of Frankenberg's quote in your own words.
6. In your discussion group, share your answers to the reflection questions on our neighborhoods and teachers in this chapter. What patterns do you notice among the group? What insights do the answers give you on implicit aspects of our racial socialization?

HOW RACE SHAPES THE LIVES
OF WHITE PEOPLE

For me, I grew up in an open-minded, liberal white family and race was never an issue of any negative nature. My neighborhood was mostly white and for my elementary and middle school years I attended a parochial school, which was also mostly white. I had a very understanding family that wouldn't raise us prejudice anyway. (ASR)

My individual neighborhood growing up was not very diverse at all. All 7 or 8 houses on my cul-de-sac were white, Christian families. Only recently did we get a bit of diversity when a young Korean family moved in about 2 years ago. I grew up in a very liberal accepting family and was always taught that everyone was equal and deserves love and kindness. I am very open to people who are "different." (ASR)

In previous chapters I have provided some statistics to illustrate racist practices and policies. In the next two chapters I explore another aspect of racism; the unaware, unspoken, unmarked, and privileged aspects of white racial identity that *lead to* racist policies and practices. These aspects of white identity also ensure that I will most likely be unaware of, uninterested in, and in denial about the impact of these practices on people of color. In these chapters I explore how whites are *socialized* into a racist framework. My inability or unwillingness to acknowledge and challenge this socialization is key to holding racism in place.

I begin this chapter by describing how my own life has been shaped by my race. It has taken me many years of intensive study and practice to be able to recognize and articulate how I am shaped by being white, and this in itself is an example of whiteness (while there are exceptions, most people of color do not find it anywhere near as difficult to articulate how race shapes their lives). Notice that the way I discuss racism here is different than the mainstream conceptualization, in that it is less about anything I have "done" to perpetuate racism and more about how racism has shaped my consciousness and identity and how it has granted me unearned yet powerful advantages that *result in* disadvantages for people of color.

Although I am speaking for myself, it is a rare white person who cannot recognize most of the privileges I identify. Many of the dynamics I discuss here are developed and adapted from Peggy McIntosh's (2012) seminal work on white privilege. Thus, I will move between the individual and collective voice. Notice as you read that a person of color could not claim these same privileges.

Belonging

First, I was born into a culture in which I belonged, racially. Indeed, even *where* I was born and the conditions surrounding my birth were shaped by race. If I were born in a hospital, regardless of the decade in which I was born, any hospital would be open to me based on race. If my parents attended a childbirth preparation class, the instructor was most likely white, the videos they watched in class most likely depicted white people, and their fellow classmates with whom they built connections and community, were also most likely white. When they read their textbooks and other written materials, the pictures most likely depicted primarily white mothers and fathers, doctors and nurses. If they took a parenting class, the theories and models of child development were based on white racial identity, culture and norms. The doctors and nurses attending my birth were most likely white. While my parents may have been anxious about the birth process, they did not have to worry about how they would be treated by the hospital staff because of their race. Based on years of research demonstrating racial discrimination in health care (Schroeder & DiAngelo, 2010), I can assume that my parents were more likely to have been treated well by hospital personnel, and to receive a higher caliber of care than would people of color. At the same time, the people who cleaned my mother's hospital room, did the laundry, cooked and cleaned in the cafeteria, and maintained the facilities were most likely people of color. So the very context in which I entered the world was organized hierarchically by race and reinforced my place within this hierarchy.

As I move through my daily life, I fit in; my race is unremarkable. I belong when I turn on the TV, read novels, and watch movies. I belong when I pass by the magazine racks at the grocery store. I belong when I compare myself to standards of beauty in skin tone, hair texture, and body parts such as noses, hips, and lips. I belong when I look up at my teachers and at my classmates. I belong when I learn about the history of my country and when I am shown its heroes and heroines (McIntosh, 2012). I belong when I look at the pictures in my textbooks and on my school walls. I belong when I speak to my children's teachers, when I talk to their camp counselors, when I consult with their doctors and dentists.

In virtually every situation or context deemed "normal" or valuable in society, I belong racially. This belonging is a deep and ever-present feeling that has always been with me. Belonging has settled deep into my body; it shapes the way I move through the world, my goals and expectations, what I reach for in life and what I expect to find. Lillian Smith (1949) captures this beautifully when she states, "These ceremonials in honor of white suprem- acy, performed from babyhood, slip from the conscious mind down deep into muscles ... and become difficult to tear out" (p. 91). The experience of belong- ing is so normal and taken for granted that I do not have to think about it or notice it. Thus, the rare moments in which I don't belong racially come as a surprise—a surprise that I can either enjoy for its novelty or easily avoid if I find it uncomfortable. It is rare for most whites to experience a sense of not belonging racially, and these are usually very temporary, easily avoidable situations. Indeed, throughout my life I have been warned that I *should* avoid situations in which I might be a racial minority. These situations are often presented as scary, dangerous, or "sketchy." Yet if the environment or situation is viewed as good, nice, or valuable, I can be confident that as a white person, I will be seen as *racially* belonging there.

Visibility

My race is represented widely and in a vast range of roles. All of the halls of power are filled with people of my race: the House of Representatives, the Senate, the Supreme Court, the *Fortune* 500 CEOs, the professors, the managers, the teachers, the doctors and lawyers: in other words, the decision makers. In 2015, the House is 80% white, the Senate is 94% white, and the Supreme Court is 77% white. From the founding of the country until 2008, every president has reflected my race, and through today, so has every vice president. The protagonists in my literature classics and history books are overwhelmingly (if not exclusively) white, as are the statues and monuments erected to honor our cultural heroes.

As a white person I can be confident that I will be represented in virtually every form of media that is easily accessible and considered mainstream. "The Top 100 Most Beautiful People" will be at least 90% white, and "The Best New Hairstyles" will likely *all* be based on my hair texture. When a woman of color is included in these features, such as Halle Berry, her hair will be straightened based on white norms of beauty.

Figure 26. *Charlize Theron.*

In 2015 a link advertised on a CNN page was titled *The 10 Hottest Women From Around the World*. Of these 10, two were women of color (Rihanna from Barbados and Sofia Vergara from Colombia). None were Asian (the majority race of women in the world). Representing South Africa, a country that is 92% black and only 8% white, was Charlize Theron. Choosing Theron to represent South Africa is a particularly cogent example of how we are constantly reinforced to see whiteness (and repetitive and narrow representations of it) as the ideal.

In this two-page *Vanity Fair* spread, the nine "Fresh Faces of Hollywood 2010" are all white.

Figure 27. *Vanity Fair* cover.

Figure 28. Zoe Saldana (left) and Gabourey Sidibe (right).

Kristen Stewart was also on *Vanity Fair*'s "Fresh Faces" list the year before, but they didn't feature Kristen twice simply because they ran out of fresh faces, for this was the same year that Zoe Saldana starred in *Avatar*, the highest-grossing movie of all time at that point, and Gabourey Sidibe was nominated for an Academy Award for her first role in *Precious*. It cannot be argued that these two young women were left out because they starred in insignificant movies.

Figures 29 and 30 show the 2015 Hollywood edition of *Vanity Fair*. Imagine looking at these *Vanity Fair* covers from the perspective of a young woman

Figures 29 and 30. Front cover and two-page spread for the 2015 edition.

of color. Remember, these are just single images pulled from the millions of similar images that circulate daily. How encouraged do you imagine you might feel about your beauty, value, and career hopes? Yet I, as a white person, see myriad possibilities for myself. And while I may feel inadequate in terms of my weight, age, or other aspects of dominant beauty norms, as a white person I am not *fundamentally* outside the norm.

Recall from Chapter 4 that a key aspect of dominance is the ability to define what is normal, real, correct, beautiful, and valuable. Figure 31, "The World's Next Top Models," illustrates both how my race is represented in media, and the power of media to construct and promote these definitions.

The headline is also noteworthy; these women are being held up as the icons of ideal female beauty for the entire world. Notice in these magazine covers the importance of being blonde, and all that blondeness represents. This cover is also an example of how we export white supremacy around the

Figure 31. *Vogue* cover.

world. Because our movies and media have been exported globally, whiteness has worldwide currency. For example, blepharoplasty, a surgical technique to make the eyes appear more "Caucasian," is the most popular cosmetic surgery in Asia and the third most frequently requested procedure among Asian Americans (Motaparthi, 2010); light skin is advertised in countries such as India as the most beautiful, and skin-lightening cream is a huge industry around the world (Li, Min, Belk, Kimura, & Bahl, 2008).

Another racially problematic *Vogue* cover featured LeBron James posed with Gisele Bundchen in a style almost identical to those featured on King Kong posters spanning decades (note the strapless green dress).

Figure 32. King Kong images.

Readers may say that they don't read these magazines, or they don't pay attention to them. But this is to misunderstand the power of advertising and media imagery. Every time we pass these covers, in the grocery store or on a billboard, they are affecting us, whether we are aware of it or not. Advertising is a multibillion-dollar industry, and its techniques are based on copious research. There are no accidents in ads—every aspect of an ad is designed to affect us, even if we only glance at it for a moment. One of the ways that media and popular culture work to perpetuate whiteness is by normalizing racial associations. Through constant repetition, we see people enact conventional racial scripts and reinforce specific racial associations, and we internalize these scripts and the expectations that go with them.

Take, for example, three of the most successful television shows from the 1990s (and for two of them, into the 2000s): *Seinfeld*, *Friends*, and *Sex and the City*. All three of these shows took place in New York City, one of the most racially diverse cities in the United States. All three of them depicted ideal friendship circles. Yet not one featured a person of color. The whiteness of these shows reinforced the ability of whites to be surrounded by people of color and still remain segregated (ironically, it is whites who usually ask why *they* always sit together, as if *we* don't). These shows convey the message that the "perfect" friendship circle can be all white and that this is unremarkable and not problematic. For the generation that grew up with these shows, the normalcy, even *preference* for segregation was both represented and reinforced.

As a white person, this relentless representation of white as normal, beautiful, and ideal has shaped my identity and the trajectory of my life.

Represented in Childhood

Throughout my childhood and my daughter's childhood, we have been racially affirmed. Although many white people position racism as something in the past, white children who grow up today receive the same exclusive messages of belonging and affirmation as they always have. While there is more inclusion in very superficial ways, such as adding a brown face to a poster or sprinkling a few people of color in a crowd scene, it is rare for the protagonist of popular children's movies to be anything other than white. Consider that in the 20 top-grossing children's films of all time, *every* hero was white, and many featured no significant roles for people of color (these films include the *Star Wars* series, *Shrek*, *The Incredibles*, *Home Alone*, three Harry Potter movies, *The Lion King*, and two Spider Man movies). We can add other children's favorites to this list which, while they may not have been top grossing, are hugely popular and have toy and other corporate tie-ins: *Iron Man*, *The Hulk*, *Toy Story*, and others.

While it is slightly easier to find black and brown dolls and action figures than it was during my childhood, it is still difficult. When we are able to find these toys, they may still be very racially problematic. For example, in 2009, the doll in Figure 33 appeared on Costco shelves.

Throughout history people of color, and black people in particular, have been depicted as monkeys, apes, and gorillas. This is not an isolated image; it is constantly reinscribed through jokes, movies such as *King Kong*, and other social discourse.

Figure 33. Lil' Monkey.

In the Harry Potter films, virtually 100% of the main characters are white. Occasionally, as the camera pans over the dining hall, we will see a brown face, and sometimes these faces will be given a reaction shot or a line to speak. The very brief glimpses we get of these characters allow us to claim that the films are diverse, but this is rather disingenuous. From whose perspective is it diverse to have three or four non-white faces in a crowd shot of hundreds, with virtually no speaking parts? For a very brief time in one of the Harry Potter films, Harry has a love interest who is of Asian heritage (Cho Chang), but she rarely speaks. In the final two-part films, his love interest—whom he ultimately marries—is white (Ginnie Weasley).

It behooves us to reflect upon the impact of this disparity on both our conscious and unconscious minds; to either continually see yourself racially reflected if you are white, or continually be invisible if you are a person of color.

Shrek 2 was the highest grossing film of 2004. When I ask my audiences, regardless of age, who plays Fiona and Shrek in the film series, almost all know it's Cameron Diaz and Mike Myers. When I ask them who plays the donkey, they all know it is Eddie Murphy. This is important because it illustrates that we are subliminally aware of the actor behind the character, and thus these characters are racialized. While we may not think about race in Fiona and Shrek's case (because they are just "normal"), we are definitely aware that the donkey is "black." Indeed, his character fits a long-circulating representation of black men as crude, buck-toothed, leering, and stupid. Further reinforcing his blackness, rather than having a mane—as donkeys do—he actually has a small afro (see Figure 34).

The plot of *Shrek 2* involves the characters taking a secret potion that turns them into their most beautiful selves. Shrek and Fiona turn into a white man and woman. The donkey turns into a white stallion. There is even a moment when the stallion tosses his head in order to flip his silky blonde mane. Although many whites may be unaware of the sensitive relationship black people have to their hair due to white representations of it as ugly, this gesture, in which the transformed donkey shows off his newly (and temporarily) perfected blonde "hair," will likely not be lost on black children.

Figure 34. Shrek 2.

Eventually, of course, the donkey must return to his true self (and nappy head): crude and simple-minded. I am arguing that these images matter and that they reinforce important racial ideas for us. These ideas and the images that support them do not stand alone. What I see in *Shrek 2* is reinforced in countless other ways throughout society. Of course the impact of these ideas and images on white children is different than the impact on children of color.

Disney's *Frozen* has been a monumental success worldwide. It accumulated nearly $1.3 billion in worldwide box office revenue, $400 million of which was earned in the United States and Canada and $247 million of which was earned in Japan. It ranks as the highest-grossing animated film of all time, the third-highest-grossing original film of all time, the eighth-highest-grossing film of all time, the highest-grossing film of 2013, and the third-highest-grossing film in Japan.

Figure 35. Frozen Sisters.

The child in Figure 36, Kristina Piminova, has been christened "The World's Most Beautiful Girl" (*Elite Daily*, 2014; *Daily Mail*, 2014).

Consider the clear message of ideal beauty that these images convey and send worldwide. That message does not stand alone and is not lost on any child of any race.

Represented in Films

As a white person, I can expect to see my race represented widely and in a vast range of roles in film. I do not have to worry about whites being typecast, or

Figure 36. World's most beautiful girl.

worry that a white actor playing a negative character will reflect poorly on *me*. The abundance of films written, directed by, produced, edited, and starring whites provides me with role models in all aspects of life. These films affirm me and engender a sense of normalcy and belonging.

On the other hand, there are few significant roles for people of color in Hollywood, and most are extremely stereotypical. We can be confident that they will be visible in movies dealing with crime, portraying either cops or criminals. Although blacks and Latinos often play cops, it is rare for them to play the lead; they are most often in an assistant or "sidekick" role. While we may see their presence as police, detectives, lieutenants, and district attorneys as positive, at a deeper level these roles reinforce their continual association with crime, be it on the right or wrong side of the law. Other than in films focusing on crime, urban poverty, or brave white teachers who risk their lives to help inner-city children of color, I rarely see people of color depicted in films at all.

Let's look more closely at two films, both of which were extremely popular, financially successful, and critically acclaimed.

The Blind Side

The Blind Side was a hugely popular movie, and Sandra Bullock received an Academy Award for her portrayal of Mrs. Tuohy. However, many problematic racial narratives are reinscribed in the film. In fact, there are no black characters who do *not* reinforce negative racial stereotypes: Oher himself, portrayed as a big, dumb, gentle giant who lives in such abject poverty that he has never even had a bed; his drug-addicted single mother with multiple children from unknown fathers; the incompetent welfare worker; the uppity lawyer; and the menacing gang members in his drug-infested and crime-ridden neighborhood. Midway through the film, Oher returns to the "ghetto" seeking a reunion with his birth mother. As he walks down the street of his old neighborhood, he is surrounded by a drug lord and his gang who try to intimidate him into joining them. While he considers his limited options, Mrs. Tuohy arrives and confronts the drug lord, who backs down and retreats. Oher is whisked out of the ghetto and back to their safe suburban home, signifying that the only way Oher could be saved from the terrors of his own black family and community was through the kindness of a white family.

Oher is discussed by white professionals as if he is developmentally disabled (he certainly comes off as such—he is passive and inarticulate throughout the movie). His teachers note that on his IQ test he scored in the bottom percentile in "ability to learn" but in the 98th percentile in "protective instinct"! As a professor of education who has never heard of a test measuring "protective instinct," I have been unable to find evidence of this bizarre measurement. It is highly problematic that Oher, as a black male, is portrayed as severely lacking in *intellectual* abilities but exceptional in something *instinctual*. Oher's limited intellectual capacity is reinforced throughout the film, for example when the youngest child of the Tuohy household has to teach Oher how to play football. The body language and positioning in this photo from the film capture these dynamics.

Oher is never able to understand how to play football, so Mrs. Tuohy appeals to his "protective instinct" by telling him to pretend one of his new white family members is going to be hurt. Once his instincts are engaged (rather than his intellect), he is unstoppable on the field. In a particularly insulting scene, this same white *child*, who apparently possesses skills and intellect far beyond Oher's, negotiates a contract for him with highly powerful adult men while Oher sits in the background, mute.

Figure 37. The Blind Side.

This film, told from the white perspective and enthusiastically received by audiences, reinforces some very important dominant ideologies (Sensoy & DiAngelo, 2012):

- White people are saviors of people of color.
- Some black children may be innocent, but black adults are morally and criminally corrupt.
- Whites who are willing to save/help people of color, at seemingly great personal cost, are noble and courageous.
- Individual people of color can overcome their circumstances, but usually only with the help of white people.
- Urban spaces and the people of color living in them are inherently threatening, dangerous, and criminal.
- Virtually all blacks are poor, belong to gangs, are addicted to drugs, and are bad parents.
- The most dependable route for black males to escape the "inner city" is through sports.

- White people are willing to deal with individual "deserving" people of color, but whites do not become a part of the black community in any meaningful way (beyond charity work and soup kitchens).
- White people who are willing to "deal with" individual people of color are morally superior to other white people.

Of course Oher also brings redemption to the whites who save him. The film actually ends with a voice-over from Mrs. Tuohy, a Christian, claiming it was *God's will* that *this* boy be *saved* (presumably because his talent on the field made him more profitable and thus valuable to white people). The Tuohys, of course, are the good whites, who have to deal with the prejudice of the individual bad whites they encounter at the country club and other places. In this way the film also reinforces the racist = bad/not racist = good binary (For another example of good whites versus bad, see the popular 2011 film *The Help*).

When I have raised these issues with students, they often reply, "But it's a true story!" This idea that films can be "true" is a common one. Yet no story in film is a "true story." Films can only ever be *based* on a true story, and still only represent a limited and particular *perspective* on events. Many decisions are made along the way that impact what gets told, and from whose perspective. How much was rearranged, added, or subtracted in order to create the dramatic pacing a movie requires, and who made these decisions? These decisions are made by the writers, producers, and director (in this case, all white people). Thus, whose story is *The Blind Side*? From whose perspective is the story true? Whose perspectives are missing? Are all of the elements true, or were some of those elements (such as the neighborhood being overrun by gangs or Michael's mother being an addict) added to make the story more exciting or "real" (appealing to a mainstream audience who has come to expect these tropes)?

Finally, in developing racial literacy, we can ask: What stories do we choose to tell, and why? Whose vision of the world do these stories serve? Why is this story so familiar and *beloved* by white people? Why might it also be popular with some black audiences? What racial scripts get reinforced by this story? A story, and the film based on it, can only ever be someone's interpretation of an event, re-interpreted by the writers, directors, and editors. (For a more in-depth analysis of *The Blind Side* see Gooding, 2009).

Lord of the Rings

Lord of the Rings was an immensely popular film trilogy; the first segment alone garnered an unprecedented 12 Academy Awards. It was seen by millions of people across the world. Let's consider it through the lens of white supremacy. First, *100%* of all of the various creatures (or, in Tolkien's terms, races) that were portrayed in the film as inhabiting the top of the earth were white. The elves were all white, the wizards were all white, the hobbits were all white, and the "men" were all white. As the camera panned across various crowds in different scenes, the casting agent had not even sprinkled in *one* brown face. No other images exist in the film except for white, until the evil orcs, created by the bad wizard Saruman, rise up from under the ground, through the dirt and mud.

Figure 38. An orc.

While the orcs overall are monstrous and, as the series continues, appear to be of a range of races, the first orcs we see are black (and the only blacks we see in the entire film are orcs). They are menacing, hideous, and clearly evil. They have brown skin, long locked hair, and face paint that looks very "primitive." Peter Jackson, the white male director of *Lord of the Rings*, is from New Zealand. The aboriginal people of New Zealand are the Maori. The painted faces of the black orcs are reminiscent of Maori, who tattoo their faces.

Further, our heroes are trying to get to a place literally called "The White City," and to do so they must escape the reaches of the Dark Lord Sauron who lives in Mordor, a city protected by the Black Gate. In the final film of the trilogy, during the battle scene between the good creatures and bad, we also see characters that appear to be Asian, riding elephants. These characters are, of course, on the Dark Lord's side. While one of the evil wizards is also white, his whiteness does not reinforce the same problematic racial scripts because there is an overwhelming abundance of other positive white role models in the film. This wizard is the exception among many, not the rule. Yet there are *no* exceptions to the rule of black characters presented as monstrous and evil. Recall that it is the nature of stereotyping to take in information that confirms our beliefs and associations and disregard information that counters them. One evil white wizard will be seen as an individual, and will not stand in for all whites in the same way that people of color do.

That these aspects of whiteness are so unremarkable for so many illustrates their power. Again and again, the relentless whiteness of things depicted as good and the relentless darkness of those depicted as bad reinforce our racial frames. We don't have to be conscious of the racialization of these images and narratives for them to be at play in our psyches.

> **Remember:** While I am focusing on specific examples, none of these examples stand alone. They are recognizable (or conversely, so normal as to be invisible to us) precisely because they connect to all that has come before.

When I show these images to groups and offer this analysis, I am occasionally approached by people afterward who want to explain to me that the white supremacy of the films isn't anybody's "fault"; they are simply being true to the white supremacy Tolkien was arguing for in the books. Still others have explained to me that Tolkien was calling upon the nations of Europe to band together to fight fascism, and in so doing unintentionally used white supremacy to represent the forces of good. Actually, these rebuttals are important, but not because they show the fallacy of my analysis. Whether Tolkien's white supremacy was intentional (which is problematic), or an unexamined backdrop to his case against fascism (which is also problematic), generation after generation has been weaned on Tolkien's white supremacist story. This only reinforces my point. Further, every director has and makes choices as they adapt a story for film. For example, the black orcs that arise from the dirt and mud beneath the earth were not in the book; they were added by the director. That Jackson chose to leave the white supremacy of the series intact (and even *amplify* it visually)—regardless of Tolkien's original intentions—is a decision to keep white supremacy alive and circulating in the culture at large.

While Tolkien might be excused for writing at a time in which white supremacy wasn't questioned as it is now, what is Jackson's excuse? This retelling of the story keeps it connected to the generations that went before it, reinforcing and reproducing the original white supremacy. I don't believe that Jackson made a conscious or direct decision to deliberately reproduce white supremacy (although the black orcs are pretty blatant), but again, this is its power. White supremacy is so normalized and taken for granted by most whites that it isn't even noticeable. The *absence* of people of color (except in the most repetitively negative representations) also shapes us, for that absence sends powerful messages about value and worth, while continually limiting our understanding of a multitude of perspectives.

It is also important to consider what happens when the issue of white supremacy in these films is raised. This is another key aspect of how racism works. Because we come from a racist = bad/not racist = good binary framework, to suggest that there is racism in the images and story lines of these films causes many people (and white people in particular) to feel defensive. "If you are saying the film was racist and I liked the film," the reasoning goes, "you must be saying I am racist." This defensiveness makes it very difficult to think critically about race and works to hold it in place. While I can see the brilliance of films such as the *Lord of the Rings* trilogy, I can also see the racism in the films (and that racism does makes it harder for me to enjoy them). But I am less concerned with judging people based on whether or not they enjoyed the films, and more interested in developing the ability to recognize and discuss the racism in them. We can't challenge or resist it if we can't (or won't) see it.

The Human Norm

One of the ways in which my life has been shaped by my race is that my race is held up as the norm for humanity. Whites are "just people"—our race is rarely if ever named. Think about how often white people mention the race of a person if they are not white; my *black* friend, the *Asian* woman. I, on the other hand, am just *a woman, a teacher, a friend*.

To use an example from school, consider the writers we are all expected to read; the list usually includes Hemingway, Steinbeck, Dickens, Dostoevsky, Twain, and Shakespeare. These writers are seen as representing the "universal human experience." If this is not stated explicitly, it is implicit in their ubiquitous presence in the canon. We read them precisely because they are presumed to be able to speak to us all. Now consider the writers we turn to during events such as "Multicultural Authors Week." These writers usually include Maya Angelou, Toni Morrison, James Baldwin, Amy Tan, and Sandra Cisneros. We go to them for the black or Asian perspective; Maya Angelou is always seen as a *black writer*, not just a writer. But when we are not looking for the black or Asian perspective, we return to white writers. This reinforces the idea of whites as *just human*, and people of color as particular kinds (racialized) of humans. This dynamic also allows white (male) writers to be seen as not having an agenda or any particular perspective, while racialized (and gendered) writers do.

Virtually any representation of "human" is based on white people's norms and images. "Flesh-colored" Band-Aids (McIntosh, 2012), "nude" colored panty-hose, educational models of the human body with white skin and blue eyes. The picture in Figure 39 is from the front page of the science website, *Discovery News* (http://news.discovery.com/human/perfect-face-120426.htm). It is captioned: "Is This the Scientifically Perfect Face?"

This one example illustrates several concepts discussed thus far: positionality; the white racial frame; whiteness as the human norm; whiteness as ideal

Figure 39. The scientifically perfect face?.

beauty; and, whiteness as naturally superior. Not only is this racially problematic in its own right, but it rests on and reinforces the backdrop of an earlier era of scientific racism.

Many of us may have taken a psychology course or other course related to human development. These courses and the textbooks and theorists they use present human development as if it is universal. Think about how we are given models for child development and its stages, and how our culture talks about children as a universal group. Occasionally we may distinguish between boys and girls, but even then the categories are presumed to include *all* boys or *all* girls. Now consider all of the dynamics I have discussed thus far. Is an Asian or black child's development the same as a white child's, within the context of white supremacy?

What do you imagine is the race of the vast majority of researchers, and of the children they studied? For example, Jean Piaget, one of the most famous and well-read child development theorists, based his infant development research on his observations of his own children. These theories are purported to apply to all children with no acknowledgment of the racial context in which we develop and come to know who we are.

Psychic Freedom

Because I have not been socialized to see myself, or to be seen by other whites as having a race, I don't carry the psychic burden of race. In other words, I don't have to worry about how others *feel* about my race. I don't have to worry that my race will be held against me. I feel free to go wherever I want (especially any place seen as belonging to a higher class or status). I am assumed to belong in these settings. I take for granted that I won't be followed in a store because someone assumes I am prone to stealing. Almost anyone in a position to hire me will share my race, and once hired, I don't have to deal with my co-workers' resentment that I only got the job because I am white; I am assumed to be the most qualified (McIntosh, 2012). Thus, I am able to focus on my work and productivity. This is an example of Harris's concept of whiteness as property discussed in Chapter 6—whiteness has psychological advantages that translate into material advantage.

In general, race just isn't my problem. While I am aware that race has been used unfairly against people of color, I haven't been taught to see that as *my* problem, as long as I personally haven't done anything wrong. This actually affords me a level of racial relaxation and emotional and intellectual space that people of color are not afforded as they navigate mainstream society. Let me be clear that this is not just because they are members of a numerical minority and I am not. It is because they are members of a racially minoritized group in a culture of white supremacy—a culture in which they are seen as inferior, if they are seen at all. If race didn't matter and everyone were truly seen as equal, minority/majority numbers would not matter. It is this deep-seated assumption of white superiority that people of color must navigate and that takes up so much of their psychic energy.

Freedom of Movement

I am free to move in virtually any space seen as normal, valuable, or high status. While I might worry about my class status in some settings, for example when attending a "high society" event such as a museum opening or art auction, I will not have to worry about my race. In fact, my race will work in my favor in these settings, granting me the initial benefit of the doubt that I belong there (McIntosh, 2012). I also will certainly not be the only white person there, unless the event is specifically organized by or celebrating people of color.

I return to the text in the ad for Costa Rica I introduced in Chapter 4 to illustrate positionality (Figure 13). The ad shows a white nuclear family, enjoying the view of a vast open space. In addition to positionality, this ad illustrates several dimensions of white supremacy. First, from whose perspective was Costa Rica "discovered" in 1502? Certainly not from the perspective of those already living there. This text positions the white reference point as the only one that exists. In so doing, it renders other people invisible and irrelevant. During the "Age of Discovery" Indigenous peoples were viewed as savages, barely distinguishable from plants and animals (Zinn, 2005), as though they were the same thing and of equal worth. Ads such as this one keep alive the concept of Indigenous people as just part of the landscape. Second, the ad conveys the idea that this land is *ours* to consume; that we have a right to it. As long as we can afford to buy it, or are strong enough to dominate it, we can have it. Missionary work and the embedded assumption of Christian superiority also convey this idea.

A Romanticized Past

As a white person, I can openly and unabashedly reminisce about "the good old days." Romanticized recollections of the past and calls for a return to former ways are a function of white privilege. This privilege manifests in the ability to remain oblivious to our racial history. For whom was the past better? Consider any time period in the past from the perspective of people of color: slavery, the attempted genocide of Indigenous people, Indian removal acts, reservations, indentured servitude, lynching, share-cropping, Chinese exclusion laws, Japanese American internment, Jim Crow, medical sterilization and experimentation, red-lining, and you can see how a romanticized past is strictly a white construct. As comic Louis CK quips:

> I'm not saying white people are better, I'm saying that *being* white is better. Here's how great it is. I could get in a time machine and go to any time, and it would be … awesome when I get there! That is exclusively a white privilege. Black people can't [mess] with time machines! A black guy in a time machine is like, "Hey, anything before 1980, no thank you I don't want to go." But I can go to any time. The year 2. I don't even know that was happening then, but I know when I get there, "Welcome! We have a table right here for you sir." Thank you. If you're white and you don't admit that it's great, you're an asshole!

Louis uses humor to chide white America about this idealized narrative of a past that was always better than the present. He reminds us that although racism is still alive and well, in the past it was even more blatant and explicitly accepted.

Romanticized former family values are also racially problematic. White families created what is termed white flight, wrote covenants to keep schools and neighborhoods segregated, and forbade cross-racial dating. At the minimum, this idealization of the past is another example of *white* experiences and perceptions positioned as representing everyone's experience and perceptions. It is also an insensitive denial of our racial history; how might this nostalgia sound to a person of color?

A lucid example of this romanticization is the popular country music group Lady Antebellum, whose debut album went platinum in the United States. When asked about the choice of name, lead singer Hillary Scott (2010) explained:

> So we wanted to take pictures to put on MySpace to get people's attention, and we ended up going out outside of Nashville to this little town. It's this historic town called Franklin, Tennessee, and there's tons of antebellum homes with the columns, like, from *Gone with the Wind*. And we ended up in front of these houses, and Charles, the other lead singer in the group, he kind of looked back through the pictures and said, "Wow, that's a really beautiful antebellum home." And I said, "What does that

mean?" I didn't know what it meant. But after he explained it to me, I was like, "Oh, yeah. It is. It's really pretty." And he goes, "Isn't that a cool word?" And then we just put a bunch of words in front of it, and "Lady" is what stuck.

One wonders how Charles explained what antebellum meant, given Hillary's response (antebellum refers to the pre-Civil War South under slavery). In fact, his explanation *reinforces* her sense that the houses are pretty. Now that they have a shared definition, they describe the word as "cool." Nowhere is the fact that antebellum *literally* means the South *under slavery* acknowledged or problematized. This statement demonstrates several aspects of whiteness: the lack of historical knowledge; the ability to participate in racial discourse while remaining oblivious that you are doing so; a romanticized past, in this case *slavery*; the ability to disconnect the means from the ends, in this case seeing only beautiful houses with complete disregard that they were *only made possible* by slave labor; the lack of critical media literacy, in this case the unanalyzed glorification of the racist film *Gone with the Wind*; the absolute centrality of the white experience and perspective; white solidarity demonstrated by the support of fans; and obliviousness to cross-racial insensitivity. I do not know how the band has responded to criticism of the name, but based on my long-term experience I suspect that their response, along with that of their fans, will illustrate still another aspect of whiteness: defensiveness, trivialization, and dismissal of racial implications.

The ability to erase my country's racial history and to actually consider the past as better than the present has shaped my identity, both as an individual white person and as a national citizen. It has also shaped my relationship to people of color, personally and collectively.

Rewarded for Racial Silence

White solidarity is the unspoken agreement among whites to not talk openly and honestly about race and to avoid causing other whites to feel racial discomfort by confronting them when they say or do something racially problematic. Sleeter (1996) describes this solidarity as White "racial bonding": "interactions in which whites engage that have the purpose of affirming a common stance on race-related issues, legitimating particular interpretations of groups of color, and drawing conspiratorial we-they boundaries" (149). White solidarity requires silence about anything that exposes the meaning of race, as well as the tacit agreement to remain racially united in protection of white privilege and white supremacy. By maintaining this silence, we maintain group solidarity. To break the silence is to break rank. Certainly people of color experience our silence as a form of racism, wherein we do not hold each other accountable, challenge racism when we see it, or support them.

> **White Solidarity**: The unspoken agreement between whites to maintain silence, not challenge each other, keep each other comfortable, and generally maintain the racist status quo and protect white privilege.

The following examples may illustrate white solidarity and the role it plays in the maintenance of white silence. Imagine that a white mother and her white child are in the grocery store. The child sees a black person and shouts out, very loudly, "Mommy, that man's skin is black!" How do you imagine that the mother would respond? Most whites, when asked this, immediately put their finger to their mouth and say, "Shush!" When asked what the mother might be feeling, most agree that she will likely feel anxiety, tension, and embarrassment. Indeed, many of us have had similar experiences, wherein we were taught not to talk openly about race. When I use this example with my students, sometimes one will say that the mother is just teaching her child to be polite. In other words, naming a person of color's race is seen as being impolite. But why? What is wrong with being black? The mother is conveying a sense of shame to the child; this man's skin is something we should pretend we don't notice (Tatum, 2008). The same process would likely happen if the man had a visible disability of some kind, or was obese.

Now imagine that the child had shouted out how handsome the man was, or how strong. The child would not be shushed for loud statements that we consider compliments. These statements would likely be met with chuckles and smiles. If the child had seen a white person and shouted out, "Mommy, that man's skin is white!" it is unlikely that the mother would feel the anxiety, tension, and embarrassment that would accompany the first statement.

This example illustrates several aspects of white racial socialization. First, the taboo against openly talking about race. Second, teaching that we should pretend not to notice those things about people that make them *less than* (a large birthmark on someone's face; a person using a wheelchair). We can see how these teachings manifest later in life when adults drop their voices before naming the race of someone who isn't white, as if their race is shameful or the word is itself impolite. If we add all of the comments made in private about people of color, where we are less careful, we may come to understand a little more about how white children are taught to navigate race.

White solidarity also requires an agreement not to "embarrass" other whites when they make racist statements or engage in racist behaviors. We see this at parties, at the dinner table, and in work settings. Most white people can relate to the big family dinner, in which old Uncle Bob says something racially offensive, but no one challenges him in order to avoid conflict. Or the party where a friend or acquaintance says something racist but we keep silent because we don't want to ruin the fun (or be accused of being "PC" and told to lighten up). In the workplace setting, we avoid naming racism for the same reasons, in addition to the desire to be seen as a team player and to avoid anything that may jeopardize our employment. All of these familiar scenarios are examples of white solidarity—the tacit agreement among whites not to talk openly and honestly about race, or cause other whites to feel racial discomfort by confronting them when they say or do something racially problematic.

White solidarity is maintained, in part, by virtue of the very real consequences for breaking it. We really do risk penalties from other whites, such as being accused of being PC and ruining everyone's fun, or being perceived as angry, humorless, combative, and not suited to go far in an organization. In my own life, these penalties have worked as a form of coercion to prevent me from breaking white silence. Seeking to avoid conflict and wanting to be liked, I have chosen silence all too often. Conversely, I have been rewarded when I remain silent and granted social capital such as being seen as fun, cooperative, and a team player. Notice that within a white supremacist society, I am *rewarded* for not interrupting racism, and *punished* in a range of ways—big and small—when I do. My silence protects and maintains my white privilege.

Allowed Racial Innocence

Raised to see ourselves as "just human" or "just an individual," we are able to position ourselves as not having a race. Race is what *they* have. Not seeing

ourselves as having a race, we don't see ourselves as having the problems associated with race. Living in racial segregation, we can tell ourselves that we
believe that everyone is equal, but that we *just happen to* live separately. When
people of color are present and more explicit racism surfaces, we can say "we
didn't have these problems until you came here." This positions people of
color as the problem, which validates our desire for segregation.

An interaction I had may serve to illustrate the concept of white racial
innocence. I attended an educational panel of white antiracist activists with
a friend who is a woman of color. The purpose of the panel was for the white
activists to share their motivations, strategies, and experiences in working
against racism, and hopefully to educate and motivate other whites to do the
same. One man on the panel stood out for me. In sharing the story of his
journey toward antiracist practice, he said, "I am like a 7-year-old child, just
learning." His point was that he had not been educated about racism, and he
was still "young" in terms of his learning process. I was very impressed by this
particular man, positioning himself as child-like. That was something I had
not seen a man do before, and I thought it was a great contradiction to traditional masculinity. I saw him as humble and open.

As my friend and I were walking to the car after the presentation, I shared
with her how impressed I was with this panelist, and his vulnerability in positioning himself as a child. I was surprised to discover that she, on the other
hand, was disturbed by his comment. "How am I supposed to hold a 7-year-old
accountable?" she asked. "He is not a child, innocent of race. I need him to
take responsibility for his role in the system and speak from that position."
This was a powerful moment for me as I considered both the difference in
racial perspective between my friend and me, and the racial impact of the
panelist's statement. I realized that although he was well intentioned, he had
reinforced several racially problematic concepts.

First, this panelist reinforced the idea that whites do not know about
race, and thus are child-like in the face of it. This, of course, is simply not
true. We are not innocent of race at all. On the contrary—we have been
deeply socialized into the racial construct, and navigate it every day. In fact,
most white people I have met feel perfectly qualified to argue with people of
color about race and how it works, or with other whites who study race. It
would appear that in most situations, we don't see ourselves as innocent of
race at all, but as quite knowledgeable. So this begs the question, just *when*
do we position ourselves as innocent, and what does this accomplish? For
my friend, the impact was that the panelist was not taking responsibility; he

was claiming ignorance. In so doing, he was reinforcing the idea of whites as *outside* of race. People of color, who are not positioned as outside of race, are thus left to speak to issues of race. This claim enables us to sit back and listen to people of color as they take very real risks in sharing their stories (which is more than most whites are willing to do), but does not require us to take our own cross-racial risks.

Yet whites do, in fact, have expertise on aspects of race and racism, and we can certainly speak to many aspects of how race works in our lives, messages we have received, privileges we enjoy, how we came to be socialized to feel superior (while denying that we feel this way), and our challenges in countering racism. Perhaps the more constructive use of a child-like positioning would be the willingness to talk openly and honestly as children often do. Although the panelist clearly was committed to antiracist practice, and I am confident that he would be open to considering the impact of his statement, the narrative of white racial innocence is not benign; it has material consequences because it allows whites to deny the impact of racism on people of color while enjoying its benefits.

Because whites are socially positioned as individuals, or "just people" (the writer, the man, the friend), while people of color are always positioned as members of a racial group (the Latino writer, the Asian man, the black friend), we have the privilege of seeing ourselves as outside of race and thus unfamiliar with it. The white claim that one does not know much about race is particularly problematic because while it positions whiteness as innocence, it simultaneously reinforces the projection of race onto people of color (and all the problems associated with it); they have race, not us, and thus are the holders of racial knowledge. In so doing, we position ourselves as standing outside of hierarchical social relations—as if the oppression of people of color occurs in a vacuum.

Conversely, positioning whites as innocent taps into classic discourses of people of color as *not* innocent. Racist images and resultant white fears can be found at all levels of society, and myriad studies demonstrate that whites believe that people of color (and blacks in particular) are dangerous (Feagin, 2006; Myers, 2003; Johnson & Shapiro, 2003; Dyer, 1997). These beliefs are fueled by the mass media via relentless representations of people of color associated with criminality. Indeed, much of white flight and the resulting segregation in housing and schooling can be attributed to this representation. This discourse distorts reality and the actual direction of danger that has historically existed between whites and people of color. Thus the history of extensive and brutal explicit violence perpetrated by whites—slavery, lynching, whipping, genocide, internment, forced sterilization, and medical experimentation to mention a few—and their ideological rationalizations, are all trivialized through white claims of racial innocence. The power and privilege we wield and have wielded for centuries is thus obscured. The discourse of innocence is powerful in part because it rests not only on the current structure of white supremacy, but also on this vast backdrop of historical white supremacy.

Two newspaper photos released during the reporting on Hurricane Katrina illustrate another aspect of the concept of racial innocence: how whites and blacks are represented in relation to crime (see Figure 40). Both photos were published on **August 30, 2005.**

The first photo shows a black man, up to his chest in water, with a carton of soda under his arm and a bag of groceries at his side. The caption reads: "A young man walks through chest deep flood water *after looting a grocery store* in New Orleans on Tuesday, Aug. 30, 2005" (AP Photo/Dave Martin; emphasis added).

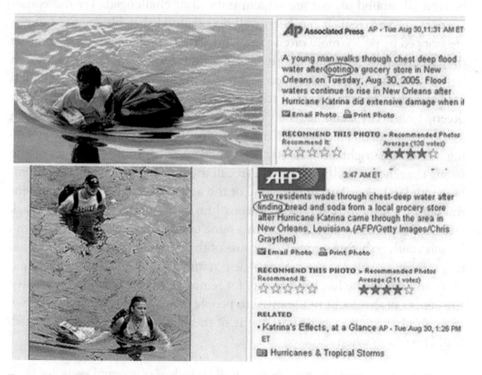

Figure 40. Katrina.

The second photo features two people who appear to be white. They are also in chest-deep water, and one can be seen carrying a bag of food in her hand. The caption reads: "Two residents wade through chest-deep water *after finding bread and soda from a local grocery store* ..." (AFP/Getty Images/Chris Graythen; emphasis added).

There is a very significant difference in the stories these pictures are used to tell. Because all my life I have seen images of black people involved in crime and associated with looting, it seems normal to me—even expected— when I read that a black man is looting. This narrative reinforces my racial frame. I don't even stop to ask myself how getting desperately needed food from an abandoned grocery store in the aftermath of a natural disaster can fairly be described as looting. In the second photo, released on the same day, people who appear white are engaged in exactly the same survival activities as the black man, but are described as "finding" bread and soda. These people are presented as victims instead of criminals, evoking very different responses from the reader and reinforcing very different narratives.

These blatant differences in the ways blacks and whites are depicted can be seen all around us, but are seldom noticed or challenged. Yet the consequences are very real. It has been well documented that blacks and Latinos are stopped by police more often than whites for the same activities, and that they receive harsher sentences than whites do for the same crimes. Research has shown that a major factor accounting for this racial disparity is the beliefs held by judges and others about the *cause of* the criminal behavior (Bridges & Steen, 1998). For example, the criminal behavior of white juveniles is seen as caused by *external* factors—he comes from a single-parent home, he is having a hard time right now, he just happened to be at the wrong place at the wrong time, he was bullied at school (recall the reasons offered for the Columbine murders). Attributing the cause of the action to external factors lessens the person's responsibility and positions him as a victim himself. But black and Latino youth are not afforded this same understanding. When black and Latino youth go before a judge, the cause of the crime is more often attributed to something *internal* to the person—he is naturally more prone to crime, he is more animalistic, he has less capacity for remorse. Whites continually receive the benefit of the doubt not granted to people of color—our race alone serves to establish our innocence. This is one of the "credit cards" Peggy McIntosh (2012) refers to when she says:

> I have come to see white privilege as an invisible package of unearned assets that I can count on cashing in each day, but about which I was "meant" to remain oblivious.

White privilege is like an invisible weightless knapsack of special provisions, assurances, tools, maps, guides, codebooks, passports, visas, clothes, compass, emergency gear, and blank checks. (p. 1)

My life has been profoundly shaped by having these privileges and the psychological support and freedom of movement they allow me. One of these privileges is being positioned as racially innocent—as outside or innocent of race—and thus granted the benefit of the doubt where racialized others are not.

No Sense of Loss in Racial Segregation

As a white person, my life has been deeply shaped by racial segregation. Of all the racial groups, *whites* are the most likely to choose segregation, and are also the group in the social and economic position to do so (Dawkins, 2004; Johnson & Shapiro, 2003). Growing up in segregation (e.g., schools, workplaces, neighborhoods, shopping districts, places of worship, entertainment, social gatherings), we are given the message that our experiences and perspectives are the only ones that matter. We receive this message day in and day out.

Segregation is often lessened somewhat for poor urban whites who may live near and have friendships with people of color on the local level. But segregation is still operating on the macro level. This segregation informs our collective perspective on what kind of space is most valuable. Whites from the lower classes who may have more integrated lives on the micro level still receive the message that achievement means moving out of poverty and away from the neighborhoods and schools that define us. Upward mobility is the great class goal in the United States, and the social environment gets tangibly whiter the higher up one goes. Whiter environments, in turn, are marked as the most socially and economically valuable. For upwardly mobile whites, reaching toward the most valuable places in society usually means leaving friends and neighbors of color behind.

Despite the claims that opportunity is equal and anyone can succeed if they try hard enough, we know that neighborhoods and schools are demonstrably not equal; they are separate and unequal. Tax bases, school resources, and the quality of the teaching force differ widely between school districts. Who is not aware of where the "good" schools and neighborhoods are, and the primary race of those in them? Race is most often the determining factor in our perceptions. For example, in a study on school choice, Johnson and

Shapiro (2003) interviewed approximately 200 white families in Boston, St. Louis, and Los Angeles on how they made school choices for their children. They found that race was a primary factor, if not *the* primary factor, in determining white decisions on community and school choice. They argue that within the context of a deeply unequal society, the opportunity to choose is a primary mechanism through which segregation and inequality is reproduced today.

Without white interest or effort invested in changing a system that serves them at the expense of others, advantage is passed down from generation to generation. Rather than challenge this inequality, whites take advantage of it and abandon children of color to schools they would never allow their own children to attend. McGraff and Kuriloff (1999) found that upper-middle-class parents often block parents of color from school involvement and push for more tracking and other mechanisms that will separate their children from lower-status children when they *do* attend school together. We don't want inferior conditions for *our* children, but rather than change these conditions so that public education is equal for all, we allow other people's children to endure them.

Further, the way we talk about "good schools" and "good neighborhoods" makes it clear that the absence of people of color is, in large part, what defines our schools and neighborhoods as good. I am confident that my readers have heard schools and neighborhoods discussed in these terms and know that this talk is racially coded; "urban" is code for "not-white" and therefore less desirable. When we discuss these places in these terms, we are engaged in racial discourse. In the United States, we are actually returning to pre-integration levels of racial segregation; schools and neighborhoods are becoming *more* racially separated, not less (Lichter, Parisi, & Taquino, 2015). Even when whites live in physical proximity to people of color (and this is exceptional outside of a lower-class urban neighborhood), segregation is occurring on many other levels in the culture (and often in the school itself).

White flight is a major mechanism of racial segregation. White flight is the term used to describe the phenomenon of whites moving out of neighborhoods when they perceive that there are "too many" people of color (and blacks in particular) in the neighborhood. On attitude surveys, most whites say they would prefer neighborhoods that are no more than 30% black. More than half of whites say they would not move into a neighborhood that is 30% black or more. Studies of actual mobility patterns not only confirm these preferences, but show that whites downplay them. White flight has been shown to be triggered when a formerly white neighborhood reaches 7% black (Bonilla-Silva, 2002) and that in neighborhoods with more than a few black families, white housing demand tends to disappear (Quillian, 2002). Whites consistently move out of neighborhoods with growing black populations, ensuring that many of these newly integrated neighborhoods will soon become segregated again. White flight is the primary reason that racial integration has not been achieved; the majority of whites, in both the expression of their beliefs and the practice of their lives, do not want to integrate with blacks.

White flight is often justified by beliefs that people of color (and blacks in particular) are more prone to crime, and that if "too many" blacks move into a neighborhood, crime will increase, home values will go down, and the neighborhood will deteriorate. Research matching census data and police department crime statistics show that this is not true, but these statistics do not quell white fears. For most whites, the percentage of young black men in a neighborhood is directly correlated with perceptions of the neighborhood crime level. For example, the white families in Johnson and Shapiro's study consistently discussed fear of crime and associated crime with people of color. In their minds, the more people of color in an area (specifically, blacks and Latinos), the more dangerous the area was perceived to be.

Although there is a deep association between the two in most whites' minds, and the media keeps these associations alive with the ways in which they define and report crime and with prison-based "reality" shows, consider the following:

- Crime rates (including violent crime) in the United States are actually decreasing, not increasing (FBI Uniform Crime Reports, 2014).
- Although crime rates have fluctuated over the last 40 years, the imprisonment of blacks and Latinos has consistently risen. In other words, the increasing incarceration of men of color is not related to crime rates.
- Most men of color are incarcerated for drug offenses. People have been sentenced to life imprisonment for first-time marijuana offenses, and the Supreme Court has refused to intervene in these sentences.

Most Americans, and white Americans in particular, are woefully misinformed about race and crime.

Although many whites see spaces in which more than a few people of color are present as undesirable and even dangerous, consider the matter of perspective. I have heard countless people of color share stories of what it was like to be one of only a few people of color in their schools and neighborhoods, and it was most often described as a miserable, painful experience for them. Although many parents of color want the advantages granted by attending predominantly white schools, they also worry about the stress and even danger they are putting their children in by sending them to white schools. These parents must also worry about a predominantly white teaching force. This teaching force has little if any authentic knowledge about children of color and has been socialized (often unconsciously) to see children of color as inferior and even to fear them. This perspective turns the "dangerous places" narrative on its head; imagine how unsafe *white schools*, which are so precious to whites, might appear to people of color.

The most profound message of racial segregation for whites may be that there is no real loss in the absence of people of color from our lives. Not one person who loved me, guided me, or taught me ever conveyed that there was loss to me in segregation; that I would lose anything by not having people of color in my life. I could live my entire life without a friend or loved one of color and not see that as a problem. In fact, my life trajectory would almost certainly ensure that I had few, if any, people of color in my life—especially if I was upwardly mobile. Perhaps I met some non-white people when I played sports in school, or there "just happened" to be a person of color or two in my class, but when I was outside the context of a class or game, I did not have any authentic, long-term cross-racial relationships. Most whites who describe having a friend of color in childhood rarely keep them into adulthood. Yet I am confident that if my parents had thought it was *valuable* to have cross-racial relationships, I would have had them.

Pause for a moment and consider the magnitude and profundity of this message: *We lose nothing of value by not having cross-racial relationships.* In fact, the absence of people of color in our lives is in large part what defines our schools and neighborhoods as "good."

In conclusion, for those of us who work to raise the racial consciousness of whites, simply getting whites to acknowledge that we have privilege—that we have had unfair advantages not granted to people of color—is a major effort. The defensiveness, denial, and resistance is deep. But acknowledging privilege is only a first step, and as often happens with movements for social change, it too can be used in a way that renders it meaningless and allows for inequality to continue. For example, I have often heard whites say, "*Just because of the color of my skin*, I have privilege. ..." Yet this describes privilege as if it's a fluke—something that *just happens* to us as we walk through life, with no involvement or complicity on our part. This description of privilege as a fluke also obscures the systematic and institutional dimensions of racism that are deeply embedded in our society and actively and passively, consciously and unconsciously, maintained. The "just because" narrative also maintains the concept of white racial innocence.

Based on everything I have discussed so far, I want to push well beyond the concept of privilege as an accident or something I can't help. As a white person, my psychosocial development was inculcated in a white supremacist culture in which I am in the valued group. I was raised in a society that taught me that there was no loss in the absence of people of color; that in fact their absence was a good and desirable thing that should be sought and maintained. This has shaped every aspect of my identity and what I think of as my "self" or personality: my interests and investments, what I care about or don't care about, what I see or don't see, what I am drawn to and what I am repelled by, what I can take for granted, where I can go, how I think about myself and how others think about and respond to me, and what I can ignore. All are shaped by my development in the water of white supremacy. I benefit from racism and I am invested in it, and from this acknowledgment I must fight it.

> **Remember:** Racism is a historical, social, cultural, political, and institutional relationship between white people and people of color. This relationship is built into the very fabric of society. No one who resides in society is outside this relationship.

But let me be clear. I do not view myself as a bad person and do not feel guilty about racism. Racism is a system that I inherited but did not create. I do not believe that most of us would choose to be socialized into racism and white supremacy. Unfortunately, we didn't have that choice. So I must take responsibility now that I can see it. This means working to challenge racism both within and without me. (Concrete steps for how to do this will be discussed in Chapter 16.)

Discussion Questions

1. The author traces some of the specific ways that her life has been shaped by racism. Consider your own socialization. In what specific ways has your life has been shaped by racism?

2. What are the earliest racial messages you can recall? We receive many more *implicit* messages than explicit messages. If you are white, try to move beyond what you were openly told or your first interactions with people of color and work to identify *implicit* messages.

3. Consider your education, the media, health care, the military and other social institutions from the perspective of the white racial frame. What messages were conveyed specifically from these institutions?

4. How are the messages identified in questions 2 and 3 conveyed in your current life?

5. In what settings have you experienced the expectation of white solidarity/racial silence? How has that expectation been communicated to you? How have you responded? How might you respond differently in the future?

6. Consider the bulleted list following the author's analysis of *The Blind Side*. Why is this story so appealing to white people? Whose vision of the world do these stories serve? What racial scripts get reinforced by these stories? Where else have you seen these racial scripts?

7. The author describes the power of segregation. She argues that segregation is "active." What does she mean? Discuss how various patterns of segregation across your life span shape your racial frame.

· 1 0 ·

WHAT MAKES RACISM SO HARD FOR WHITES TO SEE?

> I am white. My neighborhood and town growing up was (pretty much) all white. Therefore race wasn't discussed much or wasn't that much of an issue growing up because there really wasn't any diversity. (ASR)

> I mostly lived in all-white neighborhoods. We are all equal, regardless of what we look like, because at the end of the day we are all human. Until we can learn to see our differences as unique characteristics and not defining qualities, it will continue to be an issue. Honestly, I cannot see specifically how my race has shaped my life. I personally see myself as an individual, not a white female in her early 20s. My race exists, but it does not define who I am, it merely adds to the description. (ASR)

The vast majority of whites cannot answer the question "How has race shaped your life?" beyond the most superficial of platitudes. So what makes racism so difficult for whites to see?

The Racist = Bad/Not Racist = Good Binary

In Chapter 2, I introduced the concept of the *racist = bad not racist = good* binary (see Figure 2) and how it sets whites up to feel personally accused and defensive about the suggestion of any association with racism; we hear these suggestions as unfair accusations that we are fundamentally bad or immoral people.

This binary certainly obscures racism and makes it difficult for us to see or understand. Another problem with the binary concerns the impact of such a worldview on our actions. If, as a white person, I conceptualize racism as a binary and I see myself on the "not racist" side, what further action is required of me? No action is required at all, because *I am not a racist*. Therefore racism is not my problem; it doesn't concern me and there is nothing further I need to do. This guarantees that, as a member of the dominant group, I will not build my skills in thinking critically about racism or use my position to challenge racial inequality. Further, if I conceptualize racism as an either/or proposition, any suggestion that I have racist thoughts or feelings places me on the "wrong" side of the binary. As a result, all of my energy will go to denying and negating this possibility rather than to trying to understand what these thoughts and feelings are and how they are manifesting in my actions.

If you are white and have ever been challenged to look at an aspect of yourself related to racism—perhaps you told a problematic joke or made a prejudiced assumption, and someone brought it to your attention—it is common to feel very defensive. This defensiveness reveals the binary that informs our understanding of racism; we interpret the feedback to mean that we have done something bad and are thus being told that we are bad people. This binary, which is the foundation of whites' understanding of racism (Trepagnier, 2010) and the defensiveness it triggers are primary obstacles preventing us from moving forward in our understanding. As African American scholar and filmmaker Omowale Akintunde (1999) says:

> Racism is a systemic, societal, institutional, omnipresent, and epistemologically embedded phenomenon that pervades every vestige of our reality. For most whites, however, racism is like murder: the concept exists, but someone has to commit it in order for it to happen. This limited view of such a multilayered syndrome cultivates the sinister nature of racism and, in fact, perpetuates racist phenomena rather than eradicates them. (p. 1)

The dominant paradigm of racism as discreet, individual, intentional, and malicious acts makes it unlikely that whites will see or understand racism.

Individualism

In my years as a white person co-facilitating antiracism workshops for primarily white audiences within the United States, I have come to believe that the ideology of Individualism is one of the primary barriers to well-meaning (and other) white people understanding racism: as long as I don't see myself as *personally engaged* in acts of racism, I am exempt from it. Individualism is so deeply entrenched that it is virtually immovable without sustained effort. A recent interaction may illustrate the depth of this narrative.

I was co-facilitating a mandatory workplace training entitled "Race & Social Justice." Two key components of this training are my presentation, as a white person, on the dynamics of white privilege, and my co-facilitator's presentation, as a person of color, on the dynamics of internalized racial oppression. Included in my presentation is a list of common barriers that prevent whites from seeing racism (these barriers are discussed in detail in this chapter). One barrier is that we see ourselves as individuals, outside of social groups. I had just finished presenting this list and had called for a break, during which a white woman, "Sue," who had been sitting next to a white man, "Bill," approached me and declared, "Bill and I think we should all just see each other as individuals." Although in my work moments like this occur frequently, they continue to disorient me on two interconnected levels. First, I had just stated that seeing each other as individuals was a perspective only available to the dominant group. Yet Sue's statement implied I had never heard or considered this most simple and popular of "solutions" to racism, even though I had just raised and critiqued it. I was left wondering, yet again, what happens cognitively for many whites that prevents them from actually hearing what is being presented. Second, why did she, as a white person, feel confident to declare the one-sentence "answer" to the profoundly complex and perennial dilemma of racism? Why not consider my background in the field and instead engage me in a deeper dialogue on the matter? I did my best to reiterate why individualism is problematic when discussing race, but to no avail. By the afternoon break, Sue had walked out.

So what was Sue and Bill's point? In my experience as a white person facilitating countless college courses and workshops over the past 15 years, in a range of academic, corporate, and government institutions across the United States, Canada, and the United Kingdom, when white people insist on Individualism in discussions about racism, they are in essence saying:

> My race has not made a difference in my life, so why do we have to talk about it? It is talking about race as if it mattered that divides us. I don't see myself as a member of a racial group; you shouldn't see me that way, either. In fact, by saying that my group membership matters, you are generalizing. Generalizing discounts my individuality; unless you know me, you can't profess to know anything about my life and all of the

ways I am an exception to the rules. Further, I am objective and view others as individuals and not as members of racial groups. For example, if I were hiring I would hire
the best person for the job no matter what their race was. Racism will disappear when
we all see each other as individuals. Or, it has, in fact, disappeared because I already
see everyone as individuals.

Individualism is a storyline or narrative that creates, communicates, reproduces, and reinforces the concept that each of us is a unique individual and
that our group memberships, such as race, class, or gender, are not important or relevant to our opportunities. Individualism claims that there are no
intrinsic barriers to individual success, and that failure is not a consequence
of social structures but of individual character. According to the ideology of
individualism, race is irrelevant. Yet in reality, we *do* occupy distinct race,
gender, class (and other) positions that profoundly shape our life chances in
ways that are not natural, voluntary, or random; opportunity is not equally
distributed across race, class, and gender. Individualism—when applied to
racism—obscures several key dynamics of racism.

Dynamic One: Denies the significance of race and the advantages of being white

While scientific research has shown that there are no biologically or genetically distinct races as we have traditionally understood them, race has profound meaning as a social category. This meaning has created consistent,
predictable patterns related to one's life outcomes based on the racial group
society assigns to people. On every measure: health, education, interaction with the criminal justice system, income and wealth, there is disparity
between white people and people of color, with people of color consistently
relegated to the bottom and white people holding the consistent advantage.
Regardless of the intentions of white people, and regardless of the other social
groups to which they may belong (such as class, gender, sexual orientation,
religion, and ability), whites as a group benefit from a society in which racism
(white advantage) is deeply embedded. Whites need not hold consciously
racist beliefs or intentions in order to benefit from being white. Insistence
on pretending that we see everyone as an individual and ignoring the significance of group membership denies the reality that not all individuals have
the same access to resources based on whether they are perceived as white or
a person of color.

Dynamic Two: Hides the accumulation of wealth over generations

Seeing ourselves as individuals erases our history and hides the way in which wealth has accumulated over generations and benefits us, as a group, today. Our country was founded on slavery (as well as genocide), and racism did not end when slavery ended. Legal exclusion of people of color, in addition to illegal acts of terrorism against them such as lynching, continued all the way through the 1960s. For example, people of color were denied Federal Housing Act (FHA) loans in the 1950s that allowed a generation of whites to attain middle-class status through home ownership. Home ownership is critical in the United States because it is the way in which the "average" person builds and passes down wealth, and provides the starting point for the next generation. People of color were systematically denied this opportunity, and today the average white family has *13* times the wealth of the average black or Latino family (Kochhar & Fry, 2014). Excluding people of color from wealth-building mechanisms continues today through illegal but common practices such as higher mortgage rates, more barriers to loans, being steered away from "good" neighborhoods by real estate agents, discrimination in hiring, and unequal school funding. Insistence on Individualism (exemplified by superficial and simplistic platitudes such as "I didn't own slaves so I have not benefited from racism") hides the reality of white advantage at every level of our past and present society.

Dynamic Three: Denies the social and historical context

Discourses are an interrelated "system of statements which cohere around common meanings and values ... [that] are a product of social factors, of powers and practices, rather than an individual's set of ideas" (Hollway, 1984, p. 231). These statements are embedded in a matrix of past statements, stories, and meanings—they connect to, expand, extend, and refer back to discourses already circulating in the culture. If they did not connect to existing discourses, we could not make sense of them. Removing these historical dimensions from the analysis prevents an understanding of all that has occurred in the past and denies that we are products of our historical lineage. This denial also prevents us from understanding how the past bears upon the present and how it has led us to the current conditions in which we find ourselves. The individual is thereby positioned as a unique entity—one that emerged from the ether, untouched by socio-historic conditioning—rather than as a social, cultural, and historical subject. To be able to think critically about the phenomenon of racism, we must be able to think socio-historically about it. Individualism falsely positions us as existing outside of social history.

Dynamic Four: Prevents a macro analysis of the institutional and structural dimensions of social life

Insisting that we should see ourselves solely as individuals prevents us from seeing and addressing racism as an institutionalized system. Outcomes are traced to group membership on every indicator of quality of life, and these outcomes are well documented and predictable (Weber, 2010; Wise, 2015). Limiting our analysis to the *micro* or individual level prevents a *macro* or "big picture" assessment. It also reinforces the conceptualization of racism as individual acts of meanness that only some "bad" people commit. At the micro level, we cannot assess and address the macro dimensions of society that help hold racism in place, such as practices, policies, norms, rules, laws, traditions, and regulations. For example, in the United States, people of color have historically been barred by laws and by discrimination from participating in government wealth-building programs that benefit white Americans. Individualism keeps our focus on isolated exceptions to the rules and allows us to deny the significance of the rules themselves, who makes the rules, and whom the rules benefit.

Consider, for example, the fact that schools are primarily funded through the property tax base of the community in which they are situated. Given that, due to systematic and historical racism, youth of color disproportionately live in poor communities and their families rent rather than own, youth of color are penalized by this policy, which ensures that poor communities will have inferior schools. In turn, this practice ensures that middle- and upper-class students, who are more likely to be white, will get a superior education and will have less competition in the future workplace—an example of both institutional racism and its result: individual white privilege. Given the many possible creative options for funding schools in ways that ensure that every child gets equal access to quality education, funding schools in this particular way and the social acceptance of this tradition is an example of institutional racism.

Individualism also allows whites to exempt ourselves personally from these patterns and the resulting network of race-based advantage. In other words, as a white person, if I personally do not agree with receiving advantages, Individualism allows me to deny that I receive them. This also presumes that a desire that resides in my head can affectively ward off the society in which I am embedded. Of course, even if it were possible to simply decide not to benefit from racial advantages, I cannot ward off the myriad ways in which society grants privilege to whites automatically and at both individual and institutional levels, regardless of my personal desire.

Dynamic Five: Denies collective socialization and the power of dominant culture (media, education, religion, etc.) to shape our perspectives and ideology

Individualism allows us to present ourselves as unique and original, outside of socialization and unaffected by the relentless racial messages we receive on a daily basis from films, advertising, textbooks, teachers, relatives, shared stories, silence, the absence of information, segregated schools and neighborhoods, and countless other dimensions of social life. Individualism, which places us outside of culture and history, is further developed and refined through modern-day advertising and consumerism, which depends on this conceptualization. Individualism helps us maintain the illusion that we are unaffected by media, and that our consumer choices reflect our unique tastes and preferences. At the same time, we believe that the brands we have been conditioned to use represent us and make us special. Advertisers certainly see us as group members with specific and predictable patterns, and have effectively built a multibillion-dollar industry on these patterns. Advertisers need us to see ourselves as individuals who are unaffected by the culture around us in order to maintain the illusion of free choice. The irony of advertising, of course, is that this illusion of free choice is necessary precisely in order to manipulate group behavior.

Dynamic Six: Functions as neo-colorblindness and reproduces the myth of meritocracy

If we use the line of reasoning that we are all individuals and that social categories such as race, class, and gender do not matter and are just "labels" that stereotype and limit us, then it follows that we all end up in our own "natural" places. Those at the top are merely a collection of individuals who rose under their own individual merits, and those at the bottom are there due to individual deficiencies. Group membership is thereby rendered inoperative, and racial disparities are seen as the result of essential character attributes rather than the result of consistent structural barriers.

According to Individualism, it is either just a fluke that those at the top are a very homogenous collection of individuals, or else white, middle-, and upper-class men and sometimes women are consistently "the cream of the crop." According to Individualism, white privilege is not a factor because we do not see color anyway; we see each person as a unique individual, and we treat him or her as such. This ideology is particularly popular with white teachers. Thus, Individualism not only upholds the myth of meritocracy—that success is solely the result of ability and hard work—but it also upholds the belief in the superiority of those at the top. Individualism naturalizes the social order and relations of inequality.

Dynamic Seven: Makes collective action difficult

Based on the ideology of Individualism, we see ourselves as different from one another and expect others to see us as different, too. Not having a group consciousness, whites often respond defensively when grouped with other whites, resenting what they see as unfair generalizations. Individualism prevents us from seeing ourselves as responsible for or accountable to other whites as members of a shared racial group that collectively benefits from racial inequality. Individualism allows whites to distance themselves from the actions of their racial group and demand to be granted the benefit of the doubt, as individuals, in all cases. Since we don't see the racism of other whites as our problem, we leave people of color with the responsibility of challenging other white people. Challenging white people is much more difficult for people of color to do, for they are often dismissed with a variety of accusations including: playing the race card, having a chip on their shoulder, seeing race in everything, or being overly sensitive or angry. These dismissals are painful because they add to a lifetime of being invalided by whites. When whites break racial solidarity and speak up to challenge racism, we are seen as more credible and more objective. Further, when the resistance comes—while often uncomfortable—it does not trigger a lifetime of racial invalidation for whites. Given that whites hold social and institutional power and benefit from racism, racism is essentially a *white* problem. We need to take collective action for and among ourselves.

Many whites depend on the ideology of Individualism to position ourselves as standing outside of hierarchical social relations. At stake is our very identity—a sense of ourselves as fair, open-minded, and hard-working. Thus we must deny our investment in racism. If we can sustain a denial of ourselves as members of groups, social inequity and its consequences become personally moot, and so, too, does any imperative to change this inequity.

> **Individualism**: The ideology that we are all unique, therefore categories such as race have no meaning and provide no more or less opportunities. Thus success or failure is not a consequence of social structures but of individual character.

In conclusion, let me be clear: I am not arguing that we are not individuals in the general sense of the word. Rather, I am arguing that white insistence on individualism *in regard to race* prevents cross-racial understanding and denies the salience of race and racism in white people's lives. Further, being viewed as an individual outside of race is a privilege only available to whites. In other words, people of color are almost always seen as "having a race" and described in racial terms (e.g., "a black guy," "an Aboriginal director"), whereas whites are rarely defined by race (e.g., "a man," "a director"), thereby allowing whites to move through society as "just people." Individualism also allows whites to see ourselves as objective and people of color as having "special" or biased group interests and agendas.

Of course, to see oneself as an individual is a very different dynamic for people of color. While for whites individualism is often a strategy for *resisting* acknowledging that their race has meaning, for people of color it can be a strategy for *coping* with always being seen in racial terms. Because people of color are denied individuality by dominant society, individualism can actually be a way to challenge racism for them and an important contradiction to the relentless imposition of racial identity. Individualism can also be a way for people of color to "push away" the onslaught of racism and carve out psychic space and autonomy (denying racism may be a similar strategy). Because the social and institutional positions are not the same between whites and people of color, the ideological dynamics of individualism are not the same. Thus to challenge a particular form of oppression requires different tasks based on one's position in that form of oppression. If we fall into the dominant group, one of our tasks is to look beyond our sense of ourselves as individuals and to examine our group history and socialization. If we fall into the minoritized group, one of our tasks is to move beyond our group identification and claim individual complexity—that is, to challenge the way in which society has focused solely on our minoritized identity, and denied us a sense of individuality.

Universalism

Because whites are taught to see themselves as "just human" and thus outside of race, we see our perspectives as objective and representative of reality. The belief in objectivity, coupled with the positioning of whites as the norm for humanity, allows whites to view themselves as universal humans who can represent all of human experience. Within this construction, people of color can only represent their own racialized experience. I refer to this ideology as Universalism, and it functions in ways that are similar to Individualism. But instead of declaring that we all need to see each other as individuals (everyone is different), the person declares that we all need to see each other as human beings (everyone is the same). Of course we are all humans and I am not denying universalism in that regard, *but when applied to racism*, it denies the social and institutional realities of race and racism in a society in which race matters profoundly. Once again, the significance of race and the advantages of being white are denied.

Universalism often manifests in an unracialized identity which functions as a kind of blindness, an inability to think about being white as something that would or could have an impact on one's life. Universalism assumes that whites and people of color have the same reality, the same experiences in the same context (i.e., I feel comfortable in this majority white classroom, so you must too), the same responses from others, and that the same doors are open.

> **Universalism**: The ideology that because we are all human, categories such as race have no meaning and provide no more or less opportunities.

White people tend to invoke these seemingly contradictory discourses—we are either all unique or we are all the same—interchangeably, but both discourses work to deny white privilege and the significance of race. Of course, I am working toward the day when both individualism and universalism are the social reality, but we are not in that society, and to claim that we are simply hides the realities of racism while protecting white privilege.

We Feel Entitled to Cross-Racial Trust

Because most whites see themselves as individuals, we take exception to being "lumped together" with other whites. I encounter this again and again in my work—white people who feel that my generalizations about white people are unfair. These people want to be seen as individuals; in other words, they want to be seen as they see themselves. Given that most whites see themselves as "not racist," this means that they expect other people to see them that way, too. "I didn't own slaves" or "I don't see color," or "I am working-class (or gay, etc.) so I don't have race privilege," thus I cannot be included in any generalized claims made about white people. Further, because whites are not socialized to see ourselves collectively, we don't see our group's history as relevant. Therefore, we expect people of color to trust us as soon as they meet us. We don't see ourselves as having to *earn* that trust.

Many times I have heard white people complain about the unfairness of not being trusted immediately by people of color. "How dare they assume I would be racist, or that I would be like other white people they have met!" What we don't understand is that in this very response—taking umbrage that we should have to demonstrate we are different from other whites rather than have it assumed—we are actually demonstrating how similar we are to other whites, and how much we don't understand about how racism works. We don't realize that we are not solely unique individuals, unaffected by social dynamics; rather, we are profoundly shaped by our collective experiences as whites. We don't understand that this expectation simply demonstrates the privilege we have enjoyed throughout our lives. We have not had to understand the experiences of people of color, or see ourselves as more than just individuals.

We bring our collective group histories with us, and for most people of color, this is a history of harm. People of color are wise not to give us the benefit of the doubt and make themselves vulnerable to our unaware racism. It is a rare white person who demonstrates sensitivity or understanding about race. It would be foolhardy for people of color to assume we are sophisticated about race just because we see ourselves as such. We need to demonstrate that we can be trusted, and expecting this trust without earning it, or expecting to not be seen as *white*, does not demonstrate racial sophistication (or that we "get it").

We Are Taught to Deny That Race Matters within a Deeply Racialized Society

Many whites believe that not talking about race is evidence that race doesn't matter to them. Yet for all the white insistence that race doesn't matter, whites have fairly strong emotions when it comes to race. These emotions are often triggered by the racist = bad/not racist = good binary—for example, a suggestion that I am involved in anything perceived as racial means that I am a bad person. But these emotions are also caused by the internal conflict between internalized feelings of superiority and the moral imperative that we deny them.

Scholars have argued that whites split off from themselves and project onto blacks (in particular) character aspects that we don't want to own in ourselves (Van Dijk, 1993; Bonilla-Silva, 2002; Morrison, 1993a). For example, slave masters consistently depicted their slaves as lazy and child-like, even as they toiled under back-breaking work from sunup to sundown (building, among other things, those antebellum mansions). Today, we depict blacks (for example) as dangerous, which perverts the actual direction of violence between whites and blacks since the founding of this country. This causes very negative feelings toward blacks on one end of the emotional continuum, and feelings of superiority on the other end, neither of which we can acknowledge in the current racial construct. I am speaking of the collective consciousness; an individual white person may not be aware of these feelings, but I am often amazed at how quickly they surface with even the slightest challenge.

Denying that race matters is irrational in the face of segregation and all of the other forms of obvious racial inequity in society. It is even more irrational to believe that it is *whites* who are at the receiving end of racial discrimination. Maintaining this denial of reality takes tremendous emotional and psychic energy. Most of the time, race doesn't come up in conversation, so the demands of denial are minimized. But when confronted directly with matters of race, the work of denial is much harder, and white people often erupt in anger and resentment. These feelings prevent us from engaging in thoughtful or sensitive ways that could allow for constructive engagement, self-knowledge, and growth.

We Feel Entitled to Racial Comfort

As a facilitator of countless discussions of race with predominantly white groups, I have often heard white people say that they "don't feel safe" in cross-racial discussions. I believe that they mean they want to feel *comfortable* in the discussion, as whites often confuse comfort with safety. Yet this call for safety minimizes our history of brutality toward people of color and distorts the reality of that history. Because we don't think with complexity about racism, we don't ask ourselves what safety means from a position of societal dominance. Nor do we consider the impact of our request for safety on people of color. Given history, whites' insistence that safety be created for them before they can merely talk about racism is highly trivializing.

In the dominant position, whites are almost always racially comfortable and thus have developed an unchallenged expectation to remain so. Whites have not had to build tolerance for racial discomfort, and thus when racial discomfort arises, whites typically respond as if something is "wrong," and blame the person or event that triggered the discomfort (usually a person of color). This blame results in a socially sanctioned array of moves against the perceived source of the discomfort, including penalization, retaliation, isolation, ostracization, and disengagement. Since racism is necessarily uncomfortable in that it is oppressive, white insistence on racial comfort guarantees racism will not be faced except in the most superficial of ways.

Antiracist educator Darlene Flynn exposes how the expectation that whites should feel safe or comfortable when discussing race is a function of white privilege when she replies, "You mean you usually feel safe racially? That must be a great feeling. It's not something people of color can take for granted or expect, much less demand."

We Are Racially Arrogant

Racism includes strongly positive images of whites as well as strongly negative images of racial "others" ("I worked hard for what I have, why can't they?"). For whites, this self-image engenders a sense of entitlement to the resources of society. Because whites are not educated about racism in schools or mainstream culture, and because it benefits us not to do so, we have a very limited understanding of racism. Yet racial dominance leads to racial arrogance, and in this racial arrogance, whites have no compunction about debating with people who have thought complexly about race. Whites generally feel free to dismiss these informed perspectives rather than acknowledge that they are unfamiliar, reflect on them further, or seek more information.

Because of white social, economic, and political power within a white supremacist culture, whites are in the position to legitimize people of color's assertions of racism. Yet whites are the least likely to see, understand, or be invested in validating those assertions and being honest about their consequences. This leads whites to claim that they disagree with perspectives that challenge their worldview when, in fact, they don't understand the perspective—thus confusing not understanding with not agreeing. The issue is that we don't understand racism. Declaring that we don't agree presumes that we are in an informed position that qualifies our disagreement.

Further, this racial arrogance, coupled with the need for racial comfort, also has whites demanding that people of color explain racism in the "right" way. The right way is politely, without any show of emotional upset. When racism is explained in a way that white people can see and understand, then its validity may be granted. While we rarely acknowledge our own racism, we are occasionally receptive to acknowledging someone else's. These patterns prevent us from assuming the humility necessary for cross-racial understanding.

We Focus on Intent and Ignore Impact

A common white reasoning is that as long as we didn't *intend* to perpetuate racism, then our actions *don't count* as racism. In other words, we focus on our intentions and discount the impact of our behaviors, thereby invalidating the experience of people of color. We then spend a great deal of energy explaining to people of color why our behavior is not racism at all. This enables us to deny responsibility for our behavior's *impact* in both the immediate interaction, and the broader, historical context. This focus on intent rather than impact often surfaces when a person of color tries to give a white person feedback. The white person deflects the feedback by responding, "but, I didn't mean to." The "but" in the sentence conveys that it shouldn't matter because it wasn't intended. The person is essentially saying, "Yes, I did do that, BUT I didn't mean it as racism so you should not be hurt and I should not be held accountable." It's much more productive to say, "While I didn't mean to hurt you in that way, I see that I did, and I am sorry."

Focusing on intentions rather than impact is reinforced institutionally. In order to legally substantiate a claim of racism, one must prove intentions, which is virtually impossible to do. Notice that legally, the impact or outcome of behavior is not as relevant—intent is what must be proven. Unless someone explicitly admits that they intended to perpetrate racism (and few people can or will admit this), how can you prove that they did? This is one example of what it means to say that racism is institutional. The system is set up in a way that makes addressing racism very difficult, while not appearing on its face to be racially biased. In fact, on its face it appears racially fair—we now have policies that protect against racial discrimination! Yet the need to demonstrate intent has made it very difficult for people of color to get legal recourse or justice in cases involving racism. This policy is rooted in a white understanding of racism: the racist = bad/not racist = good binary, from which only a bad person would intend to have a racist impact. We can assume that the people who crafted such a policy were primarily white, because whites hold the institutional positions that enable them to make policies such as this.

We Are Not Aware of Our Racial Power

Many white people cannot relate to the idea of racial power because we don't *feel* it; we aren't aware that we have power over other people. Indeed, in many areas of our lives we may feel deeply disempowered as we struggle against others who have power over *us*—such as a supervisor or parent. If we are in a minoritized group somewhere else in our lives—perhaps we are gay or lesbian, or Jewish, or have a disability—we definitely are not socially and institutionally powerful in those areas of our lives. But so much of racism is internalized for whites; it is not on a conscious level. Of course when we are telling a racist joke or discussing how much better our neighborhoods are, we are outwardly manifesting superiority, but most of white superiority is internalized and unconscious.

We often expect that power will be something that we are aware of, rather than something that we can take for granted. The issue of social power is where being in a minoritized position other than race often becomes confused with a lack of racial privilege. For example, in discussions about race I often hear white working-class men protest that they don't have any social power. They work long and grueling hours, often in jobs in which they have no long-term security, and come home feeling beaten and quite disempowered. These men cannot relate to the concept of holding social power. But if being able to *feel* racial privilege is required before whites can acknowledge its reality, we will not be able to see (and thus change) it. The key to recognizing power is in recognizing *normalcy*—what is not attended to or in need of constant navigation. These men are indeed struggling against social and economic barriers, but race is simply not one of them; in fact, race is a major social current running in their direction and not only moving them along, but helping them navigate their other social struggles.

If we think about power a little differently, it may be easier to see and acknowledge. Conceptualize power as the *absence of struggle* in a key area of life. For example, we may be dealing with a boss who is a bully, but we are not *also* dealing with their racism toward us. We may be dealing with heterosexism or ableism, but we are not *also* dealing with racism. In other words, a person who uses a wheelchair will have a different experience, depending on whether they are white or a person of color. White people who use a wheelchair will not *also* be dealing with the racism of whites they depend on to meet their daily needs. White gay or lesbian people will not *also* be dealing with racism, including the racism of the whites in their own gay community.

We Live Segregated Lives

In Chapter 9, I discussed the power of segregation to shape my identity. Because I see segregation as one of the primary manifestations of modern racism, in this chapter I want to discuss segregation in more depth. Drawing upon many concepts previously discussed, I will analyze one of the anonymous student essays written in response to the question, "How has your race shaped your life?" This student wrote:

> I was really lucky. I grew up in an all-white neighborhood and went to mostly white schools, so I didn't learn anything about racism. My family taught me that everyone is the same. (ASR)

As may be seen from the other excerpts I have reproduced throughout this book, this response is not an anomaly; some variation on this theme is very common in response to the question of the meaning of race in a white person's life. As such, it provides a powerful illustration of the ways white people make sense of racism. First, the idea that to grow up in an all-white environment is to avoid race and racism reveals the belief that whites are *outside* of race; we are just human (universalism). We see race as what people of color have (or *are*). If people of color are not present, race is not present. Further, if people of color are not present, not only is race absent, so is that terrible thing: racism. Ironically, this positions racism as something people of color have and bring to whites, rather than a system which whites control and impose on people of color. To place race and racism on people of color and to see race and racism as absent in an all-white neighborhood also reinforces the idea of whiteness as innocence.

Second, an all-white neighborhood is not the product of luck (or a benign preference to be with one's own, or a fluke or accident); all-white neighborhoods are the end result of centuries of racist policies, practices, and attitudes, which have systematically denied people of color entrance into white neighborhoods. In the past this was done legally. Today this is accomplished through more subtle mechanisms such as discrimination in lending; real estate practices that steer homebuyers into specific areas; not funding public transportation that could make suburbs more accessible; funding schools based on real estate taxes, which penalize those who don't own homes and keep them out of "good" neighborhoods; narratives that associate white space with goodness and safety; and white flight. All-white neighborhoods and schools don't happen naturally; they are actively constructed and maintained.

The third problem with this statement is the student's sense that this environment was racially neutral, rather than racially active. Socialization is a concept that is hard for many of us to understand. Living in a culture that elevates the individual and teaches us that we can be anything if we just try hard enough, we have the sense that we can merely decide to reject our socialization and that this decision is all it takes. Those who are able to acknowledge that we are shaped by socialization usually see it as in the past—messages we received as children but are no longer receiving. We also tend to see it as solely taking place in our families—whatever our families explicitly taught us is the only conditioning we believe we have received. Popular discourse furthers this idea by constantly declaring that it all comes down to "the parents." If you come from a "good" family you will do well, but if you come from a "bad" family you will do poorly.

Because many of us see socialization as something that only happens to us when we are young (if at all), it is difficult for us to recognize the forces that continue to socialize us throughout our lives. Given this, it can be very difficult to understand that an all-white environment is affecting us. But a segregated environment is racially *active*. Race has not been removed from that space—race is at play in the very perception that it is absent. To live, work, study, and worship in segregation sends powerful messages about what—*and who*—is normal, good, and valuable. The more time we spend in segregation, the more comfortable and familiar it becomes to us. We know less about and become less interested in the perspectives of people of color; policies and practices we develop will reflect this myopic view. We rely more and more on superficial and racist representations of people of color from the media and from those around us. Our own racial perspectives become more and more limited while becoming more and more validated by the culture at large. Segregation reinforces racism within and without us in each and every moment. *Segregation is not neutral;* it is *lived* and, as such, is socializing us in every moment.

When I discuss racial segregation in schools with my virtually all-white classes, they are quick to respond that although there were only a few kids of color in their school, "no one had an issue with them." Often the person telling me this will also mention a "good friend" who is a person of color. My students' responses are in keeping with surveys that show that 80% of whites claim to have black friends. But research shows differently. A 2014 study by the Public Religion Research Institute showed that 91% of the average white American's closest friends and family members are white, and just 1% are black (2013 American Values). When asked to name their closest friends and family members, 75% of white Americans did not name even one person who was not white. Yet most of my white students insist that they *do* have black friends.

After some reflection on this phenomenon, I think that the elevation of black sports and music idols may have created a false sense of having cross-ra-cial relationships for many white youth: I love your CDs; I read about you and follow your career; I talk about you with my friends; I have your poster on my wall and look at your image every day; and I *feel like I know you.*

When I point out racism in toys and dolls, students counter by offering the American Girl doll series, which has dolls of color. For these students, the dolls are evidence that children today are racially open. A white girl can buy the exact clothes worn by her Native American or black doll, and these outfits are advertised as allowing a girl and her doll to become "best friends." I think these dolls and idols give young people a false sense that they have relationships with people of color that they don't actually have in their real lives. Even when they do have real friends of color, the sense of closeness is not mutual.

Notably, when students of color who went to mostly white schools talk about their experiences, these experiences were almost always very painful, even traumatic. When so much of whiteness is invisible to whites, how can we say the few kids of color in our schools had no issues? There is a great deal of research documenting the differences between how students and faculty of color experience schools and how white students and faculty experience it (see Lee, 2005; Olsen, 2008). Generally, whites see their schools as places that welcome diversity and affirm all students. Lee and Olsen found that far from affirming diversity, the dominant norms of schools privilege whites and exclude students of color. When whites do perceive racial tensions in school, they attribute the cause of these tensions to people of color. Kailin's findings (2002) confirm that most white teachers operate from a very limited consciousness about racism. In her study, the majority of teachers assigned blame for racism to blacks. She also found that of those who noticed racist behavior by their white colleagues, the majority remained silent and did not challenge this behavior. Many white teachers and administrators believe that if they are not aware of racial tension, there is none. At the same time, faculty of color who raise racial issues are seen as the problem and accused of being racist toward whites for suggesting that racism is present. This puts people of color in a double bind: they either have to endure racism or be penalized for challenging it.

This is yet another example of our lack of humility in the face of our racial blindness. It is also an example of our narrow definition of racism as explicit acts such as beatings or cross burnings (although these things also happen), rather than as a deeply embedded system shaping our lives. People of color learn very early that trying to talk to white people about race goes nowhere, and often makes the situation worse. An African heritage colleague of mine has a 21-year-old son who attended predominantly white schools. She explains:

> The kids of color do not believe that their white "friends" can deal with anything related to race, so they don't bring it to them. And of course, the white kids don't initiate those kinds of conversations—except by accident when their racism slips out. Then the kid of color has to make a decision about how valuable her/his white "friend" is. If they do feel that they are valuable, the comments are endured, unless they are just completely unbearable. But their standard for what a friendship can be with a white peer remains low. When they're with other kids of color they talk about how clueless the white kids are. (anonymous email correspondence, 12/8/2011)

These dilemmas for people of color who have friendships with whites are in part the result of whites living the bulk of their lives in segregation. This segregation prevents the development of cross-racial understanding and communication skills within a society that cannot admit that segregation has meaning.

In addition to reinforcing many problematic racial ideologies, living in segregation also maintains ignorance of how racism impacts the lives of people of color. Many whites believe that people of color are doing much better than they actually are. Indeed, many whites believe that *they* are now the disadvantaged minority (Wise, 2015). This misperception causes us to minimize and invalidate the experiences of people of color. It also causes us to feel resentful at our imagined disadvantage, and thus actually be punitive toward people of color in our policies and practices. For example: giving greater penalties to those who use crack cocaine than those who use powder cocaine; not allowing someone convicted of a felony to vote, even after they have served their time; and the elimination of Affirmative Action and other programs intended to ameliorate the impact of racial discrimination.

Returning to the student quoted above, contrary to her assertion that she didn't learn anything about racism, she learned a *great deal* about racism in her neighborhood and schools. The entirety of her childhood education of race occurred in a racially segregated environment. Even if we grant that she only grew up in segregation and never heard or saw an explicitly racist comment or image (which is virtually impossible), by what means did she come to define and understand race? There is a profound contradiction in saying to our children, "Everyone is the same" yet never having a person of color sitting at your dinner table as a friend and equal. Conveying to our children that living in a white neighborhood makes them lucky, rather than conveying to them that they have *lost* something valuable, is to teach them a great deal about race.

In Conclusion

In this chapter I have discussed some of the dynamics that obscure racism and make it difficult for whites to see and understand. But of all these dynamics, the two that I believe most powerfully obscure racism for whites are individualism and the racist = bad/not racist = good binary. Readers may notice that again and again I return to these two dynamics in explaining misconceptions

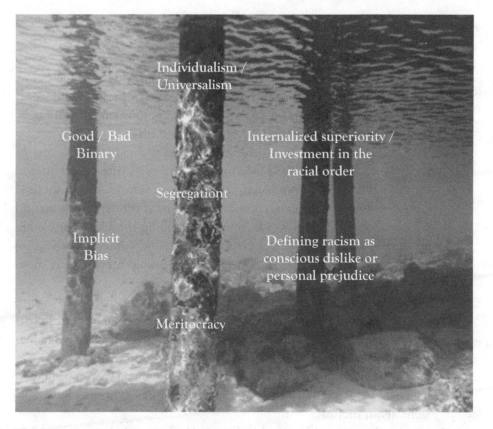

Figure 41. Pier Supports.

about racism. Readers who may have felt defensive at various points through-out this book may also notice that the bulk of defensiveness can be traced to a challenge to one of two dynamics: seeing oneself as an individual; or a sense that I am suggesting that they are "bad." So I repeat: 1. Racism is a complex and multidimensional system in which we are all immersed. This system is reinforced both within us (in terms of our socialization) and outside of us (in terms of institutions). 2. This system is not our fault, and I do not see whites as bad people. But I do see us as responsible for changing this system from which we unfairly benefit. Institutionalized racism is the societal default; to not act *against* it is to collude *with* it. Returning to the pier metaphor, we can now identify the key pillars that prop of new racism.

Discussion Questions

1. If you are white, when was the last time someone challenged you to look at an aspect of yourself related to racism? How did you feel? How did you respond? What insights did/can you gain from the exchange? If no one has ever challenged you or not in a very long time, what might that tell you about how whiteness shapes your life?

2. The author contends that "the ideology of Individualism is one of the primary barriers to well meaning (and other) white people understanding racism." In what ways is this ideology transmitted in society? Consider figures of speech, cultural norms, institutional practices, and popular culture. When you imagine challenging the idea that we are all unique and that if you don't know someone you can't generalize about them, what thoughts and feelings come up for you? Do these thoughts and feelings support or challenge racism?

3. The author suggests that one of the most significant barriers to white people developing racial literacy is the Good/Bad binary (e.g. *Racists are bad. If I am good I cannot be racist. If you suggest I am involved in racism you are saying I am a bad person*). How have you seen this binary at play in white people? If you are white, how have you seen it at play in yourself? How might you respond when the binary surfaces in discussions about racism?

4. Discuss the pillars identified in Figure 41. Try to explain each one in your own words. Provide examples of these pillars on both the individual and societal levels.

5. Using an antiracist framework, how would you respond to a white person who said, "You just want me to feel bad and guilty about something that I had nothing to do with"?

· 1 1 ·

INTERSECTING IDENTITIES—
AN EXAMPLE OF CLASS

> The true focus of revolutionary change is never the oppressive situations which we seek to escape, but that piece of the oppressor which is planted deep within us.
>
> —Audre Lorde

Intersectionality is the term scholars use to acknowledge the reality that we simultaneously occupy multiple groups—both oppressed and privileged positions—and that these positions intersect in complex ways (Crenshaw, 1991). It is a very rare individual who is in dominant groups in every aspect of social life. For example, poor whites, while oppressed through classism, are also elevated by race privilege, so that to be poor and Asian, for example, is not the same experience as being poor and white. Further, because of sexism, to be a poor white female will create barriers that a poor white male will not face due to gender privilege. However, while the poor white female will have to deal with sexism and classism, she will not have to deal with the racism that a poor Latina female will face. Thus, while all women experience sexism, they experience it differently based on its interaction with their other social group identities. Facing oppression in one area of social life does not "cancel out" your privilege in another; these identities will be more or less salient in different situations. The challenge is to identify how our identities play out in shifting social contexts. In this chapter, I trace how another key identity—class—intersects with race through the example of my own life.

Intersectionality: The understanding that we simultaneously occupy multiple social positions and that these positions do not cancel each other out, they interact in complex ways that must be explored and understood.

Growing up, I always knew I was poor. While my class oppression has been relatively visible to me, my race privilege has not. In my efforts to uncover how race has shaped my life, I have gained deeper insight by placing race in the center of my analysis and asking how each of my other group locations has socialized me to collude with racism. In so doing, I have been able to address in greater depth my multiple social locations and how they function together to hold racism in place. Thus my exploration of what it means to be white is inseparable from what it means to be poor, for my understanding of race is inextricably entwined with my class background. I now make the distinction that I grew up poor *and* white, for my experience of poverty would have been different had I not been white. For whites who experience oppression in other areas of our lives (such as class, gender, religion, or sexual orientation), it can be difficult to center a location through which we experience privilege. When leading discussions in multicultural education courses, I find that white students often resist centering racism in their analysis, feeling that to do so invalidates other identities in which they are minoritized. These students feel that these minoritized identities make them "less" racially privileged. But rather than ameliorating my race privilege, my oppressed class location was a primary avenue through which I came to understand the meaning of whiteness. As I work to unravel my internalized racial dominance, I have found two key questions useful: how does internalized dominance function collectively for whites, regardless of our other social locations, and how did I learn racism *specifically through my class oppression* (DiAngelo, 2006).

I was born to working-class parents; my father was a construction worker and my mother occasionally found work as a telephone operator. When I was two, my parents divorced and my mother began to raise us on her own. As she was a single mother without a college education, steady job, or health care, we soon fell into poverty. When I was 7 she was diagnosed with leukemia, making it ever more difficult for her to hold a job (she died in a military hospital, 5 years later, at the age of 37). I have never understood people who say, "We were poor but we didn't know it because we had lots of love." Poverty hurts. It isn't romantic, or some form of "living simply." Poor people are not inno- cent and child-like. The lack of medical and dental care, the hunger, and the ostracization, are concrete. The stress of poverty made my household much more chaotic than loving.

We were evicted frequently, and moved 4–5 times a year. There were peri- ods when oatmeal was the only food in our house. I had no medical or dental care during my childhood, and today all of my front teeth are filled because by the time I was 10 they had visible cavities. My teacher once held my hands up to my 4th-grade class as an example of poor hygiene, and with the class as her audience, told me to go home and tell my mother to wash me. If we got sick, my mother would scream that we could not get sick because she could not afford to take us to the doctor. We occasionally had to live in our car, and once I was left with relatives for 8 months while my mother tried to secure housing for us in another state.

I used to stare at the girls in my class and ache to be like them—to have a father, to wear new and pretty clothes, to go to camp, to be clean and get to sit with them. I knew we didn't have enough money, and that meant that I couldn't be in their circle at school or go to their houses or have the same things they had. But the moment the real meaning of poverty crystallized for me came when we were visiting another family. As we were leaving I heard one of the daughters ask her mother, "What is wrong with them?" I stopped, riveted. I, too, wanted to know. Her mother held her finger to her lips and whispered, "Shhh, they're *poor*." This was a revelatory moment for me. The shock came not just in the knowledge that we were poor, but that it was *exposed*. There was something wrong with us, indeed, and it was something that was obvious to others and that we couldn't hide, something shameful that could be seen but should not be named. It took me many years to gain a structural analysis of class that would help shift this sense of shame.

From an early age I had the sense of being an outsider; I was acutely aware that I was poor, that I was dirty, that I was not *normal*, and that there was something "wrong" with me. But I also knew that I was *not* black. We were at the lower rungs of society, but there was always someone just below us. I knew that "colored" people existed and that they should be avoided. I can remem- ber many occasions when I reached for candy or uneaten food laying on the street and was admonished by my grandmother not to touch it because a "col- ored person" may have touched it. The message was clear to me: if a colored person touched something, it became dirty. The irony here is that the marks of poverty were clearly visible on me: poor hygiene, torn clothes, homelessness, hunger. Yet through comments such as my grandmother's, a racial Other was formed in my consciousness—an Other through whom I became clean. Race was the one identity that aligned me with the other girls in my school.

I left home as a teenager and struggled to survive. As I looked at what lay ahead, I could see no path out of poverty other than education. The decision to take that path was terrifying for me; I had never gotten the message that I was smart, and academia was a completely foreign social context. But once I was in academia, I understood that a college degree is not conferred upon those who are smarter or who try harder than others. It comes through a complex web of intersecting systems of privilege that include internal expectations as well as external resources.

Raised in poverty, I received a clear message from society that I was inferior to other white people from higher social classes. At the same time, I received another message: I was superior to people of color. This message was delivered on the individual level, through comments and stories I was told about people of color, and from the society at large, through cultural representations of people of color, as well as their absence. As I reflect back on the early messages I received about being poor and being white, I now realize that my family and I *needed* people of color to cleanse and re-align us with the dominant white culture from which we had been separated by our poverty. I now ask myself how the classist messages I internalized growing up led me to collude in racism.

For example, as a child who grew up in poverty, I received constant messages that I was stupid, lazy, dirty, and a drain on the resources of hard-working people. I internalized these messages, and they still work to silence me. Unless I vigilantly work to uproot them, I am less likely to trust my own perceptions or feel like I have a "right" to speak up. I may not attempt to interrupt racism because the social context in which it is occurring intimidates me (for example, the social context of academia or professional business meetings). My fear on these occasions may be coming from a place of internalized class inferiority, but in practice my silence colludes with racism and ultimately benefits me by protecting my white privilege and maintaining racial solidarity with other white people. This solidarity connects and realigns me with white people across other lines of difference, such as class. I am also prone to use others to elevate me, as in the example with my grandmother. So while my specific class background mediated the way I learned racism and how I enact it, in the end it still socialized me to collude with the overall structure.

   A story from Greek mythology may help us to visualize how intersection-ality works. Sisyphus was a king who was being punished by the gods. He had to roll an immense boulder up a hill. As soon as he got it to the top, it rolled back down and he had to start over again, for eternity. My diagram shows two of my "boulders"—classism and sexism—barriers that I have had to struggle against in order to get where I am today. These boulders can be thought of as my *internalized* oppression (lack of self-confidence) as well as the *external* limitations (institutional barriers) I have had to navigate based on my class and gender. But there is a major boulder that I do not have to push, and that is racism. In fact, the "wind" generated by others who do push that boulder has helped me get mine up the hill. In other words, my white privilege has helped me deal with my class and gender oppression, and has elevated me over others, some of whom were also raised poor and female but are not white. Now that I am in academia I fit in. I look like and *I am assumed to* belong, and I do not have to push against and navigate racism every day as my colleagues of color do. Indeed, I am more likely to succeed in academia if I don't challenge racism, thereby maintaining white privilege and solidarity. Figure 42 illus-trates my Sisyphean struggle regarding three of my key social identities.

   It is my observation that class dictates proximity between whites and peo-ple of color. Poor urban whites are often in close proximity to people of color because they tend to live in the same or nearby neighborhoods. I hear the

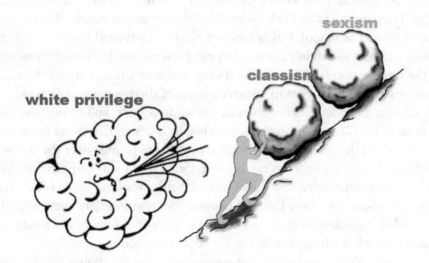

Figure 42. My Sisyphean struggle.

term "white trash" frequently. It is not without significance that this is one of the few expressions in which race is named for whites. I think the reason for this is the proximity of the people labeled as white trash to people of color; race becomes marked or "exposed" by virtue of a closeness to people of color. In a racist society, this closeness both highlights, and pollutes, whiteness. That people of color are seen as trash is implied and needs no racial qualifier. The popularity of shows such as Jerry Springer and Maury Povich rests on their mockery of poor people. Note that these shows are highly racially diverse in terms of white people and people of color, and the white guests behave in exactly the same stereotypical manner as do the black guests: unwed mothers of multiple children who don't know who the fathers are; fathers with babies by several women who don't pay child support; barefoot women cursing and fist-fighting over men; mothers sleeping with their daughters' boyfriends; cousins in love with each other; welfare cheats. In aligning poor blacks and poor whites in these behaviors and coaching the guests to behave in extremely negative and stereotypical ways, these shows reinforce the concept of white trash. I ask my readers to think about a term that refers to any human being as "trash," and the profound classism and racism inherent in using this term for people who are marginalized in society through race and poverty.

Owning-class people may also have people of color near them because people of color are often their domestics and gardeners—their servants. But they do not interact socially with people of color in the same way that poor whites do. Middle-class whites are generally the furthest away from people of color. They are the most likely to say that "there were no people of color in my neighborhood or school. I didn't meet a black person until I went to college" (often adding, "so I didn't learn anything about racism"). These are examples of the intersection between race and class and how whites can use their class positions and socialization to unravel aspects of their racial socialization.

Class is much less flexible than we are led to believe, and throughout their lives most people remain in the same class into which were born. Still, class is one of the social groups that it is possible to change over the course of one's life. For example, I am no longer poor. While I still carry the marks of poverty, those marks are now only internal. Still, they limit me beyond what I believe I deserve or where I think I belong; they also interfere with my ability to stand up against injustice. As long as I believe that I am not as smart or as valuable as other white people, I won't challenge racism.

I believe that in order for whites to unravel our internalized racial dominance, we have two interwoven tasks. One is to work on our own internalized oppression—the ways in which we impose limitations on ourselves based on the societal messages we receive about the inferiority of the lower-status groups to which we belong.

The other task is to face the internalized dominance that results from being socialized in a racist society—the ways in which we consciously or unconsciously believe that we are more important, more valuable, more intelligent, and more deserving than people of color. I cannot address the interwoven complexity of other white people's social locations. However, after years of facilitating dialogues on race with thousands of white people from a range of class positions (as well as varied gender, sexual orientation, religious, and ability positions), and bearing witness to countless stories and challenges from people of color about my own racism and that of other whites, I have come to see some very common patterns of internalized dominance. These patterns are shared across other social positions: regardless of one's other locations, white people know on some level that being white in this society is "better" than being a person of color, and this, along with the very real doors opened by whiteness, serves to mediate the oppression experienced in those other social locations.

I have found that a key to interrupting my internalized racial dominance is to defer to the knowledge of people whom I have been taught, in countless ways, are less knowledgeable and less valuable than I am. I must reach for humility and be willing to *not know*. I may never fully understand the workings of racism, as I have been trained my entire life to perpetuate racism while denying its reality. I do not have to understand racism for it to be real, and my expectation that I could is part of my internalized dominance. Reaching for racial humility as a white person is not the same for me as being mired in class shame.

My class position is only one social location from which I learned to collude with racism. For example, I have also asked myself how I learned to collude with racism as a Catholic and a woman. How did it shape my sense of racial belonging, of racial *correctness*, to be presented with God, the ultimate and universal authority, as white? How did the active erasure of Jesus's race and ethnicity shape my racial consciousness? How did the universalization of Catholicism as the true religion for all peoples of the world engender racial superiority within me when all the authorities within that religion were white like myself? At the same time, how did my conditioning under Catholicism not to question authority lead me to silently collude with the racism of other whites?

As a white woman, how did I internalize racial superiority through the culture's representation of white women as the embodiment of ultimate beauty? What has it meant for me to have a key signifier of female perfection—whiteness—available to me? How have images of white women in the careers deemed valuable for women shaped my goals? How has mainstream feminism's articulation of white women's issues as universal women's issues shaped what I care about? At the same time, what has it meant to live under patriarchy and to be taught that as a female I am less intelligent, that I should not speak up, that I should defer to others, and at all times be nice and polite? How have all of these messages ultimately set me up to collude in the oppression of people of color? By asking questions such as these I have been able to gain a much deeper and more useful analysis of racism. Rather than denying my other minoritized positions, I find that centering racism has been a profound way to address the complexity of all my social locations.

Discussion Questions

1. Consider some aspects of your positionality other than race (i.e., gender, sexual orientation, religion, class, ability, nationality, age). What did you learn about race and racism through these social locations?
2. If you are white, reflect on the patterns of internalized oppression that you developed as a result of a group wherein you are minoritized. What are these patterns and how do they set you up to collude with racism?
3. If you are part of a social group that is targeted with oppression (other than or in addition to racism), how does that form of internalized oppression impact your ability to work against racism?
4. How can challenging a form of oppression you benefit from help address the internalized oppression you developed as a result of being in a minoritized group?
5. There have been social media critiques of "white feminism." What are some examples of "white feminism"? What would an intersectional approach look like?

· 1 2 ·

COMMON PATTERNS OF
WELL-MEANING WHITE PEOPLE

> My town is not racially diverse at all so I would say that I never really focused on my
> own race at all. My family, school, and neighbors have all given messages of tolerance
> regarding race when I was growing up, and I was taught to treat everyone equally. I
> was taught to always be sensitive to race by using P.C. terms when speaking about
> race. (ASR)

Although we are taught to see ourselves as individuals, we are socialized collectively. This collective socialization results in predictable group patterns of engagement. For over 15 years I have led white people in discussions of race, allowing me an exceptional opportunity to observe some of these patterns. This chapter explores some of the most common.

Guilt

Guilt is a common response for whites when they begin to take racism seriously. White guilt can be a general reaction to the realization that racism is a system from which they benefit while others suffer. White guilt can also be a response to a more specific incident; perhaps a white person has been given feedback (or has realized independently) that they have just said or done something with a racist impact. Guilt is, of course, a normal response and in and of itself is not problematic. However, it is what we do with the guilt that matters. We can use our guilt to avoid further engagement ("It just makes me feel too bad so I don't want to deal with it") or become resentful ("You are making me feel guilty and that is not fair!") or we can become incapacitated ("I am such a bad person—I give up"). Notice that all of these responses exempt us from any further action and thus protect our position and privilege while indirectly blaming people of color or antiracist whites who "cause us" to feel guilty.

Racism and our involvement in it cannot be avoided, and that is not our fault. We did not choose to be born into a culture in which racism was embedded, nor did we choose to be socialized into entitlement and superiority. I believe that most of us would not have chosen this socialization if we had been given the choice. But racism is real and we are involved in it, so we must take *responsibility* and work against it. Guilt and responsibility are not the same thing. The best antidote to guilt is accountability and corrective action.

Seeking Absolution

When given specific feedback about our racism we can become subservient ("I'll do anything you ask to make up for how terrible I am") or we can beg for absolution ("I am so sorry, please tell me everything is OK and you are not mad at me"). However, these responses are not constructive. They put an unfair burden on the person who named the issue, and when that person is a person of color, that burden is particularly problematic. Asking for absolution puts the focus back on you and demands more time and attention from the injured party, essentially demanding more energy from them than it took to give the feedback in the first place. Although not intentional, this is like a second injury or micro-aggression. Micro-aggressions are the myriad slights that people of color endure on a daily basis, most often from well-intentioned whites (see Sue et al., 2007).

> **Micro-Aggressions**: The everyday slights and insults that people of color endure and most white people don't notice or concern themselves with.

Giving feedback to whites on racism is very risky because we are so often defensive and unreceptive. We need to appreciate the risk taken, sit with our feelings, and give the other person some space for theirs. Then, when we are ready, we need to do whatever is necessary to move forward. Sometimes what we need to do is as simple as listening.

Feeling Indignant/Unfairly Accused

While it is certainly ubiquitous, white superiority is also unnamed and denied by most whites. We whites who see ourselves as "against racism" often base our identities in a denial of the racially based privileges we hold. We more often opt to protect what we perceive as our moral reputations, rather than recognize or change our participation. This is why pointing out white advantage will often trigger patterns of confusion, defensiveness, and righteous indignation. These responses enable us to protect our moral character against what we perceive as an accusation while deflecting any recognition of culpability or need of accountability. Focusing on restoring our moral standing through these tactics, we are able to avoid the question of white privilege.

For most whites the worst thing to be called is "racist." This is due to many of the dynamics I've already discussed: misconceptions about what racism actually is; the racist = bad/not racist = good binary; the internalization of racial superiority coupled with the need to deny it; our investment in racism; and our investment in ideologies such as meritocracy and individualism. Thus the response to the suggestion of racism is usually highly emotional and defensive. This defensiveness works on multiple levels to: position the white person as morally superior while obscuring the true power of social locations; blame others with less social power for their discomfort; falsely position that discomfort as dangerous; and reinforce the narrative of white racial innocence. Positioning ourselves as the victims of antiracist efforts, we cannot be the beneficiaries of white privilege. Claiming that it is *we* who have been unfairly treated by the very *suggestion* that we are implicated in racism, we are able to demand that more social resources (such as time and attention) be channeled in our direction to help us cope with this mistreatment.

> **Remember:** Racism is more than individual racial bias. Racism is a multilayered system into which we are all born and socialized in the United States. No one can avoid this socialization. To say that a white person has done something that has a racist impact is not the same as saying they are bad.

Objectifying

Objectifying refers to the white tendency to overemphasize the race of people of color. Whites may constantly ask them questions related to race, make racial jokes or comments they don't normally make with white people, ask personal questions about their racial experiences, ask them to speak on behalf of their group ("What's the black perspective on that?") and generally bring up race in ways they don't with fellow whites. Whites may also emphasize how beautiful a person of color is, and make comments about their hair or skin, which objectifies and exoticizes people of color. This happens in personal relationships, but also in organizations, wherein people of color are made highly visible. They may be continually asked to appear in photos in order to make the organization appear more diverse than it is, or they may be invited to sit on every committee so that the committee "has diversity," or they may be asked to handle anything in the organization related to diversity or multiculturalism. This places a great burden on the person while reinforcing many problematic dynamics, such as the continual reduction of people of color to their race, the perception that people of color represent their race (but whites do not), and the idea that racial or multicultural issues are the domain of people of color, but "normal" issues are the domain of white people.

When people of color do sit on committees, they are in the awkward position of having to represent the "racial perspective," while whites are not asked to represent the "white perspective." There is great diversity within and between groups of color, and representing them all is impossible. Further, whites are often satisfied with just one person of color (feeling that they are "covered"), but this form of "window dressing" generally stops there and does not recognize the dynamics that will inevitably play out in the group. Often, the perspectives of that one person on the committee are not heard or validated, especially if it's a perspective that is unfamiliar or one that feels threatening to the status quo.

To illustrate, imagine a typical white-dominated organization. There are a few people of color scattered throughout. A work committee is formed, consisting of 10 white people and 1 person of color. A woman of color is invited to the committee in order to give the "multicultural perspective." That is problematic enough, but the dynamics present in the group will likely be even more problematic. Given the patterns of white dominance, what might that group feel like to her? Will she risk giving her perspective if it is contrary to everyone else's? Will she be heard? Will she be allowed to name the patterns she sees and not risk her job? If she challenges these patterns will she be seen as angry, combative, or "always playing the race card?" Most likely, her "multicultural" perspective will only be welcome if it doesn't challenge the status quo in any significant way. While the intention of inviting a "minority" to participate may be good, there are skills and perspectives that need to be developed on the part of the *white* members of the group. Without these skills and perspectives on the part of whites, people of color in organizations have to deal with a significant level of racial stress and may quickly burn out.

When people of color are asked to be the face of a white-dominated organization in order for it to appear more diverse, they are put on the spot to promote something that is false. An example of this is when people of color are vastly underrepresented on a college campus, but their faces appear in the college's promotional materials in order to attract more students of color. While I understand the dilemma—the campus wants to attract more students of color and avoid reinforcing whiteness in their promotional materials—the practice is still a form of false advertising that places an unfair burden on the student who is continually asked to be in the photos and promote the appearance of a campus climate that doesn't exist. There are many consultants available who can assist the college in attracting racial diversity in more meaningful and effective ways.

Rushing to Prove Ourselves

Rushing to prove ourselves refers to the white pattern of wanting to prove to people of color that we are "not racist." This pattern rests on the racist = bad/not racist = good binary and the need to be seen as a good person. Many years ago I fell headlong into this trap. My partner and I went out to dinner with another couple who were friends of hers. This couple was black. At this point in my life I had rarely spent time with people of color and in my excitement, I wanted them to know that I was "not racist." I quickly began telling them how racist my family was, and my grandmother in particular. I then proceeded to tell them all of the incredibly racist things I had heard my grandmother say. I thought this would show how progressive I was, since unlike my grandmother, I knew these things were racist and I would never say them. The couple looked very uncomfortable and I knew something was wrong, but this incident took place years before my journey toward antiracism and I had no idea what I had done.

I realize now that I had engaged in several problematic cross-racial dynamics. First, I had objectified them by immediately bringing the conversation to race. I would never have done this if they were not people of color, and that fact was not lost on them. I emphasized their race and reinforced the idea that race is only a topic of interest when people of color are present—whites don't discuss race because we are outside of race and would only bring it up to make a joke or discuss some incident in the news. But worse, in sharing racist things that other whites had said, I was still forcing the couple to hear these racist comments. It didn't make any difference where the comments originated. They were awful and I repeated them to this couple. That did not make me look "not racist," but racially clueless. Imagine what a depressing evening that was for them, as I subjected them to the re-telling of countless racist comments.

I have seen this dynamic play out in other, perhaps less obvious ways: a white person going through the check-out line of a cashier who is a person of color, and takes out their family pictures in order to show the cashier—a complete stranger—that there are people of color in their family; throwing a high-5 when we wouldn't throw one to a white person; referring to a black person as "my brotha"; gushing about our trip to China or other country we assume they are from; or telling the person that we had a Latino housekeeper and she was just like a member of the family. While these actions may be well intended, they work to objectify people of color, make their race hyper-visible, and put them on the spot. If they don't respond graciously, or if they try to point out what is problematic about our behavior, we accuse them of being oversensitive or of playing the race card. An irony is that these actions take place in a culture that professes colorblindness.

The need to prove ourselves also comes from what I believe is our genuine desire to be connected to people of color. Racism is taught—we are not born knowing that it is "better" to be white and to live separately from people of color. Many of my students report having had a friend or two of color when they were children, but having lost these friends when they got older—perhaps because they moved away or they reached dating age and their parents disapproved of cross-racial relationships. These students often feel some pain about the loss of these friendships. There are many contradictions within racism, and one is that we can feel superior to people of color while also "missing them" and desiring deeply to be connected. Still, rushing to prove ourselves is not useful. It is best to relax, earn trust, and slowly build authentic relationships.

Ignoring

People of color often report that white people ignore them, and that this is hurtful and insulting. Whites ignoring people of color can have several causes: we may actually not notice them, especially if they are from a racial group which is more "invisible" in dominant culture, such as people of Asian heritage;

we may be trying to act as if their race doesn't matter to us; we may feel uncomfortable or unsure how to interact cross-racially; we may fear making a "mistake"; we may be trying to pretend we are colorblind; or we may be manifesting unconscious racism that causes us to devalue them and their presence. All of these motivations are problematic in different ways, but ultimately serve to isolate the person of color, give them less social resources, and convey that we do not value them. While we don't want to go to the other extreme and objectify people of color, we should try to acknowledge their presence in the same way we acknowledge others, and in whatever way is appropriate in the setting.

Assuming People of Color Have the Same Experience We Do

As previously discussed, because we are taught that our social groups don't matter, we often assume that our experience is the same as people of color's. In other words, because race doesn't matter, if I feel comfortable in my community, so will they, or if I have only had positive experiences with the police, so have they, or if my race has not appeared to matter in my life, neither has theirs. Living in segregation where we are not exposed to the perspectives of people of color, and within a culture that centralizes the white perspective (in history, media, etc.), leads to this assumption. On the occasion that we do have the opportunity to hear the perspectives of people of color, we often don't listen, or not understanding their experiences, we minimize and discount them. This prevents us from understanding the differences in our perspectives and experiences.

For example, I recently attended a conference on white privilege. I thought the conference was wonderful—I found it very exciting to be among people who cared about the same issues that I did, I made many important connections, and I received much valuable information. During a break, I went on about how exciting the experience was to a group of friends of color who were also attending the conference. I just assumed that they would share my enthusiasm. But they did not find the conference exciting and energizing as I did. Being confronted head-on with the reality of white privilege in workshop after workshop was painful. Further, they were experiencing all kinds of slights from the white participants; just because the conference was about challenging white privilege didn't mean that it was free from it. Of course these slights were not apparent to me (indeed I had just committed one of my own). While for me it was more of a stimulating intellectual experience, for them it was much more emotionally demanding. Not having the history of harm from racism, I could "enjoy" the conference in a way that they could not. They are supporters of this conference and find it valuable, yet we have vastly different experiences of it based on our races. I try now to be much more sensitive to that fact, and instead of making universal declarations with which I assume they will agree, I speak for myself and ask them for their perspective.

In Stacey Lee's (2005) excellent ethnographic study of Hmong immigrant students in a U.S. school, *Up Against Whiteness: Race, School, and Immigrant Youth*, she found that the perceptions of the primarily white faculty were at odds with those of the students of color. While the faculty expressed pride in the school's diversity, they continually differentiated students of color from the white student population and measured their success against the school's ideal of whiteness. School officials viewed Hmong students as culturally deficient, which allowed faculty to position the students' needs as being too difficult to meet. They expected the language teachers to be responsible for them—even when the students were native English speakers (an example of the way racism manifests for Asian Americans—it is commonly assumed that they do not speak English and are all new immigrants—thus, they are ignored and excluded (Sue et al., 2009). As is common in many contexts, having some people of color present allowed whites to claim the social benefits of diversity (e.g., being seen as socially progressive and welcoming), while not actually being inclusive in any meaningful way.

By guiding readers through a specific context from the perspective of people of color, Lee provides an exceptional view into the everyday workings of whiteness. She illuminates the contrast between how whites perceive cross-racial dynamics and how people of color experience them. Developing white racial literacy requires an understanding that whiteness is present in all contexts, and a willingness to consider that an environment that feels racially comfortable for whites will often not feel that way for people of color. When we can recognize aspects of the environment that we take for granted but which are exclusionary for others, we can begin to change them.

Pretending Our Preference for Segregation Is Accidental

A common exercise in antiracist workshops is termed "Racial Caucusing" (or sometimes referred to as "racial affinity groups"), wherein participants are separated into their own racial groups to discuss the specific ways that racism manifests for their group. Whites meet together, biracial and multiracial people meet together, African heritage people, Asian heritage people, and so on. Separating by race allows the groups to discuss the specific ways that racism impacts them without the pressure of worrying about how their discussion might impact another group. Typically, the white group discusses internalized dominance, and the groups of color discuss internalized racial oppression.

As an illustration of how we experience society differently, people of color usually appreciate this exercise because it provides a rare opportunity to talk openly with their fellow group members about racism without having to worry about how whites are reacting, and gives them a break from the white patterns they have been dealing with throughout the workshop. Yet whites tend to find this exercise very uncomfortable. I think this is because this exercise interrupts individualism, universalism, and colorblindness, and it is likely the only time they have been so explicitly seen and named as *white people*, rather than as *just individuals* or *just people*. In other words, separating by race exposes them as white. Further, whites often feel disconcerted by not knowing what the other groups are talking about (are they talking about us? are they plotting something?); these are historical white fears.

I find it very interesting that whites live so much of their lives in racial segregation and appear to not only be comfortable with that segregation, but to prefer it, *as long as it isn't named as such*. If it appears to *just happen*, or be a *fluke*, or is just *human nature*, or is the only way to get our kids into the better schools, segregation is fine, because none of these rationales makes our racial segregation appear *intentional*. But if we are asked to intentionally separate by race, even if it's a temporary and strategic request *made in the name of challenging racism*, we often express upset and discomfort.

Only Acknowledging Racism in Other Whites, Not in Ourselves

Even white people who are willing to acknowledge the existence of racism and white privilege will still typically locate it in any white person other than themselves. For example, the most predictable pattern that will surface in a white caucus is that whites will immediately want to talk about the racism of *other* whites—whites who are not present in the group. In workshops, when I go over common patterns of white people, many whites will want to provide examples involving their co-workers or friends. At the end of the workshop they will say, "I sure wish so-and-so were here—*they* really needs this!" It is extremely rare for a white person to be willing to apply the information to *internally*. A group may be receptive to the workshop, open and engaged in all of the exercises, and ready and willing to point out problematic racial patterns in other people. But if the facilitators try to point out something racially problematic happening in the room—which is not uncommon because racism is ever present—the room breaks down.

A recent experience may illustrate this inability for many whites to look at themselves and their own racial patterns, rather than at others. I was co-leading an antiracist workshop with a woman of color. The group of 40 participants was racially diverse (approximately half people of color and half white) and tightly packed into a small training room. It was just before lunch and we were one-third of the way through an all-day session. I had just finished an in-depth presentation on white privilege that appeared to have gone well; the group listened attentively, and no challenges were raised. Next, my co-facilitator led the corollary presentation to the previous one: the impact of racism on people of color. She prefaced her talk with the statement, "I will now be specifically engaging the people of color in the room on the topic of how systematic white racism impacts us. This is a very sensitive conversation for us to have in the presence of white people, and I ask the white participants to simply listen."

Yet as she began presenting a list of ways that people of color are impacted by racism, a white woman repeatedly questioned her. My co-facilitator did her best to speak to the woman's questions, but the interruptions continued. Finally, the white woman declared, "I think it's more complex than that." Hopefully, at this point my readers can see for themselves why the white woman's engagement was very racially problematic: this is a sensitive discussion for people of color and white people were asked to just listen; she was dominating the discussion with repeated interruptions; she was undermining the leadership of the facilitator of color and derailing the presentation; she positioned herself as more knowledgeable than the facilitator—a person of color—on issues of internalized racial oppression; and she implied that the facilitator—an African heritage woman—was intellectually limited in her analysis. At this point, I leaned in and quietly asked my co-trainer if she would like me to intervene. She said yes, and I spoke up. As diplomatically as possible, I attempted to point out to the white participant what was racially problematic about her behavior. The woman was shocked and expressed outrage at the "accusation" that her actions could have a racist impact. The room erupted in emotion, dividing along the lines of whether the woman had been "mistreated" or not, with many people speaking at once. Other participants nervously withdrew from the discussion.

It should be clear that internalized dominance was manifesting in the white woman's interactions with my co-facilitator. The racist = bad/not racist = good binary was manifesting in the response to my pointing that out. The internalized dominance that the woman manifested was a result of socialization by the culture at large. *It is just a pattern*, not a measure of her morality or goodness. These patterns, while harmful to others, are not our fault, but need to be interrupted nonetheless. But the good/bad binary makes it impossible to look at, learn about, and change these patterns of internalized dominance. Until we can replace the binary with a new conceptualization of racism, we cannot move forward. If a workshop or other discussion can *only* go well as long as no evident white pattern is *ever* pointed out, racism will remain protected and intact.

Explaining Away/Justifying/Minimizing/Comforting

I believe that very few white people want to deliberately hurt a person of color. In my experience, when we realize that we *have* hurt them—when we can let our defenses down enough to take this in—we are truly remorseful and want to remedy the harm. It is also difficult for us to hear about how another white person hurt a person of color through their unaware racism, and it is common to want to support and comfort the person who was hurt. Unfortunately, in our attempts to do so, we often end up minimizing or invalidating the harm. I have been in countless cross-racial discussions in which a person of color shares an experience of white racism, and a white person then tries to explain to them that it wasn't really racism because the person didn't mean it that way, or that the person of color misunderstood the situation in some other way. While these responses may come from a desire to minimize the harm—in other words, "if you just understood that they didn't mean that, it wouldn't hurt you so much"—these responses only make the situation worse.

Consider the underlying messages to people of color when we attempt to explain away or interpret their racial experiences for them:

- Even though I wasn't there, I understand what was happening in that interaction.

- I know the correct way to respond to this situation—you got it wrong.
- It's really not that bad—you are overreacting.
- You see racism where it doesn't exist.
- I understand racism better than you do.

All of these responses minimize not only the experience, but also the intellectual capability of the person of color, and invalidate the reality of white racism. Though well intentioned, this is arrogant and demeaning on our part. Without ongoing study and antiracist practice, we actually *do not* know more about the reality of racism than people of color. This is a significant reason why people of color often don't bother sharing their experiences with us. Not only do we not hear them, we also re-target them by invalidating these experiences. We need to acknowledge our blind spots and have the humility to *not know*; we do not have to understand a person of color's experience for it to be real. We also need to build the capacity to just sit with the discomfort and pain of the story rather than try to block it or sweep it away with denial, minimization, and invalidation.

I witnessed a powerful example of minimizing during a workshop on racism I attended several years ago. Volunteers were invited to come to the front of the room and give testimony on how racism manifested in their lives. An African American woman came up and shared how terrifying it was to have black sons and the fear she lived with every day that they would be beaten or killed by the police. She told us about the day she had to "break their hearts" by letting them know that although she saw them as beautiful and good, society at large did not. She had to prepare them for the inevitable interactions they would have with the police and how to be safe when pulled over, to keep both hands visible at all times, to make eye contact, etc. She began to sob, and her grief spread around the room as the other African American mothers broke down in recognition of what she had shared.

The expression of grief was intense, and as I sat among these sobbing women, I had a powerful realization that *I had no idea* of how all-encompassing racism was for people of color. I just could not know. For me, the relationship between children and police was embodied in "Officer Friendly," our partner and helper. As a white mother, I did not have the history of police brutality toward my family. I was not able to see the countless unarmed black men and women killed by police and vigilantes as potentially my own children. (The few cases I am only recently aware of due to the benefits of video and social media are only the tip of the iceberg of what black people have endured in this country at the hands of police.) That I could not identify with these mothers was my first realization. But then as I watched the room, I had a second realization. I saw many of the white women turn to comfort the black women, trying to hold them and tell them it would be OK. Although motivated by compassion, this seemed deeply inappropriate to me. How could I, as a white mother who did not know and did not *have to know* this pain, tell them it was going to be OK, pat them on the back or give them a hug? How could I, from the position of historical and current social and institutional privilege, comfort them? I cannot know how the mothers felt about the offers of support from some of the white women. For me, it was their moment to express their grief with each other and my moment to bear witness.

Insisting That If "They" Won't Teach Us, "We" Can't Know

I vividly remember a day during the 5-day train-the-trainer sessions I attended in preparation for becoming a diversity trainer for the Department of Health and Social Services in the 1990s. A heated argument had broken out between some of the trainers of color and some of the white trainers over whose job it was to teach the white trainers about racism. The trainers of color were insisting that it was not their job to teach the white trainers, and they refused to do it, while the white trainers were arguing that if people of color didn't teach them about racism, how were they supposed to learn? Emotions were high, and as I sat there, I felt angry, too. Although I lacked the courage (or authenticity) to speak up, I agreed with the white trainers and couldn't understand what the trainers of color were saying. It just didn't make sense: they experienced racism, not us, so how could we know what it was like if they didn't explain it to us? (Of course we felt qualified and informed enough to apply for the job, even while we openly acknowledged—without fear of repercussions—that we were "innocent" of racial knowledge. This may give some insight into why people of color often see whites as arrogant and entitled, and our claims that we have earned our positions through hard work as disingenuous). The white pattern of interrogating people of color about their racial experiences—asking them to teach us about racism—is common. But now I understand the perspectives of the trainers of color, and today would support them in refusing to explain it to us, rather than silently collude with the white trainers as I did that day.

The expectation that people of color teach whites about racism reinforces several problematic dimensions of racism. First, it reinforces the idea that racism is something that happens to people of color, but that it doesn't have anything to do with *us* and thus we cannot be expected to have any knowledge of it. This framework denies that racism is a *relationship* in which both groups are involved. Second, this request requires nothing of us and reinforces unequal power relations by asking people of color to do our work for us (there is plenty of material written on the subject by people of color who *are* willing to share the information; why haven't we sought it out prior to this conversation?). Third, this request assumes that I don't have any knowledge about how white racism works, thereby reinforcing the concept of my racial innocence. Fourth, this request does not recognize the historical dimensions of racial relations— in other words, how often people of color have tried to tell us about what racism is like for them and how often we have minimized or invalidated them. To ask people of color to tell us how they experience racism without first building a trusting relationship is a red flag that we are not skilled in antiracist practice; that we *don't get it.*

So how do we gain this information if we don't ask people of color to give it to us? We get it in several interconnected ways. We can seek out the information from books, websites, films, and other available sources. Many people of color are committed to teaching whites about racism (on their own terms) and have been offering this information to us for decades, if not centuries. It is our own lack of interest or motivation that has prevented us from receiving it. We can also demand that we be given this information in schools and universities, and that we not be required to take special, elective courses to be exposed to it. We can get involved with multiracial organizations and white organizations working for racial justice. And we can build authentic cross-racial relationships and be willing to watch, listen, and learn. Sometimes, within the context of these relationships, we can ask direct questions and ask for explicit information, but this is not always necessary. Simply by virtue of living an integrated life and paying attention, we will learn what we need to know.

Focusing on Delivery

Sometimes when I am asked to mediate a cross-racial conflict I will encounter a white person who is willing to acknowledge that they said or did something cross-racially problematic. The sticking point, however, is *the way they received feedback* about it. "Why did the person have to be so angry? Why couldn't they have been nice about it?" Until the person of color changes their tone or approach, the white person cannot or will not move on.

There are several key understandings and corresponding skills that the person is missing:

- We bring our histories with us—this communication is not occurring solely between two different individuals, but also across two different positions of social and institutional power.
- It is extremely difficult and entails great risk for a person of color to give feedback to a white person on racism, especially when the white person is unaware of or does not acknowledge the differential in racial power.
- While we may see our mistake as small or isolated, for a person of color it is often one among many and represents the entirety of whiteness. Our one act may just be the proverbial straw.
- Given the risk it takes to give us feedback, many people of color let a great deal of white racism go unchecked and will only speak up when they are really upset. Insisting that they wait until they are calm pressures them to give up and (yet again) endure the slight.
- Consider what you believe to be the "rules" for how a person of color should give you feedback about your racism. Ask yourself how you came to have these rules and how they function in terms of bridging cross-racial divides. While they may be the norm in some areas of communication, these rules likely do not translate to cross-racial dynamics given the context of unequal power. (These unspoken "rules" will be discussed in more depth in Chapter 13).
- In some ways a person of color who is willing to show you the impact of racism is conveying a sense of trust. Perhaps you have demonstrated that you are worth the risk. Consider it an invaluable learning opportunity. Build your skills and endurance for bearing witness to their pain.

Over the years, as I have been involved in antiracist education, I have had countless people of color express upset with me. I keep in mind that on the one hand I have done something problematic and I need to take responsibility for it. On the other hand, I remember that when emotions are high they are likely not all about me but also about what I represent. This actually helps me move forward more easily as I take the upset less personally. To use tone or delivery as a reason to refuse to bridge the conflict is an unfair demand that keeps us from moving forward.

A white colleague of mine shared a related pattern she has observed in herself and other whites when communicating with people of color. "When I'm working with my colleague who is African American and she says something I don't understand, I have often assumed—because I see myself as smart—that *she* is the one who is not being clear, rather than any number of alternatives, which may include but are not limited to:

- My lack of the basic education needed to comprehend her racial perspective
- An emotional response (conscious or not) which is clouding my thinking and making it hard for me to process what she is saying
- My lack of experience and practice communicating outside my dominant cultural context."

She continues, "Several times in our relationship I have asked her to repeat or rephrase something. I distinctly remember one meeting with several other white people wherein we kept asking her to do this. She stopped and said, 'No. You need to look at why you can't seem to hear what I am saying. What gets in the way for you that prevents you from taking in my voice?'"

From an antiracist perspective, several dynamics are illustrated in this exchange. The first is that we *do* have racial filters that impact how we view, hear, and respond to people of color. As has been demonstrated over and over, we don't perceive objectively across race. Second, it is *our* responsibility to identify these filters and how they impact our cross-racial communication, rather than continually expect people of color to adapt until they "get it right" by our norms. Third, our insistence that our lack of understanding laies in their inability to make sense reinforces racist assumptions about who is or isn't intelligent. Not only does this reinforce our intellectual superiority, but it reinforces their internalized oppression—we are engaged in "the dance."

I have also seen this happen regarding people of color who have accents, even very mild ones. White people often lose interest and claim that they can't understand the person, when what is happening is a refusal to expend effort—to *try*.

I asked my friend if communication with her colleague has improved. She explained, "If I focus on understanding every single word, I am anxious and often can't track her very well. When I let my mind relax I can take in the whole of what's being said—even though I didn't understand every part. I am also much more engaged and connected in the dialogue. I notice that the more connected I am, the more I truly understand."

Dismissing What We Don't Understand

I was once asked to provide one-on-one mentoring for a white male teacher who had made inappropriate racial comments to a black female student. When the girl's mother complained, the teacher became defensive, and the conflict escalated. The incident ended up in the newspaper, and potential legal action was discussed. I will call this teacher Mr. Smith. During one of our sessions, Mr. Smith told me about his colleague, a white female teacher, who recently had two black students at her desk. She prefaced something she said to one of them with, "Girl, ..." The student was clearly taken aback and asked, "Did you just call me girl?" The other student said it was OK; the teacher called all her students girl.

In relaying this story to me, Mr. Smith expressed the anger that he and his colleague felt about having to be "so careful" and not being able to "say anything anymore." They perceived my intervention with Mr. Smith as a form of punishment and felt that because of the incident with him, students of color were now "oversensitive" and complaining about racism where it did not exist. For these teachers, the student's reaction to being called girl was an example of this oversensitivity. This is a familiar white narrative, and in this instance, it was rationalized based on the following: (1) The teacher called all her students girl and so the comment had nothing to do with race, and (2) One of the students didn't have an issue with the comment, so the student who did was overreacting. The white teachers' response illustrates several dynamics of whiteness:

- The teachers never considered that in not understanding the student's reaction, *they* might be lacking in knowledge.
- The teachers did not demonstrate curiosity about the student's perspective or why she might have taken offense.
- The teachers did not demonstrate concern about the student's feelings.
- The teachers do not know their racial history.
- The teachers did not understand that actions or words that may not be problematic with the dominant group can have a very different impact when used with the minoritized group.

- The teachers were not able to separate intentions from impact.
- In spite of the fact that Mr. Smith was so lacking in cross-racial skills and understanding that he was involved in a racial violation with potential legal repercussions, he remained confident that he was right and the student of color was wrong.
- His colleague, aware that Mr. Smith was in serious trouble regarding a cross-racial incident, still maintained white solidarity with him by validating their shared perspective and invalidating the student of color's.
- The teachers used the student who excused the comment as proof that the other student was wrong; she was the "correct" student because she denied any racial implications.
- The teachers used this interaction as an opportunity to increase racial divides rather than as an opportunity to bridge them.

Unfortunately, the teachers' responses are all too familiar. Like most of us who are white, they are culturally incompetent. They had an invaluable opportunity to increase their cultural competency, but they used it to maintain their limited worldview rather than expand it. Further, they used it as an opportunity to increase their racial resentment toward people of color who raise racial issues. Imagine how the interaction could have gone if the teacher had replied, with openness and sincerity, "It seems I offended you. I'm sorry. I use that term a lot. Can you help me understand why it's problematic?" Seeking understanding would not have necessitated agreement; we don't have to agree with or understand someone's offense in order to support and validate them. However, neither I nor any colleague I know who is involved in antiracist education had any difficulty understanding why the student reacted as she did. While the term "girl" may not be offensive to most young white women, it was historically used to demean and infantilize black women (as "boy" was used in the same way against black men) and has a different impact when used by whites to describe women of color. While most whites may not know this history, some humility about that lack of knowledge and the ability to focus on impact rather than intent would have made for a very different and much more constructive interaction.

Carefulness

Racism is a very complex, multilevel system. There are no easy and concise answers or solutions to it. While we need to develop strategies for challenging racism, no single strategy will work in every situation, and some strategies, if taken to the extreme, can become non-constructive. For example, *thoughtfulness* is an important strategy. Thoughtfulness can include being cognizant of the history we bring to racial encounters, being considerate about the language we use, being sensitive to group dynamics, and being attentive to our patterns and blind spots. But thoughtfulness taken to an extreme can become *carefulness*, in which we are so cautious about making a mistake or offending that we end up engaging disingenuously. This was brought home to me during a workshop I was planning with a colleague of color. One of the exercises we would be leading the group in was designed to illustrate the unavoidable internalization of stereotypes. In this exercise, participants are paired up, they choose a minoritized group that neither of them belongs to, and together they explore their stereotypes about the group.

In discussing this exercise with my colleague, I shared my fear of blurting out something racist. I told her I thought the goal was to be careful not to expose these stereotypes, rather than publicly air them in an exercise. She paused and looked at me for several moments and then said, "Robin ... *do you think we can't tell when you are being careful?*" Chagrined, I had another fish-out-of-water moment. I suddenly felt *uncovered* as a white person. I realized that I expected my friend to see me as I saw myself—outside of race. I also had a sudden realization of what it must look like for people of color when whites are being careful around them. We look stiff, uncomfortable, uptight, and reserved. As I pictured myself being careful around people of color in this way, I also saw why they experienced that as racism. I certainly wasn't warm, relaxed, sincere, or open when I was being careful.

For me, this was a great example of my own unaware and unintended racism, and made clear why people of color so often shared that whites were reserved and cold around them and how awful that felt. This behavior *is* rooted in racism in that we are acting differently around people of color. This difference in behavior can be attributed to factors such as segregation, fear of people of color, and not valuing our relationships with people of color enough to build comfort with them. My friend's question caused me to realize that while I needed to be *thoughtful* about what I said and not just blurt out every racist thought in my head, *carefulness* was not useful. I have come to realize that people of color expect us to make mistakes and are less concerned about that than about how we respond when these mistakes are pointed out, what we are willing to do to "clean them up," and what we learn from our mistakes and do differently in the future.

In Conclusion

An experience I had with a group studying racism may bring together and illustrate several dynamics discussed in this chapter. Deborah Terry-Hays, a friend and colleague who is a black woman, was involved in an organization committed to critical self-awareness. While this organization is primarily white, heterosexual, and middle-class, they work hard to educate themselves on various aspects of oppression and their role in them. Deborah was a member in one of the organization's weekly study groups. She was the only person of color in the group of twelve. At some point, the group's facilitator, a white male, informed her that for the next week they would be studying racism and asked her if she would teach that session. She told him she needed to think about it, and then she called me, very distressed. She was torn: on the one hand she wanted to give them this information because they desperately needed it; on the other hand, to be the only person of color in the group and have to explain to them how racism manifested—both in general and in the group—was terrifying. In so doing, she risked experiencing many of the white patterns discussed in this chapter: minimization, defensiveness, anger, objectification, invalidation, being ignored, and white guilt. She told me that she would share her experience as a person of color if I would come with her and speak to them—specifically as a white person—about white patterns of racism, since whites are generally more receptive to hearing about racism from other whites. My presence would also ensure that she had a trusted ally at her side. I agreed.

As the days passed and she prepared her presentation, she called me many times to vent her fear and anxiety. This request to teach an all-white group about racism took a tremendous toll on her. In addition to the emotional work she was doing, she spent hours preparing her presentation so that it was clear in a way that could be understood by white people, and was as indisputable as possible so it could not be negated. Being in front of an all-white group also triggered her internalized oppression—as a black woman she had a lifetime of messages from schools, white teachers, and society at large that she was unintelligent and had no knowledge of intrinsic value.

Finally the evening came. The group listened thoughtfully and then asked questions or made comments. One member of the group stated—in a way somewhat critical of the organization—"I am so glad this organization is finally teaching us about racism. I have been waiting for them to do that." This statement triggered in me another fish-out-of-water moment in which I could see a cross-racial dynamic I had not seen before. I had watched the tremendous amount of emotional and intellectual work Deborah had done in order to make this presentation. Now, watching this group sitting comfortably on their chairs and effortlessly receiving Deborah's presentation, I saw a metaphor for *colonialist* relations (one more powerful group occupies the land of another and exploits and profits from the resources and work of the people of that land).

Sherene Razack (1998), writing about whiteness and the pattern of study-ing those who are seen as "different," states that, "The cultural differences approach reinforces an important … cornerstone of imperialism: the colo-nized possess a series of knowable characteristics that can be studied, known, and managed accordingly by the colonizers whose own complicity remains masked" (p. 10). Using this metaphor, the group was in essence saying, "We will observe you and seek to understand you. In doing so, we will relax while you work. You will provide us with the fruits of your labor. We will receive these fruits and consider them; we will decide what to keep and what to reject—what we deem worthy of consideration and what we don't. We thank the organization for bringing you to us, for we have desired your knowledge. But if you were not brought before us, we would not (as we have not up until now) expend any effort in seeking it for ourselves." Further, this group mem-ber positioned this as a shortcoming of the organization rather than of himself, so that he also managed to elevate his own moral standing. Still, his credit went to the organization, not to Deborah. While I am quite sure that this is not what the person *meant* to say or do, I do think that his response illustrates the dynamics of internalized colonialism (or internalized dominance).

Antiracist education challenges our worldview and our sense of ourselves in relation to others. It asks us to connect ourselves to uncomfortable con-cepts such as prejudice, discrimination, racism, and oppression. It challenges deeply held ideals such as treating everyone equally and not seeing color. Understandably, it can feel overwhelming—even impossible—to get it right. It would be so much easier if we had a list with easy-to-understand dos and don'ts. Yet such an approach would avoid the life-altering changes antiracist education asks of us. Developing an antiracist perspective and practice takes a lifetime. One of the greatest challenges we face is the lack of humility our position engenders—thinking that we can live our lives primarily in segrega-tion and then learn how to bridge this separation (and the blindness it pro-duces) quickly, easily, and without making mistakes. In light of this, the single most effective skill we need as we begin this journey is the ability to accept our inevitable mistakes and be willing to learn from them.

Discussion Questions

1. Which of the patterns discussed in this chapter challenge you the most? Why?

2. If you are white, which of the patterns discussed in this chapter have you seen in yourself? How might you address these patterns?

3. Choose a pattern from this chapter. In your own words, practice explaining to a white person what is problematic about that pattern.

4. In the section titled "Dismissing What We Don't Understand," the author provides an example of two teachers and lists the ways that they dismissed what they didn't understand. Discuss this list. How have you seen or participated in these forms of dismissal?

5. The patterns discussed here are addressed at the interpersonal level overall. How have you seen these patterns manifest institutionally? In the society at large?

WHITE FRAGILITY

I am a white woman. I am standing beside a black woman. We are facing a group of white people who are seated in front of us. We are in their workplace, and have been hired by their employer to lead them in a dialogue about race. The room is filled with tension and charged with hostility. I have just presented a definition of racism that includes the acknowledgment that whites hold social and institutional power over people of color. A white man is pounding his fist on the table. His face is red and he is furious. As he pounds he yells, "White people have been discriminated against for 25 years! A white person can't get a job anymore!" I look around the room and see 40 employed people, all white. There are no people of color in this workplace. Something is happening here, and it isn't based in the racial reality of the workplace. I am feeling unnerved by this man's disconnection with that reality, and his lack of sensitivity to the impact this is having on my co-facilitator, the only person of color in the room. Why is this white man so angry? Why is he being so careless about the impact of his anger? Why are all the other white people either sitting in silent agreement with him or tuning out? We have, after all, only articulated a definition of racism.

When ideologies such as colorblindness, meritocracy, and individualism are challenged, intense emotional reactions are common. There are many complex reasons why whites are so defensive about the suggestion that we benefit from and are complicit in a racist system. These reasons include:

- Social taboos against talking openly about race
- The racist = bad/not racist = good binary
- Fear and resentment towards people of color
- Our view of ourselves as objective individuals
- Our guilt and knowledge that there is more going on than we can or will admit
- Deep investment in a system that benefits us and that we have been conditioned to see as fair

As I have discussed throughout this book, all of these reasons serve to protect and shelter white people from an honest exploration of racism, while allowing us to live in a social environment that protects and insulates us. This insulated environment of racial privilege builds our expectations for racial comfort while at the same time it lowers our tolerance for racial stress.

For many white people, a single required multicultural education course taken in college, or required "cultural competency training" in their workplace, is the only time they may encounter a direct and sustained challenge to their racial realities. But even in this arena, not all multicultural courses or training programs talk directly about racism, much less address white privilege. It is far more the norm for these courses and programs to use racially coded language such as "urban," "inner city," and "disadvantaged," but rarely use "white" or "over-advantaged" or "privileged." This racially coded language reproduces racist images and perspectives while simultaneously reproducing the comfortable illusion that race and its problems are what "they" have, not us. Reasons that the facilitators of such training may not directly name the dynamics and beneficiaries of racism range from the lack of a valid analysis of racism by white facilitators and the personal and economic survival strategies for facilitators of color to the overall pressure from management to keep the content comfortable and palatable for whites.

However, if and when an educational program does directly address racism and the privileging of whites, common white responses include anger, withdrawal, emotional incapacitation, guilt, argumentation, and cognitive dissonance (all of which reinforce the pressure on facilitators to avoid directly addressing racism). So-called progressive whites may not respond with anger but still insulate themselves via claims that they are beyond the need for engaging with the content because they "already had a class on this" or "already know this." These reactions are often seen in antiracist education endeavors as forms of resistance. These reactions do indeed function as resistance, but it may be useful to also conceptualize them as the result of the reduced psycho-social stamina that racial insulation inculcates. I call this lack of racial stamina *white fragility* (DiAngelo, 2011).

Triggers

White fragility is a state in which even a minimum amount of racial stress becomes intolerable, triggering a range of defensive moves. These moves include the outward display of emotions such as anger, fear, and guilt, and behaviors such as argumentation, silence, and leaving the stress-inducing situation. These behaviors, in turn, function to reinstate white racial equilibrium. Racial stress results from an interruption of what is racially familiar. These interruptions can take a variety of forms and come from a range of sources.

The following are examples of the kinds of challenges that trigger racial stress for white people:

- Suggesting that a white person's viewpoint comes from a racialized frame of reference (challenge to objectivity)
- People of color talking directly about their racial perspectives and experiences (challenge to white taboos on talking openly about race)
- People of color choosing not to protect the racial feelings of white people in regard to race (challenge to white racial expectations and need for/entitlement to racial comfort)
- People of color not being willing to tell their stories or answer questions about their racial experiences (challenge to the expectation that people of color will serve us/do our work for us)
- A fellow white not providing agreement with one's racial perspective (challenge to white solidarity)
- Receiving feedback that one's behavior had a racist impact (challenge to white racial innocence)
- Suggesting that group membership is significant (challenge to individualism)
- An acknowledgment that access is unequal between racial groups (challenge to meritocracy)

- Being presented with a person of color in a position of leadership (challenge to white authority)
- Being presented with information about other racial groups through, for example, movies in which people of color drive the action but are not in stereotypical roles, or racial justice education (challenge to white centrality).

In a white dominant environment, each of these challenges becomes exceptional. In turn, we are often at a loss for how to respond in constructive ways, and resort to withdrawal, defensiveness, crying, arguing, minimizing, ignoring, and in other ways push back to regain our racial position and equilibrium. We have not had to build the cognitive or affective skills or develop the stamina that that would allow for constructive engagement across racial divides.

White fragility may be conceptualized as a response or "condition" produced and reproduced by the continuous social and material advantages of whiteness. When disequilibrium occurs—when there is an interruption to that which is familiar and taken for granted—*white fragility* functions to restore equilibrium and return the resources "lost" via the challenge. Resistance towards the trigger, shutting down and/or tuning out, indulgence in emotional incapacitation such as guilt or "hurt feelings," exiting, or a combination of these responses results. These strategies are often not conscious but rather are reflexive (automatic). Given that white people hold the social, economic and cultural capital, our strategies for maintaining our racial position or "balance" trump those of people of color.

What Does White Fragility Look Like?

At the same time that it is ubiquitous, white superiority is also unnamed and denied by most whites. If we become adults who explicitly oppose racism, as do many, we often organize our identity around a denial of the racially based privileges we hold that reinforce racist disadvantage for others. What is particularly problematic about this contradiction is that white moral objection to racism increases white resistance to acknowledging complicity with it. In a white supremacist context, white identity in large part rests upon a foundation of (superficial) racial toleration and acceptance. Whites who position themselves as liberal often opt to protect what we perceive as our moral reputations, rather than to recognize or change our participation in systems of inequity and domination. In so responding, whites invoke the power to chose when, how, and how much to address or challenge racism. Thus pointing out white advantage will often trigger patterns of confusion, defensiveness and righteous indignation. This enables defenders to protect their moral character against what they perceive as accusation and attack while deflecting any recognition of culpability or need of accountability. Focusing on restoring their moral standing through these tactics, whites are able to avoid the challenge (Marty, 1999).

Those who lead whites in discussions of race may find the discourse of self-defense familiar. In this discourse, whites position themselves as victimized, slammed, blamed, attacked, and being used as a "punching bag" (DiAngelo & Sensoy, 2014). Whites who describe the interactions in this way are responding to the articulation of counternarratives; no physical violence has ever occurred in any inter-racial discussion or training that I am aware of. These self-defense claims work on multiple levels to: position the speakers as morally superior while obscuring the true power of their social stations; blame others with less social power for their discomfort; falsely position that discomfort as dangerous; and, reinscribe racist imagery. By positioning themselves as the victim of antiracist efforts, they cannot be the beneficiaries of whiteness. Claiming that it is they who have been unfairly treated via a challenge to their position or via an expectation that they listen to the perspectives and experiences of people of color, they are able to demand that more social resources (such as time and attention) be channeled in their direction to help them cope with this mistreatment.

A cogent example of *White fragility* occurred recently during a workplace antiracism training I co-facilitated with an inter-racial team. One of the white participants left the session and went back to her desk, upset at receiving (what appeared to the training team as) sensitive and diplomatic feedback on how some of her statements had impacted several of the people of color in the room. At break, several other white participants approached us (the trainers) and reported that they had talked to the woman at her desk, and that she was very upset that her statements had been challenged. (Of course this was not how it was framed. It was framed as her being "falsely accused" of having a racist impact). Her friends wanted to alert us to the fact that she "might be having a heart-attack." Upon questioning from us, they clarified that they meant this *literally*. These co-workers were sincere in their fear that the young woman might actually physically die as a result of the feedback. Of course when news of the woman's potentially fatal condition reached the rest of the participants, all attention was immediately focused back onto her and away from engagement with the impact she had had on the people of color. As Vodde (2001) states, "If privilege is defined as a legitimization of one's entitlement to resources, it can also be defined as permission to escape or avoid any challenges to this entitlement" (p. 3).

This lack of stamina results in the maintenance of white power because the ability to determine which narratives are authorized and which are suppressed is the foundation of cultural domination. Further, if whites cannot engage with an exploration of alternate racial perspectives, they can only reinscribe white perspectives as universal.

White Fragility and the Rules of Engagement

You can't wake a person who is pretending to be asleep

—Navaho Proverb

As a professor, facilitator, and consultant I am in a position to give white people feedback on how their unintentional racism is manifesting. This has provided me the opportunity to observe countless enactments of *white fragility*. One of the most common is outrage: *How dare you suggest that I could have said or done something racist!* Outrage is often followed by righteous indignation about the manner in which the feedback was given. I have discovered (as I am sure have countless people of color) that there is apparently an unspoken set of rules—rooted in white fragility—for how to give white people feedback on our inevitable and often unaware racism. In this section I will overview these "rules."

After years of working with my fellow whites, I have found that the only way to give feedback correctly is *not to give it at all*. Thus, the first rule is cardinal:

1. **Do not give me feedback on my racism under any circumstances.**

   If you break the cardinal rule:

   1. Proper tone is crucial—feedback must be given calmly. If there is any emotion in the feedback, the feedback is invalid and does not have to be considered.

2. There must be trust between us. You must trust that I am in no way racist before you can give me feedback on my racism.

3. Our relationship must be issue-free—if there are issues between us you cannot give me feedback on racism.

4. Feedback must be given immediately, otherwise it will be discounted because it was not given sooner.

5. You must give feedback privately, regardless of whether the incident occurred in front of other people. To give feedback in front of anyone else—even those involved in the situation—is to commit a serious social transgression. The feedback is thus invalid.

6. You must be as indirect as possible. To be direct is to be insensitive and will invalidate the feedback and require repair.

7. As a white person I must feel completely safe during any discussion of race. Giving me any feedback on my racism will cause me to feel unsafe, so you will need to rebuild my trust by never giving me feedback again. Point of clarification: when I say "safe" what I really mean is "comfortable."

8. Giving me feedback on my racial privilege invalidates the form of oppression that *I* experience (i.e., classism, sexism, heterosexism). We will then need to focus on how *you* oppressed *me*.

9. You must focus on my intentions, which cancel out the impact of my behavior.

10. To suggest my behavior had a racist impact is to have misunderstood me. You will need to allow me to explain until you can acknowledge that it was *your* misunderstanding.

The contradictions in these rules are irrelevant; their function is to obscure racism, protect white dominance, and regain white equilibrium, and they do so very effectively. Yet from an understanding of racism as a system of unequal institutional power, we need to ask ourselves where these rules come from and whom they serve.

Many of us actively working to interrupt racism continually hear complaints about the "gotcha" culture of white antiracism. There is a stereotype that we are looking for every incident we can find so we can spring out, point our fingers, and shout, "You're a racist!" While certainly there are white people who arrogantly set themselves apart from other whites by acting in this way, in my experience of over 20 years, this is not the norm. It is far more common for sincere white people to agonize over when and how to give feedback to a fellow white person, given the ubiquity of white fragility. *White fragility* works to pun-ish the person giving feedback and essentially bully them back into silence. It also maintains white solidarity—the tacit agreement that we will protect white privilege and not hold each other accountable for our racism. When the person giving the feedback is a person of color, the charge is "playing the race card" and the consequences of *white fragility* are much more penalizing.

Racism is the norm rather than an aberration. Feedback is key to our ability to recognize and repair our inevitable and often unaware collusion. In recognition of this, I follow these *guidelines*:

1. How, where, and when you give me feedback is irrelevant—it is the feedback I want and need. Understanding that it is hard to give, I will take it any way I can get it. From my position of social, cultural and institutional white power and privilege, I am perfectly safe and I can handle it. If I cannot handle it, *it's on me* to build my racial stamina.
2. Thank you.

The above guidelines rest on the understanding that there is no face to save and the jig is up; I know that I have blind spots and unconscious investments in white superiority. My investments are reinforced every day in mainstream society. I did not set this system up but it does unfairly benefit me and I am responsible for interrupting it. I need to work hard to recognize it myself, but I can't do it alone. This understanding leads me to gratitude when others help me.

In my workshops I often ask people of color, "How often have you given white people feedback on our unaware yet inevitable racism and did that go well for you?" Eye-rolling, head-shaking, and outright laughter follow, along with the general consensus of *never*. I then ask, "What would it be like if you could simply give us feedback, have us graciously receive it, reflect, and work to change the behavior?" Recently a man of color sighed and said, "It would be *revolutionary*." I ask my fellow whites to consider the profundity of that response. *Revolutionary* that we would receive, reflect, and work to change the behavior. On the one hand it points to how difficult and fragile we are. But on the other hand, how simple taking responsibility for our racism can be.

If we can't listen to, or comprehend, the perspectives of people of color, we cannot bridge cross-racial divides.

Discussion Questions

1. What does it mean to say that white people live in a social environment that insulates them from racial stress? How have you seen white fragility at play in discussions of race and racism? If you are white, how have you seen it in yourself?
2. Discuss each item on the list of triggers. Explain in your own words what each item is challenging.
3. How have you seen the "rules" at play when whites are receiving feedback on unaware but inevitable racism? What beliefs about racism is each rule rooted in? What do white people have to "give up" in order to challenge the factors that lead to white fragility? Discuss the statement the author quotes from a man of color who says that for whites to graciously receive feedback on their unaware but inevitable racism, reflect on the feedback, and seek to change the behavior would be *revolutionary*.

· 1 4 ·

POPULAR WHITE NARRATIVES
THAT DENY RACISM

In my neighborhoods it has only been white people. Ever since elementary school, I have always been taught to treat everybody equally and that just because you have a different skin color doesn't mean that you are different or should look down on anyone. I always learned about slavery in history classes and how it was many years ago. Society has gotten much better now and society and schools are trying to teach everyone not to be prejudice. I am proud to treat everybody equal. (ASR)

My particular neighborhood was not very racially diverse but surrounding neighborhoods were. I have always been taught to treat everyone equally. Although my neighborhood was not racially diverse, my high school was. Even though it was, most of the people I hung around with are white. This is not saying I wouldn't be friends with someone of a different race, it just happened like that. (ASR)

There are many common white narratives about racism that I have attempted to clarify throughout the previous chapters. However, given their tenacity, I want to explicitly address a few key ones here. These misconceptions limit rather than expand understanding of what racism is and how it works, and thus function to protect rather than to challenge racism. In this way they can be conceptualized as ideologies of white supremacy.

"Racism is in the past. I didn't own slaves"

Most white people are woefully uninformed when it comes to both the history and continuing presence of racism. "I didn't own slaves" is an extremely popular albeit extremely simplistic white narrative. It reinforces the following claims:

- Racism is synonymous with slavery and *only* slavery: racism = slavery.
- Racism ended the day slavery ended, in 1865.
- Only slave owners were involved in slavery/racism.
- I wasn't a slave owner; therefore I have not been involved in racism.
- My ancestors weren't slave owners; therefore, I have not been involved in racism.
- There is nothing more to discuss.

Racism has been and continues to be perpetrated against all groups of color in the United States. For example, in 1862, the Homestead Act was passed, allowing any U.S. citizen to file an application and lay claim to 160 acres of surveyed government land. This land had been taken from Native Americans and was a large-scale government redistribution of land from autonomous tribes to taxpaying farmers, a process carried out directly on Indian territories. In 1882 the Chinese Exclusion Act was passed, which banned Chinese immigration (at the same time that European immigration was exploding). This act placed the most significant restrictions on free immigration in U.S. history. In 1942, approximately 110,00 Japanese were forcibly interned, losing their homes and businesses. These are just a few notable ways in which racism has manifested throughout our history.

   As for slavery, it wasn't only slave owners who were involved in the enslavement of kidnapped Africans. This is the equivalent of saying that only Nazis were complicit in the Holocaust and accomplished their goals without the tacit support of German citizens, the Catholic Church, the press, the military, the policies of other countries such as the United States who turned Jews away and/or turned a blind eye, and so on. Similarly, white people and the institutions they control were complicit in slavery at every level of society. But racism against blacks most definitely did not end when slavery ended.

   The period following emancipation is termed Reconstruction. Legal and institutional exclusion of people of color, in addition to unpunished illegal acts of terrorism such as lynching and dismemberment, were rampant during Reconstruction. Between 1882 and 1968, there were 3,446 recorded lynchings of blacks in the United States (Tuskegee Institute, 2012). In the West, Chinese, Mexicans, and Indians were also lynched in this period. This is the period in which Jim Crow laws were instituted in the South (legal racial segregation, e.g., whites only; separate "colored" sections) in order to limit the rights of former slaves through law. *Plessy* v. *Ferguson* (1896) is a legal case that played a key role. Plessy was arrested for sitting in a whites-only section of a train. His attorney argued that the separate car laws violated his civil rights. But Judge Ferguson found Plessy guilty. The case went to the Supreme Court, which held that the law of separate cars was constitutional, and ruled that "separate but equal facilities" were appropriate under the Fourteenth Amendment.

It was not until *Brown* v. *Board of Education* in 1954 that "separate but equal" was overturned in education. The winning argument posited that separate was inherently unequal. Kenneth Clark's research with black children and dolls, discussed in Chapter 8, played a role in making this argument. This research led Chief Justice Earl Warren to write in the *Brown* v. *Board* opinion, "To separate them from others of similar age and qualifications solely because of their race generates a feeling of inferiority as to their status in the community that may affect their hearts and minds in a way unlikely to ever be undone" (Benjamin, 2007). Chief Justice Warren here acknowledges that the effects of racism do not end when an act of racism ends. These effects are ongoing and shape generations.

In the United States, people of color have been formally—and now informally—prevented from participating in government wealth-building programs that benefit white Americans. The New Deal and The Fair Deal were denied to blacks. People of color were denied Federal Housing Act (FHA) loans as recently as the 1950s. Today, it has been documented that blacks and Latinos were targeted for sub-prime mortgages, even when they qualified for better loans. Excluding people of color from the mechanisms of society that allow wealth building continues today through illegal but common practices such as higher mortgage rates, more difficulty getting loans, real estate agents steering them away from "good" neighborhoods, discrimination in hiring, and unequal school funding. The Drug War and its policies has had a profound impact on the massive incarceration of blacks and Latinos; it functions as a modern manifestation of Jim Crow (Alexander, 2010).

Racial group membership has been and continues to be consistently traced to inequitable outcomes on every indicator of quality of life. Insisting that we could not have benefited from racism because we personally didn't own slaves is dismissive and shallow, and serves to hide the reality of both individual and collective white advantage at every level of our past and present society.

At the same time, we should not minimize the profound significance of living in a society that was built upon and maintained slavery for centuries. The first African slaves arrived in Hispaniola (Haiti and the Dominican Republic) in 1501, and slavery was legal in all 13 colonies by 1750. This means that every foundational aspect of our country was developed in the context of slavery. Thomas Jefferson wrote the Declaration of Independence while holding over 200 slaves. The Constitution and the Bill of Rights were all written by slave-holders, and slavery did not end in the United States until 1865. If it is important for us to study in depth the founding of our country in schools, why do we minimize the impact that over 300 years of slavery had on the hearts and minds of the founders and the populace? If political and economic systems such as democracy and capitalism are understood to be fundamental in shaping our consciousness and thus worthy of in-depth study, how can we deny that slavery and the white supremacy that developed from it have also been fundamental in shaping us as a society, and where we are today in terms of national identity and race relations? How can we ignore the monumental role that slavery played in the building of U.S. wealth? The relations of slavery are deeply encoded in the national psyche.

For some whites, it is possible that one's ancestors owned slaves, as very few whites actually know if their families were slave owners or not. This information has not been passed down historically, especially in the North. If one's ancestors were slave owners, why would that information be suppressed? How might direct involvement in slavery, as well as the denial of that involvement, be relevant to one's family history?

> **Remember:** White ignorance is not born of innocence, is not benign and is not simply a matter of not knowing. White ignorance is highly effective at protecting our investments in racism and thus, actively maintained in the society at large.

Glibly dismissing the impact of slavery and refusing to trace its impact into the present is a form of willful ignorance. This is not to say that we should educate children about how bad white people were/are and impose guilt upon them. But if we want to understand who we are and how we got here, we should teach an honest and complete account of our past practices and their impact on the present, rather than deny them. I cannot do justice here to the vast manifestation of racist policies and practices that permeated society *following* slavery and continue today. Anyone seeking to develop racial literacy must educate themselves on U.S. racial history.

"Slavery has always been around. In fact, Africans engaged in slavery too. They are the ones who sold the slaves"

While it appears that human slavery has always existed, and it is heinous in all of its forms, it behooves us to consider the unique manifestation of slavery in the United States. To do so sheds light on the specific trajectory of our nation: the process of citizenship and the rights accorded; the development of identity in various citizen groups; the construction of and response to difference; the ideology of human objectivity and belief in the scientific method; the accumulation of national wealth; the motivations for wars; the professed ideals of human equality and freedom; the persistent racial inequality in the face of those ideals; and the ideological mechanisms by which moral contradictions are navigated.

Slavery in African countries was not based on concepts of inherent superiority and inferiority, a notion developed as justification for the enslavement of blacks in America. African slaves were acquired through wars and conflicts and served for a limited time or until death, but their status was not handed down to the next generation (Akomolafe, 1994). In America, a slave's caste status was inherited, generation-to-generation, for hundreds of years.

American slavery was unique in another very important aspect. America was one of the first nations to declare the rights of the individual: that all men are born free and created equal. Yet these concepts, of which our nation is rightly proud, contrasted radically with the practice of slavery: that a person could be defined as less than a human being, owned as property by other people, forced to work against their will for the entirety for their life, be sub-jected to ongoing torture and murder, and be forced to breed children to be taken away and placed into the same unending chattel servitude. There is something unparalleled about being enslaved in the "Land of the Free." How did white people manage this profound contradiction? How did centuries of slavery shape all of us? How has racial oppression, from the founding of the nation into the present time and in its various forms, structured today's race relations?

In light of how fundamental slavery is to the identity and trajectory of the nation, it is important to reflect on what is accomplished by the rebuttal, "Africans engaged in slavery too. They are the ones who sold the slaves." In other words, what point is the person declaring this trying to make? That Africans are equally complicit in the 300 years of American slavery? And so? Or perhaps the point is that slavery is a function of human nature? If so, why do we no longer practice it? Is the claim meant to justify U.S. slavery? Or per-haps to suggest that it is irrelevant to understanding the distribution of wealth today? This is not a benign discourse and warrants some personal reflection on the part of those making it.

"I know people of color, so I am not racist"

Aside from the rather ridiculous suggestion in this claim that a racist could not tolerate knowing, working next to, or walking among people of color, many whites have no cross-racial friendships at all, so having a friend of color is important. But the person who makes this claim is still invoking the racist = bad/not racist = good binary. They see their friendship as proof that they are on the "not racist" side of the binary. However, cross-racial friendships do not block out the dynamics of racism in the society at large, which continue unabated. The white person will still receive white privilege that their friend does not, even as they go about activities together. Nor do these friendships block out all of the messages we have internalized and that are reinforced as a result of living in this society. In fact, dynamics of racism invariably manifest *within* cross-racial friendships as well, through unaware assumptions, stereotypes, and patterns of engagement. Using an antiracist theoretical framework, it is not *possible* for racism to be absent from your friendship. I have not met a person of color who has said that racism *isn't* at play in their friendships with white people. Some white people are more thoughtful, aware, and receptive to feedback than others, but no cross-racial relationship is free of racism.

Many whites believe that if they are not talking about racism with their friends of color or if their friends are not giving them feedback about racism, then there is no racism. But just because you and your friend don't talk about racism does not mean it isn't at play. Indeed, this silence is one of the ways that modern racism manifests, for it is an *imposed* silence. Many people of color have shared that they initially tried to talk about racism with their white friends, but their friends got defensive or invalidated these experiences, so they stopped sharing them. People of color are not free of internalized racial oppression, and it may also be possible that they are not aware of how racism is playing out themselves. It is highly likely that they have not been taught about how racism works by the society at large, and like many whites, they may not have the vocabulary to address it. If racism is not coming up as a topic of discussion between a white person and a person of color who are friends, this may be an indication of *less* cross-racial trust.

"I was the minority at my school, so I was the one who experienced racism"

The person making this claim does not understand that racism is a system of unequal historical, cultural, and institutional power between white people and people of color. While anyone of any race can be prejudiced and can discriminate against someone of another race, only whites are in the position to oppress people of color collectively and throughout the whole of society. This claim positions racism as a function of numbers, which changes direction based on each group's ratio in a given situation. While a white person may have been picked on—even mercilessly—by being in the numerical minority in a specific context, they were experiencing race *prejudice and discrimination*, not racism. This distinction is not meant to minimize their experience, but to clarify in order to prevent rendering the terms interchangeable and thus meaningless.

Further, the society at large is still reinforcing white supremacy, and *everyone* in the school was impacted by it. It is likely that white students at such a school were treated better by teachers, and higher expectations were held for them. Their textbooks, the curriculum, the administration, still reinforced whiteness. Outside the school (and in many aspects within it), they were still granted white privilege as they moved through society.

For most whites, being the minority in their school or neighborhood is usually temporary. They are likely no longer the minority in their environment, as upward mobility generally entails moving away from integrated spaces or those in which people of color are the majority.

> **Remember**: Minoritized group members can be prejudiced and discriminate against dominant group members, but this is temporary and contextual. Only the dominant group has the institutional power to oppress the minoritized throughout the society by denying them access to resources.

"People of color complain too much and play the race card"

The race card discourse is highly problematic because it implies cheating. Someone who is playing this card is dealing from the bottom of the deck. It is an accusation that is meant to invalidate people of color's assertions about racism. People of color's motivations for speaking up about racism are also suspect; they are taking advantage of whites by playing on their sympathies. Yet I haven't witnessed much white sympathy for people of color's assertions of racism, and as white antiracist activist Tim Wise counters (2008), the race card is the equivalent of the two of diamonds; in other words, it isn't much of a card to play, as it rarely gets anywhere with whites.

In addition to invalidating people of color's understanding of racism by reducing it to some kind of trick played on whites, this phrase also positions whites as the experts on race. We are the ones to decide whether or not racism is real in any given context, even though we are the least likely to understand racism or be invested in seeing it. In other words, based on our socialization within a white supremacist culture, without focused study and practice in cross-racial awareness and skills, whites are completely unqualified to assess whether racism "happened" or not. Dei, Karumanchery-Luik, and Karumanchery (2004), addressing the race card discourse, state, "… the power to 'know' often mutes the recognition that *there is also power in not knowing*" (pp. xi–xii) [emphasis mine]. The very concept of a "race card" at all, in a society so deeply unequal by race, is a powerful example of white insensitivity and denial.

Most people of color learn very early that "complaining" about racism to whites usually ends in defensiveness, invalidation, and dismissal. It's been my observation that the vast majority of racism goes unmentioned by people of color, because trying to talk to white people about it is just too hard. The white card of dismissal always trumps.

"People of color are just as racist as we are"

If you define racism as merely race prejudice, then yes, people of color have just as much race prejudice as whites. But people of color are not and cannot be just as *racist* as whites because they do not hold institutional power. People of color do not control the institutional mechanisms that would allow them to back their prejudice and infuse it throughout the whole of society. We must reserve some language to capture this magnitude of difference between preju- dice and institutional power. Without this language, we obscure the reality of power and render the concepts meaningless.

Also consider why and when white people make this claim. It is usu- ally said defensively and with resentment, in order to minimize and deny the impact of white supremacy. Where can you go in response to a claim such as this? It functions to block reflection and end discussion. A person making this claim is usually refusing to engage with the issue and thus maintaining willful ignorance.

"I am all for equality but I don't want anyone to have special rights. Now there is reverse racism"

There is empirical evidence that people of color are discriminated against in hiring and have been since the ending of slavery and into the present. In the late 1960s, a program was instituted to help ameliorate this discrimination: Affirmative Action. There is a great amount of misinformation about Affir- mative Action, which most people are referring to when they bring up "spe- cial rights." Common misinformation about the program usually includes the beliefs that if a person of color applies for a position, they must be hired over a white person, and that a specific number of people of color must be hired in order to fill a quota. This is patently untrue. Affirmative Action is a tool to ensure that *qualified* minority applicants are given the same employment opportunities as white people. It is a flexible program—there are no quotas or requirements as commonly understood. No employer is required to hire an unqualified person of color, but they are required to be able to articulate why they didn't hire a *qualified* person of color. Further, several states have eliminated Affirmative Action, and it may be assumed that before long, the rest of the country will follow suit.

While the 2009–2016 U.S. president was biracial—and this is very significant—consider that 236 years after the first Congress was formed, of 100 senators there is one Latino, one Japanese American, one Native Hawaiian, and one African American. Of the 100 members of the Senate in 2015, two are African Americans, three are Latino, and one is Asian American. None is Native American. Of the 9 members of the Supreme Court, only two are not white. The vast majority of CEOs, *Fortune* 500 executives, managers, professors, doctors, lawyers, scientists, and other prestigious positions of leadership and decision-making are whites. While whites are the majority of people in the United States, their overrepresentation in leadership does not match their numbers in society. This overrepresentation is the result of roughly 300 years of Affirmative Action for whites. This white Affirmative Action has not been in the form of current Affirmative Action programs, which are only guidelines in employment and education, but in the form of concrete discrimination across all institutions of society.

For example, white men with a criminal record are slightly *more* likely to be called back for a job interview than black men with no criminal record, even when they are equally qualified (Pager, 2007). In addition to unconscious preference for white applicants, another way racism manifests in the workplace is through the concept of "fit." This is the tendency to prefer people whose cultural style matches the workplace culture. But fit is a very effective way to maintain the status quo and block diversity. Unless the culture of the workplace is owned by people of color, it will likely be more accepting of and conducive to whites.

Further, *white women* have been the greatest beneficiaries of affirmative action, although the program did not initially include them. Favoring white women over people of color in employment has helped form what some have called a persistent *white ceiling*. Further, corporations are more likely to favor white women and people of color (of elite backgrounds) from outside the United States than within when choosing their executives (Reed, 2011). I think it's worthy to reflect upon why, when pushed, white men have been more receptive to opening the workplace up to white women than to people of color. I see this as a function of white solidarity; when white men were forced to open domains previously only open to white men (fire-fighting, policing, and other trades), gender trumped race. Granting access to white women, who were their daughters, wives, and sisters, was ultimately more beneficial to white men and thus easier to accept.

Unfounded beliefs that Affirmative Action programs require people of color to be hired over whites increases cross-racial conflicts in the workplace. These problems include white resentment caused by the assumption that a person of color got a job through a quota, and not because they could possibly have been the most qualified. If we truly value diversity in the workplace, we might consider the following: if two candidates are equally qualified, but one is a person of color and the other is white and the workplace is not racially diverse, the person of color is actually *more* qualified because they bring a perspective to the workplace that is missing.

While many of us want to believe that we would hire the best person for the job regardless of race, our racial filters skew that assessment and protections such as Affirmative Action, although very minimal, remain necessary (recall the resume study).

"My parents were not racist and they taught me not to be racist"

Whether you define racism as racial prejudices and individual acts (as most people do) or as a system of racial inequality that benefits whites at the expense of people of color (as antiracists do), it is not possible for your parents to have taught you not to be racist, or for your parents to have been free of racism themselves. This is not possible because racism is a social system embedded in culture and its institutions. We are born into this system and don't have a say in whether or not we will be affected by it. Someone who understands what racism is could not make this statement. Indeed, only someone who defined racism as racial prejudice, and then misunderstood the nature of prejudice, could make this statement.

Let's imagine what the person really meant was that their parents were not racially prejudiced and taught them not to be racially prejudiced. This statement would still be false because it is not humanly possible to be free of prejudice. All humans have prejudice to varying degrees based on the culture in which they were raised. This statement simply indicates that the person is uneducated about the socialization process and the inescapable dynamics of human culture. One's parents might have *said* that they were not prejudiced, and thus denied their prejudice. They may have told their children that *they* should not be prejudiced, the result being that like their parents, the children deny their prejudice. They may have sincerely hoped and believed that they were raising their children not to be prejudiced. But we can't actually teach humans to have no prejudice at all. The human brain just does not work that way as we process information about others. We can only teach our children not to *admit to* prejudice. Ideally, we would teach them how to recognize and challenge prejudice, rather than deny it.

Given the unavoidability of both personal prejudice and the current system of institutional racism that has developed from it, the best we can do is to continually challenge our prejudices in order to change the actions they inform. We can do this both personally and institutionally.

"Race has nothing to do with it"

How often have we heard someone preface a story about race with the statement, "Race had nothing to do with this *but* ... " or "She *just happened* to be black. ..." We might consider why the person feels that it is necessary to make this opening point, as it usually illustrates just the opposite. The racist = bad/not racist = good binary is reflected in this need, because according to the binary, if race had anything to do with it, then the person telling the story would be implicated in a racial matter and thus no longer positioned as colorblind or outside of race. Further, if the story is about a conflict between the storyteller and a person of color, then the storyteller might sound racist, and that would mean that they are a bad person. If, however, you understand racism as a social and institutional system into which we are all socialized, then you wouldn't make this disclaimer because you understand that it is not possible for race to have nothing to do with the conflict. We bring our racial histories with us; contrary to the ideology of individualism, we represent our groups and all that has come before us. Our identities are not unique but "constructed" or produced through social processes. Further, we don't see through clear or objective eyes—we see through racial lenses. On some level, race is always at play, even in its supposed absence.

Imagine a workplace meeting or a house party. Everyone in the meeting or at the party is white (this is not an uncommon scene). Most of these people would not see race as present or at play in these settings.

> **Remember:** While we are of course all human, we don't live in a world in which race doesn't matter. Until we attain that world, insisting that one sees everyone as *just human* denies the reality of racism and white privilege, and falsely assumes that everyone has the same experience, regardless of race.

Consider when the white people would think that race had "entered" the picture. Most likely, when a person(s) of color entered the room. Why is race absent from the room before the person of color enters, but present afterward? This reinforces the idea that *they* have race, and they bring race with them, to *us*, who are outside of race. Second, an all-white meeting or party is not an accident; it is the result of decades of policies and practices, including racial discrimination in hiring and white flight, which have resulted in continuing racial segregation at work and home. Third, race is at play in the *acceptance* of the all-white group—the lack of interest in or concern about the absence of people of color.

If a person of color were to enter the previously all-white space, I am confident that every white person would notice, and that they would unavoidably be reading that person through racial lenses.

> **Remember:** There is no human objectivity. We see each other through socialized filters based on our group memberships.

To further illustrate the point, reflect on *when* whites want to insist they don't notice race, and when we want to emphasize how "diverse" a given context is. The way we navigate race in terms of when we say we notice it and when we say we don't is directly related to the *politics* of race and its *social meaning*, not to what we actually do or don't see.

Of course the person of color will also be aware that they are the only person of color among white people, and they too will be reading the room through their own racial lenses. Now imagine there is a conflict between the person of color and a white person in the room. Can we honestly say that race (and our stereotypes, ideas, beliefs, and past experiences related to race) will not be at play in the conflict? Acknowledging that race plays a role in the dynamics of the interaction does not mean that the white people are bad, or that in any conflict with a person of color, the white person is always wrong. But it does mean that one must consider how race impacted each person's perception of the conflict, especially if they want to understand their own and others' responses. Countless studies demonstrate that whites react to people of color differently than to other whites, and react most negatively to blacks. Refusal to acknowledge this and consider its implications is willful ignorance.

"It's racist to talk about race"

The idea that to talk about racism is itself racist has always struck me as odd. It is rooted in the concept that race doesn't matter; thus, to talk about it gives it a weight it should not have. Yet the energy behind this response belies the claim. There are many things that we talk about every day that don't really matter. Yet precisely because these topics of conversation don't matter, they are easy to talk about. It seems clear that we know race matters a great deal, but for many of the reasons already discussed, we feel the need to deny this. Ironically, this denial is a fundamental way in which we *maintain* unequal racial power; the denial only serves those who hold racial power, not those who don't.

I have heard this response many times in the context of cross-racial discussions, most often occurring at the point in which white racial power is named. Many whites see the naming of white racial power as divisive. The problem for those who see it this way is not the existence of power itself, but the *recognition* of it. This recognition breaks the pretense of unity and exposes the reality of racial division. Even though participants of color repeatedly state that *not* naming power maintains dominance and that *this* is what keeps them divided, white participants continue to insist that denying power is necessary for maintaining unity. Although the participants are purportedly engaged in these discussions in order to explore differences in racial perspectives and experiences, as soon as these differences actually appear, many whites react as if there has been a violation. Of course, white norms *are* violated by naming white power. But unequal power relations cannot be challenged if they are not named and acknowledged. Refusing to engage in an authentic exploration of this reality erases (and denies) alternate racial experiences and positions.

The following dynamics underlie the false idea that to talk openly about racism is itself racist:

- Lack of understanding of what racism is and how it works
- White racial taboos against acknowledging that one notices race
- The white pretense that race doesn't matter
- The sense that only people of color have race and we should pretend we don't notice this "flaw"
- White solidarity and the pressure to protect white privilege by keeping it insulated and unnamed
- The need for racial divisions to appear natural rather than constructed and imposed
- The imposition of a white reality onto others—if we block out other realities by not discussing them, we can pretend that they don't exist
- Universalism and its presumption of a shared racial experience
- Individualism and the need to be seen as different from others and outside of collective socialization and group experience
- White Fragility and the need to maintain racial comfort and equilibrium (see Chapter 13)

While it isn't comfortable for most whites to talk about racism, it is necessary if we want to challenge—rather than protect—racism. To not talk about racism can only hold our misinformation in place and prevent us from developing the necessary skills and perspectives.

"It's just human nature; somebody has to be on top"

"Is it nature or is it nurture?" How much of human behavior is biology and how much is socialization is an ongoing debate. As we saw in the earlier discussion of race science, how we generate and interpret data is based on our cultural beliefs. Thus, as a sociologist I lean more toward socialization. However, it is virtually impossible to separate the two and prove what is natural and what is socialized. Therefore, when considering a claim such as this I am less interested in establishing whether it is true, and more interested in how the claim functions in the discussion. Usually, I hear this after I have explained what oppression is. Obviously, claiming that oppression is human nature conveys acceptance—for example, it's going to happen no matter what because it's natural, so what can you do about it? It does appear that groups of people have dominated other groups of people across history, so it may indeed be human nature. But people have also resisted domination and struggled to create more just societies across history, so that, too, appears to be human nature. Further, the reasons we have dominated others are arbitrary. For example, in some societies the elderly are valued and treated with respect, and in others—such as ours—they are devalued and discarded. In other words, humans construct reasons to oppress others, and thus we can deconstruct those reasons. I would argue that seeking to end domination and create a just society is the more evolved goal. It's certainly the goal I choose to support. Which side of this ongoing struggle do *you* choose to support?

It is also useful to consider who is more likely to make the claim that oppression is just human nature—those who are oppressing or those being oppressed? I don't think I have ever heard someone from an oppressed group rationalize their oppression by saying it's just human nature. This discourse only serves the interests of the dominant group.

"The real issue is class. If we addressed class, racism wouldn't be an issue"

Again, when considering claims in discussions of race such as this one—that the true oppression is class—I ask myself how the claim functions. Does it open and expand the discussion? Does it seek to add more insight and analysis? Does it convey humility and a willingness to engage in self-reflection? Or does it work to close off, end, or derail the discussion? Since the person making this claim is essentially saying that race is not an issue or that racism would disappear if class were addressed, it clearly functions to deny the validity of racism. It also moves the discussion off the topic of racism (in antiracism education we call this "channel-switching"). While ultimately all forms of oppression are about the distribution of resources, we could say that all oppressions are ultimately rooted in classism. But that does not negate the reality and salience of racism and how it *deepens and intensifies* the inequitable distribution of resources.

As someone who was raised poor, I know that my experience of poverty was different because I am white. I was both implicitly and explicitly taught that I was above people of color, regardless of my poverty. I also know that I will have the advantage in the job market, workplace, and as I navigate institutions. Poor whites and poor people of color are not exactly "all in the same boat." Barbara Major, speaking on behalf of the *Bring Back New Orleans Mayoral Commission* (2007), puts it succinctly: "Race trumps anything in this country. You give me class, race gonna trump it. You give me anything ... and as bad as your situation is you put some color on it and see if it isn't worse."

"How can you say only whites can be racist? There is racism all over the world! Look at Rwanda!"

Yes, racism occurs in other countries. If a group that holds institutional power in a society oppresses another group in that society based on race, they are engaged in racism. For example, the Chinese can be racist toward the Tibetans without any involvement from white people. I am not saying racism doesn't occur in other societies. I am saying that in the West—Europe, Canada, and the United States—whites are the racial group holding long-term historical institutional power over people of color. And since that is where I am situated as I write this book, that is the context I am addressing. I assume that my readers are also situated in the United States or other Western contexts, and thus they, too, should be addressing their own context. Similar to the rebuttal that people of color are "just as racist" as whites, this rebuttal—that other countries are just as racist as the United States—blocks self-reflection and derails the discussion.

"How dare you accuse me of racism! I am a good person!"

In the early days of my work co-facilitating antiracist trainings, I was taken aback at how angry and defensive so many white people became at any suggestion that they were connected to racism in any way. The very idea that they would have to attend a workshop on racism was outrageous to them. They entered the room angry and made that anger clear to us throughout the day as they slammed their notebooks down on the table, refused to participate in exercises, and occasionally told us off. At that point in my learning, I just couldn't understand the anger or lack of interest in learning more about such a complex dynamic as racism. These reactions were especially perplexing when there were few or no people of color in their workplace. Wouldn't that indicate a problem? Or at least indicate that some perspectives were missing? Or that they might be undereducated about race due to their lack of exposure to cross-racial interactions? Thus, wouldn't an educational workshop on racism be appreciated?

It took me several years to see beneath this anger. At first I was intimidated by it, and it held me back and kept me careful and quiet. But over time, because it was so predictable—so patterned and consistent—I was able to stop taking it personally, get past my own survival mode, and reflect on what was behind it. The more familiar it became the more clearly I was able to think about it. I began to see what I think of as the "anchors" of whiteness—the pillars that prop up our racial concepts. I could see the power of the racist = bad/not racist = good binary, as well as how individualism allowed white people to exempt themselves from racism. I could see how we are taught to think about racism only as acts that individual whites do, rather than as a system. And based on countless expressions of resentment toward people of color that whites expressed, I realized that we see ourselves as entitled to and deserving of more than people of color; I saw our *investment* in a system that serves us. I also saw how hard we worked to *deny* all of this. My personal reflections on my own racism, my viewing of media and other aspects of culture with more critical eyes, and my exposure to the perspectives of people of color all helped me to "see" how these aspects of racism worked. Figure 43 is intended to illustrate perceiving feedback about racism as an accusation, rather than as valuable information.

I could only respond with outrage to suggestions of my involvement in racism if I think it is not possible for me to commit an act of racism. Thus, I will feel "accused," as the term accused implies unfair or false. The racist = bad/not racist = good binary makes it virtually impossible for whites to reflect upon our problematic racial patterns.

Remember: Being a good person and being complicit in racism are not mutually exclusive. We may be good people, but have still been socialized into unaware racist perspectives, investments, and behaviors.

Figure 43. Barrier.

If, however, I understand racism as a system into which I was socialized, I can actually receive feedback on my problematic racial patterns as a kind of gift, from which I can learn and grow.

Imagine walking out of a public restroom and not realizing that a long strip of toilet paper is affixed to your shoe. Someone approaches you to let you know. Most people, while slightly embarrassed, would appreciate being informed so that they could remove the paper and avoid further embarrassment. They would thank the person who told them. It's not likely that someone would respond with outrage and insist that there is no toilet paper and that everyone better carry on as if it's not there. Once we truly integrate an understanding of racism as unavoidable, we understand that it is *not possible* for us to be completely free of problematic racial patterns, and we actually come to see feedback about it (while still somewhat embarrassing), as ultimately something valuable from which we can learn. Figure 44 is meant to illustrate this conceptual frame and the more constructive response it engenders.

When we understand social power, we understand what it takes for a person from a minoritized group to give feedback to a member of the dominant group. In other words, it's very difficult for a person with a disability to tell an

Figure 44. Bridge.

able-bodied person that they have just done something ableist, or for a woman to tell a man that he has just said something sexist, or a person of color to tell a white person that they have just done something racist. Giving feedback to dominant group members from the minoritized position is difficult because dominant group members are simultaneously uninformed about the oppression and highly defensive. Dominant group members' responses typically include: dismissal, trivialization, denial, hurt feelings, anger, and punishments such as withdrawal, exclusion, or telling others how difficult and oversensitive the minoritized group member is. Sometimes dominant group members will go to other members of the minoritized group and try to get them to agree that their fellow member was wrong. These reactions put minoritized group members in a very difficult spot, and they often choose to endure the slight rather than be targeted further.

Recall the bitter laughter when people of color are asked if they have ever had a positive experience trying to talk to whites about our racism. Many people of color report trying to have these conversations, but they are so consistently invalidated that they stop bringing them up. But this does not mean there is no longer racism manifesting in the relationship; it just means that the relationship is not as close as the white person may believe. This should be a red flag to whites who have relationships with people of color—if you are not talking about race and racism, it may be an indicator that there is a lack of trust in the relationship.

In this chapter I have attempted to address many common white narratives about racism. I am confident that these narratives are familiar to my readers. This familiarity illustrates that opinions are not just personal, benign, or merely uninformed; they are rooted in unexamined ideology and serve to actively reproduce racism by rationalizing and/or denying its reality. While rationalizing and denying racism may not be the conscious intention of those making these claims, such claims do function this way. If we are sincere about challenging the racism circulating in the culture at large, we must be willing to challenge our worldviews. This requires us to explore the ideology that informs our worldview, and the impact of that ideology.

Discussion Questions

1. Which of the narratives that deny racism are the most challenging for you to speak back to? Why? How can you work to be more comfortable speaking back to narratives that challenge you? Practice speaking back to these narratives using the concepts in this book.

2. Which of the narratives have you held yourself, or still hold? If you could speak back to yourself with the voice of the author, how would you counter the narrative?

3. How do these narratives illustrate several of the concepts discussed thus far: socialization; implicit bias; internalized dominance; ideology; the white racial frame?

4. How can a white person still enact racism in a close relationship with a person of color? Doesn't the close relationship itself prove that they are not racist? Explain how and why enacting racism in a close relationship with a person of color is not only possible but inevitable.

5. The author states that white ignorance is not born of innocence and is not simply a matter of not knowing, and that it is highly effective at protecting our investments in racism and thus actively maintained. Discuss this statement. If you are white, how have you seen willful ignorance in yourself? In other white people?

· 1 5 ·

STOP TELLING THAT STORY! DANGER DISCOURSE AND THE WHITE RACIAL FRAME

I am a white professor. I teach in a program that is 97 percent white. We are located 10 miles away from Springfield, MA, a city that is approximately 57 percent black and Latino. I am walking down the hallway towards the classroom where I am teaching a course titled "Schools in Society." In this course, we take an institutional perspective on schools as primary sites of socialization and explore the role that schools play in the maintenance and reproduction of social inequality. On the second day of class, during an introductory exercise wherein students share aspects of their frames of reference, a student shares that she and her boyfriend had been "mugged by a black man in Springfield." I am dismayed that she chooses to tell us this, and that she doesn't follow it with any point or connection, but don't see how I can challenge her story so early in the course. Now, 8 weeks later, we have finished reading James Loewen's Lies My Teacher Told Me *and are halfway though Michelle Alexander's* The New Jim Crow: Mass Incarceration in an Era of Colorblindness. *My students have responded very well to both texts and I am feeling hopeful that they are beginning to understand the multidimensional nature of racism and how it is structured into society. As I walk towards the classroom, a group of students is sitting in the hall and as I approach, I hear their conversation. "I grew up in a really sheltered neighborhood so I am scared to do my placement there." "Oh, I used to live in New Haven where I heard gunshots at the dance club, so Springfield doesn't scare me."*

"Wow! Growing up in a small town, I've never had anything like that happen to me." The conversation continues in this vein.

Toni Morrison (1993b) uses the term "racetalk" to capture the explicit insertion into everyday life of racial signs and symbols that have no meaning other than positioning African Americans into the lowest level of the racial hierarchy. Casual racetalk is a key component of white racial framing because it accomplishes the interconnected goals of elevating whites while demeaning people of color; racetalk always implies a racial "us" and "them." How we *think* and *speak* about people of color is a fundamental foundation for how we *treat* people of color. Discourse that specifically positions people of color as inherently dangerous, while simultaneously positioning whites as inherently innocent, has material consequences in the larger society. My goal here is not to add to the body of evidence for racetalk, but to make a clear and compelling case, based on a familiar and representative example, for whites to *stop* racetalk.

As I consider my students' racial narratives, it is important to remind readers again that these narratives do not stand alone. They represent a vast network of similar narratives; comments, images, and representations that whites are exposed to and circulate on a daily basis and that position whites as superior (recall the 2007 Picca & Feagin study on racial discourse among college students). I term the particular form of racetalk illustrated in the opening vignette *danger discourse*.

In the vignette of danger discourse above, we can see white racial framing and white solidarity at play in several familiar and more or less racially explicit statements. While the opening claim of the student in the hall, *"I grew up in a really sheltered neighborhood …,"* is less explicit than the mugging story, it is still clearly racially coded. It is a very important narrative for whites, as it opens many white racial narratives and is relentlessly reinforced by news stories that position any primarily white suburban community in which a major crime occurs as "sheltered." It is a claim that begs the question, "Sheltered from what and in contrast to whom?" Of course sheltered is always in contrast to spaces that are not sheltered, which are by default urban and filled with people of color (black and brown people in particular).

Conversely, positioning white spaces as sheltered and those who are raised in them as racially innocent taps into classic discourses of people of color as *not* innocent. The second part of the claim reinforces the first, *"… so I am scared to do my placement there."* Racist images and resultant white fears can be found at all levels of society, and myriad studies demonstrate that whites believe that people of color (and blacks in particular) are dangerous (DiAngelo & Sensoy, 2014). These beliefs are fueled by the mass media via relentless representations of people of color associated with criminality. Indeed, much of white flight and the resulting segregation in housing and schooling can be attributed to this representation. Danger discourse distorts reality, trivializes the true direction of violence and positions whites as innocent.

The discourse of innocence is powerful in part because it rests not only on the current structure of white supremacy, but also on this vast backdrop of historical white supremacy. Whites rarely consider how sheltered and safe their spaces may be from the perspective of people of color. For example, students of color attending primarily white schools often experience them as unsafe. Treyvon Martin was a young Black man who was walking home from the store in a gated white community when he was presumed to be a threat, shot and killed. Although that community, because it was gated, was likely viewed as "safe" from the white perspective, Treyvon's murder within those gates turns that discourse on its head. Because it is such a bald perversion of the true direction of racial danger, whiteness as innocence may be one of the most perniciously clever of racist discourses.

The opening claim is followed by this statement: *"Oh, I used to live in New Haven where I heard gunshots at the dance club, so Springfield doesn't scare me."* Contrary to the first speaker, this speaker is positioning herself as jaded rather than innocent. She isn't afraid to go to an urban space because she has been initiated; she has ventured outside of sheltered communities, been exposed to the danger, and survived. Her narrative works powerfully to reinforce the belief in the inherent danger of black and brown spaces for those who have no cross-racial experience—she has witnessed the danger firsthand and can confirm it. She has been to places *even worse than Springfield*, and she is not afraid. But her lack of fear does not come because she can now testify that there is nothing to be afraid of. She has not built relationships with the inhabitants of these spaces; she has no stories to tell that would humanize them. This is not a narrative of integration. No, her social capital is generated from the fact that she has seen the danger, and can attest to it. Her narrative, while in contrast to the first speaker, still positions her firmly inside of whiteness as she testifies for the white collective gathered there that their fears are legitimate.

"Wow! Growing up in a small town, I've never had anything like that happen to me." The "wow!" indicates that our second speaker has indeed accrued the social capital of "racial experience." Her narrative is met with a kind of white

racial awe. This speaker has been reinforced in her fear of racial others. The statement that follows the "wow!" brings us back to the narrative of white racial innocence and the reinforcement of white spaces as inherently safe by virtue of the absence of people of color—these things happen "out there" where *they* are but not "in here" where *we* are (I feel compelled to point out that we are located 75 miles from Newtown, CT, the site of the Sandy Hook shooting). These students bond over their collective recognition of spaces inhabited by black and brown people as *other* to their own, simultaneously reinforcing racist images and weaving the threads of white solidarity.

The statement made by a student on the second day of class, "*My boyfriend and I were mugged by a Black man in Springfield*" functions similarly to that above, but holds perhaps more shock value and thus more social capital; racetalk has a "certain allure" and "spices up conversations in enjoyable ways" (Myers, 2003, p. 4). While I assume that this is a true statement (and that her boyfriend is white), discursively it is deeply problematic in this context. It is shared in an exercise in which students have been asked to articulate how various aspects of group identity shape their perspectives. This student does not talk about being white; that a black man mugged her is the sum of her racial narrative. Yet, it is critical to this student's story that she name the mugger's race. This naming happens in a context in which many whites (and younger whites in particular) insist that they don't see color, or that it has no meaning for them.

The one-sided racial naming of this story powerfully highlights the racial binary while serving as a cautionary tale. Through her narrative, she rein-scribes the white racial frame, reinforces Black danger and white innocence, reinforces we-they boundaries, and maintains white solidarity in this all-white space. She too gains the social capital accrued from racial experience that is unmarred by testimony that could disrupt the narrative of black danger.

These stories are told in a context of extreme segregation. In fact, my students' life trajectories (as with most middle-class/upwardly mobile whites) almost certainly ensure that they will have few, if any, enduring relationships with people of color. This segregation is justified and reinforced by danger discourse.

There is nothing special about these students (although it is important to note that they will go on to become teachers). These narratives have been well documented across many white contexts (see Bonilla-Silva, 2009; Picca & Feagin, 2007). I have been to countless conferences wherein white teachers preface their comments with a description of their schools as "rough" or in "bad neighborhoods." These are simply more racially coded forms of danger discourse, and while they are socially acceptable, they are also highly reductive and paint whole communities with a very broad and negative brush. These narratives carry discursive capital and connect to countless supporting narratives stretching across history that they are keeping alive and in circulation. The examples here provide a momentary freeze-frame of the ongoing and adaptive racial (and racist) social context we are all immersed in. As Myers (2003) states, "dominant ideologies help whites to maintain power by manufacturing consent" (p. 144). Danger discourse links and reinforces the *ideology* of white supremacy with the resultant *practices* of white supremacy.

Returning to the vignette that opens this chapter, I addressed the comment in class the following week, after I had time for further reflection. I decided to take race off the table in order to diminish defensiveness in this all-white class. Instead, I focused on an identity that I knew they had sympathy for based on previous discussions. In this case, it was sexual orientation. I had them imagine someone telling a negative and deeply stereotypical story about a gay man over and over. I asked them to trace what other discourses about gay men this story would connect to and reinforce in order to illustrate that no story stands alone. We mapped these out on the board to reveal how the story functioned not only as a cautionary tale to prevent gay men from entering the teaching field, but also to reinforce heterosexuality and binary gender roles as normative and inherently superior.

Next we discussed why people repeat these stories, and what they would need to give up if they stopped telling them. It became clear that reinforcing the social position of the storyteller was an integral but unmarked function of the story; the contrasting relationship between the storytellers' identities and the object of their derision was inseparable. We ended with the question, "Would you be willing to give up such a story, or ask another to do so, given your understanding of how the story functions?" Everyone agreed that they would be. I then raised what I had heard in the hall, why I was distressed about it, and asked them to please stop telling that story. Their reflection papers the following week indicated that this had been a powerful session.

I understand that the stories we as white people tell about cross-racial encounters may be "true," but I want to make a case for us to stop telling them in contexts and ways in which they can only function to reinforce white solidarity and white supremacy. Of course one may tell about a mugging to the police, and to one's family when in need of emotional or physical support. But in a predominately white public forum (and with no antiracist analysis), sharing this story is deeply problematic. Challenging whiteness requires breaking white solidarity and giving up the social capital accrued from the oppression of people of color. It requires us to think intentionally and strategically about what we are doing and how that functions to either maintain or reinforce racism. We must ask ourselves, "What do I lose by not telling this story?" and use the answer to that question as an entry point into examining and breaking our investments in racism and white supremacy.[1]

Discussion Questions

1. The author argues that although a racial story may be true, we should not tell it in certain contexts. Explain why.
2. How is the white racial frame reinforced through danger discourse?
3. What forms of social capital do white people gain through danger discourse?
4. Have you engaged in danger discourse, either as the story teller or the receiver? How did you feel when you were in these roles? What can those feelings help illustrate about how danger discourse works to reinforce racism? How might you respond the next time you hear danger discourse?
5. How do you see danger discourse circulating on the societal and institutional levels? What role does it play in maintaining explicit bias and the racist policies and practices that are informed by implicit bias?

Note

1. An earlier version of this chapter appears in Carr, P., Lea, V., & Lund, D. (Eds.) (2015). *Critical multicultural perspectives on whiteness.* New York: Peter Lang.

· 16 ·

A NOTE ON WHITE SILENCE

To me being white means no more to me than if I was any other race. This is what I was taught all through school. I have been taught not to be judgmental. Although I did grow up in an almost completely white-population town, I have never felt any sense of racism apparent in myself or my peers. However, the older generation where I grew up did seem to be a little judgmental and particular to their own race. Growing up I just chose to ignore things said/taught to do with race from these people. (ASR)

My colleague and I are facilitating a workshop. She has just made a presentation on the impact of racism on people of color. She leads the participants of color in a follow-up discussion. Now she turns and asks the white participants for their thoughts. She explains how important it is in terms of trust building for the people of color to hear what the white participants gained from the discussion. She'd also like the chance to clarify any misunderstanding. No white participants respond. She tries again, explaining that she and the participants of color have made themselves vulnerable by exposing the pain of racism, and that it is important for them to know how they have been heard. One white participant speaks up and shares her thoughts. My co-facilitator thanks her and asks to hear from a few more people. Silence. After a very long wait, I try. I explain how critical it is for us to practice speaking across race, take risks, and show ourselves. I point out that in the face of a direct request from a person of color for feedback, their silence has a racist impact, and may even feel hostile. Could just a few more people share their thoughts so the people of color can get a sense of where they are? The silence continues. Given that the worst fear of most whites is that they be perceived as being racist, and they have just been given direct feedback that this is the effect their silence is having, how can they continue to hold back? What's going on?

Because I lead discussions about race and racism on an almost daily basis, certain patterns of white engagement have become predictable to me. In Chapter 12, I discussed several of these patterns. In this chapter, I want to introduce and discuss a specific white pattern in a specific context: whites' tendency to remain silent in racial discussions. By analyzing white silence in racial discussions, I hope to illustrate and challenge many common white rationales and the patterns that result from them.

Two fundamental premises of antiracist practice are: (1) the need to continually educate yourself, and (2) the need to build cross-racial relationships. White silence limits our ability to accomplish either of these goals. If readers are engaging with this book in order to discuss it with others—perhaps it was assigned in a class or workshop related to these issues, or they are working on racial equity in the workplace or other organization—addressing this pattern will be especially relevant.

In cross-racial discussions it is easy to be distracted by white participants who dominate; indeed, facilitators spend a lot of energy strategizing about how to rein in these participants. For example, in the excellent and award-winning educational film *The Color of Fear*, in which a racially diverse group of men discuss racism, the white man who continually dominates the discussion and invalidates the men of color receives the greatest amount of attention in every post-film discussion I have led. Yet there is another white man in the film who is at the other end of the participation spectrum, one who rarely speaks and has to be asked directly to join in. This participant receives little if any attention following the film, but his role in the discussion is no less racially salient. I want to direct our attention to the often-neglected end of the participation continuum—white silence. I hope to challenge white participants who are silent in cross-racial discussions. My goal is to unsettle the complacency that often surrounds this silence and motivate silent whites to speak up.

> **Remember:** The racial status quo is not neutral; it is racist. Therefore, anything that works to maintain the status quo rather than challenge it maintains racism. Because whites are usually most comfortable not talking about race, remaining silent when given the opportunity to discuss race supports the status quo.

Within the current racial construct, white racial comfort and sense of racial equilibrium are rooted in norms and traditions that uphold relations of inequality; one of these norms is to avoid talking openly about race, especially in mixed-race groups. When white normative taboos against talking directly about race are broken, especially within the context of deliberately challenging racial inequality, it is uncomfortable and destabilizing for many whites. Seeking to regain our comfort and sense of racial stability is a predictable response. In a racial discussion, white moves that are intended to maintain racial comfort or equilibrium necessarily work to maintain traditional racial relations. In this context, when whites employ silence to maintain a degree of comfort, that silence functions (albeit implicitly) as a means to regain dominance and control.

Overall Effects of White Silence

In racial dialogue, white silence functions to shelter white participants by keeping their racial perspectives hidden and thus protected from exploration or challenge. Not offering your perspective for exploration serves to ensure that it cannot be expanded. While one can, of course, gain deeper understanding through listening, there are several problems with this being one's primary mode of engagement. Listening alone leaves everyone else to carry the weight of the discussion. And, of course, if everyone chose this mode, no discussion (and hence no learning) would occur at all. On the other hand, one may have something to say that is insightful and that could contribute to everyone's learning, but if a lack of confidence can't be overcome, everyone loses.

In the context of particularly difficult discussions, white silence serves to embolden explicitly resistant participants because it establishes that no challenge will be forthcoming, and can even imply agreement. Even if whites who are silent find the behavior of their peers problematic, their silence allows vocally resistant participants to continually dictate the agenda of the discussion and rally resources around themselves as facilitators (and others) work to move them forward. At a minimum, the resistant participants receive no social penalty from other whites, and the silence effectively maintains white solidarity. Although silent whites might recognize and be troubled by the behavior of some of their white cohorts, they ultimately maintain their white privilege by not contesting this behavior.

Silence has different effects depending on what move it follows. For example, if white silence follows a story shared by a person of color about the impact of racism on their lives, that silence serves to invalidate the story. People of color who take the social risk of revealing the impact of racism only to be met by white silence are left with their vulnerability unreciprocated. Whites could offer validation, for example, by sharing how the story impacted them or what insight they gained from hearing it. Conversely, when white silence follows a particularly problematic move made by a white participant, that silence supports the move by offering no interruption. When white silence follows a white antiracist stand (such as challenging one's fellow whites to racialize their perspectives), it serves to isolate the person who took that stand. This isolation is a powerful social penalty and an enticement to return to the comfort of white solidarity.

When is white silence a constructive move in racial dialogue?

White silence, when used strategically from an antiracist framework, can be a constructive move in racial discussions. Indeed, too much white participation simply reinscribes the white dominance and centrality embedded in the larger society. What differentiates constructive use of white silence from a reinforcement of white racism is that the person is using their best judgment, based in an antiracist framework and *at each phase of the discussion*, to determine the most constructive way to engage, with the goal of deepening racial self-knowledge, building antiracist community, and interrupting traditional racist power relations. No one way for whites to engage is likely to be effective in all contexts, but antiracist white engagement asks that one *continually grapple* with the question of how best to interrupt white power and privilege. The following are generally good times for whites to just listen when in inter-racial groups:

- When people of color are discussing the sensitive issue of internalized racial oppression
- When one tends to take up a lot of airspace, and in recognition of the history of white dominance, is trying to pull back and have a less dominant voice
- When other whites have already spoken first and at length to an issue
- When intentionally trying not to speak first and most in the discussion
- When a person of color has spoken and we feel drawn to re-explain, clarify, or "add to" their point (and thereby "say it better" and have the last word on the matter)
- When a facilitator asks for whites to just listen, hold back, or not go first

The above list addresses silence in the context of racially mixed groups. In all-white settings, the dynamics are different because whites are not navigating their relationships to people of color in the group. In the context of all-white groups, white silence results in a missed opportunity to explore one's racial perspectives, feelings, blind spots, and assumptions. To not take advantage of a structured discussion about race in an all-white group prevents community-building and antiracist alignment among whites and fails to support those whites who are actively taking risks in the pursuit of antiracist growth. In this context, the main reason for white silence should be for periods of personal reflection, and to provide time and space for other, more reticent whites who need a slower pace to speak up. These forms of silence can more authentically be seen as active listening.

Rationales for White Silence and an Antiracist Challenge

"It's just my personality; I rarely talk in groups"

Our personalities are not separate from the society in which we were raised. All whites in the United States are socialized in a white dominant society. Our patterns of engagement are not merely a function of our unique person-alities, they are developed within a social and political context and occur in relationship with social others. By focusing on ourselves as individuals, we are able to conceptualize the patterns in our behavior that have a racist impact as "just our personality" and not connected to inter-group dynam-ics. For example, I might be an extrovert and talk over people when I am engaged in a discussion. I can say, "that is just my personality, I do that to everyone. That is how we talked at the dinner table in my family. And because I do it to everyone, it can't be racism." However, when I talk over a person of color, the impact of that behavior is different because we bring the racial history of our groups with us. While we tend to see ourselves as individuals, not representing a race, people of color tend to see us as *white* individuals. Thus the *meaning* of cutting off or talking over a person of color is very different.

Antiracist action requires us to challenge our patterns and respond differ-ently than we normally would. The freedom to remain oblivious to that fact, with no sense that this obliviousness has any consequences of importance, is a form of white privilege. In effect, we are saying, "I will not adapt to you or this context, I will continue to act the way I always act and you will have to adapt to me."

Participants of color seldom see themselves as having the option to disengage or withdraw from a cross-racial discussion based solely on their personal preferences for engagement. They understand that dominant culture does not position them as individuals and has a different set of stereotypical expectations for them. If they hold back, they reinforce these expectations, a concern that puts constant pressure on them. Not speaking up due to personal preference—*without penalty*—is a privilege they are not afforded; if they remain silent they don't challenge the racism that constricts their lives. This pressure illustrates the difference in the way white people and people of color often conceptualize themselves. Whites tend to see themselves as unique individuals and not members of a racial group whose actions represent that group. People of color, who don't have that luxury, want whites to meet them halfway—to understand white patterns at the group level and push through the temporary discomfort of not engaging in their "preferred" mode in order to challenge those patterns. Challenging whiteness requires whites to engage differently in order to interrupt problematic racial dynamics.

"Everyone has already said what I was thinking," or "I don't have much to add"

Perhaps others have expressed our general sentiments, but no one will express them the way that we will. It's essential to the discussion to hear everyone's voice, and even vocalizing one or two sentences makes a difference. If an antiracist perspective has been offered, it is important to support that perspective. Further, it is important to give people of color a read of the room; they do not know what we are thinking. In fact, given the history of harm between white people and people of color, people of color may assume whites haven't spoken because they are *not* aligned with an antiracist perspective and don't want to reveal that misalignment. It is important for us to contribute our thoughts in order to demonstrate to people of color that what they have shared has made a difference in terms of helping increase our understanding. If we are moved or if we gained insight from what someone shared, we should say so, even if others have also said it.

Sometimes the reticence to speak is based on a perception that those who have expressed similar thoughts are far more articulate, and that we won't be as eloquent. In my experience, openness, humility, and vulnerability are the most important aspects of participation, not perfection. Positioning ourselves as having less of value to contribute than others in the group may be rooted in dominant culture's expectation that knowledge should be a form of "correct" information. Yet sharing what we are thinking, whether "right" or "wrong," articulate or clumsy, is important in terms of building trust, conveying empathy, or validating a perspective.

"I am trying to be careful not to dominate the discussion"

While it is important not to dominate discussions in general and important for a white person not to dominate an inter-racial discussion in particular, this strategy needs to remain flexible. Antiracist practice asks us to think strategically—to be *racially* attentive to the person who is talking, when, how much, and for how long. As a white person in the discussion, we need to ask ourselves when it is a constructive time to speak up, and when is it most constructive to just listen. The more practiced we become in racial discussions, the more easily we will be able to make sound strategic judgments about where and when to enter. When we remain silent we leave the weight of the dialogue on either people of color or other, more dominant whites. If these dominant whites are expressing hostility, we aren't challenging them; if they are taking risks, we aren't supporting them. When one is trying not to dominate the discussion and so never joins in, one errs on the opposite side of domination—passive collusion.

"I feel intimidated by people in this group who have power over me"

Complex socio-political power relations circulate in all groups, and there are other identities besides race at play in any discussion. While one is in a power position as a white person, there are other identities that may obscure that sense of power because they are minoritized—namely, gender or class. Because we "swim against the current" in our minoritized identities, they are generally more salient to us. However, that our race may not be salient to us does not mean it is inoperative; indeed, much of the power we derive from whiteness is in its unremarkable, taken-for-granted status. In a setting in which I feel intimidated because I am more aware of my minoritized identities, this feeling of intimidation may indeed be coming from a place of internalized inferiority. In practice, however, my silence colludes with racism and ultimately benefits me by protecting my white privilege and maintaining racial solidarity with other white people. When I work to keep my race privilege salient and push myself to speak up in this context, I not only break white solidarity, I simultaneously interrupt (and thus work to heal the "lie" of) my internalized inferiority where I am also in a minoritized position.

In situations in which we fear there may be repercussions because someone is present who holds more power in the specific *context*—for example, I am a staff worker and my supervisor is in the room—a different kind of courage is needed. This is the courage to put our integrity to do the right thing above the *possibility* of repercussions. Ultimately, we have to make an ethical decision: Do I protect myself and maintain white solidarity and power, or do I authentically engage in antiracist practice and accept the risks that may go with it?

"I don't know much about race so I will just listen"

Many whites have not thought about racism in the way that antiracist education conceptualizes it, but once we are introduced, it's important to share our thoughts. If I have never thought about these issues before, what am I thinking about them now as a result of the discussion? What information is new to me? What questions do I have? What insights am I having? What emotions am I feeling? Why might I have never thought about these issues before, and what role might this play in keeping racism in place? In other words, how might racism depend on white people not thinking about these issues? Being new to the concepts is not an end point or a pass to only listen and not speak; it is a key entry point into the discussion and into further self-knowledge.

While as white people we may not have thought explicitly about race from an antiracist perspective, we do have knowledge of the ways in which we are socialized into denial of ourselves as racialized. We can speak to why we believe we don't know anything about race—for example, if we don't know much about it, who do we believe does know about it, and why do they have this knowledge when we do not? Further, why have we not sought out this knowledge prior to this conversation? Explorations such as these have the potential to reveal our racial paradigms, an essential precursor to antiracist action; they are a great place to start engaging in the discussion without depending on people of color to teach us.

"I already know all this"

While the previous rationale positions the listener as racially innocent and thus only able to absorb the discussion, this rationale positions the listener as so sophisticated that she is *beyond* the discussion. This claim gives the message to the people of color in the group that there is nothing to be gained from what they might share—their stories, experiences, perspectives, or feelings. This claim is particularly problematic because it conveys superiority by rein-scribing the historical invalidation of people of color as having no knowledge of value to white people, while simultaneously elevating oneself above other whites in the group and the potential to work together with them against racism.

The antiracist framework holds that racism is a deeply embedded, complex system that will not end in our lifetimes, and that *certainly* will not end through our complacency. I have been studying racism in depth for many years, and there are vast amounts I have yet to learn and ever more transformative action I have yet to practice. I don't understand white people who think they are done "dealing with" racism because they took a class, or read a book, or have a friend, or live in a "diverse" town, or are just cool and progressive people. If one sincerely believes that their understanding of racism is more advanced than the discussion allows (which can happen when the majority of the white participants are very new to the concepts and the facilitators assess that they must move at a slower pace), then the antiracist way to engage is to make strategic points which will help guide the other white people. Whites who have more knowledge than the majority of the group are in an excellent position to mentor from the sidelines. They can share their own process and how they came to their current understanding, validate the struggle while reinforcing its worthiness, take the discussion deeper, and back up the facilitators and participants of color.

We may have an intellectual grasp of the dynamics, but awareness of racial inequity alone is not enough. White people, served well by the dynamics of whiteness, are also in a prime position to interrupt it, yet to do so we must take unambiguous action. Claiming that "we already know" is meaningless without demonstration of that knowledge, and remaining silent is not a demonstration of antiracist action or understanding. People of color involved in antiracist endeavors generally assume that all whites have a racist perspective unless demonstrated otherwise (Sue, 2003; Tatum, 2008). To not explicitly take up an antiracist stance in such a context can only reinforce the perception that we are choosing to align with whiteness. Being "advanced" is not a reason for us to disengage; the disengagement itself makes the claim unconvincing.

"I need time to process"

In my experience, participants who use this rationale seldom return after processing to share the results, suggesting that this may be a deflection based in self-protection rather than an expression of a sincere difference in how people process information. We may indeed need time to process, but taking that time is a privilege not everyone can afford. At the minimum, we can try articulating what we are hearing that we need to process, and then let the group know that these are new ideas, that we are feeling overwhelmed, and we want to let things settle in. We can let the group know *why* we need the time to process and *what* we will be processing, rather than remain silent and leave others to wonder. When we have had time to process, we can share the results with the group.

It's also helpful to distinguish between the need to process and the need to sound controlled, correct, and coherent. If composure is what we are waiting for, we are working at cross-purposes to the discussion. Confusion, inner conflict, and inarticulation are all usually welcome in racial discussions. Vulnerability and openness build trust, and while thoughtfulness and respect are critical, control and composure are not necessary and can be counterproductive.

"I don't want to be misunderstood"

To remain silent with the goal of preventing possible misunderstanding is to protect our perspective from deepening or expanding. Given the institutionalization of racism in society, it is not possible for white people to be free of problematic racial assumptions and blind spots. Of course it is uncomfortable and even embarrassing to see that we lack certain forms of knowledge, but if we don't take risks, we will never gain that knowledge. It is imperative that we enter the discussion with a willingness (even an enthusiasm) to have our assumptions uncovered so that we can increase our knowledge and cross-racial skills. How will we realize that we have misconceptions and only a partial view if we don't share our views and open them up to exploration?

When whites feel misunderstood in a racial discussion, it is usually because we were given feedback on a racial assumption or blind-spot. Based on the racist = bad/not racist = good binary, we *must* have been misunderstood because we couldn't *possibly* have done anything racially problematic. Sadly, pointing out gaps in a white person's understanding is often experienced as being attacked or judged. When we insist that we were misunderstood, rather than engage with the possibility that *we* are the ones with limited understanding, we close ourselves off to further learning. We place the responsibility for the "misunderstanding" onto those who we believe have misunderstood us— usually the participants of color. If the only way one will engage in cross-racial discussion is to never be challenged, there is minimal point to the discussion.

"I don't feel safe/I don't want to be attacked/I don't want to be judged"

The safety discourse, while one of the most familiar and understandable, is also one of the most problematic. On the surface, it conveys a kind of vulnerability and desire for protection. Unfortunately, it is based in a lack of understanding of historical and ongoing institutional, cultural, and inter-personal power relations between white people and people of color. While the feelings may be real for white people struggling with a sense of safety, it is important to clarify between actual safety and what is more realistically a concern about comfort. If one does not fear that one is in actual *physical* harm, then reflection on what one actually fears can offer much insight. Because we have been taught that only bad people participate in racism, we often fear that if it is somehow revealed that *we* participate in racism, we will lose face.

Many white people feel very uncomfortable in racial discussions, but this discomfort is actually a positive sign, for it indicates that the status quo (unnamed and unexamined racism) is being challenged. It is therefore critical that we feel uncomfortable, and not confuse discomfort with danger. As for being judged, there is no human objectivity—all people judge, and we cannot protect ourselves from judgments. But feeling judged, while dismaying, should not be confused with safety.

Further, the language of safety is not without significance in this context. By implying potential victimization, we obscure our power and privilege. People of color seldom have the luxury of withdrawing because they don't feel safe. It doesn't benefit people of color to remain silent, as it does us. To not put themselves "out there" makes them complicit in their own oppression. People of color cannot depend on white people to advocate for them, as has been amply demonstrated time and again in racial discussions (often via white silence). While having our worldviews challenged by people of color can be very uncomfortable, that discomfort is key to the stretching and growing that is necessary for authentic change.

"I don't want to offend anybody"

Similar to "I don't want to be misunderstood," this rationale allows one to protect oneself against alternative perspectives, responses, constructive conflict, or taking the risks that could potentially expand one's awareness. This rationale is unfair to people of color because if we fear offending, it may be assumed that we are having offensive thoughts or are hostile toward what is being said. If this is the case, to not share our thoughts denies the group the ability to respond to our hostility.

If we are not hostile to what is being said but just worried that we may inadvertently offend someone, how will we learn that what we think or say is offensive if we don't share it and open ourselves up to feedback? In effect, by not taking this intentional opportunity to discover which ideas we hold are offensive, we protect these ideas and enable them to surface at a later date and offend someone else. In the unique and often rare learning environment of racial discussions, to remain silent so as not to offend is to offend twice—once through our silence and again in our unwillingness to discover and change racially problematic aspect of our thinking. If unsure, we can simply offer our thoughts with openness and humility rather than as declarations of certainty or truth—for example, "This is what I am thinking in response to what was just said ... can you help me understand what I may be missing ...?" "I have often heard ... what are your thoughts on that?"

"Anything I say won't be listened to because I am white"

At the point that this narrative emerges, we have usually been challenged in the way we conceptualize race—either directly or via the content of the dialogue, and we are unable to rise to that challenge. Clearly we have not understood the objectives of the discussion or the theoretical framework that it rests on: there is a relationship of unequal power between white people and people of color in which all of us participate but that only white people benefit from. One way that antiracist education tries to interrupt this relationship is by acknowledging the power differential and affirming the perspectives of those whose voices dominant society seldom hears or validates. In turn, challenging white perspectives is necessary because the way that dominant culture under-stands race actually functions to hold racism in place. The issue is not that we won't be listened to because we are white; the issue is that—counter to what we are accustomed to—our perspectives *will be* challenged at times and are not going to be affirmed *just because* we are white.

A Note on the Silence of People of Color in Racial Discussions

Although this analysis is limited to a white person addressing white silence in racial discussions, I would be remiss if I did not at least raise the issue of the silence of people of color and offer some preliminary thoughts. First, as should be clear via my argument thus far, the silence of whites has a very different foundation and impact than the silence of people of color, based on the unequal positioning of the two groups in society; these silences are not equivalent. For people of color, silence is generally not seen as a viable option. However, there are several key reasons why people of color may at times choose silence in a racial discussion, including:

- As a response to resistance or hostility expressed (consciously or not) by white participants (this unconscious expression of hostility could include silence based on many of the reasons discussed above)
- Lack of trust based on well-founded experience that one will be penal-ized for challenging white perspectives
- A sense of hopelessness in the face of white denial
- Taking risks and being vulnerable about one's racial experiences and perspectives and being met with silence, argumentation, explanation, or guilt, all of which function as forms of invalidation
- Being out-numbered in ratio to white people and assessing that there are no allies present for support were one to challenge white privilege
- Being acutely aware of the power differentials and choosing to protect oneself in the face of inevitable hurt.

In a recent exchange on the issue of white silence, Anika Nailah, a Native and African American woman and antiracist educator, writes:

The clearest way I can communicate to you what can be going on when people of color are silent in these discussions is to say that we experience white silence in a cross-racial space as: 1) collusion with whatever racist views have been stated or implied; 2) an affirmation that when things get hard, white solidarity wins; 3) a clear message that the views that we have stated are not important enough to white people to risk the most minimal vulnerability to respond to—the message is that we are not important enough to communicate with beyond the most superficial of levels. When I am met by white silence I have to decide if I am going to break the silence by sharing my perspectives. This decision will be based, in part, on whether I am invested enough in the white people to take the risk. Because of institutional white power, which most white people are unaware of, this is a very difficult, anxiety-producing, and energy draining decision to have to make, and yet again puts me in the one-down position, laying the burden and the risk for challenging racism on me. Bottom line—no matter how scared the white people might be, or how well-intended their silence is, I experience it as unsupportive and in collusion with racism. Given that, some days I am going to choose to play it safe too. (Anika Nailah, personal communication, July 25, 2009)

It is important to keep in mind that so much of white racism's operation is invisible to and/or denied by white people. A room that seems perfectly comfortable to white people may not feel that way to people of color—in fact, given white racism as the status quo, the more comfortable a space is for white people, the more likely it is to be harmful to people of color. Further, because we are deeply invested in white privilege materially, psychically, socially, and politically as the producers and beneficiaries of it, the very behaviors we think are benign or even supportive may be the behaviors that are toxic to people of color. When our identity as good people is contingent on not seeing our racism, we will need to keep it protected and intact. In this context, it should be apparent why people of color might choose silence.

In Conclusion

It may be clear at this point that much of the rationale for white silence is based on the dominant paradigm that posits racism as isolated to individual acts that only some people commit. This conceptualization of racism as isolated, intentional, and malicious acts makes it unlikely that whites will see their silence as a function of, and support for, racism and white privilege. Yet to challenge one's most comfortable patterns of engagement in a racial dialogue is necessary to interrupt one's racial socialization. From an antiracist perspective, we can assume that our racial socialization has not prepared us to be competent in cross-racial relationship building. Although silence in racial discussions feels benign to those who practice it, no form of white engagement that is not informed by an antiracist perspective is benign. Challenging white comfort, while difficult, is necessary and will result in the least harmful and most authentic and rewarding engagement.

Discussion Questions

1. Which of the rationales for white silence were the most challenging for you? Why?
2. The author argues that you may be an introvert in most settings but if you are white and you behave as an introvert in a discussion on racism, it is different and problematic. Explain her argument.
3. The author says that our personalities are not outside of race. Explain this statement.
4. If I talk over everyone regardless of their race, then I am not treating anyone differently based on race. So how can I be enacting racism when a person I am talking over is a person of color?
5. Why is white silence in racial discussions different from the silence of people of color?

· 17 ·

RACISM AND SPECIFIC
RACIAL GROUPS

> The first thing you do is to forget that i'm Black
> Second, you must never forget that i'm Black
>
> —Pat Parker (1990)

> To be completely honest, race hasn't meant a whole lot to me in my life. My parents
> have always taught me that it doesn't matter what your skin color is. What matters
> is the kind of person you are. I grew up in a neighborhood that was filled with mid-
> dle class families, most of which were white. One of my best friends on the street is
> milado [sic] (I'm not sure if this is politically correct?) and the other was Caucasian.
> In my eyes, we are all just people with beating hearts. (ASR)

Throughout this book I have been discussing race in general terms: white
people and people of color. For the purposes of challenging many problematic
dynamics of racism, such as individualism and color-blindness, it is important for us as white people to be able to suspend our focus on ourselves as
unique and/or outside of race and intentionally focus on our *collective* racial
experience. Exploring our group identity interrupts a key privilege of dominance—the ability to see oneself as a unique individual, outside of the forces
of socialization. Therefore, discussing white people in general terms may be
seen as an interruption of the normal dynamics of racism.

However, for people of color, being seen (and seeing themselves) as unique individuals outside of race is not a privilege that can be taken for granted. So while talking about race and racism in general terms such as "white and people of color" may be constructive for whites, it reinforces something problematic for people of color—the continual focus on their group identity. Further, it collapses many diverse racial groups into one big category, thereby denying the specific ways that different racial groups experience racism in the larger society. For whites wanting to continue on the journey of antiracism, it is important to also recognize how racism manifests for specific groups of color. While there are shared dynamics of racism for people of color overall, there are also variations based on a specific group's history, how people within a group have learned to adapt to racism in order to survive, how they are represented, and the "role" the group is assigned by dominant society. The experience of a person whose family has been in the country for many generations will be very different than for those who are immigrants or whose parents were immigrants. Some people of color have been adopted and raised by white families, and these families often take a "colorblind" approach to raising these children. Thus, they will have a very different experience and sense of identity than people who were raised by their own racial group. Antiracist practice involves ongoing education about how race works, and flexibility and skill in navigating its many facets and nuances.

In Chapter 3, I gave the example of a white woman entering a parking garage and seeing a man standing between her car and the car next to it. I discussed how the race of the man will impact the level of fear she may feel. This difference in the level of fear is due to the messages she has received about different racial groups. For example, while I have received constant messages throughout my life that black men are dangerous and more criminally prone, I have also received constant messages that Asian men are not. While not seeing Asian men as dangerous may seem like a positive stereotype, it isn't, because it sets Asians and blacks into a good/bad binary. If Asians are the "good" racial group, which is the "bad" one? So-called positive racial stereotypes are often used to blame other groups—"If they can make it, why can't you?" These stereotypes are also used by dominant society to deny that Asians experience racism. Positive stereotypes still objectify and exoticize people, and make social beliefs appear to be genetic, such as the belief that blacks are "naturally" better athletes, singers, and dancers. Further, dominant society has different responses to different races based on these stereotypes. Asian heritage people are often much more "comfortable" for whites to be around, while numerous studies show that blacks are generally the least comfortable for whites (Johnson & Shapiro, 2003; Bonilla-Silva, 2003; Hunter, 2007).

But there are still more layers of complexity in dominant society's relationship to blacks and Asians. I have observed that while whites are more comfortable with Asian Americans, they tend to ignore recent Asian immigrants with complaints such as "I can't understand their accents." Conversely, whites are often much more comfortable with African immigrants than they are with African Americans. This may be due to the fact that we do not have an oppressive history of racism *directly* between us (although we do have an oppressive history of colonization indirectly between us), and recent African immigrants will not have the patterns of internalized racial oppression and adaptations to racism that African Americas have had to develop for survival over centuries. African immigrants are often represented in mainstream media as victims of poverty, starvation, and war, as well as innocent and child-like or exotic (for example, in films such as *The Gods Must Be Crazy* and *In America*). This representation often causes sympathy and interest we don't often feel for African Americans, who are not represented this way. Thus the interaction between a white person and an African immigrant may not be representative of white interactions with African Americans overall. So while we should welcome and support new African immigrants, if whites do not have African *American* friends they are not challenging the racial relations they have been socialized into as a result of living in *this* society.

Returning to the parking garage example, my response to the black man also shows the contextual nature of racism. While I might feel *curious* to discover I have a black male professor when he walks into class on the first day, my *fearful* reaction to this same professor in the parking garage—before I know he is my professor—will be based upon my socialization about black men in general. The infamous story of Oprah Winfrey, one of the world's wealthiest women, unable to hail a cab in New York City, speaks to the contextual nature of racism. Until she is recognized as Oprah (or the man as "Professor"), she is just another black woman and has to navigate the same racist stereotypes as any other black woman.

Remember: Racism is a complex and multilayered system of social stratification. Challenging this system requires ongoing and sustained study and practice, and is not accomplished solely through good intentions, open-mindedness, taking a class, or reading a book.

While people of color don't choose to experience racism, they tend to be very familiar with it because they must navigate it on a daily basis. Further, people of color's familiarity with racism occurs in the context of a society whose structures and institutions perpetuate it while being unwilling to acknowledge the impact that it has on individuals and communities. Given this, perhaps the most effective way that whites can navigate racial dynamics in an anti-racist way are (1) learning to accept and validate feedback, information and leadership from people of color, and (2) educating yourself on the history and analysis needed to recognize and challenge white superiority and institutional racism in all areas of your life. These two skills alone have the potential to promote social change in ways that will ultimately interrupt the cycle of racism.

Because I cannot do justice to the complex histories and dynamics of each major racial group in an introductory text, I will provide a general overview and encourage my readers to educate themselves well beyond this book.

The Power of Language

Language is not neutral. In other words, a noun or verb is not simply an objective description of a thing or action (recall the racial impact of the photos captioned "finding" groceries versus "looting" groceries). This is especially true of terms used for various racial groups. For this reason, not all people who identify with a specific group will agree to the same terms for that group. It is best to continually educate yourself about the politics of language, and how specific groups identify at a given historical moment, and how specific individuals identify *within* groups. For example, in my lifetime all of the following terms have at some point been considered appropriate in mainstream society: Negro, Colored, Black, African American, African heritage. Note that today the terms Colored and Negro would be considered highly offensive. Also note that each of these terms conjures different images and associations in one's mind, some positive and some negative. These different images illustrate the political dimensions of language and how it changes over time as people's political awareness changes. However, not all people who are considered members of this group agree on which term they prefer. The most acceptable terms in this list currently are black or African American. African heritage is a newer term that is not yet familiar to most people.

The general guidelines regarding language and terms to identify people of color are: (1) Ask yourself why you are naming the person's race. Is it relevant to what you are speaking about? If it is not relevant, don't name it, as this only reinforces the concept of people of color as racialized and whites as not. (2) If naming the group is relevant to your story, then use the most mainstream term. (3) If appropriate (e.g., you have or are building a relationship with someone), ask them how they identify racially, and then use that term, even if it's not the same as another friend of yours from the same group prefers. For example, while I tend to use the term black in general, I have some friends who refer to themselves as black, some who use African American, and others who prefer African heritage. I simply strive to remember and use their preferred terms when I'm with them and it's relevant to the conversation.

> **Remember:** What follows is only an introductory overview, the goal of which is to start a process of ongoing study and practice. In no way should this overview be interpreted as definitive or conclusive. It also cannot be assumed that these overviews "speak" for the groups addressed or would be agreed to by all members of the group.

White Racism and Asian Heritage People

(with Darlene Lee)

The racial category recognized as Asian is very broad and encompasses people from very different cultures, ethnicities, and geographic regions, with different languages and histories. For example, this category includes South Asian (including Indian, Sri Lankan, Pakistani, Nepalese), East Asian (including Chinese, Japanese, Korean) and Southeast Asian (including Filipino, Thai, Vietnamese, Cambodian, Burmese, Laotian). Thus Asian can be a problematic term because it collapses this extremely diverse range of groups into a unified collective. Further, many people included in this category who live in the West have been here for many generations, and this is a very different experience than being an immigrant or from an immigrant family. Yet dominant culture rarely recognizes these differences. In recognition of the diversity within this category, I use the term *Asian heritage*. To say that someone is of Asian heritage is to acknowledge the larger racial category while leaving the specifics of their background open.

There is a long history of racism toward Asian heritage people in the United States. For example, Chinese immigration was initially encouraged during the building of the transcontinental railroad (to which Chinese workers made a profound contribution) and during the California gold rush, when cheap labor was needed. But when whites began to feel threatened by Chinese labor, resentment built. In 1882 the Chinese Exclusion Act was passed. Under this act, Chinese people were excluded from citizenship, regardless of how long they had lived in the United States, further immigration was banned, and Chinese workers were not able to bring their wives over or start families in the United States. Many Chinese were beaten and killed during this period. At the same time that European ethnic groups were immigrating in large numbers, the Chinese were banned. Over the years revisions were added that tightened restrictions against Chinese immigration, until the law was finally repealed in 1943.

During World War II, Japanese American citizens, many of them citizens of the United States for far more generations than European ethnic groups, were interned in concentration camps. They lost their homes, possessions, and businesses during this period. Consistently seen as foreigners regardless of their time in the United States, the internment of Japanese Americans was rationalized as necessary because their loyalty or inherent "Americanness" was questioned. In 1988 the U.S. government made an official apology and issued more than $1.6 billion in reparations to Japanese who had been interned and their heirs. This is a particularly egregious example from the past, but one of the key ways that racism manifests for Asian heritage people is through the idea that they do not belong. This perception is termed "the perpetual foreigner." Another illustrative example of the perpetual foreigner perception occurred in 1998 when American figure skater Tara Lipinski edged out American figure skater Michelle Kwan for the Olympic gold medal. The MSNBC headline read, "American beats out Kwan." The taken-for-granted assumption expressed in this headline was that Michelle Kwan could not be American.

Today, people of Asian heritage are rarely represented in television or movies, and when they are represented, it is usually in very stereotypical terms. They are often shown as passive, submissive, quiet, smart, nerdy, and good at math and science. Asian heritage men are often portrayed as effeminate or asexual. With the growing popularity of imported action films and film stars, Asian heritage men (and sometimes women) are also shown as Samurai warriors or Kung Fu fighters. Still, Asian men are rarely portrayed as sexual. For example, Jackie Chan, while very popular, is never shown kissing a woman or otherwise engaged in a romantic relationship. Conversely, Asian women are often described as "exotic" or as "dolls" and advertised to white men as available through "sex tours" in Thailand and other places. Asian women are often desired by white men who see them as "ideal": sexual but passive and receptive to domination. These stereotypes directly contribute to feelings of objectification for Asian women, emasculation for Asian men, and invisibility for Asian people in general. These feelings are accentuated by having little or no representation in politics, government, or other institutions. In turn, white people often don't notice Asian heritage people or, based on assumptions that they are culturally quiet, exclude them in conversations and discussions. In addition, being constantly asked, "Where are you from" (especially when someone may have been here for many generations) reinforces the perpetual foreigner position.

Some may be familiar with the term *The Model Minority*. This term refers to the cultural myth that people of Asian heritage are highly successful in the United States and don't experience racism. They are often held up by white culture/media as proof that with hard work and determination, anyone can succeed, and there are no racial barriers in society. According to model minority ideology, if other minority groups were as hard working and intelligent, they could also succeed. This ideology is used to further blame African Americans in particular and justify their racial oppression, while pitting them against Asian Americans. Further, the myth of the model minority does not recognize the profound differences between Asian heritage groups and the impact those differences have on their "success" in the West. Immigrating to the United States on a student visa or as a contracted worker for a large corporation is not the same as coming as a refugee from a war-torn, impoverished nation. The former has choices, resources, and "safety nets" that the latter do not. In schools, the model minority myth also causes many Asian heritage students to fall through the cracks, as teachers assume they are all naturally good students and do not need any attention. The racially based expectation of high academic performance takes a toll on Asian heritage youth. At the same time, these youth are assumed to not need support and are left to deal with these pressures on their own.

Yet in spite of historical and current racism toward Asian heritage people, they are often left out of conversations on race. In the United States, racism is often seen as a black/white issue.

The following are some suggestions for how to specifically interrupt racism against Asian heritage people:

- Notice, acknowledge, and validate the racism that exists for Asian heritage people. Challenge discussions of race that only acknowledge racism as a dynamic between blacks and whites.

- Educate yourself about the wars and political histories that impact when, how, and why people immigrate to the U.S.
- Acknowledge, explore, and challenge your stereotypes about Asian heritage people.
- Don't refer to Asian heritage people as "exotic" or use the term "Oriental."
- Don't assume that everyone who looks Asian can speak the language of their ancestors, or that they are a recent immigrant.
- Don't expect someone to speak for every person in their group.
- Do not ask, "Where are you from?" when what you want to know is someone's ethnicity. If you want to know someone's ethnicity, ask, "What is your ethnic heritage?" Also consider why you want to know someone's ethnic heritage. Is this a question you ask everyone? If not, why are you asking now? It may be a genuine way to connect with someone, but most often, this question is asked to fulfill curiosity, and it reinforces their racial difference and sense that they are outsiders.
- Don't assume silence means agreement (especially in a group)—a person may not agree but may be choosing not to argue/interrupt/speak up in that setting. Find other ways to include all voices and check in, rather than just relying on large group discussions.
- White patterns of internalized dominance can easily collude with Asian heritage cultural patterns and/or patterns of internalized oppression (pressure from living in a racist society to "keep one's head down" and not take up too much space). When this happens, whites tend to dominate, and Asian heritage people are silenced. Be conscious of these patterns and try to interrupt your role in them.
- Build authentic relationships with a wide range of Asian heritage people.

White Racism and Latino/a, Chicano, Hispanic People

(with Jacque Larrainzar)

There is great diversity and complexity within the category that dominant culture terms *Hispanic*. For example, according to the U.S. Census, a person who is Hispanic can be of any race, and therefore the Census asks for race identification as well as identification as Hispanic or Latino. Generally this group includes people of Cuban, Mexican, Puerto Rican, Central American, and South American heritage, and/or of other Spanish culture. Hispanic or Spanish are not preferred terms for antiracists because their roots are colonialist ("of Spain") and thereby merge diverse communities of people through the language of the colonizers. Latino/a can be problematic because it also blends many diverse countries together. Chicano/a is a self-applied political term for Mexican Americans who want to acknowledge that they live on lands stolen from Mexico by the United States.

The terms Hispanic and Spanish are also problematic at another level. From 1035 to 1230, the kingdoms of Castile and Leon united into one powerful entity that unified the Iberian Peninsula. Under the queen and king of Castile, the Middle Ages in Spain are often said to have ended at this time. The year 1492 marked the final acts of the Reconquista in the capitulation of the Nasrid Emirate of Granada and the Alhambra decree, ordering the expulsion of the Jews under their reign. After 600 years of Roman rule followed by 300 years of Arab rule, many of the indigenous peoples of the Iberian peninsula feel the terms Hispanic and Latin often ignore the heritage, culture, and history of the indigenous peoples of the Iberian peninsula (Basque, Catalans, and others). This brief historical overview may further illustrate why language is infused with history and politics and thus is often a site of struggle. For this overview, I will use the term Latino/a.

In discussions about racism, the focus is usually on black/white relations, or "black" stands in for all non-white groups. Thus the specific needs and experiences of Latinos/as are left out. There is little or no representation of Latino/a people in mainstream media, educational systems, politics, and other institutions. When Latinos/as are represented, it is usually in very negative and/or stereotypical roles, such as drug dealers, gang members, cops, prostitutes, gardeners, maids, and "illegals." Over and over we see Latino/a people in these roles. For example, in the highly acclaimed television series *Breaking Bad*, virtually every bad guy is Latino and every central character is white. These bad guys are members of brutal drug cartels and are repeatedly shown as ruthless murderers; their characters are seldom developed or their motives made understandable. While the central white characters also engage in these activities, their character development builds an empathy that is not developed for Latino characters. Although the white characters occasionally kill someone, it is done to save their own lives. When a white person is killed, their murder is not shown in graphic detail as the murders of Latinos are.

Depicting extreme violence against people of color without character development is a subtle but powerful way in which television and movies reinforce the idea that they are less valuable—less human. These images do not stand alone but connect to a multitude of others circulating in the culture, and as we watch these shows, deeply problematic racial images of Latinos/a are reinforced.

Latinos/as are often mocked with fake accents and portrayed as uneducated and stupid; one familiar example of this is the Taco Bell Chihuahua. A Spanish accent (unless it is on someone to be perceived as from Spain, thus European and more valuable) is usually associated with low intelligence and lack of education. A language-based hierarchy also manifests *among* Latino/a people within the United States, as those who speak English with more fluency are granted more social and institutional privilege. Rather than admire someone who can speak more than one language, Latino/a people, especially as they try to navigate the educational system, are seen as inferior by dominant culture.

Ongoing public discussions about how Latinos/as illegally cross the border to "take our jobs," and how Mexico and Cuba let their violent criminals loose in the United States all contribute to a climate of white resentment and fear. Mis-education about the politics of immigration laws, the role of corporations in the use of immigrant labor, how immigrant labor is exploited and the lives of misery many immigrant workers live, and the role immigrant labor plays in our economy underlies and exacerbates this resentment.

As with Asian heritage people, there are many different immigration histories for the diverse groups under the umbrella term Latino/a. For example, U.S. wars in Latin American countries create various refugee situations. On the other hand, some Latinos/as have been here for generations, living on lands now occupied by the United States. Historical and current dynamics of colonialism have been foundational to current dynamics of racism. Some Latino/a Americans struggle to maintain connection to their heritage, in the face of having been stripped of indigenous languages and cultures by Spanish and Portuguese conquerors. The school system and its pressure to assimilate rather than encourage bi-culturalism is one institution in particular that makes this very difficult.

The following privilege list (based on McIntosh, 2012), is adapted from a handout by the organization *Coloradans for Immigrant Rights*. It identifies some of the privileges that citizens (and those *perceived as citizens*—usually based on race) can take for granted:

- I am not worried on a daily basis about being "discovered" and deported along with, or away from, my family.
- I don't have to worry that a small misstep could lead to my deportation, even if I currently have legal papers to be in the United States.
- I can apply for a passport that will allow me to travel back and forth to most countries in the world.
- I can think nothing of crossing the border to visit Tijuana, Mexico, for a day of shopping and sightseeing, while Mexican citizens must qualify economically to obtain even a tourist visa to enter the United States, and there are a great many who do not qualify.
- If I want to get a driver's license, it's a simple matter of bringing along my birth certificate, social security card, insurance card, and taking the test. There's no need to worry about whether I have the proper documents to get a driver's license. Usually, a long line is all I have to worry about.
- If I apply for a job, I do not have to worry about what to write under "Social Security Number."
- When Social Security and Medicare are taken out of my paycheck, I have a reasonable hope that someday either my dependents or I will receive the benefit of those taxes.
- I can go into any bank and set up a checking account without fear of discrimination, thus knowing my money is safer than on my person or elsewhere.
- If a police officer pulls me over, I can be sure I haven't been singled out because of my *perceived* immigration status.
- I can be reasonably sure that if I need legal or medical advice, my citizenship status will not be a consideration.
- I can vote in any election on policies or for people who will make laws affecting my way of life and my community.
- I may consider running for political office to serve my community.
- I, or a member of my family, can apply for scholarship aid to the institutions of higher education that are supported by my family's tax dollars.
- I have not been forced to ask myself what would compel me to risk my life to enter the United States. Whether crossing a barren desert for days without food or water, traveling overseas in the hull of ship, or any other dangerous form of transport, I have not been forced to leave my family, my home, and my roots behind me to enter a country that not only feels hostile to me, but is also difficult to understand at times.

- If am treated violently or inappropriately by a federal entity, I have some hope of legal recourse.
- I can choose whether or not I take part in discussions surrounding how my lifestyle or the actions of my government have impacted the lives of those in other countries.
- If I decide to organize politically or speak out about my country's unjust policies, I am likely to be addressing systems that I was raised around and understand. Also, those in power are more likely to listen to me and credit my arguments than a non-citizen.

The following are some suggestions for how to specifically interrupt racism against Latino/a heritage people:

- Remember that there is great diversity among Latino/a people—there are many differences among Latin American cultures and countries. Learn about Latin histories and cultures.
- Educate yourself about the history of the United States in relation to Mexico and Latin America.
- Whiteness impacts the experience of whites who spend time in Latin America. Do not market yourself as an expert based on your travels.
- Notice, acknowledge, and validate the racism that exists for Latino/a people.
- Acknowledge, explore, and challenge your stereotypes about Latino/a people.
- Do not imitate or mock a Spanish accent.
- Don't assume that everyone who looks Latino/a can speak Spanish, or that they are a recent immigrant.
- Recognize that many Latinos/as have a deep value of family—don't ask them to choose between family and you/work/politics, etc.
- If there are Latinos/as involved in your work/organization, make sure they have opportunities to take leadership, and support their leadership.
- Don't expect someone to speak for every person in their group.
- Do not ask, "Where are you from?" when what you want to know is someone's ethnicity. If you want to know someone's ethnicity, ask, "What is your ethnic heritage?" Also consider why you want to know someone's ethnic heritage. Is this a question you ask everyone? If not, why are you asking now? It may be a genuine way to get closer to someone or to see if you connect around a second language you speak or

other information you have, but most often, this question is asked to fulfill curiosity, and it reinforces their racial difference and sense that they are outsiders.

- Don't assume silence means agreement (especially in a group). Silence for Latinos/as may actually indicate a conflict. Find other ways to include all voices and check in, rather than just relying on large group discussions.
- Understand that there is a range of complex reasons why someone (for whom English is not a first language) may or may not speak English to the satisfaction of native English speakers. Appreciate the skill that acquiring a new language takes. Also appreciate the importance of maintaining one's cultural heritage, and do not pressure people to assimilate in ways that deny or degrade their heritage.

White Racism and Indigenous/Native People

(with Ellany Kayce, Tlingit Tribe/Raven Clan)

The United Nations defines "Indigenous" people as pre-colonial inhabitants of any settler society, such as the United States and Canada. In the United States, it is acceptable to use the terms Indigenous and Native American. Indigenous people fall under two prominent subgroups: American Indian (various distinct tribal communities) and Alaska Native (various distinct tribal communities in the northern part of the continent).

There are four main categories that Native Americans recognize: Northwest, Southwest, Lower Woodlands, and Northeast. The Pacific Northwest would include Alaska Natives. The term "American Indian" was government imposed, and is a "legal" term. The people themselves often use Native American and Alaska Native. When possible, it is best to refer to Indigenous communities by their specific tribal affiliation. In either country, avoid using the term Eskimo, as it is not what people of the north called themselves and it is considered derogatory.

For Native Americans, the distinctions are Tribal Affiliation, Clans, what their Grandmother and Grandfather's names are, and whether they are from a Federally Recognized Tribe or a Non-Federally Recognized Tribe. Being from a Federally Recognized Tribe grants legal legitimacy and thus access to many more resources. Unfortunately, the politics of legal recognition has created hierarchies between tribes and has served to "divide and conquer" tribes and families.

Millions of acres were taken by the government in exchange for money and resources that still have not been paid. Because of this, some tribes are now considered a "landless" people. When national borders between Mexico, the United States, and Canada were created, tribes, villages, and families were split apart. When families and tribes want to reunite and participate in traditional ceremonies, it is very difficult. For example, when Native Americans want to cross the U.S.-Canadian border, they have to declare sacred items such as eagle feathers, drums, and sage. This puts them in possession of "endangered" animals because, for example, drums are made from deer or elk. The border patrol routinely confiscates these sacred items, even though the Freedom of Religion Act was passed in 1964 specifically for Native Americans.

For the most part, Indigenous people are invisible in mainstream culture, as there are very few if any positive or realistic images of them, and the history of colonization and genocide against them is absent or extremely minimized in textbooks. When Indigenous people are represented in mainstream culture, it is most often in extremely stereotypical and degrading ways. Powerful stereotypes continually circulate in mainstream culture, from portrayals in Disney movies to advertisements on television, to using Indian mascots for sports teams with racist names such as the "Redskins," to degrading imitations such as "how" and the "Toma-hawk chop." Movies such as *Avatar* portray Indigenous people as simple, loving, and "good"—in other words, as child-like.

Many aspects of Indigenous culture have been idealized and co-opted by white people, such as "dream catchers," smudge sticks," and sweat lodges. Further, many of these cultural traditions have been misunderstood and misused by whites, and Indigenous people often feel deeply degraded and insulted by these co-optations. Stereotypes include beliefs that Indigenous people are unintelligent and uneducated, lazy, alcoholic, and that all tribes own casinos and are rich. The casino stereotype often causes white resentment and a false sense that Indigenous people are doing fine and don't experience racism. In fact, only federally recognized tribes can apply for casino licenses, and even then, it is a highly political and difficult process. The vast majority of tribes do not own casinos and live in dire poverty.

The history of profound racism against Indigenous people, including attempted genocide, continues into the present via discrimination in employment, housing, and health care. Because dominant culture ignores Indigenous people, most whites are unaware of the complex legal requirements imposed on Indigenous people to prove exactly what percentage of native blood they have in order to "qualify" for government programs. The Bureau of Indian Affairs is a notoriously racist institution. Its assimilation practices have included enforced separation of families, placing Indigenous children in white families who deny them their heritage, enforced boarding schools for Indigenous children, and banning children from speaking their native languages. These practices, among others, have resulted in extreme disparity in health, education, and income between Indigenous people and whites.

Another example of institutionalized racism against Indigenous people is the celebration of Columbus Day, the myth of Thanksgiving, and Indian costumes worn at schools on Thanksgiving and Halloween. These holidays distort, minimize, and even celebrate the extreme violence done to Indigenous people through colonization and occupation, and maintain perpetual "salt in their wounds." Indian costumes, usually consisting of a headband and feathers, reinforce the reduction of Indigenous people and their diversity (as well as their humanity) to simplistic and sometimes ugly caricatures.

Pulling together all that has been discussed thus far, consider these logos for the Cleveland Indians and Washington Redskins:

Figure 45. Logos.

Regardless of our feelings about the teams themselves, there is no denying that these images and names are degrading to Indigenous people: the bright red or dark brown skin; the exaggerated facial caricature; the stereotypical feathers; the explicit and outdated reference to skin color. In addition, celebrations at games often include a mascot (usually a white person) wearing a mix of traditional Native American clothing and dancing in the field in a way they imagine a Native person would. The traditional garments Native Americans wear are called Regalia, and the designs tell the story of who they are and who their families and clans belong to. To see white people mix and match these garments, many of which have been stolen, with no knowledge of their meaning and the politics of combining them, is deeply offensive to Native people. As an illustration of white denial and entitlement, also consider how white fans of these teams have responded to continual requests from Indigenous people to change these mascots. (For an excellent documentary on one Indigenous woman's efforts and whites' responses, see Rosenstein [1997].)

Ellany Kayce, a Tlingit, in response to the question of how whites can be allies to Native people, says:

> Go to pow-wows and other cultural gatherings and get to know the elders. Sit with the elders—next to them not in front of them—and listen. It will take time to build rapport and trust. Volunteer your time to show them that you are worthy of their friendship. We've been lied to and cheated out of our homeland, language, culture, and health care, so building trust and rapport will not happen overnight. Nothing in Indian Country is "instant." Never interrupt when an elder is speaking; ask permission to take pictures; bring food to share, bring gifts to elders (elders are always served and eat first) and take the time to listen to the elder's stories. (Personal correspondence, 2011)

The following are some further suggestions for how to specifically interrupt racism against Indigenous people:

- Recognize and respect tribes as sovereign nations. This makes our relationship to them distinct from that of other racialized groups.
- Educate yourself on U.S. history. Howard Zinn's *People's History of the United States* and *Bury My Heart at Wounded Knee: An Indian History of the American West* by Dee Brown are invaluable places to start.
- Educate yourself with the tribes that are local to your community. On whose ancestral land do you live? Consider ways to acknowledge that.
- There are many different tribes and nations in North and South America. Take time to learn about different indigenous cultures, rather than assuming they are all alike.
- Educate yourself on current issues that are critical to Indigenous survival—tribal recognition issues, reservation land debates, physical and verbal harassment/racism. Build relationships with Indigenous people, listen to and believe their experiences.
- Get involved with or otherwise support organizations working for Indigenous rights.

- Recognize that Indigenous cultures may not have the same cultural conceptualizations of time or communication as dominant society does. Do not impose these norms on Indigenous people in the workplace or in schools.
- Avoid the common platitude, "We are all immigrants in this country." While well-meaning and meant to be inclusive, it denies the Native American experience.
- Reconsider the celebration of Thanksgiving and challenge the myth of the Pilgrims and the Indians.
- Educate yourself on the practices of Christopher Columbus and use this education to challenge the celebration of Columbus Day. Consider Columbus Day from the Indigenous perspective. The video at http://www.youtube.com/watch?v=il5hwpdJMcg and the Indian Country newsletter at http://preview.tinyurl.com/7oryjec are good introductions.
- Do not dress up as or otherwise imitate Indians.
- Do not co-opt or imitate Indigenous culture, "collect" Indigenous artifacts, or use Indigenous styles or symbols as fashion.

White Racism and African Heritage People

(with Darlene Flynn)

The United States was founded on slavery, and slavery was fundamental to the building of tremendous wealth in the United States. Following slavery, through the Reconstruction period, Jim Crow period, and pre-civil rights legislation, the United States continued to build wealth through the exploitation of black labor and the denial of resources and fair competition in the job market. Interestingly (and an example of the difference in white attitudes toward Asian and African heritage people), the United States did not apologize for slavery and Jim Crow until 2008. However, no monetary reparations have ever been made.

While it is not constructive to set one racial group up as more oppressed than another, blacks have always served as whites' ultimate racial "other." In virtually every measure, blacks face the highest rates of disparity. Among this group, research has indicated that whites are more comfortable with lighter-skinned blacks and reward them more in society (Hunter, 2007). This dynamic is termed *colorism*—ranking blacks in a hierarchy based on skin tone, with lighter skin being higher in the hierarchy (this also happens to Asians and Latinos/a). The darker a person's skin, the more discrimination they face (Banks, 1999). Evidence shows that lighter-skinned people of color are less discriminated against in income, education, housing, and the marriage market than darker-skinned people (Hunter, 2007). In other words, the darker a person's skin, the lower they are perceived to be in the racial hierarchy and the more racism they face. This fact has not been lost on dominant culture, where editors often digitally lighten black people's skin when they want them to look more attractive or appealing. Conversely, they also darken a person's skin if they want them to appear less appealing. As a powerful example of how our socialization shapes our perceptions, a study showed that people who approved of President Obama perceived his skin as lighter than it actually was, and those who disapproved of him perceived it as darker (Caruso, Mead, & Balcetis, 2009).

Virtually every privilege and identity-building dynamic that I discussed in Chapter 9 can be said to be the opposite for blacks: not belonging, not represented, not seen as racially innocent, not the norm for humanity, cannot enjoy psychic freedom, do not enjoy freedom of movement. For example, while European features are considered the height of beauty (blue eyes, blonde and straight hair, slim hips, small nose, light skin), characteristics associated with traditional African features are considered unattractive (in mainstream society): kinky hair, broad nose, wide hips, dark skin. Black women, unless they have very white features, such as Halle Berry and Jada Pinkett Smith (both of whom are light skinned and are biracial), are not depicted as beautiful in popular culture. The absence of black women can clearly be seen in fashion, film, and mainstream pornography, all major industries that depict idealized female beauty and sexuality.

Images of black men as criminal and violent are ubiquitous in the culture, from music videos to biased news stories, to movies and television, and copious research shows that whites associate blacks with crime and believe them to be more criminally prone. These associations are often manipulated for political gain, wherein subtle hints are made about crime, or images of blacks are darkened to promote more white fear. In addition to all of the discrimination blacks face as a result, they also have to continually monitor themselves when navigating dominant culture: keep their hands visible when stopped by police, be careful to not appear threatening to white people when seeking employment, housing, academic acceptance, and so on. This often involves men lowering their gaze, stooping over to look smaller, and generally trying to take up less space, and this behavior can have a devastating effect on pride and self-confidence. In the powerful film on race *The Color of Fear*, a black man sums up the need to monitor himself in the workplace when he states, "I used to work in corporate America. You can't be a black man in corporate America. You scare people. Walk down the halls with some pride, you scare people. Show some intelligence, you scare people. You have to shuffle."

There are deeply embedded stereotypes of blacks as being of inferior intelligence. These stereotypes continue unabated through film and media portrayals and public discussions about "the achievement gap." The challenges of black children in schools are rarely, if ever, attributed to institutionalized racism, but rather to causes that continually blame families, such as "they just don't care about education." In addition to causing many white teachers to hold lower expectations for their black students, these stereotypes cause young people to doubt their own intelligence and thinking. Further, the socially assigned "racial superiority" of white educators and their methods continues to suppress more effective alternatives promoted by black educational experts such as Dr. Jawanza Kunjufu (*Keeping Black Boys Out of Special Education*) while dismissing any critique or analysis of the practices of white teachers and administrators that track black male students into special education.

Because blacks so profoundly symbolize race in the white consciousness, any white person who wants to challenge racism and engage in antiracist practice must work to specifically address the messages they have internalized about black people.

The following are some further suggestions for how to specifically interrupt racism against African heritage people:

- Understand that racism is an ongoing condition of society, and not a one-time event. Don't position yourself as the judge of whether racism is real or whether it "occurred."
- Educate yourself about African American history—beyond Martin Luther King Jr., Harriet Tubman, Rosa Parks, and Ruby Bridges. An excellent place to start is the film series *Race: The Power of an Illusion* (2003) and *Eyes on the Prize* (1987).
- Some African heritage people are recent immigrants from Africa and identify strongly with their country of origin. Recognize that Africa is a huge continent with hundreds of different cultures and that immigrants

are learning to navigate racism from their various frames of reference, which differ significantly from those of United States-born African Americans.

- African heritage people born in the U.S. and who are descended from those brought here as slaves and stripped of their original language, spirituality, culture, and families have been impacted by a multigenerational experience that unfolded over the course of this country's history. Be mindful that in spite of the many ways that this history has oppressed African Americans, they have nonetheless contributed immeasurably to U.S. arts, culture, and industrial advancement and have largely experienced these contributions being denied, stolen, and appropriated. Educate yourself on African American accomplishments and the impacts of institutional and cultural racism on our collective awareness of their significance.

- Research the history of civilization and early African empires such as Songhai, Mali, and Timbuktu to learn more about the true origins of people of African heritage that did NOT begin with slavery.

- Challenge narratives that represent individual black people as special ("you are so articulate") and/or "making it" against the odds ("he's a credit to his race"). These stories reinforce individualism and meritocracy, while denying the power of long-term collective action and struggle.

- If there are African heritage people in your workplace or organization, support them and their leadership. If there are not many, work to integrate your workplace.

- Many African heritage people, and women in particular, are sensitive about their hair after centuries of it being viewed as ugly by whites. Never touch someone's hair without their permission, ask questions ("How do you wash it?" "How long did it take you to braid it? Did it hurt?"), or make comments ("I am surprised at how soft it is!"), as this often feels invasive and objectifying and conveys that you feel entitled to "examine" the person. If you are curious about an aspect of their appearance, educate yourself through reading and research.

- Do not compare one black person to another, for example, "You are not angry like she is," or use one to invalidate another, as in "Well my other black friend doesn't think that was racism" or compare black people to other people of color, such as "Why don't black people pull together like immigrants do when they come to this country?"

- Don't tell a black person that you don't notice that they are black, or that you don't care that they are black, or that you don't care if they are green, purple, pink, or polka-dotted. This is deeply invalidating (and the latter is dehumanizing because human beings do not come in these colors).
- Remember that different culture groups have different norms of communicating and expressing emotions. The white, middle-class norms of quiet, unemotional communication are not necessarily the best or most effective in every situation.

White Racism and People of Arab or Muslim Heritage

(with Sameerah Ahmad)

In the current political context, racism toward people perceived to fall under the broad category of "Arab" has thrived. This racism is fueled by post-9/11 resentment, fears, stereotypes, foreign policies, incidences, and general ignorance about this population. As with all racialization, perception plays a powerful role. In the case of Arabs, racialization is intensified when we add the religion of Islam. (*Islam* is the name of the religion; *Muslim* is the term for a person who practices it.) *Islamophobia* is the term for prejudice and discrimination toward the religion of Islam and Muslims who follow its teachings and practices.

An Arab person may not be Muslim, and a Muslim person may not be Arab. However, in the post-9/11 context, Arabs and Muslims have become interchangeable in dominant culture, and many think that Iranians and even Pakistanis and other groups are Arab because they may be Muslim. For example, Sikhs were targeted and even murdered after 9/11 because they were perceived as Muslim. On the other hand, African American mosques have not been targeted to the same extent post-9/11 *based on religion*, because these mosques are not perceived as related to *Arab* Muslims. Thus religion and race have intersected in important and unique ways for people of Arab heritage. Further, what we think of as Arabia, or as "the Arab World," consists of 22 different countries with their own histories and political relationships to the United States. Due to these complexities, a newer term is on the rise—SWANA—Southwest Asian and North African. This term is more encompassing than

Arab, which can leave out people that identify as Berber, Mizrahi, and so forth. For the purposes of this overview, I will use the term Arab.

Within the United States the category Arab refers to a very diverse group and includes people who are: immigrants from a range of countries, native-born, first generation bi/multilingual, monolingual, Catholic, Jewish, Muslim, and atheist. Some people of Arab heritage are perceived as and/or identify as white, and some are perceived as and/or identify as people of color (Sensoy, 2012). Those who are perceived as people of color or those with non-Western customs, language, names, and religious affiliations present a cultural and historical tradition unfamiliar to most white Americans. For example, while the majority of Arab immigrants have historically been of the Christian faith, the association of Arab culture with Islam has further fueled anti-Arab sentiment. In this way, Islam—a religion—has become racialized and is often used interchangeably with racial status.

Positionality is an important concept to keep in mind as we consider the perspectives of those categorized as Arab. While I use terms here such as the East, the West, and Middle Easterner, these concepts are from the white perspective. "Orientalism" is the term coined by scholar Edward Said to capture the dynamics of Eastern culture and history presented through the eyes of Western values and assumptions (Said, 1978). Orientalism has been the predominant framework used by the West to make sense of and position the Middle East and its people. Historical political tensions between the West and the East have been expressed in popular culture through media portrayals of the archetypal Arab as crude, barbarian, treacherous, violent, oil rich or beggar, and cruel dominator of women. Arab women have been presented as belly-dancing seductresses or voiceless victims. In general, Arab countries have been the exotic backdrop for European or American adventure films such as *Casablanca*, *Raiders of the Lost Ark*, *Lawrence of Arabia*, *Syriana*, and *The Kingdom*.

Ubiquitous images in recent years of the Arab as religiously fanatic terrorist and/or greedy and decadent oil sheik have only increased these stereotypes. Popular films continually portray Arab people in derogatory ways. For example, in a media analysis conducted by Jack Shaheen (2003) of over 900 films with Arab and Muslim characters, only 12 were positive depictions, 52 were considered even-handed, and the remainder were extremely negative. This combination of political and cultural dynamics makes the Arab the ultimate U.S. enemy—dangerous, disloyal, and untrustworthy. This has only intensified as U.S. wars in Afghanistan and Iraq have become popular contexts for films (e.g., The Academy-Award winning film *Hurt Locker*, *American Sniper*,

In the Valley of Elah, Green Zone, Redacted, Jarhead, Control Room, and *The Situation,* among many others).

Racism and official policies have intersected in ways that make daily life dangerous for people perceived to be of Arab heritage. In the name of counter-terrorism, policies have been put forth that target Arabs (and those perceived as Arabs) and allow forms of racial profiling, torture, and imprisonment that were previously (and in many cases still are) illegal. As I write this 2nd edition, the top U.S. Republican presidential candidate—Donald Trump—has just called for a complete ban on Muslims entering the U.S.

The following are some further suggestions for how to specifically interrupt racism against people of Arab heritage:

- Recognize that not all Arabs identify as people of color.
- Separate racialization from religion. Someone can be Muslim and also identify as white. Someone else can identify as a person of color or as Arab, and not be Muslim.
- Educate yourself on the history of the geographic region termed the Middle East in general, and in relation to Western interests and colonialism in particular.
- Understand that the category "Arab" is extremely diverse and includes people of color, whites, Christians, Jews, Muslims, monolingual and multilingual speakers, and people from a range of class backgrounds. Educate yourself on a person's background and incorporate this education into your interactions with them.
- Do not assume that all people of Arab heritage are Muslim.
- Challenge the false East/West binary and its rigid distinctions between "us" and "them."
- Include people of Arab heritage in diversity programs.
- Get involved in community efforts to ensure that journalists, teachers, and policy makers have accurate information.
- Challenge media typecasting.

Biracial/Multiracial People

(with Darlene Flynn)

In the United States, people who are of mixed racial heritage may identify as biracial (parents or grandparents of two different races), multiracial (parents or grandparents of two or more different races), or mixed heritage. According to these definitions, Bob Marley, whose mother was black (Jamaican) and father was white (English), was biracial. Mariah Carey, whose mother is white and father is Latino and black, is multiracial. In this section, I will use the overall term *multiracial*. However, a *multiracial* identity is not to be confused with a *multiethnic* identity. For example, while I have heritage from two European ethnic groups—Italian and English—both of these groups are considered white, and thus my *racial* identity is white.

Multiracial people, because they challenge racial constructs and boundaries, face unique challenges in a society in which racial categories have profound meaning. The dominant society will assign them the racial identity they most physically resemble, but their own internal racial identity may not align with the assigned identity. For example, while Bob Marley was multiracial, society perceived him as black and thus responded to him as if he were black. If a multiracial person's racial identity is ambiguous, they will face constant pressure to explain themselves and "choose a side." Racial identity for multiracial people is further complicated by the racial identity of their parents and the racial demographics of the community in which they are raised. For example, while a child may look black and be treated as black, she may be raised primarily by a white parent and thus identify more strongly as white.

The dynamics of what is termed "passing"—being perceived as white—will also shape multiracial people's identity, as passing will grant them the rewards of whiteness by society. However, people of mixed racial heritage who pass as white may also experience resentment and isolation from people of color who cannot pass. Multiracial people may not be seen as "real" people of color or real whites. It is worthy to note that while the term "passing" refers to the ability to blend in as a white person, there is no corresponding term for the ability to pass as a person of color. This highlights that in a racist society, the desired direction is always toward whiteness and away from being perceived as a person of color.

There are also historical and legal dimensions to racial identity. During and following slavery, people with up to one-eighth white blood could be legally classified as white as long as they "passed" as white. But in an attempt to maintain white supremacy, from 1890 to 1924 many states adopted the "one drop" rule, which meant that if you had *any* amount of black heritage at all, you were legally categorized as black and denied access to the resources granted to those who held white legal status. This is an example of Cheryl

Harris's concept of whiteness as property, discussed in Chapter 6. On the other hand, gaining federal recognition as a Native American is a very difficult and complicated process. Native Americans have had to prove their ancestry and that they have "enough" blood to legally qualify as Indian.

Multiracial people often report a lifetime of being interrogated and of having to prove or legitimize their racial identities. They are often questioned about their racial backgrounds by complete strangers who ask in ways that are demeaning ("what are you?"). When questioned by whites, many multiracial people feel a violation of boundaries and an exertion of power (I won't let you forget that you are not white and want to place you into a box that I understand). This questioning conveys that whites feel entitled to ask and believe that they have a right to know. This behavior also illustrates the need, in a highly racialized society, to be able to categorize the race of those with whom we are interacting in order to assess our position in relation to them.

Multiracial people often create racial cognitive dissonance for white people and challenge our preference for racial segregation. In his book *Uprooting Racism*, Paul Kivel (2011) points out, "Their [mixed heritage people] health and success challenge the biological and cultural justifications commonly used for the separation and inferior treatment of people of color." For example, when discussing the election of Barack Obama, the popular media sometimes made note that Obama was "not really black," pointing out that his mother was white and his father was African. At other times, he is only described as black and not multiracial. And there are those who cannot accept him as inherently American (or one of "us") and still question his place of birth, citizenship, and the legitimacy to his presidency. This illustrates the power relations and vested interests in how people are racially identified in any given context.

The preoccupation with labeling people of color serves to maintain white dominance by denying people individuality and the right to self-identify. This is particularly hard on the identity development of multiracial people. The following are some suggestions for how to specifically interrupt racism against multiracial people:

- Reflect upon your curiosity about someone's racial background. Ask yourself why you want to know.
- Never ask anyone, "What are you?" If appropriate, ask "How do you identify racially?"

- Do not question the identity of multiracial people: "Are you sure? You don't look __, you look ___."
- Consider the difference between asking someone how they identify because you are building a relationship or because it's relevant to the context, and asking a stranger who or what they are.
- Recognize that people of color should be the ones to decide when, where, and how they identify.
- Do not presume to know the racial identity or life experience of a multiracial person.
- Pay attention and adhere to the self-identification offered by an individual.
- Notice any discomfort you may feel about not knowing someone's racial heritage and use that discomfort as an opportunity to reflect on your racial socialization. *Why* is it so uncomfortable not to know? In what ways do the very existence of multiracial people challenge our assumptions about race? How is our compulsion to label a person's race related to our own white racial identity?
- Work on a daily basis to challenge and expand your racial worldview.

The Bill of Rights for People of Mixed Heritage by Maria P. Root (1993, 1994) helps counter many of the dynamics faced by multiracial people:

  I HAVE THE RIGHT

- Not to justify my existence in this world.
- Not to keep the races separate within me.
- Not to justify my ethnic legitimacy.
- Not to be responsible for people's discomfort with my physical or ethnic ambiguity.
- To identify myself differently than strangers expect me to identify.
- To identify myself differently than how my parents identify me.
- To identify myself differently than my brothers and sisters.
- To identify myself differently in different situations.
- To create a vocabulary to communicate about being multiracial or multiethnic.
- To change my identity over my lifetime—and more than once.
- To have loyalties and identification with more than one group of people.
- To freely choose whom I befriend and love.

In Conclusion

Racism manifests in a range of complex ways for various groups of color. Some of these will be consistent across all groups, and others will be specific to the group in question. For example, citizen status is a major dynamic that creates another layer of racial hierarchy between whites and people of color. White immigrants from European countries are viewed much more positively than immigrants of color from non-European countries. While white immigrants are granted white privilege and perceived as belonging regardless of how short a time they may have resided in the United States, people of color are often seen as immigrants regardless of how long they and their ancestors have been citizens.

Citizenship status also creates a hierarchy between people of color who have citizenship and those who don't, and divides groups whose interests would be better served through unity. Multicultural citizenship in an increasingly globalized society recognizes the right and need for people to maintain ties to their home countries while embracing a commitment to their current one (J. Banks, 2007). The following list, from *Coloradans for Immigrant Rights*, a project of the American Friends Service Committee, explains how whites can challenge the specific ways that racism manifests for immigrants. The list is based on Paul Kivel's excellent book, *Uprooting Racism: How White People Can Work for Racial Justice* (2011).

Support the leadership of immigrants in the movement

Do this consistently, but not uncritically, because no one needs to deal with paternalism when they are busy organizing. Don't assume that organizing isn't going on just because you don't know about it. Use the privilege you have as a citizen to work beside immigrants and refugees on common goals, but watch out for any savior mentality. Never speak on behalf of immigrants; opportunities to lift up the voices of immigrants and expose anti-immigrant sentiment and discrimination for what it is.

Learn to identify the role of race and citizenship privilege in your relationships with immigrants

Racism and citizenship privilege are pervasive in our society. One of the privileges of being a citizen, particularly a white citizen, is not having to see or deal with this reality all of the time. When you interact with immigrant friends or acquaintances, ask yourself how your citizenship status, as well as your racial/ethnic identity, may be affecting the relationship.

Notice how racism in the anti-immigrant debate is denied, minimized, and justified

Resist the argument that anti-immigrant sentiment is not about race. Learn to recognize and articulate how coded racism is at the core of the anti-immigrant debate. Notice how images and symbols are used, what fears are activated, what stereotypes are exploited, and what cultural groups are assumed to be inferior or superior.

Notice who is at the center of attention and power

Notice who speaks, and how often. Pay attention to what is said, as well as whose ideas are deemed most credible. Notice who isn't present. Be aware of code words for race or status, and the implications of the policies, patterns, and comments being expressed.

Understand the connections between anti-immigrant stances, racism, classism, sexism, and other forms of injustice

The more we know about other struggles for social justice, the more we can find common goals, work together in coalition, and share victories.

Understand and learn from this country's history of anti-immigrant sentiment

Notice how anti-immigrant sentiment has changed over time and how it has subverted or resisted challenges. Study the tactics that have worked effectively against it.

Learn something about the history of people who have worked for justice

There is a long history of both allies and people from oppressed communities fighting for justice. Their stories can inspire and sustain us. We can end injustice if we work together. Build support, establish networks, and work with already-established groups.

Take a stand against injustice

Take risks. It can be scary and difficult, but it can also be empowering. Calling out injustice may bring up feelings of inadequacy, indecision, or fear of making mistakes, but is ultimately a key part of our responsibility as allies. It is also a critical step in initiating the dialogues and movement of thought integral to change. Intervene when you see or hear racism and anti-immigrant sentiments. You will never get it right 100% of the time, but the more you try, the better you will get. Try to take criticism, feedback, and suggestions with grace.

Be strategic

Decide what is important to challenge and what's not. Look for the source of power and larger patterns. Don't confuse a battle with the war. Anti-immigrant sentiment is flexible and adaptable. There will be gains and losses in the struggle for justice and equality.

Discussion Questions

1. Which racial groups do you feel the least educated about? How might you gain more knowledge and awareness about that group?
2. Do you notice that you tend to be more comfortable with members of some racial groups rather than others? Discuss why that might be. What are the consequences of this variation in comfort?
3. What does it mean to say that language is not neutral? Why is language so important in the struggle for racial justice?
4. What is problematic about the "model minority" concept?
5. What of the guidelines offered were the most challenging for you? Why? How might you meet that challenge?

· 1 8 ·

ANTIRACIST EDUCATION AND
THE ROAD AHEAD

I am embarrassed when I think back to what I wrote on the first day of class. Like virtually everyone else, I said that race didn't matter and that I had not been affected by it. To be white is to say that race has no meaning and in the next sentence say that my neighborhood was all white. White privilege means you have the power to surround yourself by people like yourself. Reading the reflections, it became very apparent that I was blinded to my whiteness and what it meant. I have come to see that we believe that race isn't an issue because we have never been in a situation where we are not dominant. We have never had to be on the receiving end of racism. To be white is to never have to feel "not normal" in our society. On the other hand, people of color are constantly being defined by race. A very common theme in the reflections was the statement that race has not affected me and I am not racist. This comment most definitely comes from the mouth of a white person, because I can't see any way that a person of color could make that statement. Whiteness allows us to make that claim without ever having to prove it. We prove just the opposite through the practice of our lives. To be white is to sit in the middle of it even as we deny it. (Final Student Essay)

Basic Tenets of Antiracist Education

- Racism exists today, in both traditional and modern forms.
- All members of this society have been socialized to participate in it.

- All white people benefit from racism, regardless of intentions.
- Our racial socialization occurred without our consent and doesn't make us bad people.
- We have to take responsibility for racism.

Antiracist education seeks to interrupt relations of racial inequality by enabling people to identify, name, and challenge the norms, patterns, traditions, structures and institutions that keep racism and white supremacy in place. From an antiracist perspective, the question is not, "*Did* racism take place" but "*How* was racism taking place" because the assumption is that racism is always at play, always operating. This is true even in the absence of racial diversity; the absence itself is a powerful and active message. While racism is always operating, white people are not bad people and we don't need to feel guilty; we didn't choose this system and guilt doesn't help. But we *do* need to take responsibility for learning about and interrupting racism.

> **Antiracist Education:** An educational approach that goes beyond tolerating or celebrating racial diversity and addresses racism as a system of unequal power between whites and people of color.

To illustrate one of the fundamental premises of antiracist education, try this exercise: Reflect on the following and generate a few examples to illustrate each (adapted from Sensoy & DiAngelo, 2012):

- Active racism
- Passive racism
- Active antiracism
- Passive antiracism

Perhaps your examples look something like the following:

Active Racism: telling or encouraging racist jokes, excluding or discriminating against people of color in the workplace, racial profiling, and accusing people of color of "playing the race card" when they try to bring up racism.

Passive Racism: silence, ignoring incidents and dynamics that you notice, the inequitable funding of schools, lack of interest in learning more about racism, having few if any cross-racial relationships, and not getting involved in antiracist efforts or in continuing education.

Active Antiracism: working to identify internalized racial dominance if you are white, working to identify internalized racial oppression if you are a person of color, making sure there are multiple racial perspectives on an issue in the workplace, joining organizations working for racial justice, and seeking out continuing education.

But now we come to **Passive Antiracism**. If you were able to come up with any examples, reconsider them from the lens of antiracism, and you will find that they don't hold up; antiracism requires action. Antiracism, or any other endeavor to challenge injustice, is by definition not passive. As Barbara Trepagnier (2010) describes, "Anti-racism refers to taking a committed stand against racism, a stand that translates into action that interrupts racism in all of its forms, whether personal or institutional, blatant or routine, intended or unintended. Antiracism is active by definition—the opposite of passivity, which colludes with racism. If one claims to be antiracist but takes no action against racism, the claim is false" (p. 104).

It is not enough to be "open-minded" or to see ourselves as outside of racism because we are personally against racism or because we have relationships with people of color. Whites who are committed to antiracism must practice antiracism by working to challenge racism on multiple fronts. As racial justice community organizer Chris Crass says:

> My goal isn't to be a great ally. My goal is the abolition of white supremacist capitalist patriarchy and the building up of multiracial democracy, economic, gender and racial justice for all and a world where the inherent worth and dignity of all people and the interconnection of life are at the heart of our cultures, institutions, and policies. ... Strive to be a comrade with a political framework, committed to building up other people's leadership, building up collective power, being able to read situations and act for the best of our goals, rather then feeling like there is a formula to follow ... (Facebook Post, 2015)

We can begin by:

- Being willing to tolerate the discomfort associated with an honest appraisal and discussion of our internalized superiority and racial privilege
- Challenging our own racial reality by acknowledging ourselves as racial beings with a particular and limited perspective on race
- Attempting to understand the racial realities of people of color through authentic interaction rather than through the media or through unequal relationships

- Taking action to address our own racism, the racism of other whites, and the racism embedded in our institutions—e.g., get educated and act
- Continually challenging our own socialization and investments in racism
- Challenging the misinformation we have learned about people of color
- Striving for humility and being willing to not know
- Following leadership on antiracism from people of color
- Educating ourselves about the history of race relations in our country
- Building authentic cross-racial relationships
- Becoming media literate and building the capacity to identify and resist racist images
- Getting involved in organizations working for racial justice
- Breaking silence about race and racism with other whites

Let's look at one of the most important practices on this list: building authentic cross-racial relationships. What does an authentic cross-racial relationship look like? It is long-term, equal, and based on trust and commitment. In other words, these relationships are not temporary, contextual (I have a co-worker of color I hang out with at work), superficial (we don't talk about sensitive issues such as race), or easily dissolved when a conflict arises. I may be friendly with a co-worker, but if they never comes to my home, sits at my kitchen table, and breaks bread with me, as do my other friends, it is only a superficial friendship.

Further, authentic relationships cannot happen between people of unequal status—for example between an employer and an employee. I have heard many white people refer to their housekeepers, nannies, and other employees of color as friends or "family." While great feelings of fondness and affection may exist in these relationships, they are not equal, due to the differential in power between employer and employee. This power differential is both *implicit* across race and *explicit* across status in that as their boss, you have the power to dictate the rules and fire them at will. This power differential does not allow for full honesty or trust to develop; when people depend upon you for their livelihood, they are likely to be careful about what they say and do, and that limits the authenticity in your relationship.

Most white people are not socialized in ways that would make the building of authentic cross-racial relationships easy. Segregation in schools and neighborhoods makes it unlikely for us to meet or form relationships with many people of color. Dynamics of internalized superiority—reinforced by the relentless racist messages in the culture around us—and the sense that cross-racial relationships are not valuable make it unlikely that we will seek them out. Whites rarely venture outside of their social circles in ways that would make cross-racial friendships more likely. When white people do have cross-racial relationships, they are often the result of a person of color entering their existing social circle. We may also notice that these friends tend to be of the same race—in other words primarily Asian or primarily black. While this gives us some cross-racial exposure we might not otherwise have, it isn't the result of our doing anything to seek out these relationships; we aren't challenging any of the dynamics that keep us separate. This is somewhat reminiscent of the story I shared about the white person who was grateful that this organization "brought" information about race to him, but who wasn't seeking it on his own.

Building authentic cross-racial relationships usually requires that white people go beyond merely hoping that these relationships will happen. We have to interrupt the status quo of our daily lives and interactions. This will require getting out of our comfort zones, taking risks, challenging our racial apathy and our sense of entitlement to racial comfort. But most importantly, developing authentic cross-racial relationships from an antiracist perspective includes developing the skills and perspectives that enable us to engage constructively with issues of race and racism. One of the most critical and intimate of these skills is the willingness to remain in the relationship when racial tensions arise (and if the relationship is authentic, racial tensions *will* occasionally arise). Over and over I have seen or heard of whites who give up at the first sign of racial tension, who walk away and blame the person of color: they were too sensitive; they overreacted; they have a personal problem. And over and over I have heard people of color talk about how painful it is when whites give up and walk away, using the privilege of individualism and universalism to insist the issue isn't about race.

The following list (adapted from Kivel, 2011) shows what people of color have consistently asked for from white allies:

- Respect us.
- Listen to us.
- Find out about us.
- Check out your assumptions.
- Don't take over.
- Stand by my side.
- Share information.

- Let me decide what is best for me.
- Share resources.
- Be willing to make mistakes.
- Take risks.
- Honesty.
- Don't take it personally.
- Talk to other white people.
- Interrupt jokes and comments.
- Support.
- Teach your children about racism.
- Speak up.
- Don't be afraid of our anger.

In my early days doing this work, I dreaded getting feedback from people of color on my racist patterns and assumptions. But now I welcome this feedback and I actually worry if I am not receiving it. Perhaps the most powerful lesson I have learned in building cross-racial relationships is that this feedback is a positive sign in the relationship. Of course the feedback seldom feels good—I occasionally feel embarrassed or defensive. But I also understand that there isn't any way for me to avoid enacting problematic patterns, so if a person of color trusts me enough to take the risk and tell me, I am doing well overall. Further, their feedback helps me see dynamics that are difficult to see on my own, and thereby I can continually grow; this is a gift. Many people of color have shared with me that they don't bother giving feedback to white people that they don't think can hear it; they either endure the micro-aggressions or drift away from the relationship. But they do not feel close to white people to whom they can't speak openly and honestly about racism, and these relationships always have a degree of distance and inauthenticity.

> **Remember:** My inability as a white person to see or understand racism is unrelated to its reality.

Sometimes I am asked, "But what if the person of color is wrong and what they thinks is racism isn't racism at all?" To this I say that people of color are much more qualified than we are to make this determination. My not being able to see racism is unrelated to its reality. There are some aspects of racism which I am never going to understand, given my position in society. In these cases, I reach for humility and focus on impact rather than intention. Of course, it is possible for a person of color to be wrong or to have misunderstood something. But given all of the dynamics discussed in this book, our focus as white people needs to be on challenging our internalized superiority. To let go and concede the point is a powerful interruption to that superiority. In contrast to the centuries of us not validating the truth, we will be fine should that rare occasion occur.

> **Remember:** Within a racially stratified society, race is at play in all interactions, and perhaps most powerfully when it appears to be absent, as in racial segregation or all-white friendship circles. In all-white contexts, many problematic dynamics of racism are reinforced. But race is explicitly at play in cross-racial relationships. From an antiracist framework, it is impossible to insist, "Race had nothing to do with it."

Building these relationships takes time, commitment, and mutual interest. We need to challenge the desire to objectify or "use" people of color so that we can say we have cross-racial friendships. This tendency, especially for those new to antiracist practice, is very hard on people of color when every white person around wants to be their friend. This is the other extreme of ignoring; objectifying. If there are very few people of color in your environment, consider ways in which you can move outside of this environment and into more racially diverse spaces, rather than depending on a few isolated people of color to meet your needs.

Building authentic cross-racial relationships entails many of the other practices on the list that opened this chapter: continually challenging our own socialization and investments in racism; challenging the misinformation we have learned about people of color; striving for humility and being willing to not know; and accepting leadership on antiracism from people of color. In developing these practices, we will also be more likely to develop other practices as well: become media literate and build the capacity to resist racist images circulated through the media, get involved in organizations working for racial justice, educate ourselves about the history of race relations in our country, and break silence about race and racism with other whites.

However, as important as cross-racial relationships are, it is also of critical importance that whites work with other whites to raise our racial consciousness and strive for racial justice. Breaking silence with other whites is very difficult, but building cross-racial relationships and breaking silence with other whites go hand-in-hand.

As I have argued throughout this book, racism cannot be overcome through good intentions or wishful thinking, by personal self-image or simply being a nice person. We actually have to be willing to *change*. This requires great humility—a willingness to *not know* in the face of often-intense emotions, which is lifelong and ongoing work. Although I am involved in and committed to antiracist practice, I don't call my self an "antiracist white." This is because it is for people of color to determine if, in any given moment, I am behaving in antiracist ways. I am the *least* qualified to determine my antiracist qualifications. While I have *expertise*, I am not an *expert*; the position of expert implies that one's learning is complete. Antiracism for whites requires a constant state of humility. We are often at our most effective when we let go of control and are able to sit with ambiguity and contradiction.

Remember: The question is not "*Is* racism taking place?" but rather "*How is* racism taking place in this specific context?"

I remember a conversation with a friend of color in which we were debriefing a cross-racial situation. As we discussed various possible responses and the challenges and pitfalls of each, she said, "Being a white person committed to antiracism must be like being a cat on a hot roof—no matter where you step, your feet will get burned." Rather than feeling discouraged, I found this acknowledgment very supportive because it recognized how difficult it is for whites to "get it right" across race. She went on to explain that in the face of the impossibility of getting it right every time and for everyone, she appreciated that I was still trying. As a person of color, she did not expect cross-racial perfection on the part of a white person. The forces of racism that surround us at this social and historical moment make that impossible. It was my effort and willingness to *keep grappling* in the face of that impossibility—my willingness to make mistakes and learn from them—that earned her trust.

Many of my students, after just a few weeks of studying racism, grow impatient and want me to *just tell them what to do*. Sadly, their impatience is an indication that the desire for understanding may not be sincere. This is a lifelong journey without a quick fix, and for those committed to it, that should be obvious. What may be driving the desire for easy answers is a deep discomfort with *not knowing*. It can be disorienting to let go of what we were raised to believe is true before we have fully formed a new understanding. Impatience may also indicate a sense of desperation and powerlessness. All of this is understandable, yet the drive to skip over the hard work of critical analysis and self-reflection must be resisted. Even if there were a recipe for interrupting racism, it would require some sophistication to understand. Handing white people a list of quick-fix behaviors before they fully understand the issues risks making our behavior more problematic, rather than less. Further, while lists for increasing one's racial literacy do exist (and I provide several in this chapter), they are not easy to practice. Without a real commitment, many whites reject these lists because they require skills and perspectives which the person is not committed to developing.

My suggestions for continuing the work of antiracism and developing white racial literacy are as follows:

- Understand that racism is always operating in every social setting (not just when an incident occurs or a person of color is present). Continually practice observing, recognizing, and articulating how it is operating.
- Recognize that we are social beings, always in dynamic relation to one another. We interact across race within a socio-historical context and bring our group histories with us. Don't demand or expect to be seen solely as an individual.
- Focus on patterns—within ourselves and society—and grapple with a range of possible ways to interrupt these patterns.
- Let go of how someone gives you feedback. It's difficult to give feedback about racism, and emotions are often high. Focus on the content and not the tone.
- Don't position yourself as "less racist" than other whites, or otherwise position yourself as exceptional, and thus separate.
- Take responsibility for your mistakes, have humility, and be willing to admit the limitations of your knowledge.
- Let go of control and support the thinking and leadership of people of color.
- Earn trust through *action*.
- Attend trainings on antiracism. Participate in white racial caucuses and other exercises designed to help you see your racial lenses.

- Engage in activities that will expose you to differing racial views and experiences.
- Create or join a support network of other whites seeking antiracist practice. Showing Up for Racial Justice (SURJ) is a great place to begin: http://www.showingupforracialjustice.org/about
- Seek out other whites in your workplace who are also engaged or interested in antiracism. Support and learn from each other's efforts.
- Read research and scholarship on race, racism, and whiteness.
- Attend conferences. The annual White Privilege Conference is an excellent start (http://www.whiteprivilegeconference.com/)
- Subscribe to journals and websites that address racism from an antiracist perspective.
- Study race history through films and books that take a critical perspective, such as the PBS film series *Race: The Power of an Illusion* and Howard Zinn's text, *A People's History of the United States.*
- Develop genuine, long-term, trusting relationships with people of color.
- Continually seek out situations that will challenge your worldview, such as performances, book talks, marches, and cross-racial community engagement. Develop the stamina and courage to talk about race and racism in ways that are counter to your socialization.
- See racial discomfort as a positive sign.
- Think in terms of structures and patterns, not individual people and acts.
- Understand that how we respond to the world (actions/practices/solutions) comes from how we see the world (perspective/theory/consciousness). When we can see more complexity, we will have more complex responses.
- Seek out and become familiar with the myriad resources available for antiracist work. For example, Racial Equity Toolkits: http://www.racialequitytools.org/home

I do not expect racism to end in my lifetime, and I know that I continue to have problematic racist patterns and perspectives. Yet I am also confident that *I do less damage to people of color* than I used to. This is not a minor point of growth, for it impacts my lived experience and that of the people of color who interact with me. But I cannot stop there at the interpersonal level. I must also be active in ways that challenge and change institutions and their policies and practices.

In Conclusion

At the end of each semester we return to the anonymous student essays written on the first day of class. Each of us reads one aloud, and then we discuss patterns and themes. On the last day of class, I ask this question on the final essay exam, "What does it mean to be white?" The following are some of my students' answers:

> At the beginning of the course I had a whole different view of what it means to be white than I do now. Before, I had the same perception of race that most other whites do. I said that I am white, but that it doesn't make a difference in my life. I said that I don't get treated differently and that I don't see race. Looking back, I can see the many contradictions. We believe we are not affected by the media or messages in terms of race. We believe it is the older generation who is racist, and not ours. We see ourselves as accepting of everyone even as we live separately from them. We say that in schools everyone is treated equal and given an equal chance, yet we also acknowledge that money and social class gives you an upper hand in schools. We see ourselves living in a diverse society because there are a few people of color at our school, but we have the privilege of not noticing how these other students are treated. We say we worked hard to get where we are yet we also had help from money, family, networks, inheritance, and social and racial dominance. We don't see race as an issue because that is part of the privilege of being in the dominant group. It doesn't affect us negatively so it is not even noticed.

> To be white is to be privileged. It is to live each day without "realizing" race or being "affected" by it. To be white is to fit in and to be normal. Throughout this semester we have learned the privileges of being white, although we have experienced them every day unknowingly. Race affects everyone daily, though whites do not know it because it affects them in a positive way. The power relationship between whites and people of color favors white people. This causes whites to consistently deny privilege. This unconscious privilege that whites have gives them advantages and shapes their daily lives. The way I see it, because of our privileges and denial of them, whites end up disadvantaged. We live a life of denial, ignorance, and superiority. The majority of whites live their life never truly understanding the backpack they carry and why they carry it. This prolongs the segregation and injustice that remains in our society. It reinforces the denial. Because white people do not "experience" racism everyday and are blind to the systematic oppression of many people, they lack the necessary understandings to eradicate these issues. We have to realize how these ideologies affect us and how socialized we are to believe them.

> To be white is to believe that racism is over or doesn't exist. It is to believe that all people have an equal chance in this society and all you have to do is work hard and

pull yourself up by your bootstraps. We don't see our all white towns as segregated. We don't have to think about things. For most if not all of us, this class was the first time we were ever asked to analyze ourselves. But Whiteness works the most powerfully by allowing us to forget about the things we have discussed in this class. In a bigger sense, it allows us to be blind to the reality of a harsh world. Whiteness works by allowing whites to own and control this country and dictate the lives of others, from Asia to Africa and the Caribbean islands. If we don't work hard to keep seeing and remembering, we will remain in the dream of denial.

These essays are heartening, for they demonstrate that my students have grown significantly. Their analysis has deepened, they are seeing complexities and contradictions they did not see before, and their self-awareness has increased. They are able to articulate key concepts and demonstrate their increase in racial literacy. They don't exhibit defensiveness, and their openness is apparent. These changes are clear evidence that it is possible for us to move forward. How we *view* the world impacts how we *act* in the world, and as their vision takes in more complexity, their responses will become more nuanced and complex. Yet I still send them off with a caution: nothing "out there" in dominant society will support you in sustaining this awareness. In fact, just the opposite will occur, as dominant forces pressure you into forgetting, not noticing, denying, maintaining white solidarity, and protecting your investments in racism. We have to find ways to support ourselves to keep going, despite the powerful forces of comfort in the status quo.

"Getting it" when it comes to race and racism challenges our very identities as good white people. It's an ongoing and often painful process of seeking to uncover our socialization at its very roots. It asks us to rebuild this identity in new and often uncomfortable ways. But I can testify that it is also the most exciting, powerful, intellectually stimulating and emotionally fulfilling journey I have ever undertaken. It has impacted every aspect of my life—personal and professional. I have a much deeper and more complex understanding of how society works, I am able to challenge much more racism in my daily life, and I have developed cherished and fulfilling cross-racial friendships I did not have before. Of course there are many nights when I go to bed feeling hopeless. But in a society that is infused with racism, even hope is political. If I give up because it's too hard or too big or because I believe it will never end, it still serves me as a white person; the impact of my hopelessness is not the same as that of a person of color's. White hopelessness ultimately protects racism if it keeps us from challenging it. When I remember this, I find the motivation to keep going.

Discussion Questions

1. Very little if anything in the society at large supports us to persist in the work of antiracism. In fact, much pressures us *not* to continue the work. Because of this, we need to set up support for ourselves to continue. How will you set up support for yourself to stay on the journey? How will you resist complacency?

2. The author states that it isn't enough for white people to be nice people, and that in fact, racism depends on white people simply being nice and continuing on with their lives. Discuss this statement. How might this be an example of "passive" racism?

3. If we accept that racism is always operating and thus, the question is not "*Is* racism taking place?" but rather "*How is* racism taking place in this specific context?" how does that change how we think about our lives and our actions?

4. Why must white people resist cynicism and remain hopeful? At the same time, what are the pitfalls of hopefulness? What is the difference between hope and denial?

5. Discuss the author's suggestions for continuing the work of antiracism and developing white racial literacy. Which are the most challenging? How can you meet those challenges?

REFERENCES

Adelman, L. (2003). *Race: The power of an illusion*. San Francisco: California Newsreel.

Akomolafe, O. (1994). *On slavery: The retrospective history of Africa*. Hartford Web Publishing. Retrieved from http://www.hartford-hwp.com/archives/30/index-h.html

Akintunde O. (1999). White racism, white supremacy, white privilege, and the social construction of race. *Multicultural Education, 7*(2), 1.

Alexa: The web information company. (2010). *The top 500 sites on the web*. Retrieved from http://www.alexa.com/topsites/global

Alexander, M. (2010). *The New Jim Crow: Mass incarceration in the age of colorblindness*. New York: The New Press.

Ansell, D., & McDonald, E. (2015). Bias, black lives, and academic medicine. *New England Journal of Medicine, 372*, 1087–1089. doi: 10.1056/NEJMp1500832

Banks, J. (Ed.). (2007). *Diversity and citizenship education: Global perspectives*. Indianapolis, IN: Jossey-Bass.

Banks, T. L. (1999). Colorism: A darker shade of pale. *UCLA Law Review, 47*, 1705–1728.

Benjamin, L. T. Jr. (2007). *A brief history of modern psychology*. Hoboken, NJ: Wiley Blackwell Publishing.

Bernstein, D. (1983). The female super-ego: A different perspective. *The International Journal of Psychoanalysis, 64*, 187–201.

Bertrand, M., & Mullainathan, S. (2004). Are Emily and Greg more employable than Lakisha and Jamal? A field experiment on labor market discrimination. *American Economic Review, 94*(4), 991–1013.

Bonilla-Silva, E. (2002). The linguistics of colorblind racism: How to talk nasty about blacks without sounding "racist." *Critical Sociology*, 28(1–2), 41–64.

Bonilla-Silva, E. (2003). "New racism," Color-blind racism, and the future of whiteness in America. In W. Doane & E. Bonilla-Silva (Eds.), *White out: The continuing significance of racism* (pp. 271–284). New York: Routledge.

Bonilla-Silva, E. (2009). *Racism without racists: Color-blind racism and the persistence of racial inequality in America*. Lanham, MD: Rowman & Littlefield.

Box Office Mojo (2010). *All time box office worldwide grosses*. Retrieved from http://www.boxofficemojo.com/alltime/world/

Bridges, G., & Steen, S. (1998). Racial disparities in official assessments of juvenile offenders: Attributional stereotypes as mediating mechanisms. *American Sociological Review*, 63(4), 554–570.

Brodkin, K. (1998). *How Jews became white folks and what that says about race in America*. New Brunswick, NJ: Rutgers University Press.

Burd-Sharp, S. & Rasch, R. (2015). Impact of the US Housing Crisis on the Racial Wealth Gap Across Generations. *Social Science Research Council*. Retrieved from https://www.aclu.org/files/field_document/discrimlend_final.pdf

Cartwright, S. (1851). Report on the diseases and physical peculiarities of the Negro race. *Medical Surgery Journal*, 7, 691–715.

Caruso, E., Mead, N., & Balcetis, E. (2009). Political partisanship influences perception of biracial candidates' skin tone. *Proceedings of the National Academy of Sciences*, 106(48), 20168–20173.

Cavalli-Sforza, L., Menozzi, P., & Piazza, A. (1994). *The history and geography of human Genes*. Princeton, NJ: Princeton University Press.

Churchill, W. (2001). Crimes against humanity. In D. F. Eitzen (Ed.), *Sport in contemporary society* (6th ed., pp. 115–121). New York: Worth Publishers.

Clark, K., & Clark, M. (1939). The development of consciousness of self and the emergence of racial identification in Negro preschool children. *The Journal of Social Psychology*, 10(4), 591–599.

Clark, K., & Clark, M. (1950). Emotional factors in racial identification and preference in Negro children. *The Journal of Negro Education*, 19(3), 341–350.

Coates, T. (2015). *Between the world and me*. New York: Random House.

Condry, S., Condry, J., & Pogatshnik, W. (1983). Sex differences: A study of the ear of the beholder. *Sex Roles*, 9(6), 697–704.

Conley, D. (2009). *Being black, living in the red: Race, wealth and social policy in America*. Berkeley: University of California Press.

Cooley, C. (1922). *Human nature and the social order*. New York: Scribner Books.

Cooper, R. S., Kaufman, J. S., & Ward, R. (2003). Race and genomics. *New England Journal of Medicine*, 348(12), 1166–1170.

Cooper, L., Roter, D., Carson, K., Beach, M., Sabin, A., Greenwald, A., & Inui, T. (2012). The associations of clinicians' implicit attitudes about race with medical visit communication and patient ratings of interpersonal care. *American Journal of Public Health*: 102(5), 979–987. doi: 10.2105/AJPH.2011.300558

Cox, L. (2014, December 7). Laverne Cox explains the intersection of transphobia, racism, and misogyny (and what to do about it). *Everyday Feminism*. Retrieved from http://everyday-feminism.com/2014/12/laverne-cox-intersection-what-to-do/

Crass, C. (2015, November 6). Facebook entry. Retrieved from https://www.facebook.com/chris.crass.75/posts/10153789296982941

Crenshaw, K. (1991). Mapping the margins: Intersectionality, identity politics, and violence against women of color. *Stanford Law Review*, 43(6), 1241–1299.

Dawkins, C. (2004). Recent evidence on the continuing causes of black-white residential segregation. *Journal of Urban Affairs*, 26(3), 379–400.

Dei, G., Karumanchery-Luik, N., & Karumanchery, L. (2004). *Playing the race card*. New York: Peter Lang.

Derman-Sparks, L., Ramsey, P., & Olsen, J. (2011). *What if the kids are all white? Anti-bias multicultural education with young children and families*. New York: Teachers College Press.

DiAngelo, R. (2006). My class didn't trump my race: Using oppression to face privilege. *Multicultural Perspectives*, 8(1), 51–56.

DiAngelo, R. (2011). White fragility. *International Journal of Critical Pedagogy*, 3(3). 54–70.

DiAngelo, R., & Sensoy, Ö. (2014). Getting slammed: White depictions of cross-racial dialogues as arenas of violence. *Race & Ethnicity in Education*, 17(1), 104–128.

Dines, G. (2010). *Pornland: How porn has hijacked our sexuality*. Boston: Beacon.

Dominelli, L. (1989). An uncaring profession? An examination of racism in social work. *Journal of Ethnic and Migration Studies*, 15(3), 391–403.

Dovidio, J., Glick, S., & Rudman, L. (2005). *On the nature of prejudice: Fifty years after Allport*. Malden, MA: Blackwell.

Du Bois, W. E. B. (1989). *The souls of black folk*. New York: Bantam Books. (Original work published 1903)

Dyer, R. (1997). *White*. New York: Routledge.

Faber, J. (2013). Racial dynamics of subprime mortgage lending at the peak. *Housing Policy Debate*, 23(2), 328–349.

FBI Uniform Crime Report (2014). Retrieved from https://www.fbi.gov/about-us/cjis/ucr/nibrs/2014

Feagin, J. (2006). *Systematic racism: A theory of oppression*. New York: Taylor & Francis.

Feagin, J. (2009). *The white racial frame: Centuries of racial framing and counter-framing*. New York: Routledge.

Fenning, P., & Rose, J. (2007). Overrepresentation of African American students in exclusionary discipline. The role of school policy. *Urban Education 42*, 536–559.

Forbes, 2015. The highest-earning hedge fund managers and traders. Retrieved from http://www.forbes.com/hedge-fund-managers/

Frankenberg, R. (1997). Introduction: Local whitenesses, localizing whiteness. In R. Frankenberg (Ed.), *Displacing whiteness: Essays in social and cultural criticism* (pp. 1–33). Durham, NC: Duke University Press.

Frye, M. (1983). *The politics of reality: Essays in feminist theory*. Trumansburg, NY: The Crossing Press.

Ginzburg, L. (2009). *Elizabeth Cady Stanton: An American life*. New York, NY: Hill and Wang.

Gooding, F. W. (2011). *Al's notes: The blind side*. Silver Spring, MD: On the Reelz Press.

Gorski, P. (2008). Savage unrealities: Racism and classism abound in Ruby Payne's framework. *Rethinking Schools, 21*(2), 16–19.

Gossett, T. F. (1997). *Race: The history of an idea in America*. New York: Oxford University Press.

Gould, S. (1996). *The mismeasure of man*. New York: W. W. Norton & Company, Inc.

Greenwald, A. G., & Banaji, M. R. (1995). Implicit social cognition: Attitudes, self-esteem, and stereotypes. *Psychological Review, 102*, 4–27.

Greenwald, A., Poehlman, A., Uhlmann, E., & Banaji, M. (2009). Understanding and using the Implicit Association Test: III. Meta-analysis of predictive validity. *Journal of Personality and Social Psychology, 97*(1), 17–41.

Hall, S. (1997). *Representation: Cultural representation and signifying practices*. London: Sage Publications.

Harris, C. (1993). Whiteness as property. *Harvard Law Review, 106*(8), 1710–1769.

Heath, R. (2001). *The hidden power of advertising: How low involvement processing influences the way we choose brands*. London: Admap Publications.

Herival, T., & Wright, P. (2008). *Prison profiteers: Who makes money from mass incarceration?* New York: The New Press.

Hilliard, A. (1992). *Racism: Its origins and how it works*. Paper presented at the meeting of the Mid-West Association for the Education of Young Children, Madison, WI.

Hodson, G., Dovidio, J., & Gaertner, S. (2004). The aversive form of racism. In J. L. Chin (Ed.), *The psychology of prejudice and discrimination (Race and Ethnicity in Psychology)* (Vol. 1, pp. 119–136).Westport, CT: Praeger.

Hollway, W. (1984). Gender differences and the production of subjectivity. In J. Henriques, W. Hollway, C. Urwin, C. Venn, & V. Walkerdine (Eds.), *Changing the subject* (pp. 227–263). London: Methuen.

hooks, b. (1989). *Feminist theory: From margin to center*. Boston: South End Press.

Horn, J., Sperling, N., & Smith, D. (2012, February 19). Oscar voters overwhelmingly white, male. *Los Angeles Times*. Retrieved from http://www.latimes.com/entertainment/la-et-un-masking-oscar-academy-project-20120219-story.html

Hunter, M. (2007), The persistent problem of colorism: Skin tone, status, and inequality. *Sociology Compass, 1*, 237–254.

Ignatiev, N. (1995). *How the Irish became white*. New York: Routledge.

Inter-Parlimentary Union (2011). *Women in national parliaments*. Geneva: Inter-Parliamentary Union.

Jacobson, M. (1999). *Whiteness of a different color*. Cambridge, MA: Harvard University Press.

Jefferson, T. (2002). *Notes on the State of Virginia with related documents*. Waldstreicher, D. (Ed.). Boston: Bedford/St. Martin.

Jensen, R. (2007). *Getting off: Pornography and the end of masculinity*. Boston: South End Press.

Johnson, H. B., & Shapiro, T. M. (2003). Good neighborhoods, good schools: Race and the "good choices" of white families. In A. W. Doane & E. Bonilla-Silva (Eds.), *White out: The continuing significance of racism* (pp. 173–187). New York: Routledge.

Kailin, J. (2002). *Anti-racist education: From theory to practice.* Lanham, MD: Rowman & Littlefield.

Kivel, P. (2011). *Uprooting racism: How white people can work for racial justice* (3rd ed.). Gabriola, B.C., Canada: New Society Publishers.

Klein, K. (2007). *Giving notice: Why the best and the brightest are leaving the workplace and how you can help them stay.* Hoboken, NJ: Jossey-Bass.

Kochhar, R., & Fry, R. (2014). *Wealth inequality has widened along racial, ethnic lines since end of Great Recession.* Washington, DC: Pew Research Center Publications.

Kozol, J. (2005). *The shame of the nation: The restoration of apartheid schooling in America.* New York: Crown.

Kunjufu, A. (2005). *Keeping black boys out of special education.* Sauk Village, IL: African American Images.

Kunjufu, A. (2007). *An African-centered response to Ruby Payne's poverty theory.* Sauk Village, IL: African American Images.

Lee, S. (1996). *Unraveling the "model-minority" stereotype: Listening to Asian American youth.* New York: Teachers College Press.

Lee, S. (2005). *Up against whiteness: Race, school, and immigrant youth.* New York: Teachers College Press.

Li, E., Min, H., Belk, R., Kimura, J., & Bahl, S. (2008). Skin lightening and beauty in four Asian cultures. Advances in Consumer Research, *35*, 444–449.

Lichter, D., Parisi, D., & Taquino, M. (2015). Toward a new macro-segregation? Decomposing segregation within and between metropolitan cities and suburbs. *American Sociological Review, 80*(4), 843–873.

Lipsitz, G. (1995). The possessive investment in whiteness: Racialized social democracy and the "white" problem in American studies. *American Quarterly, 47*(3), 369–387.

Lorde, A. (1983). The master's tools will never dismantle the master's house. In C. Moraga & G. Anzaldúa (Eds.), *This bridge called my back: Writings by radical women of color* (pp. 94–101). New York: Kitchen Table Press.

Major, Barbara (2007). *Bring back New Orleans mayoral commission panel discussion.* Retrieved from https://www.youtube.com/watch?v=Iqp6rWpOatU

Malatesta, C., & Haviland, J. (1982). Learning display rules: The socialization of *emotion* expression in infancy. *Child Development, 53*(4), 991–1003.

Martin, K. (1998). Becoming a gendered body: Practices of preschools. *American Sociological Review, 63*(4), 494–511.

Marty, D. (1999). White antiracist rhetoric as apologia: Wendell Berry's *The hidden wound.* In Nakayama, T. K., & Martin, J. N. (Eds.), *Whiteness: The communication of social identity* (pp. 51–68). Thousand Oaks, CA: Sage.

McIntosh, P. (2012). White privilege and male privilege: A personal account of coming to see correspondence through work in women's studies. In M. Anderson & P. Hill Collins (Eds.), *Race, Class, and Gender: An Anthology.* 9th Edition (pp. 94–105). Belmont, CA: Wadsworth.

Messner, M. (1995). *Power at play: Sports and the problem of masculinity.* Boston: Beacon Press.

Miller, J., & Garran, A. M. (2007). *Racism in the United States: Implications for the helping professions.* Florence, KY: Brooks Cole.

Mills, C. W. (1997). *The racial contract.* Ithaca, NY: Cornell University Press.

Monteiro, M. B., de França, D. X., & Rodrigues, R. (2009). The development of intergroup bias in childhood: How social norms can shape children's racial behaviors. *International Journal of Psychology, 44* (1), 29–39.

Morrison, T. (1993a). *Playing in the dark.* New York: Vintage Books.

Morrison, T. (1993b). On the backs of Blacks. *Time,* special issue (Fall), 57.

Motaparthi, K. (2010). Blepharoplasty in Asian patients—Ethic and ethical implications. *Virtual Mentor: American Medical Association Journal of Ethics, 12*(12), 946–949.

Muench, U., Sindelar, J., Busch, S., & Buerhaus, P. (2015). Salary differences between male and female registered nurses in the United States. *Journal of American Medical Association, 313*(12), 1265–1267.

Myers, K. (2003). White fright: Reproducing white supremacy through casual discourse. In W. Doane & E. Bonilla-Silva (Eds.), *White out: The continuing significance of racism* (pp. 129–144). New York: Routledge.

NAACP (2015). *Criminal justice factsheet.* Retrieved from http://www.naacp.org/pages/criminal-justice-fact-sheet

Nesbit, J. (2015). Institutional Racism is Our Way of Life. *U.S. News & World Report.* Retrieved from http://www.usnews.com/news/blogs/at-the-edge/2015/05/06/institutional-racism-is-our-way-of-life

Nelson, L. & Lund, D. (2015). The School to Prison Pipeline Explained. *Anti-Defamation League.* Retrieved from http://www.adl.org/assets/pdf/education-outreach/what-is-the-school-to-prison-pipeline.pdf

Nicholson-Crotty, S., Birchmeier, Z., &Valentine, D. (2009). Exploring the impact of school discipline on racial disproportion in the juvenile justice system. *Social Science Quarterly, 90*(4), 1003–1018.

Olsen, L. (2008). *Made in America: Immigrant students in our public schools.* New York: The New Press.

Oh, S., Galanter, J., Thakur, N., Pino-Yanes, M., Barcelo, N.E., White, M.J., et al. (2015). Diversity in clinical and biomedical research: A promise yet to be fulfilled. *PLOS Medicine, 12*(12), e1001918. doi:10.1371/journal.pmed.1001918

Onwuachi-Willig, A. (2013). *According to our hearts: Rhinelander v. Rhinelander and the law of the multiracial family.* New Haven, CT: Yale University Press.

Pager, D. (2007). *Marked: Race, crime, and finding work in the era of mass incarceration.* Chicago: University of Chicago Press.

Parker, P. (1990). For the white person who wants to be my friend. In G. Anzaldúa (Ed.), *Making face, making soul* (p. 297). San Francisco: Aunt Lute Foundation Books.

Payne, R. K. (2001). *A framework for understanding poverty.* Highlands, TX: aha! Process, Inc.
2013 American values survey (2014). Public Religion Research Institute, Washington, DC.

Picca, L., & Feagin, J. (2007). *Two-faced racism: Whites in the backstage and frontstage.* New York: Routledge.

Picower, B. (2009). The unexamined whiteness of teaching: How white teachers maintain and enact dominant racial ideologies. *Race Ethnicity and Education, 12*(2,) 197–215.

Powell, J., & Godsil, R. (2012). Implicit bias insights as preconditions to structural change. Poverty & Race Action Council. Retrieved from http://www.prrac.org/full_text.php?-text_id=1363&item_id=13241&newsletter_id=119&header=Race+%2F+Racism&kc=1

Quillian, L. (2002). Why is black-white residential segregation so persistent?: Evidence on three theories from migration data. *Social Science Research, 31*(2), 197–229.

Quintana, S. & McKown, C., Eds. (2007). Handbook of race, racism and the developing child. NY: Wiley.

Rape Abuse & Incest National Network (2012). *New Survey Says Little Change in Sexual Assault Numbers.* Retrieved from https://rainn.org/news-room/new-survey-says-little-change-in-sexual-assault-numbers-in-2012

Razack, S. (1998). *Looking white people in the eye: Gender, race, and culture in courtrooms and classrooms.* Toronto: University of Toronto Press.

Reed, S. (2011). *The diversity index.* New York: AMACOM.

Rennie Center for Education Research & Policy (2011). *Executive summary. Act out, get out? Considering the impact of school discipline practices in Massachusetts.* Cambridge, MA: Rennie Center for Education Research & Policy.

Roediger, D. (2007). *The wages of whiteness: Race and the making of the American working class.* Brooklyn, NY: Verso.

Root, Maria P. (1993, 1994). *The Bill of Rights for people of mixed heritage.* Retrieved from http://www.drmariaroot.com/doc/BillOfRights.pdf

Rosenstein, J. (Director). (1997). *In whose honor? American Indian mascots in sports.* New York: New Day Films.

Ross, L. (2007). *Money shot: Wild days and lonely nights inside the black porn industry.* New York: Thunder's Mouth.

Said, E. (1978). *Orientalism.* New York: Vintage Books.

Schroeder, C., & DiAngelo, R. (2010). Addressing whiteness in nursing education: The socio-political climate project at the University of Washington School of Nursing. *Advances in Nursing Science, 23*(3), 244–255.

Sensoy, Ö. (2012). The education of Middle Eastern Americans. In J. Banks, (Ed.), *Encyclopedia of Diversity Education*. New York: Sage.

Sensoy, Ö., & DiAngelo, R. (2012). *Is everybody really equal? An introduction to key concepts in critical social justice education.* New York: Teachers College Press.

Shaheen, J. G. (2003). Reel bad Arabs: How Hollywood vilifies a people. *The Annuals of the American Academy of Political and Social Science, 588*(1), 171–193.

Sleeter, C. E. (1996). White silence, white solidarity. In N. Ignatiev & J. Garvey (Eds.), *Race Traitors* (pp. 257–265). New York: Routledge.

Smith, C. (2009). Deconstructing the pipeline: Evaluating school-to-prison equal protection cases through a structural racism framework. *Fordham Urban Law Journal, 36*, 1009–1028.

Smith, L. (1949). *Killers of the dream.* New York: W. W. Norton & Company.

Solomon, R., & Palmer, H. (2006). Black boys through the school-prison pipeline: When "racial profiling" and "zero tolerance" collide. In D. E. Armstrong & B. J. McMahon (Eds.), *Inclusion in urban educational environments: Addressing issues of diversity, equity, and social justice* (pp. 191–212). Greenwich, CT: IAP.

Steele, C. M. (1997). A threat in the air: How stereotypes shape intellectual identity and performance. *American Psychologist, 52*(6), 613–629.

Steele, C., Spencer, S., & Aronson, J. (2002). Contending with group image: The psychology of stereotype and social identity threat. *Advances in Experimental Social Psychology, 34,* 379–440.

Stepan, N., & Gilman, S. (1993). Appropriating the idioms of science: The rejection of scientific racism. In S. Harding (Ed.), *The "racial" economy of science: Toward a democratic future* (pp. 170–194). Bloomington: Indiana University Press.

Sue, D. W. (2003). *Overcoming our racism: The journey to liberation.* San Francisco, CA: Jossey-Bass.

Sue, D. W., Capodilupo, C., Torino, G., Bucceri, J., Holder, A., Nadal, K., & Esquilin, M. (2007). Racial microaggressions in everyday life: Implications for clinical practice. *American Psychologist, 62*(4), 271–286.

Sue, D. W., Bucceri, J., Lin, A., Nadal, K., & Torrino, G., (2009). Racial microaggressions and the Asian American experience. *Asian American Journal of Psychology, 1,* 88–101.

Suicide Prevention Resource Center (2011). *Suicide risk and prevention for lesbian, gay, bisexual, and transgender youth.* Newton, MA: Education Development Center, Inc.

Tatum, B. (2008). *Can we talk about racism? And other conversations in an era of school re-segregation.* Boston, MA: Beacon Press.

Tehranian, J. (2000). Performing whiteness: Naturalization litigation and the construction of racial identity in America. *Yale Law Journal, 109*(4), 817–848.

Tobin, D., Tobin, Tobin, G. & Scott, R. (2005). In every tongue: The racial and ethnic diversity of the Jewish people. Institute for Jewish & Community Research.

Tuskegee Institute (2012). *Lynchings: By state and race, 1882–1968.* University of Missouri-Kansas City School of Law.

Trepagnier, B. (2010). *Silent racism: How well-meaning white people perpetuate the racial divide* (expanded ed.). New York: Paradigm.

United for a Fair Economy (2014). *Healthcare for whom? Enduring racial disparities.* Retrieved from http://www.faireconomy.org/dream/2014

U.S. Bureau of Justice Statistics, Prisoners in 2011, 8 tbl.8 (Dec. 2012).

U.S. Department of Education (2012). *Characteristics of public and private elementary and secondary school teachers in the United States: Results from the 2011–12 Schools and Staffing Survey.*

VanAusdale, D., & Feagin, J. (2001). *The first R: How children learn race and racism.* Lanham, MD: Rowman & Littlefield.

Van Dijk, T. A. (1993). Analyzing racism through discourse analysis: Some methodological reflections. In J. H. Stanfield, & R. M. Dennis (Eds.), *Race and ethnicity in research method* (pp. 92–134). London: Sage.

Vodde, R. (2001). De-centering privilege in social work education: Whose job is it anyway? *Journal of Race, Gender and Class* 7(4), 139–160.

Weber, L. (2010). *Understanding race, class, gender, and sexuality: A conceptual framework* (2nd ed.). New York: Oxford University Press.

Weil, S. (1987). Are we struggling for justice? *Philosophical Investigations, 10*(1), 1–10.

Wellman, D. (1977). *Portraits of white racism.* Cambridge and New York: Cambridge University Press.

Western States Center (2003). *Dismantling racism: A resource book for social change groups.* Portland, OR: Western States Center.

Williams, C. L. (1992). The glass escalator: Hidden advantages for men in the "female" professions. *Social Problems, 39*(3), 253–267.

Williams, C. L. (1995). *Still a man's world: Men who do "women's work."* Los Angeles: University of California Press.

Wise, T. (2015). *Under the affluence: Shaming the poor, praising the rich and sacrificing the future of America.* San Francisco, CA: City Lights Books.

Wise, T. (2008). *Speaking treason fluently: Anti-racist reflections from an angry white male.* Berkeley, CA: Soft Skull Press.

Zinn, H. (2005). *A people's history of the United States.* New York: Harper Perennial Modern Classics.

GLOSSARY

Antiracist Education: An educational approach that goes beyond tolerating or celebrating racial diversity and addresses racism as a system of unequal power between whites and people of color.

Aversive Racism: Forms of racism that allow well-meaning white people to maintain a positive ("not racist") self-image while still perpetuating racism.

Binary: An either/or construct that positions a social dynamic into two distinct and mutually exclusive categories.

Cisgender: The term for people whose sex assignment at birth and subsequent socialization are the same as their gender identity. The majority of people are cisgender.

Colorblind Racism: Pretending that we don't notice race or that race has no meaning. This pretense denies racism and thus holds it in place.

Danger Discourse: The specific form of racetalk that positions African Americans as inherently dangerous.

Discourse: The academic term for meaning that is communicated through language in all of its forms. Discourses include myths, narratives, explanations, words, concepts, and ideology. Discourses are not universally shared among humans; they represent a particular cultural worldview and are shared among members of a given culture. Discourse is different from ideology because it refers to all of the ways in which we communicate ideology or meaning, including verbal and nonverbal aspects of communication, symbols, and representations.

Discrimination: Unfair action toward a social group and its members that is based upon prejudice about that group. Discrimination occurs at the individual level; all humans discriminate.

Hegemony: The control and imposition of dominant group ideology onto everyone in society. Hegemony makes it difficult to escape or to resist "believing in" this dominant ideology, thus this control is achieved through conditioning rather than physical force or intimidation.

Ideology: the big, shared ideas of a society that are reinforced throughout all of the institutions and thus are very hard to avoid believing. These ideas include the stories, myths, representations, explanations, definitions, and rationalizations that are used to justify inequality in the society. Individualism and meritocracy are examples of ideology.

Internalized Dominance: The result of socialization in which members of the dominant group are conditioned into their roles. This socialization causes them to see themselves as naturally superior to the relationally minoritized group and more deserving of their superior positions and the resources of society.

Implicit Bias: The largely unconscious and automatic prejudice that operates below conscious awareness and without intentional control. Implicit bias is absorbed from the messages surrounding us and results in acts of discrimination. Because implicit bias is below conscious awareness and often in conflict with what a person consciously believes, the person is unaware of the discrimination that results from it.

Individualism: The ideology that we are all unique, therefore, categories such as race have no meaning and provide no more or less opportunities. Thus, success or failure is not a consequence of social structures but of individual character.

Internalized Oppression: The result of socialization in which members of a minoritized group are conditioned into their roles. This socialization causes them to see themselves as naturally inferior to the relationally dominant group and less deserving of the resources of society.

Intersectionality: The understanding that we simultaneously occupy multiple social positions and that these positions do not cancel each other out, they interact in complex ways that must be explored and understood.

Micro-Aggressions: The everyday slights and insults that people of color endure and most white people don't notice or concern themselves with.

Minoritized: A social group that is devalued in society. This devaluing encompasses how the group is represented, what degree of access to resources it is granted, and how the unequal access is rationalized. The term "minoritized" (rather than minority) is used to indicate that the group's lower position is a function of active socially constructed dynamics, rather than its numbers in society.

New Racism: The ways in which racism has adapted over time so that modern norms, policies, and practices result in similar racial outcomes as those in the past, while not appearing to be explicitly racist.

Oppression: Group prejudice and discrimination backed by institutional power. The term "oppression" indicates that one group is in the position to enforce their prejudice and discrimination against another group throughout the society; the prejudice and discrimination have moved from the individual to the societal level and have long-term and far-reaching impacts. Prejudice + Discrimination + Power = Oppression.

People of Color: Refers collectively to all of the socially constructed racial groups who are not perceived and categorized as white and do not have access to the social, cultural, institutional, psychological, and material advantages of whiteness.

Positionality: The concept that our perceptions are shaped by our positions within society. These positions allow us to see and understand some social dynamics while obscuring others.

Prejudice: Learned prejudgment based on stereotypes about a social group that someone belongs to. Prejudice occurs at the individual level; all humans have learned prejudices.

Race: The false concept that superficial adaptations to geography (skin tone, eye shape) are genetic and biological determinants that result in significant differences among groups of human beings.

Racetalk: The explicit insertion into everyday life of racial signs and symbols that have no meaning other than positioning African Americans into the lowest level of the racial hierarchy.

Racism: A form of oppression in which one racial group dominates others. In the United States the dominant group is white, therefore racism is white racial and cultural prejudice and discrimination, supported intentionally or unintentionally by institutional power and authority, and used to the advantage of whites and the disadvantage of people of color.

Scientific Racism: The use of pseudo-scientific techniques to support the classification of individuals of different phenotypes into discrete races and to justify belief in the natural inferiority or superiority between these races.

Signifier: A sign or symbol that conveys specific cultural meaning. Signifiers connect to larger discourses that work together to construct that meaning.

Social Stratification: Ranking social groups into a hierarchy of unequal value. To say that society is socially stratified is to say that social groups are unequal and that some are seen in society as more valuable than others. This ranking is used to justify the unequal distribution of resources among social groups.

Socialization: The lifelong and multidimensional process of being trained into your culture; learning the norms, meanings and practices that enable us to make sense of the world and behave appropriately in a given context.

Socially Constructed: Meaning that is not inherently true, but agreed upon by society. Once society agrees to this meaning, it becomes real in its consequences for people's lives.

Transgender: The term for people whose sex assignment at birth is different from their gender identity.

Universalism: The ideology that because we are all human, categories such as race have no meaning and provide no more or less opportunities.

White: The "top" classification of the socially constructed and hierarchically arranged racial categories. Those perceived and categorized as white are granted social, cultural, institutional, psychological, and material advantages.

White Fragility: The result of white racial socialization. A state in which even a minimum amount of racial stress becomes intolerable, triggering a range of defensive moves. These moves include the outward display of emotions such as anger, fear, and guilt, and behaviors such as argumentation, silence, and leaving the stress-inducing situation. These behaviors, in turn, function to reinstate white racial comfort and status quo.

White Identity: To be socialized as a white person, enact whiteness by implicitly and explicitly upholding racism and white supremacy, and participate in the rewards of being perceived as white.

Whiteness: A term to capture all of the dynamics that go into being defined and/or perceived as white and that create and reinforce white people as inherently superior through society's norms, traditions, and institutions. Whiteness grants material and psychological advantages (white privilege) that are often invisible and taken for granted by whites.

Whiteness as Property: The concept that being perceived as white is more than a racial classification; it is a social and institutional status and identity imbued with legal, political, economic, and social rights and privileges that are denied to others. These translate into material gains.

White Racial Frame: The deeply internalized racist framework through which whites make racial meaning. This framework includes images, interpretations, perceptions, evaluations, emotions, and actions that position whites as superior and that are passed down and reinforced throughout society.

White Solidarity: The unspoken agreement between whites to maintain silence, not challenge each other, keep each other comfortable, and generally maintain the racist status quo and protect white privilege.

White Supremacy: The term used to capture the all-encompassing centrality and assumed superiority of people defined and perceived as white, and the practices based on this assumption.

INDEX

Z

Studies in the Postmodern Theory of Education

General Editor
Shirley R. Steinberg

Counterpoints publishes the most compelling and imaginative books being written in education today. Grounded on the theoretical advances in criticalism, feminism, and postmodernism in the last two decades of the twentieth century, Counterpoints engages the meaning of these innovations in various forms of educational expression. Committed to the proposition that theoretical literature should be accessible to a variety of audiences, the series insists that its authors avoid esoteric and jargonistic languages that transform educational scholarship into an elite discourse for the initiated. Scholarly work matters only to the degree it affects consciousness and practice at multiple sites. Counterpoints' editorial policy is based on these principles and the ability of scholars to break new ground, to open new conversations, to go where educators have never gone before.

For additional information about this series or for the submission of manuscripts, please contact:

Shirley R. Steinberg
c/o Peter Lang Publishing, Inc.
29 Broadway, 18th floor
New York, New York 10006

To order other books in this series, please contact our Customer Service Department:

(800) 770-LANG (within the U.S.)
(212) 647-7706 (outside the U.S.)
(212) 647-7707 FAX

Or browse online by series:
www.peterlang.com

Studies in the Postmodern Theory of Education

General Editor
Shirley R. Steinberg